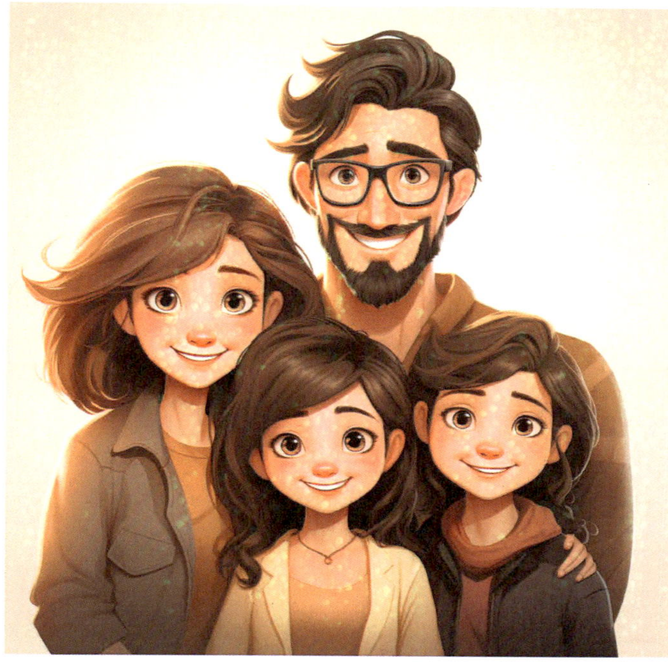

FOR MY LOVELY WIFE KRISTINA,
MY BEAUTIFUL DAUGHTER PEYTON,
AND MY SWEET BABY TAYLOR.

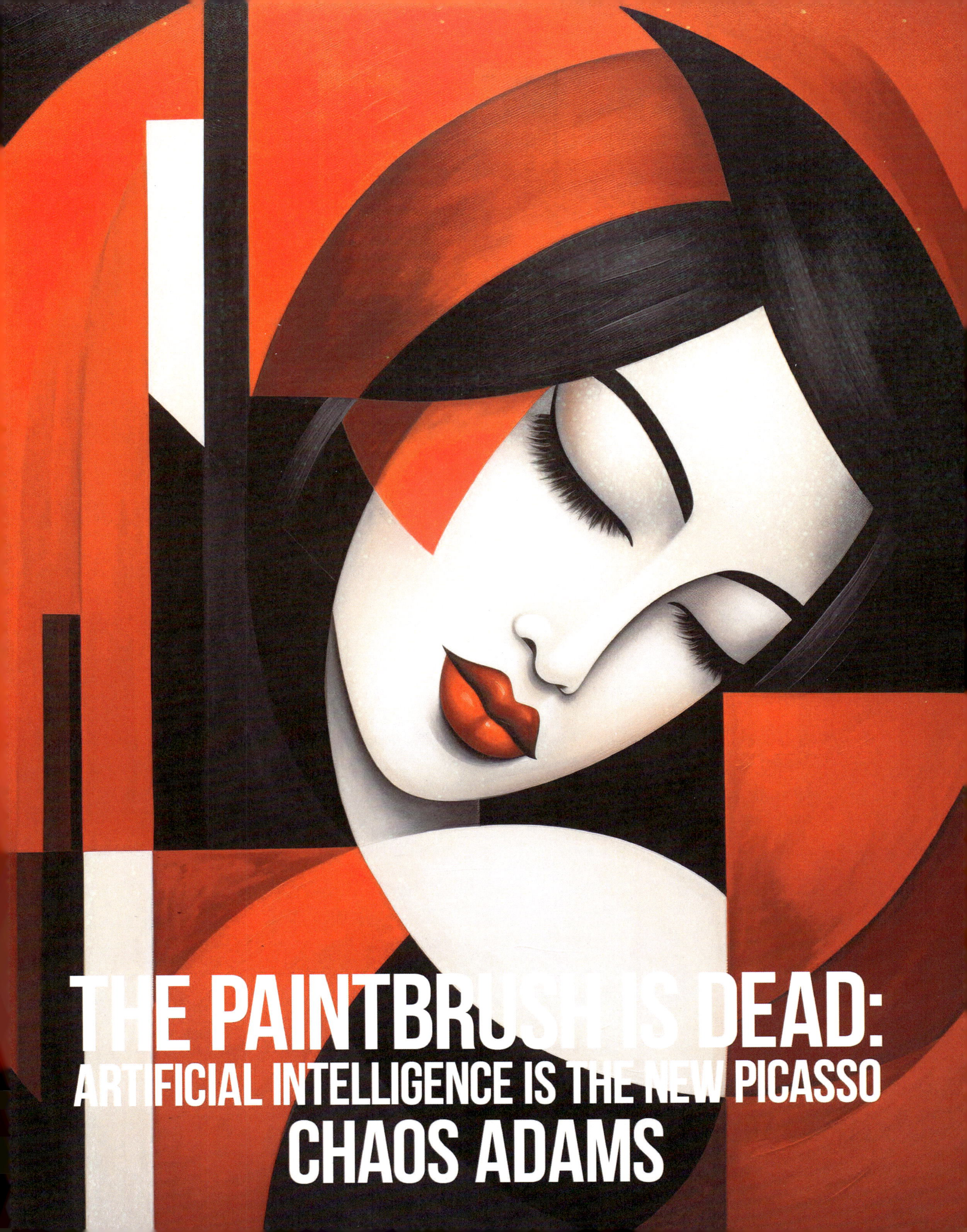

THE PAINTBRUSH IS DEAD:
ARTIFICIAL INTELLIGENCE IS THE NEW PICASSO
CHAOS ADAMS

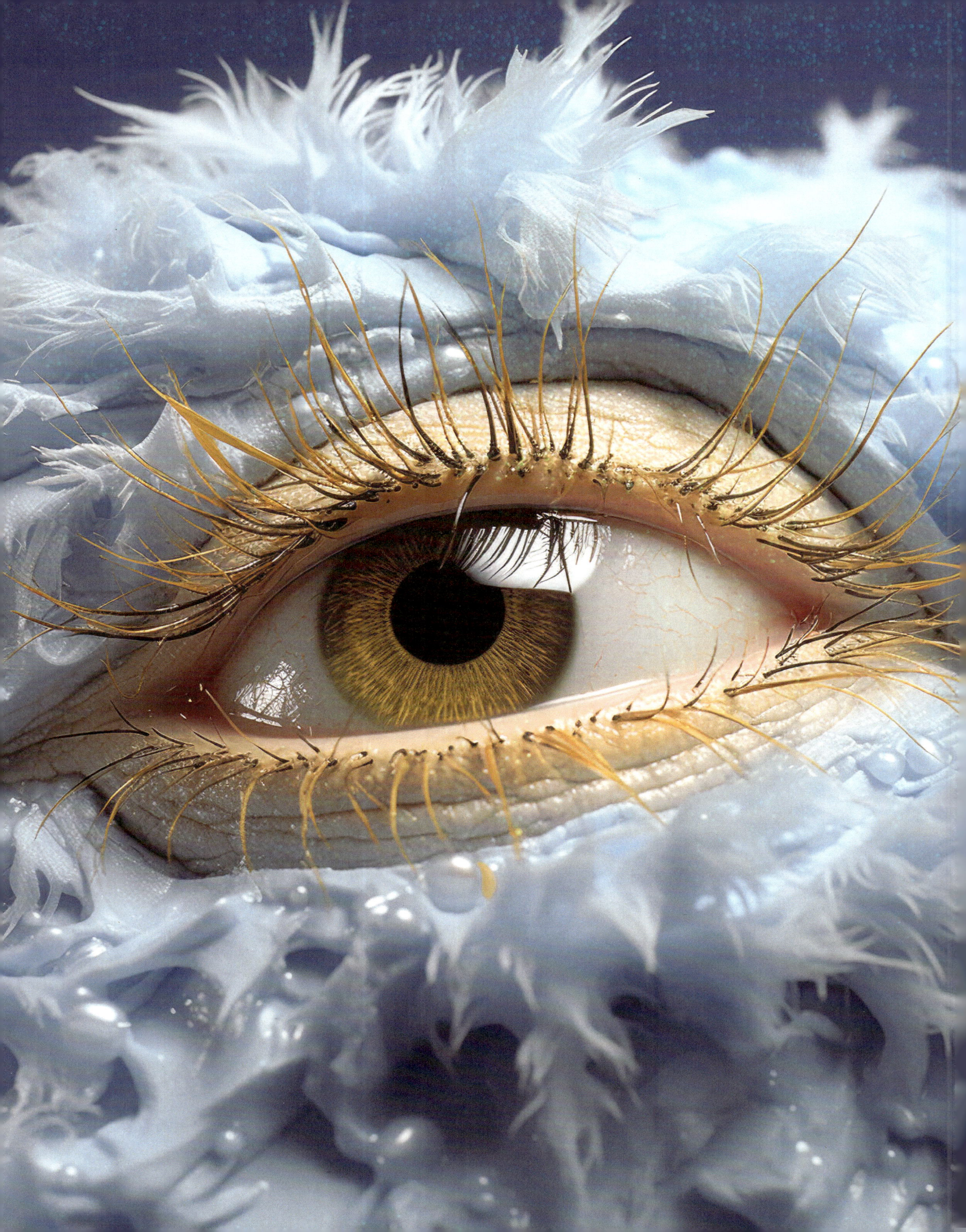

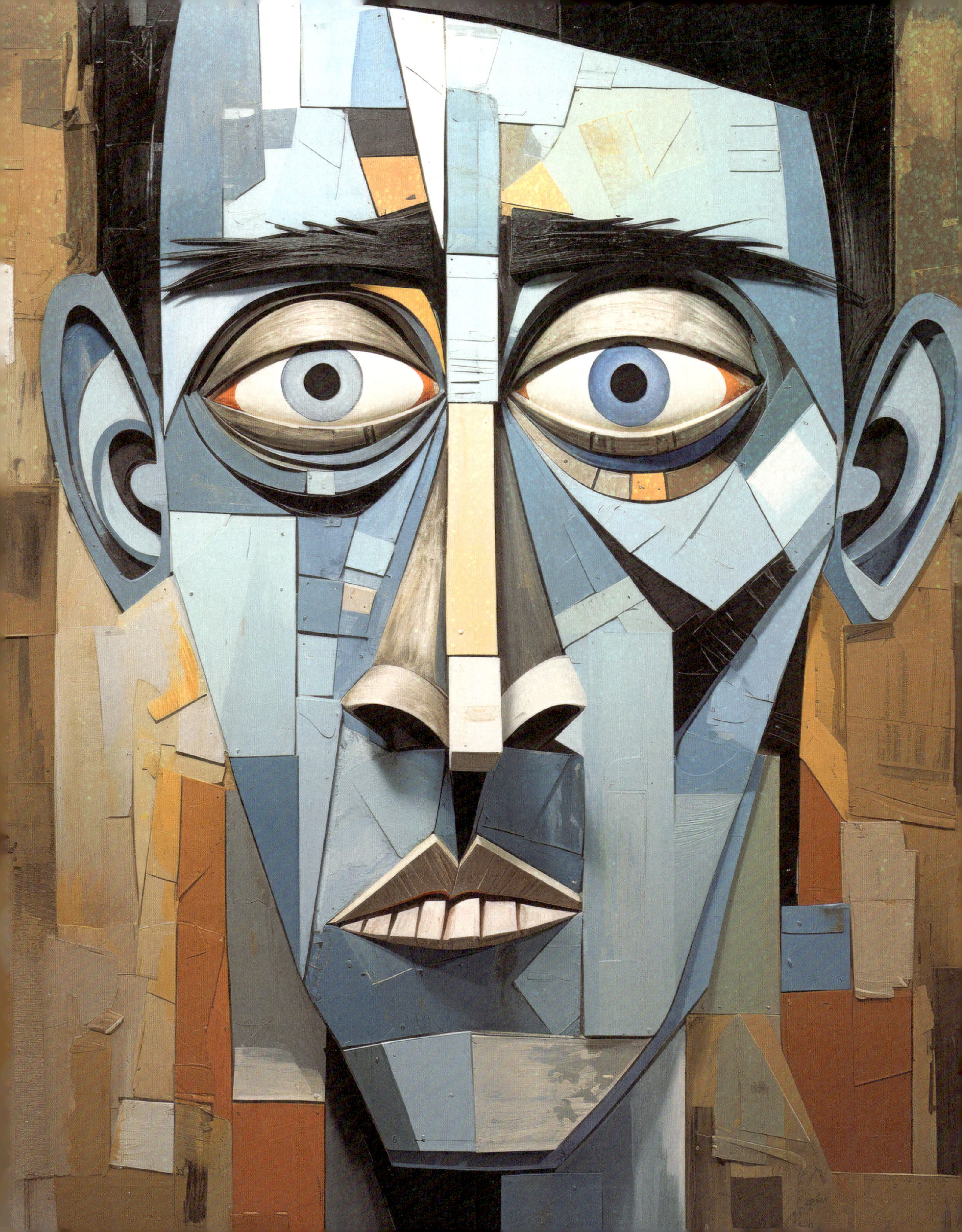

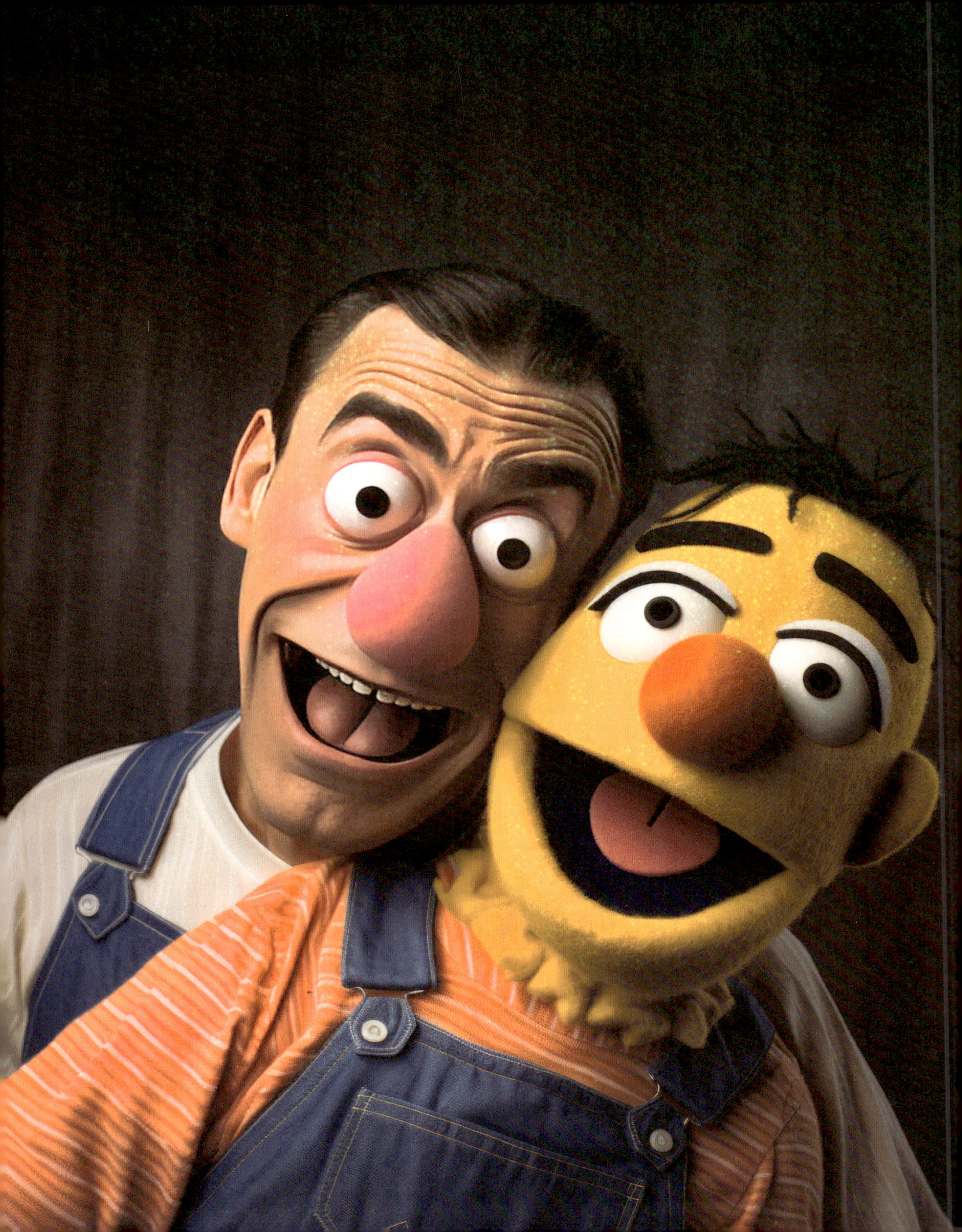

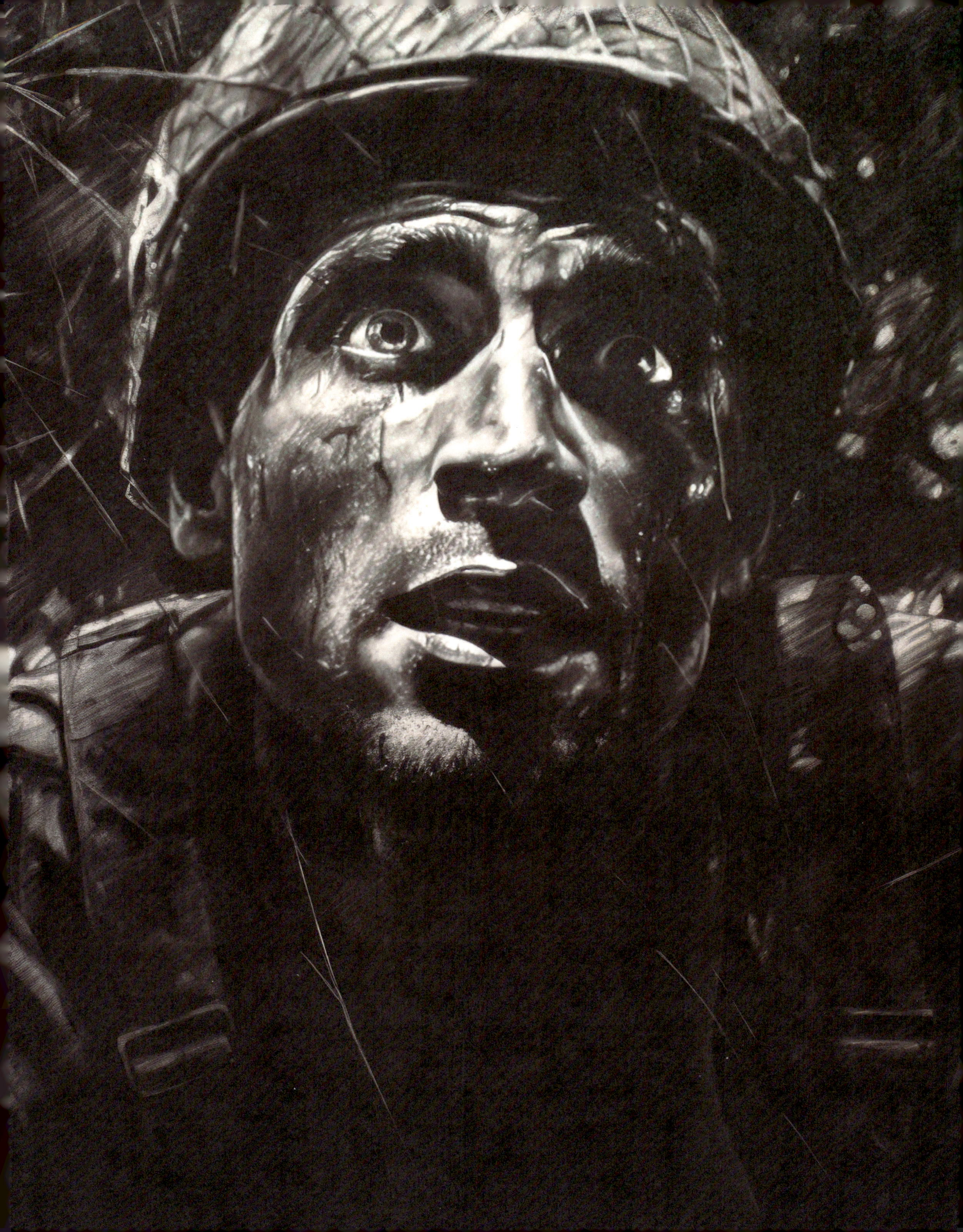

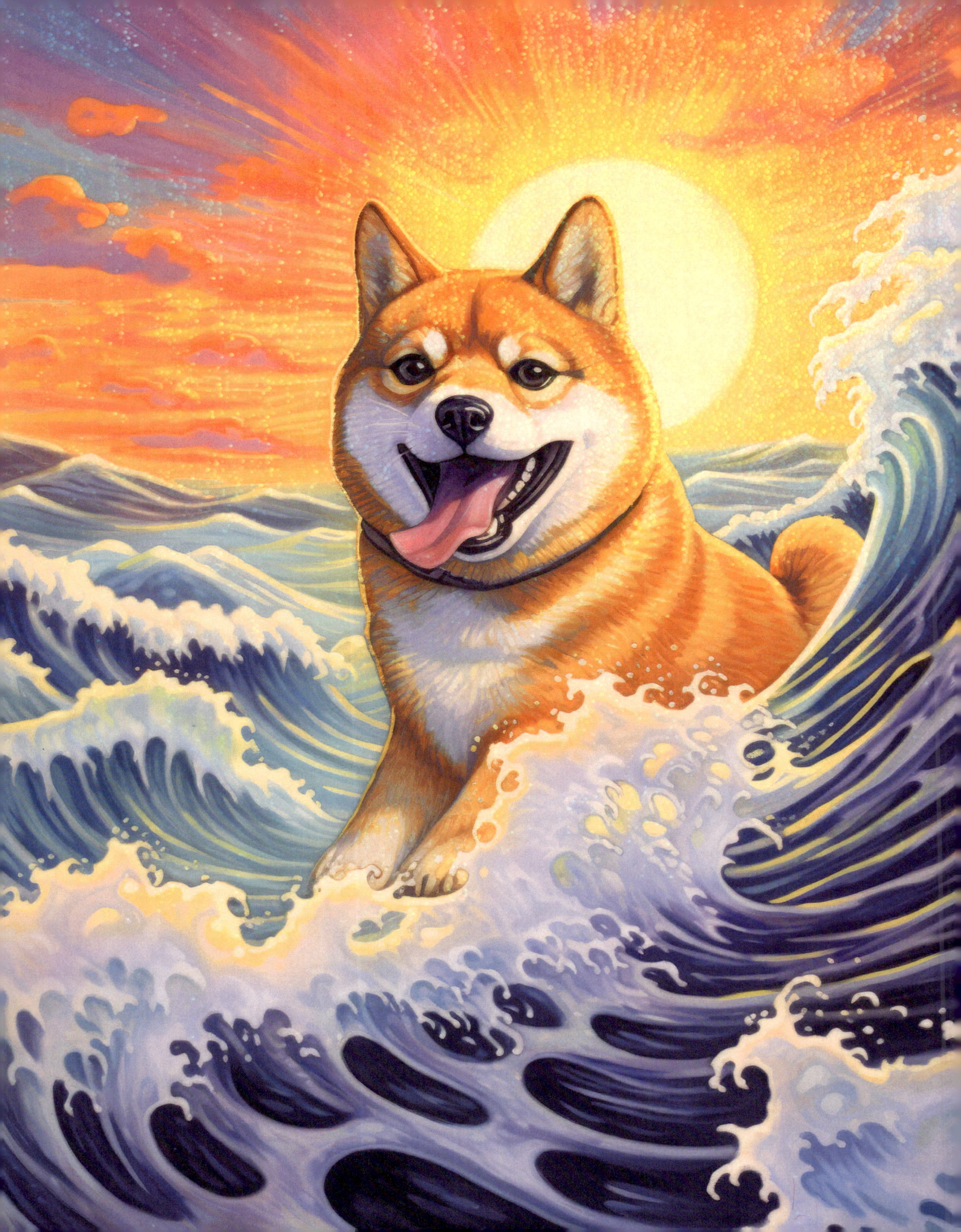

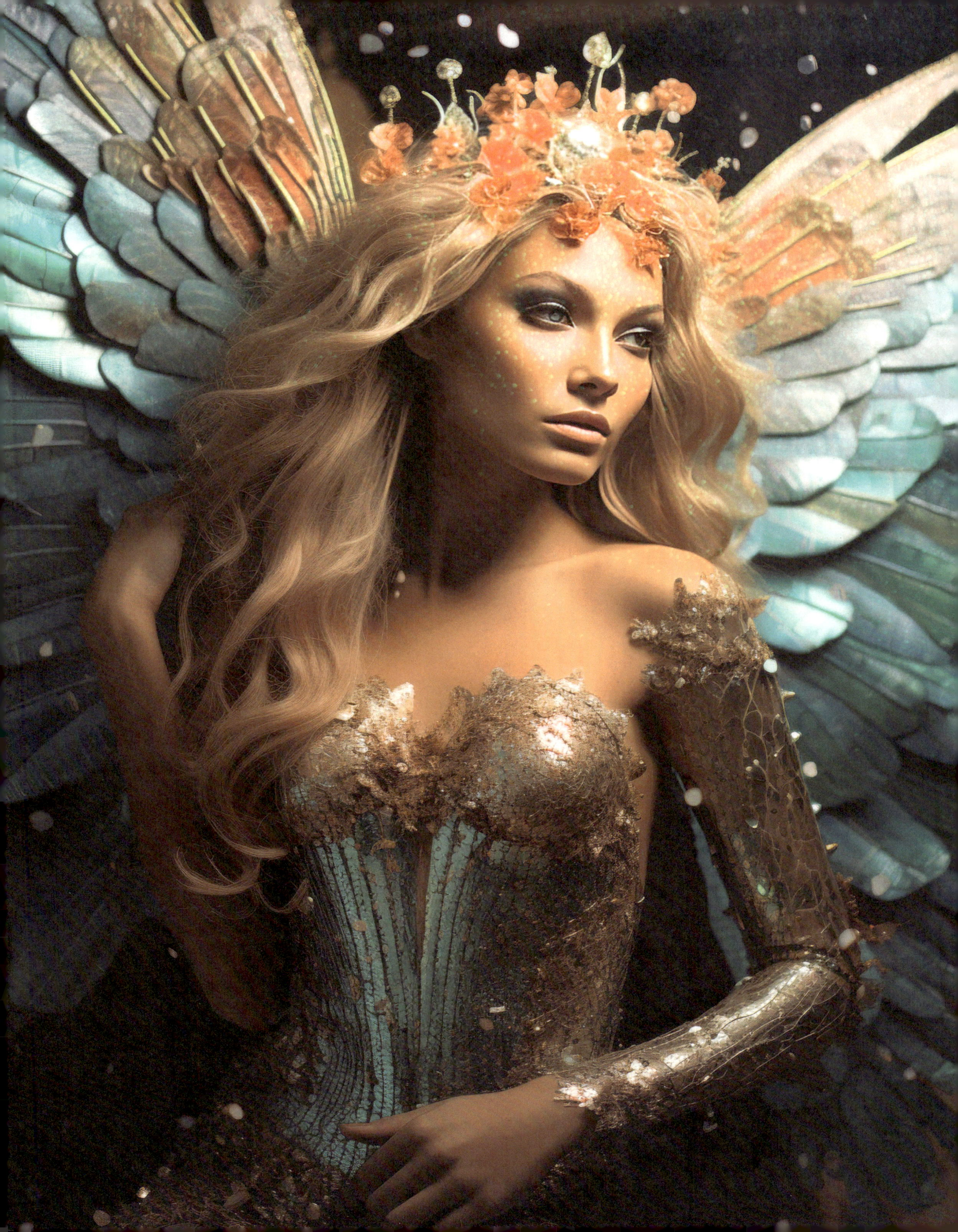

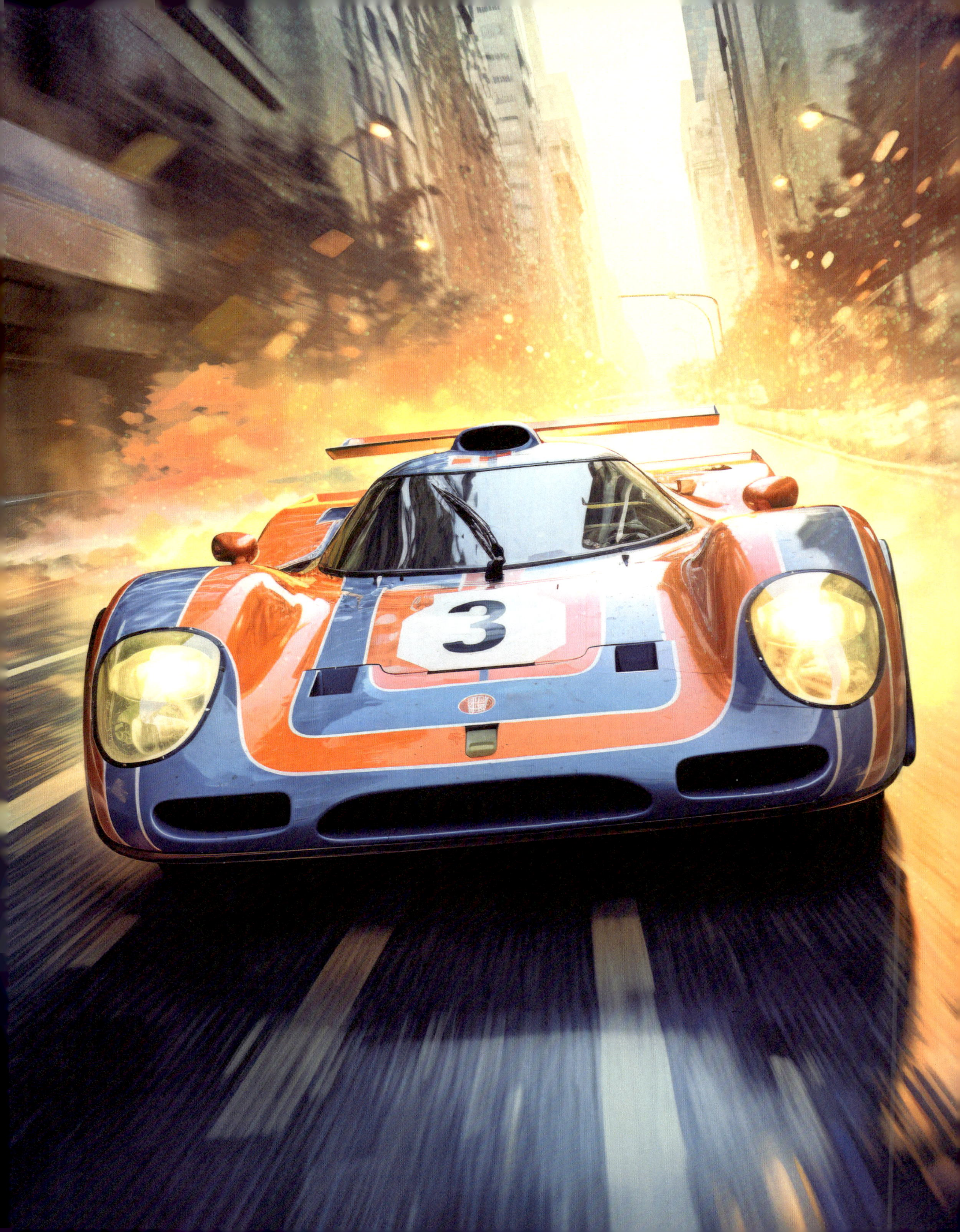

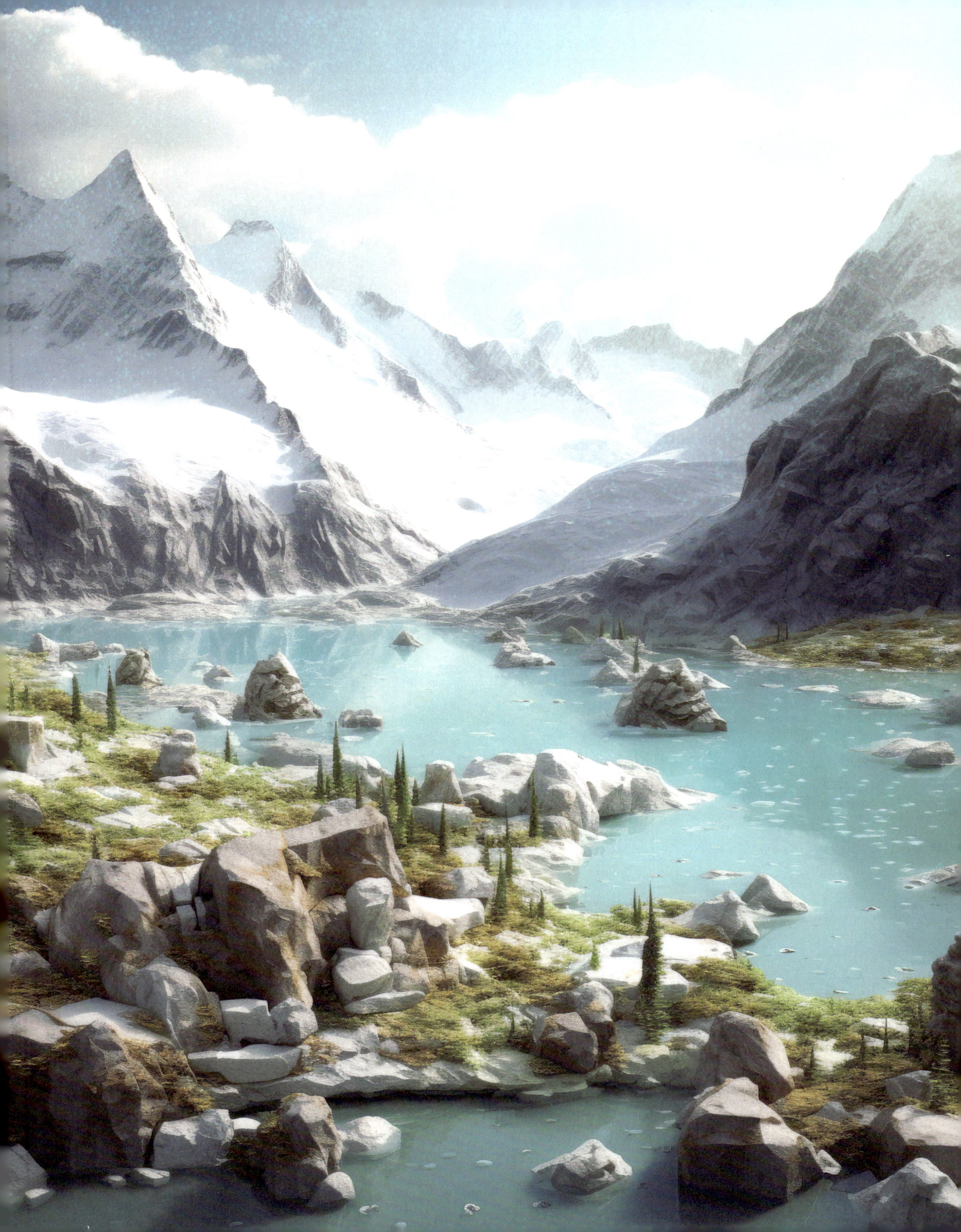

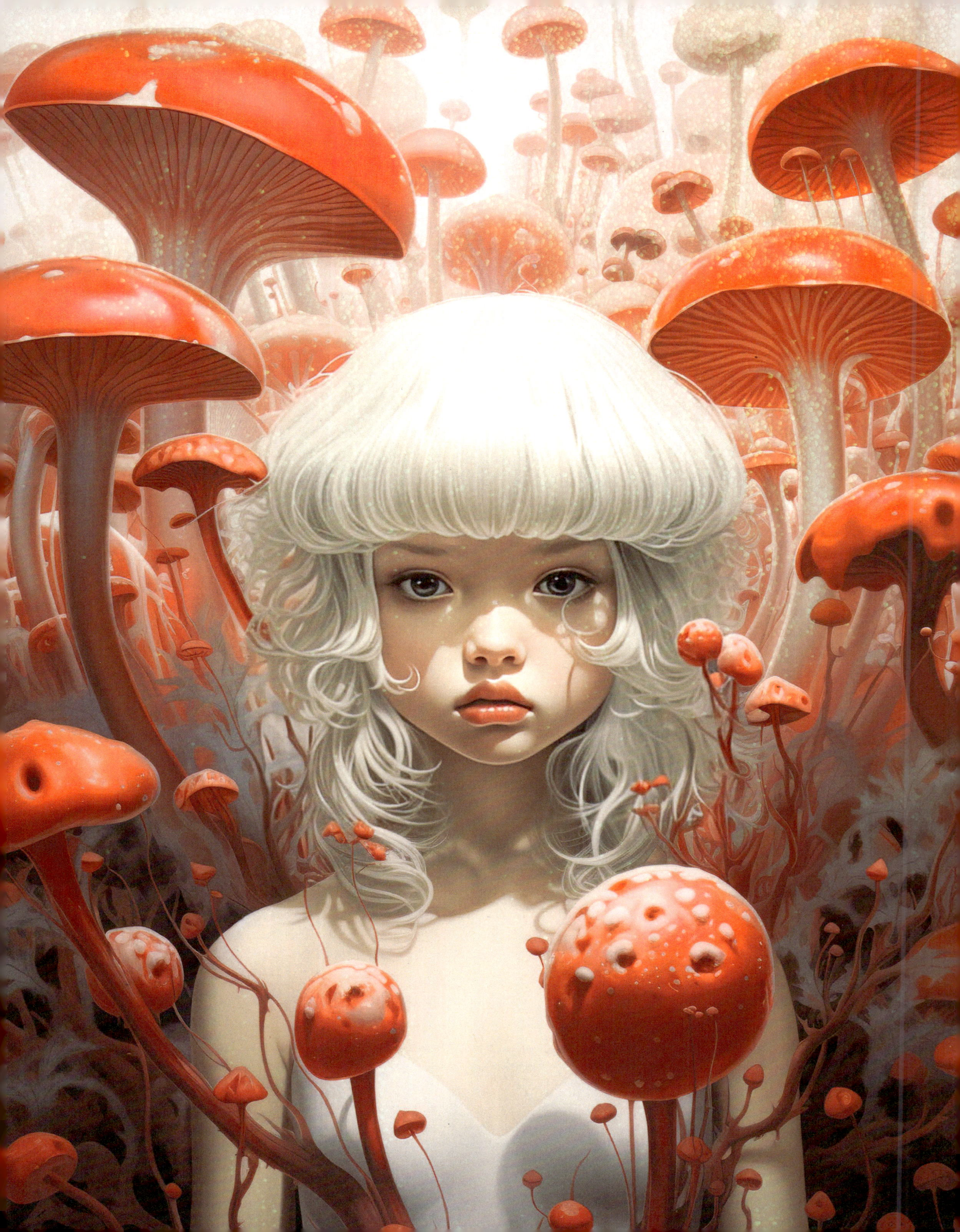

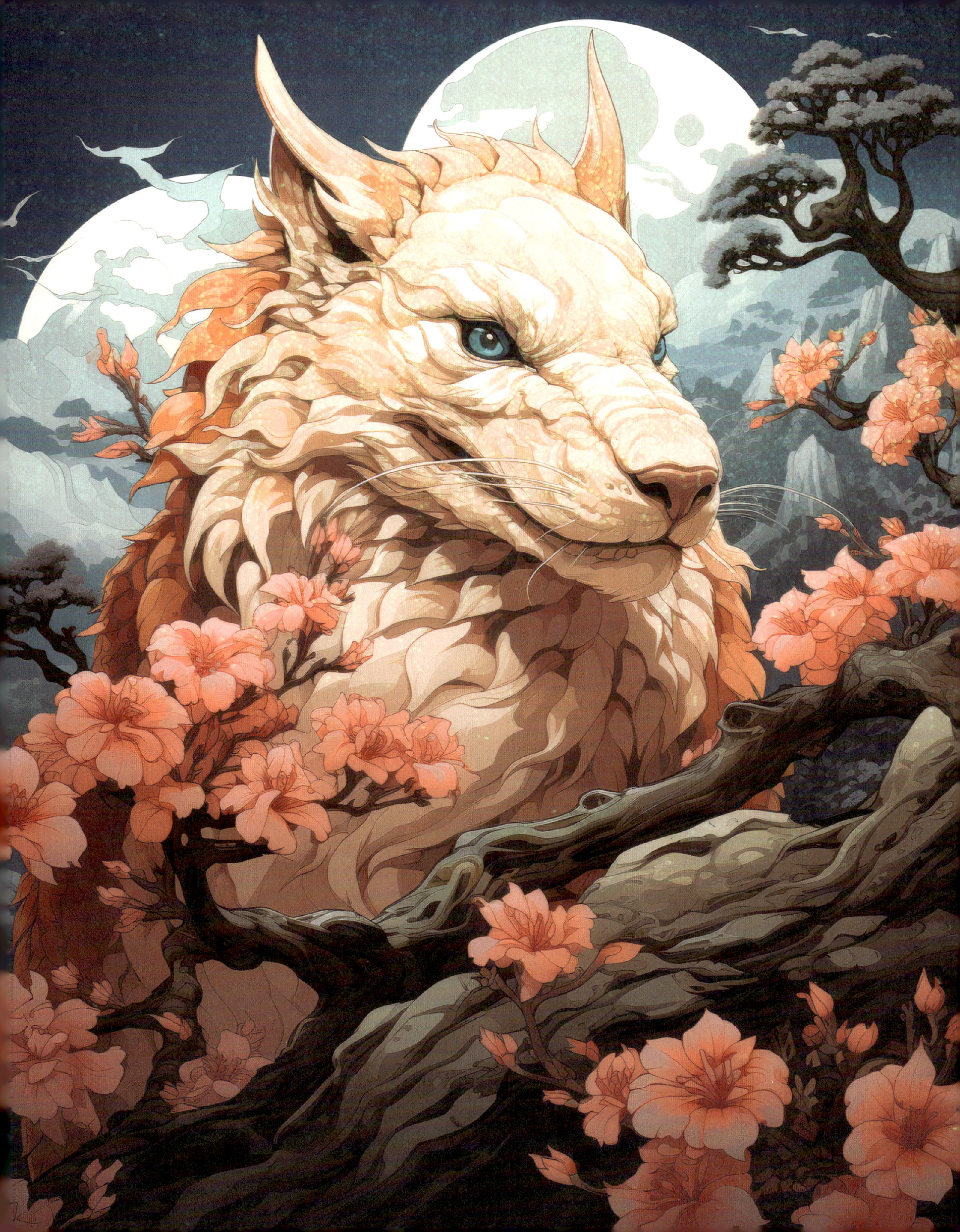

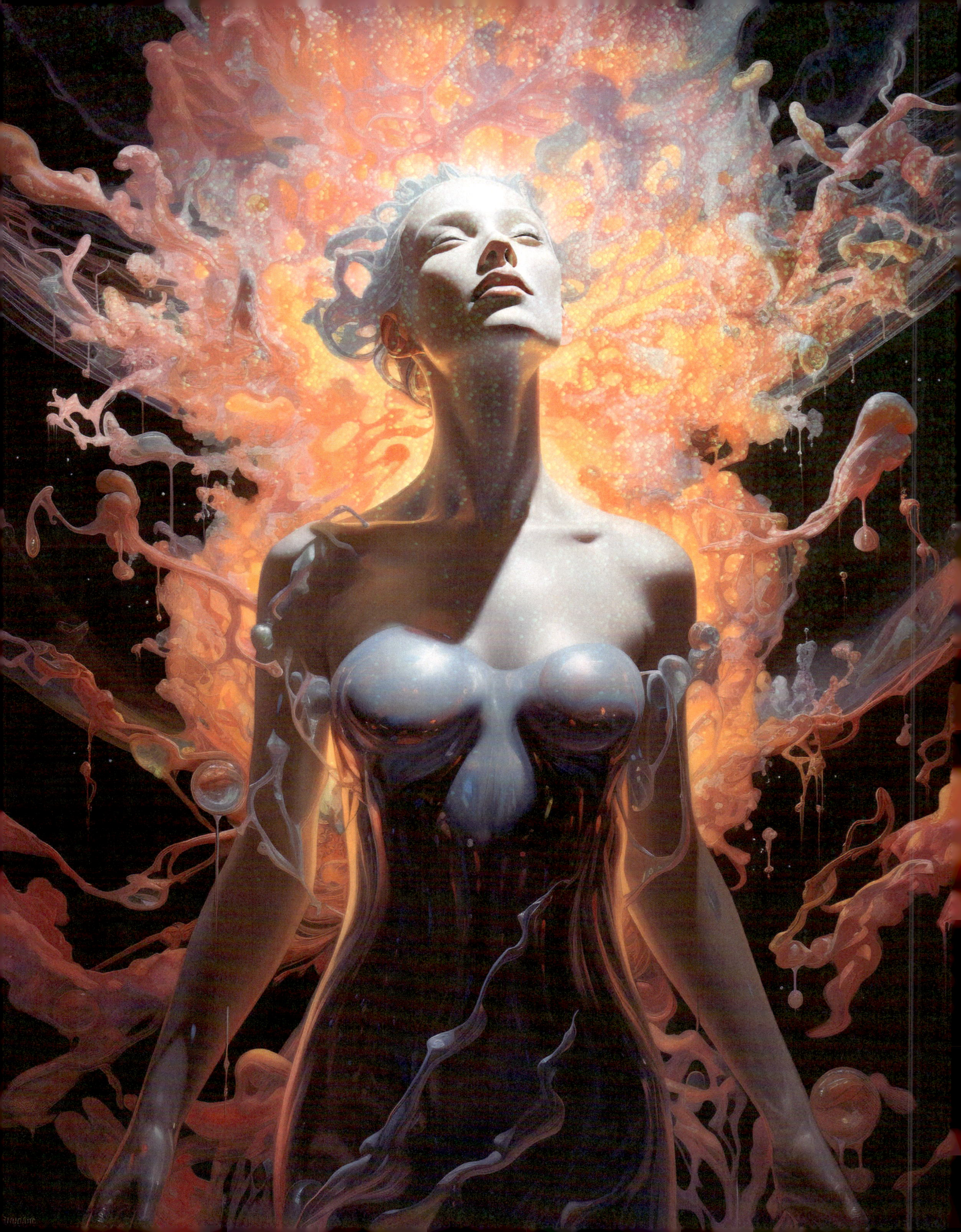

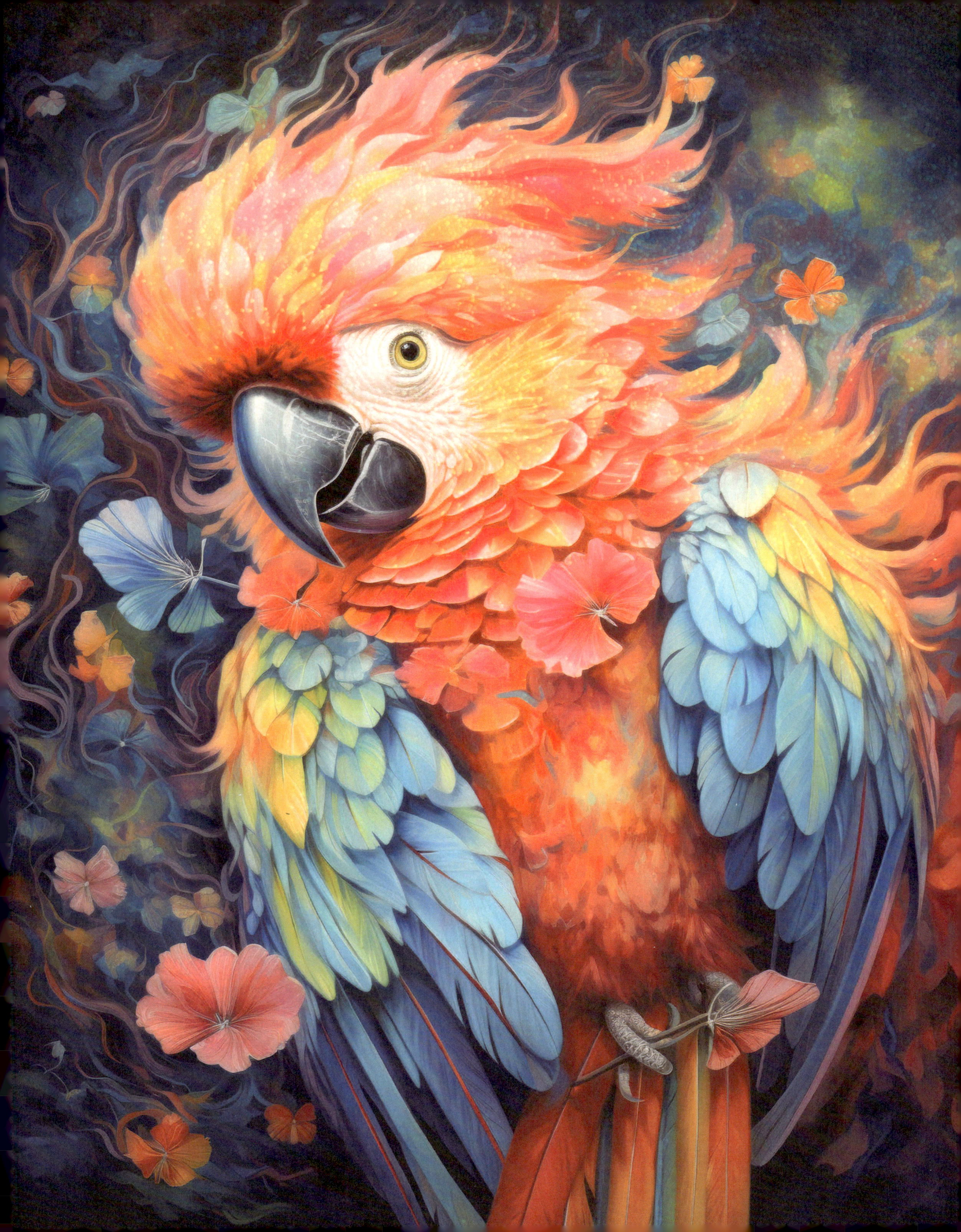

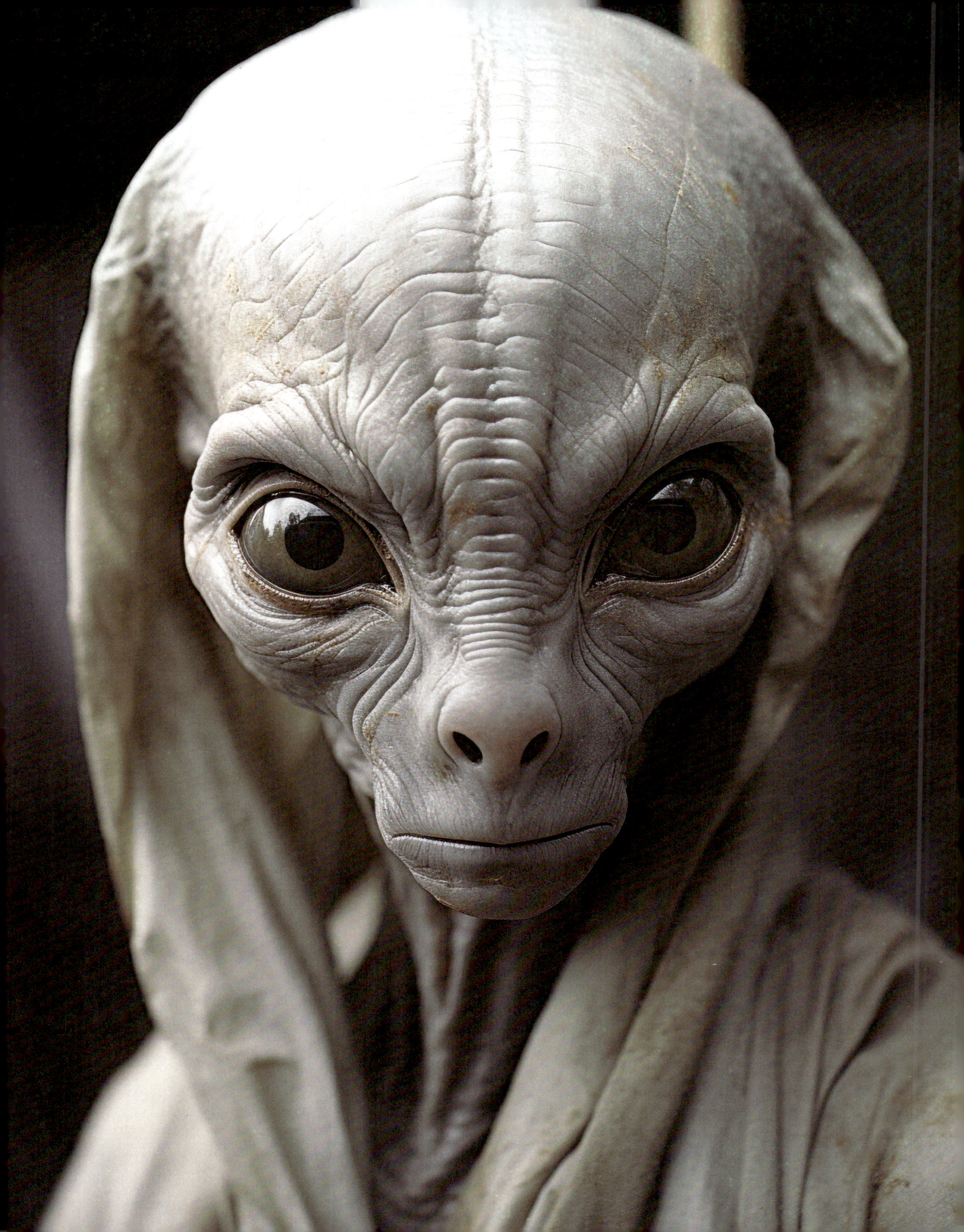

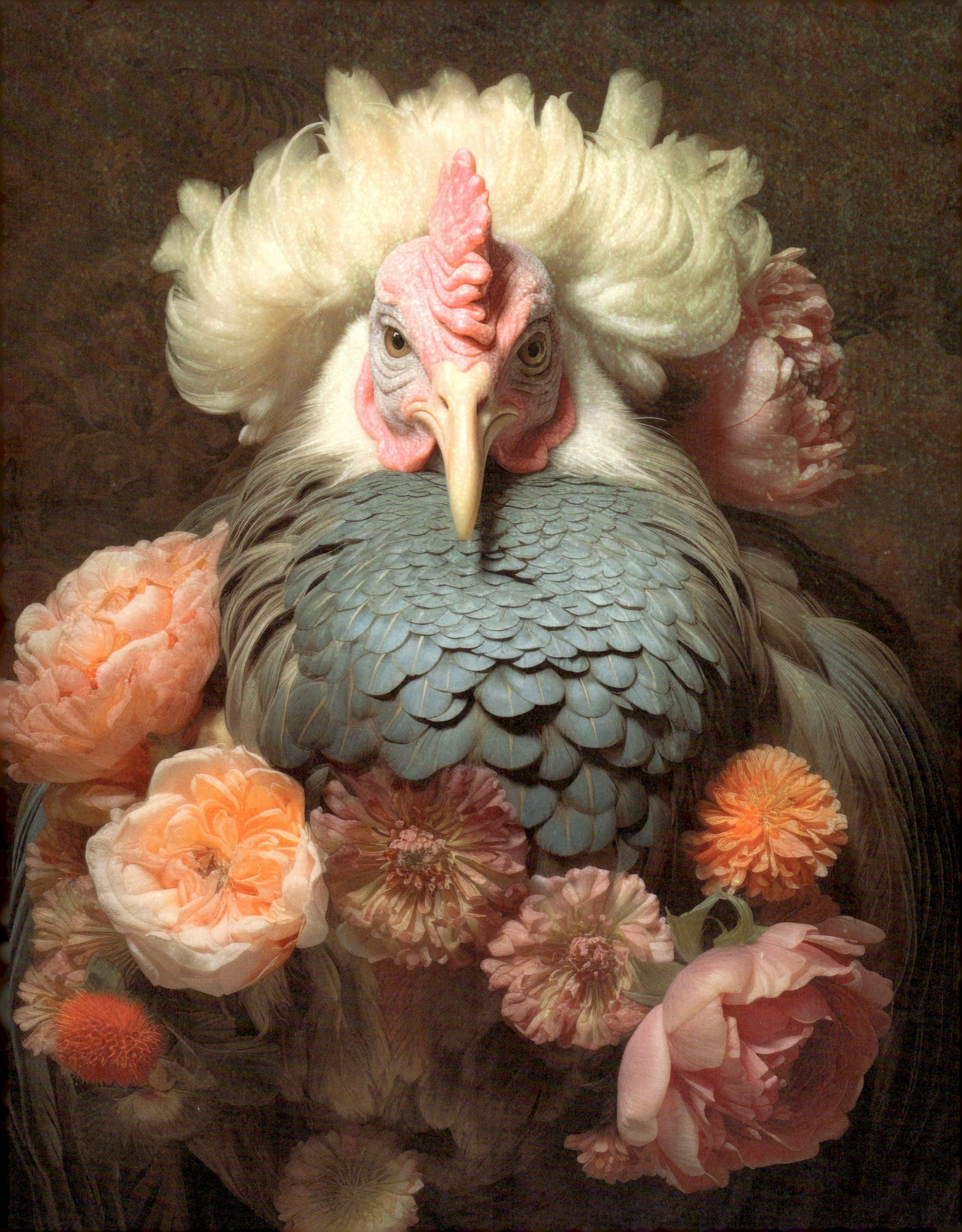

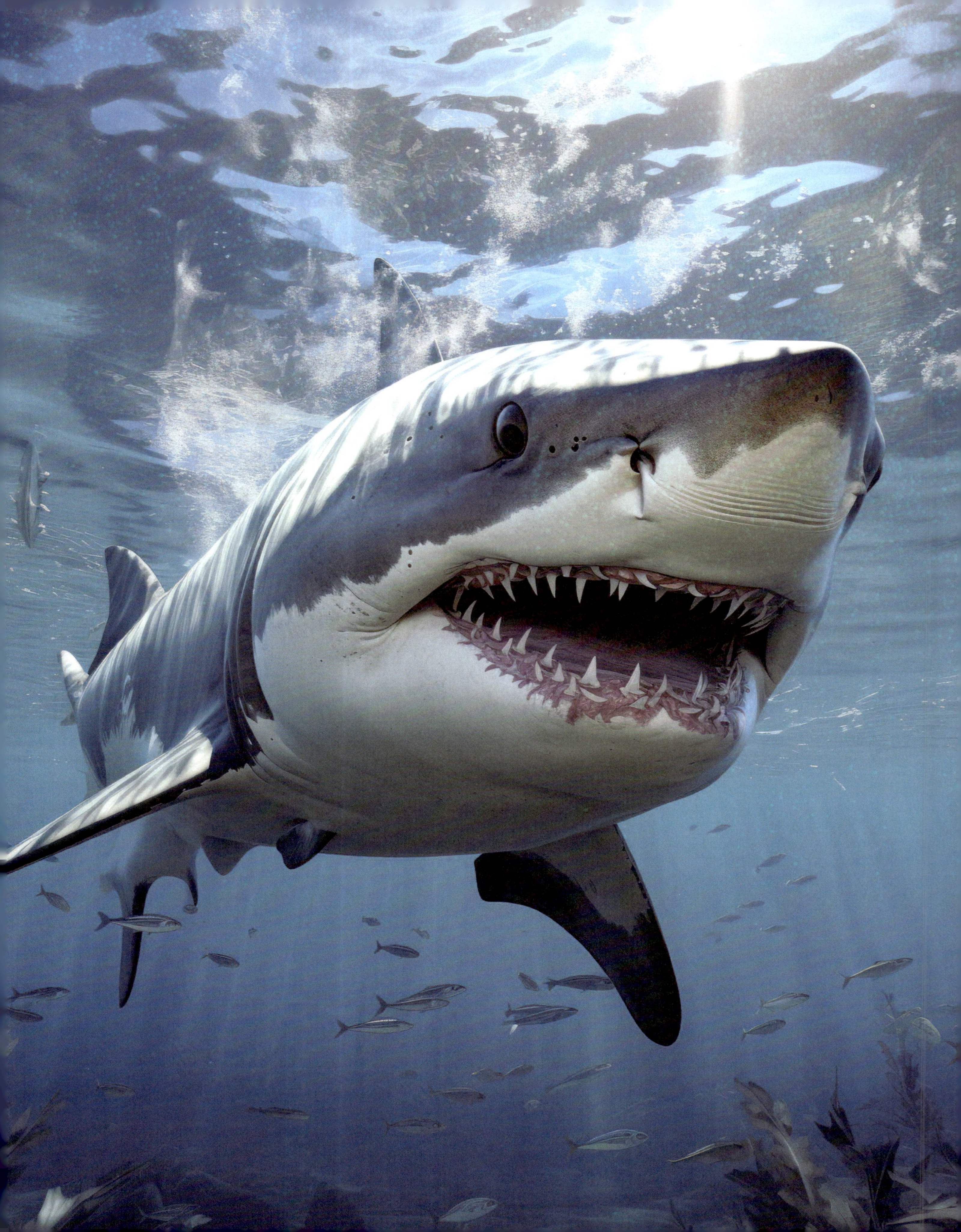

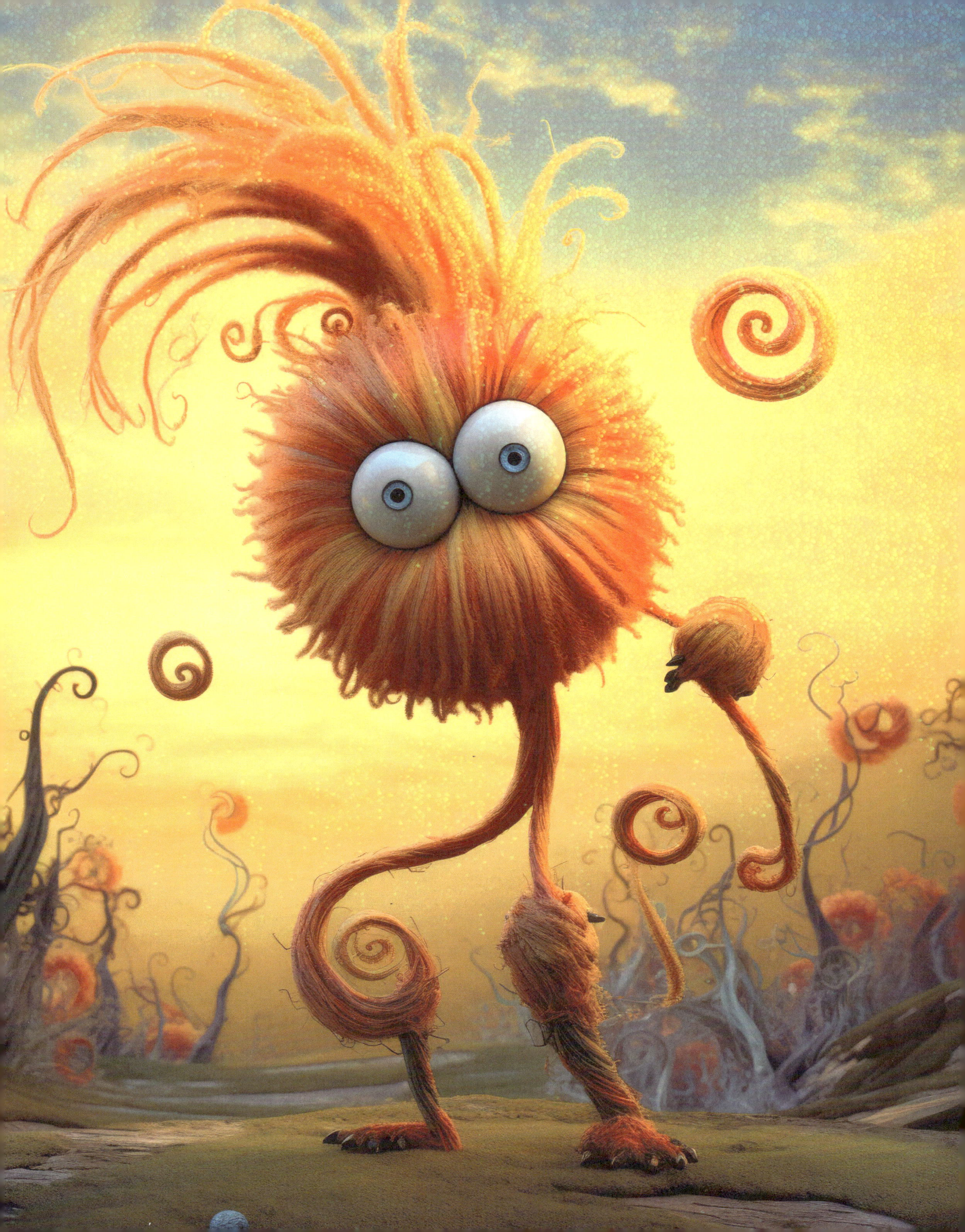

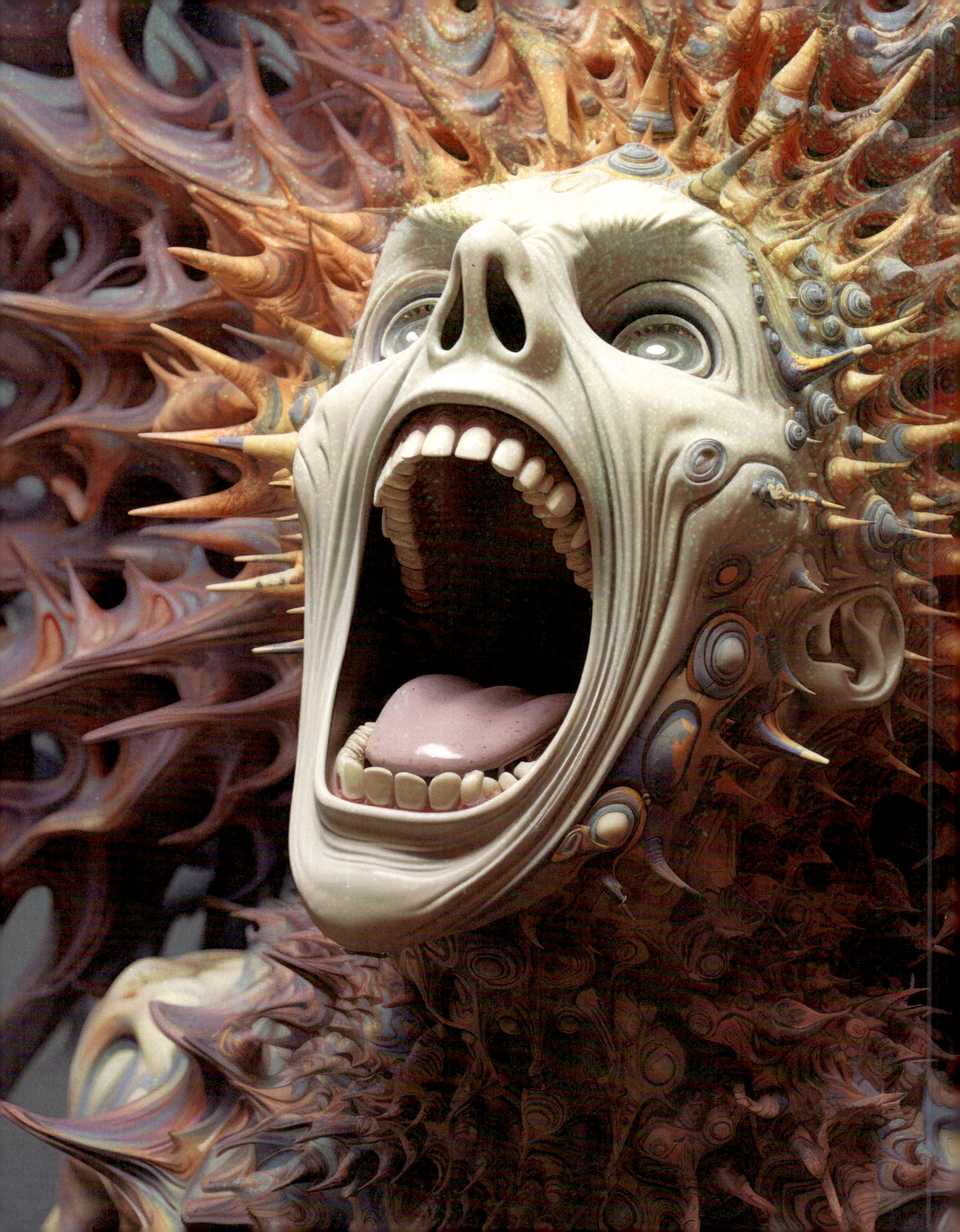

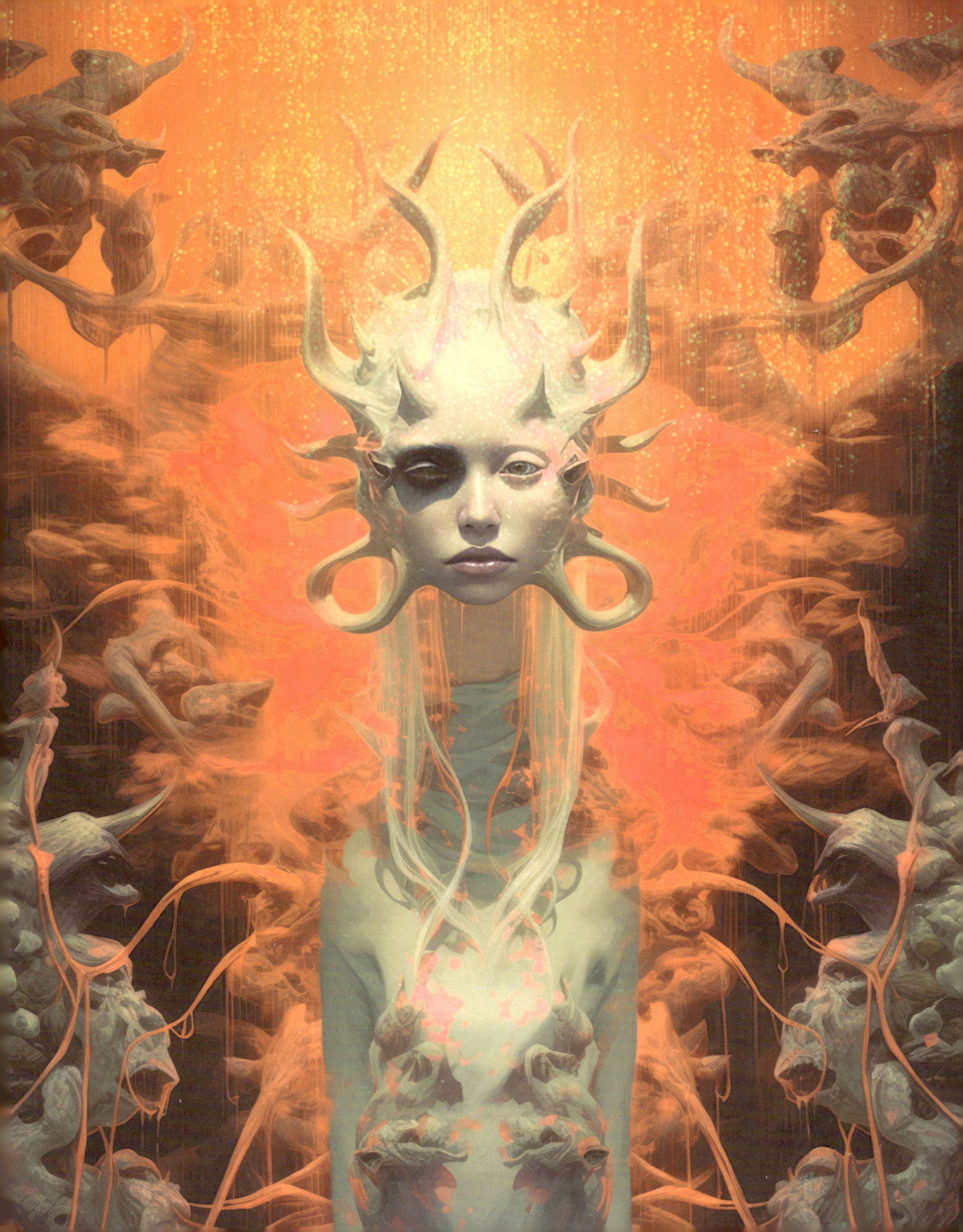

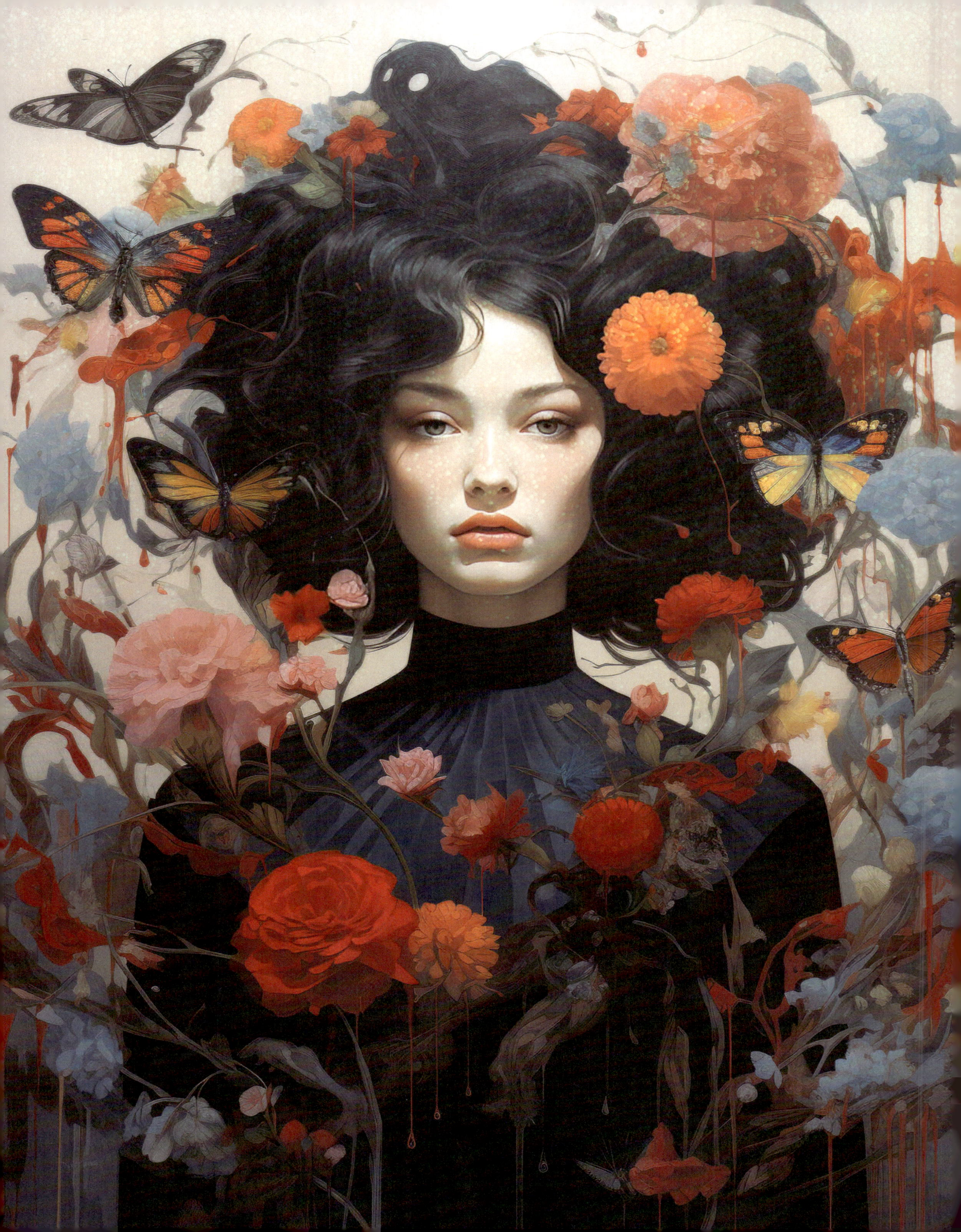

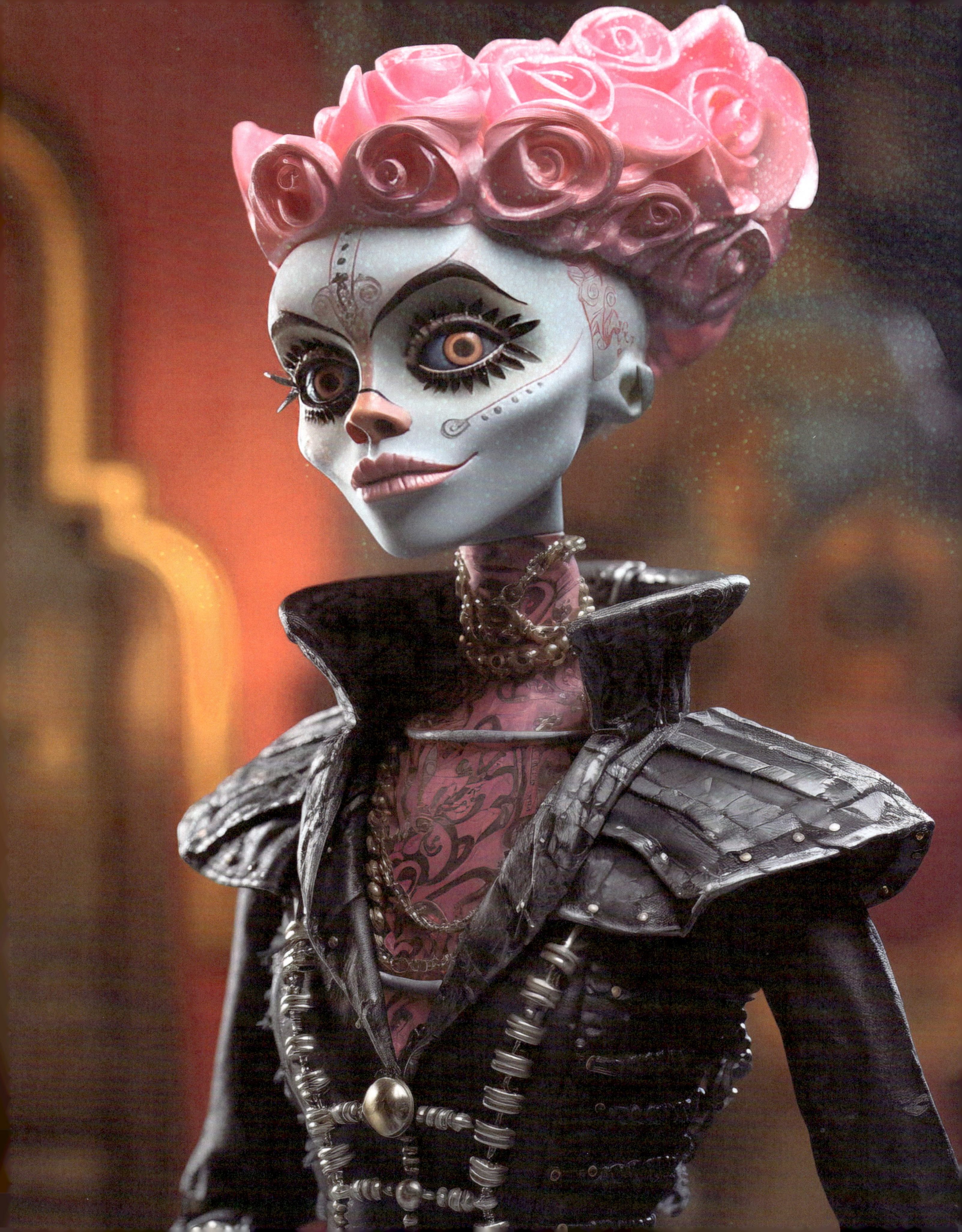

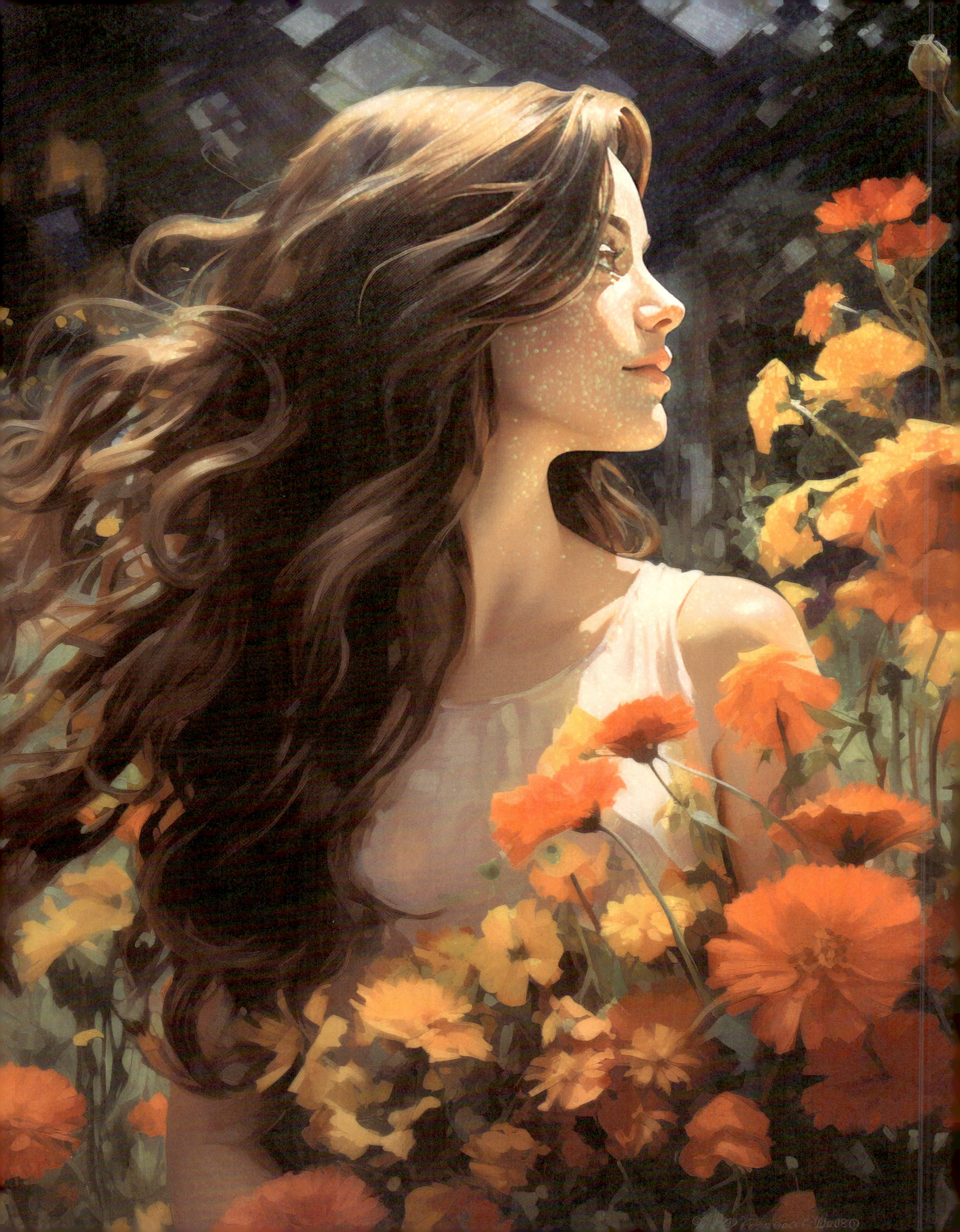

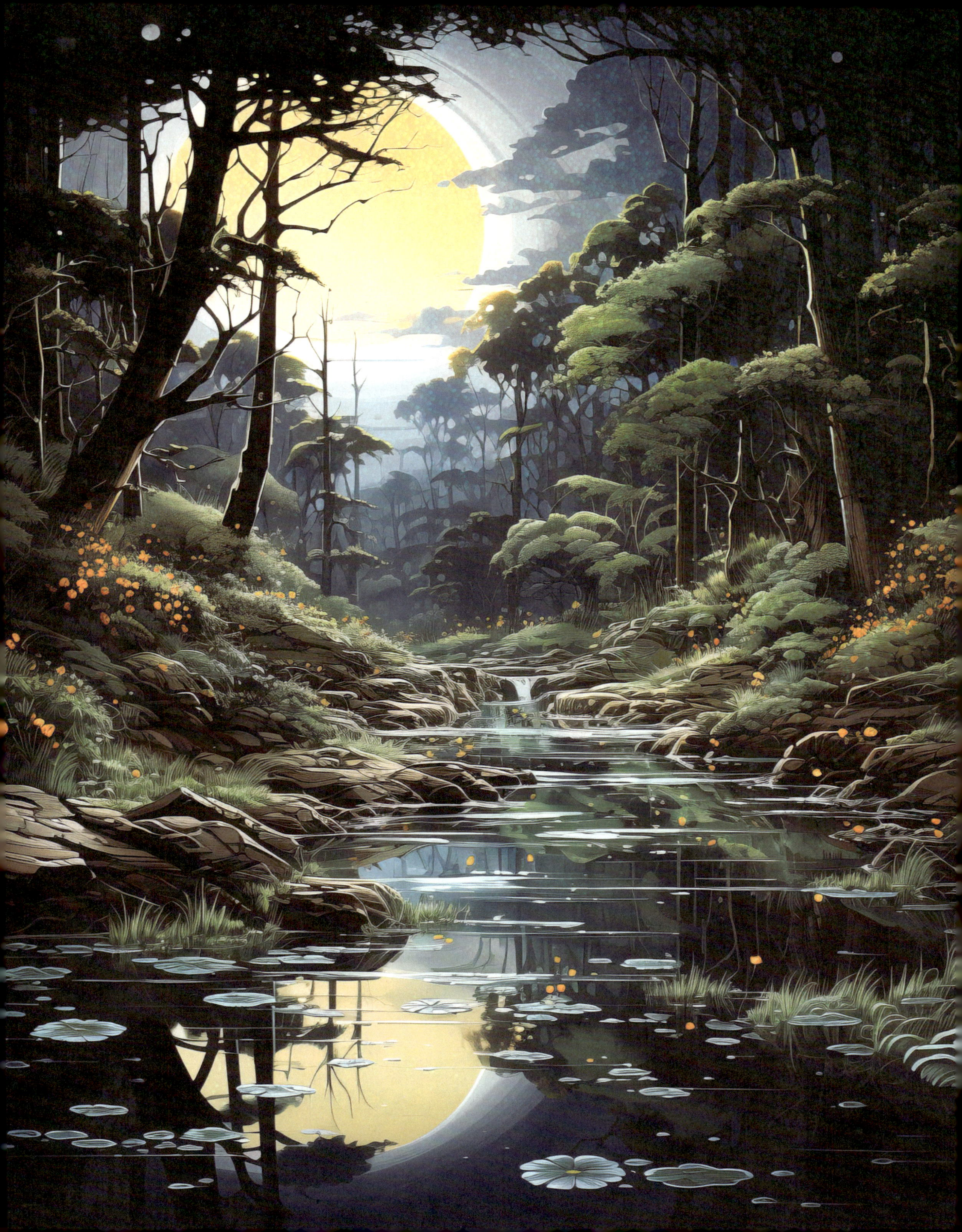

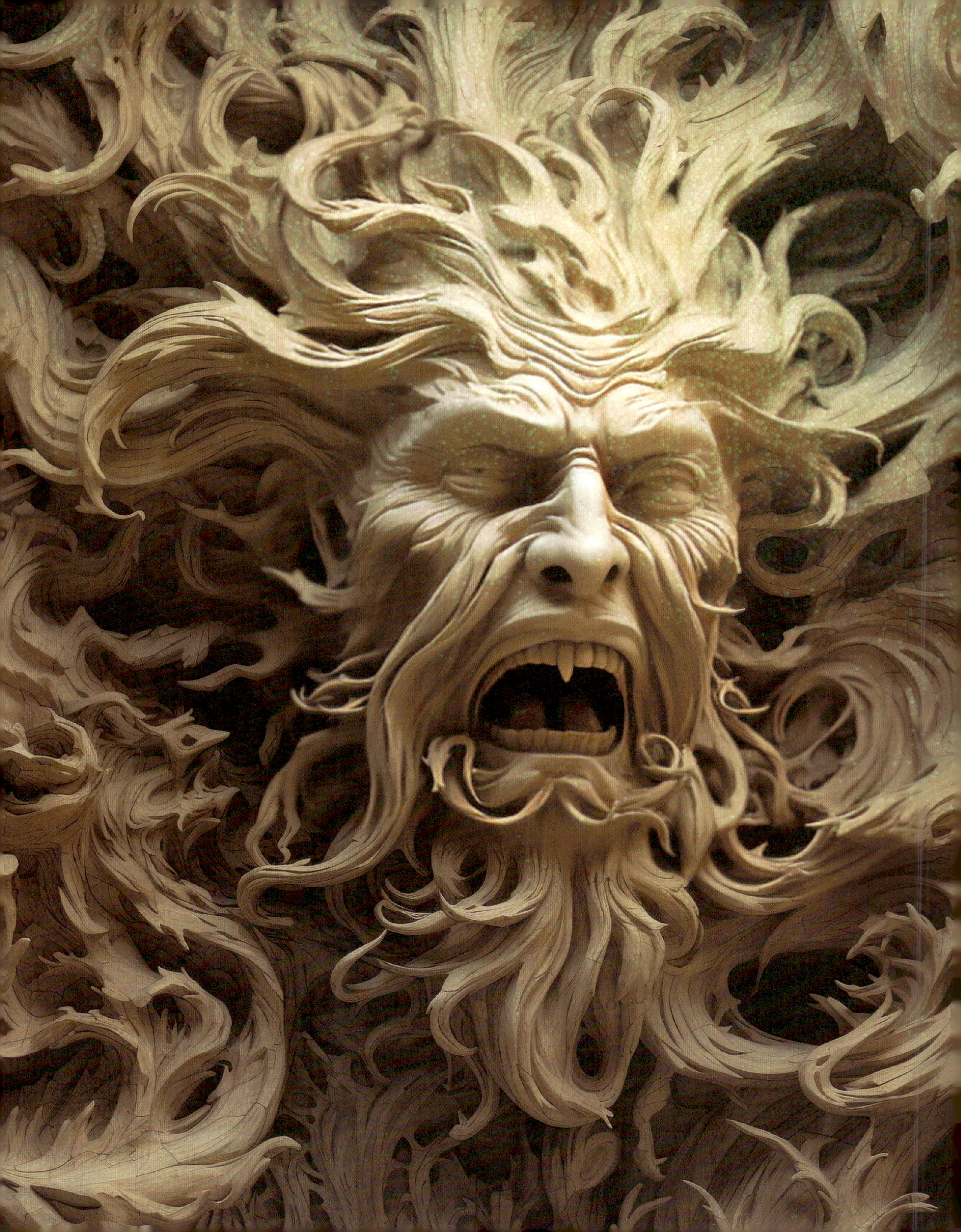

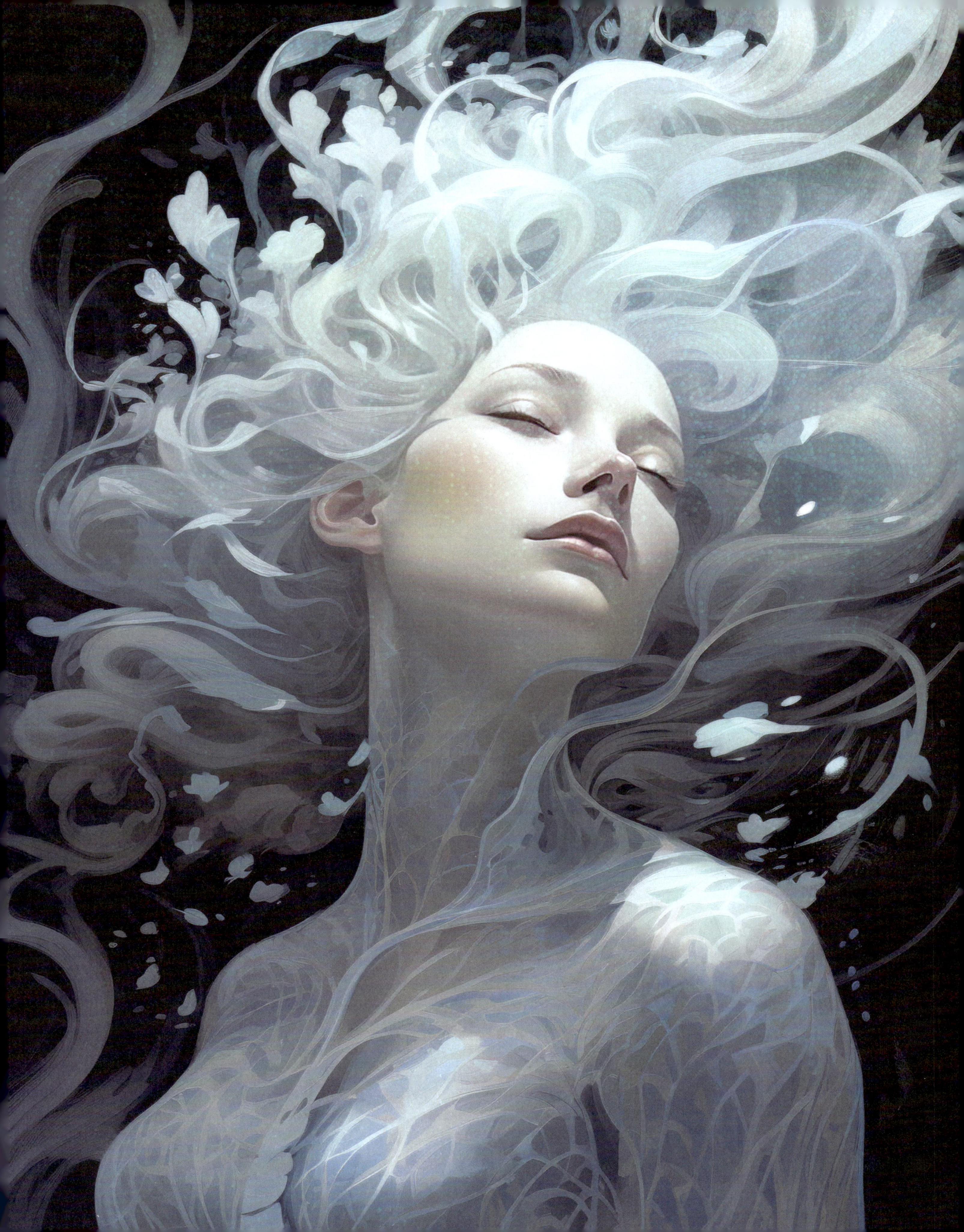

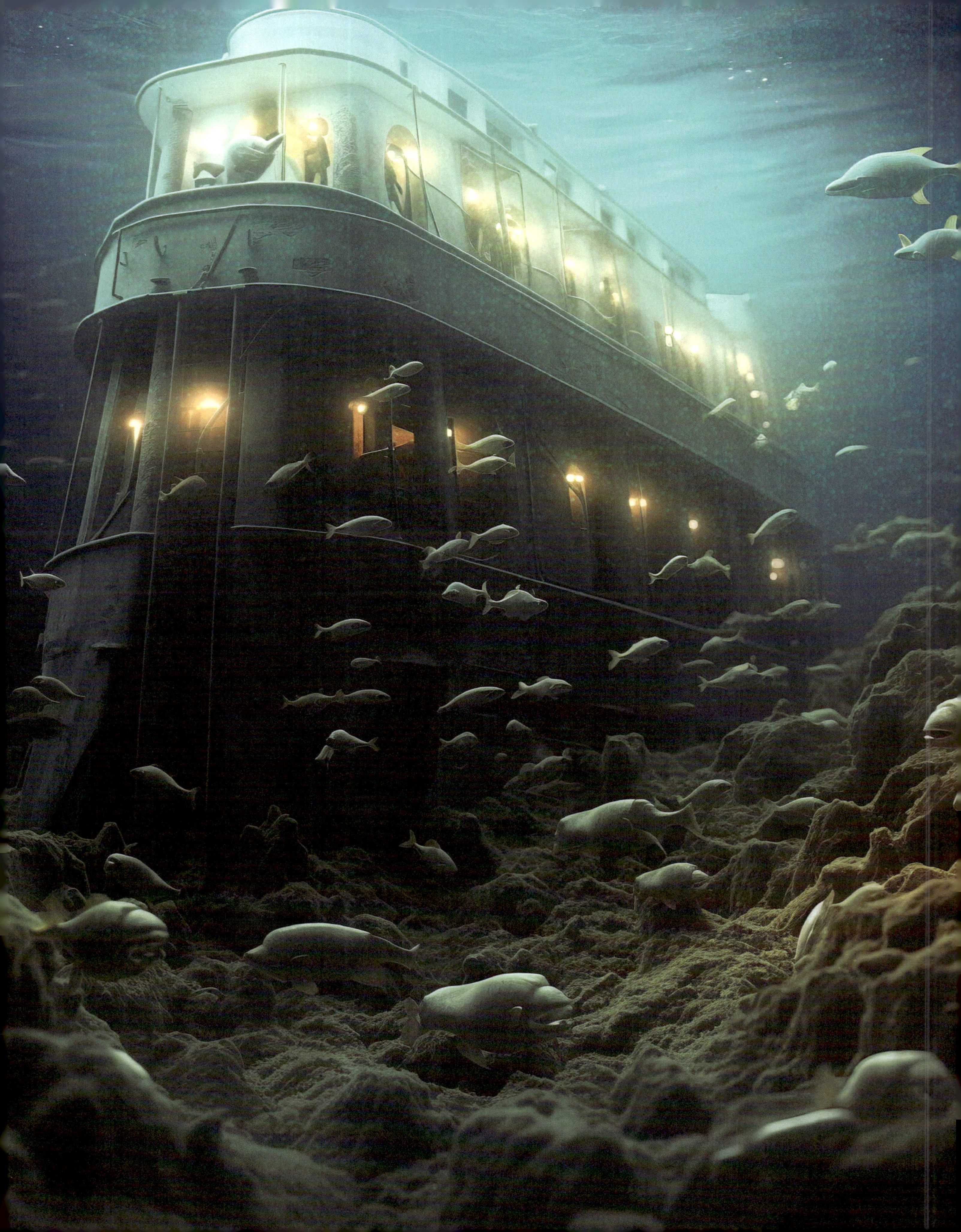

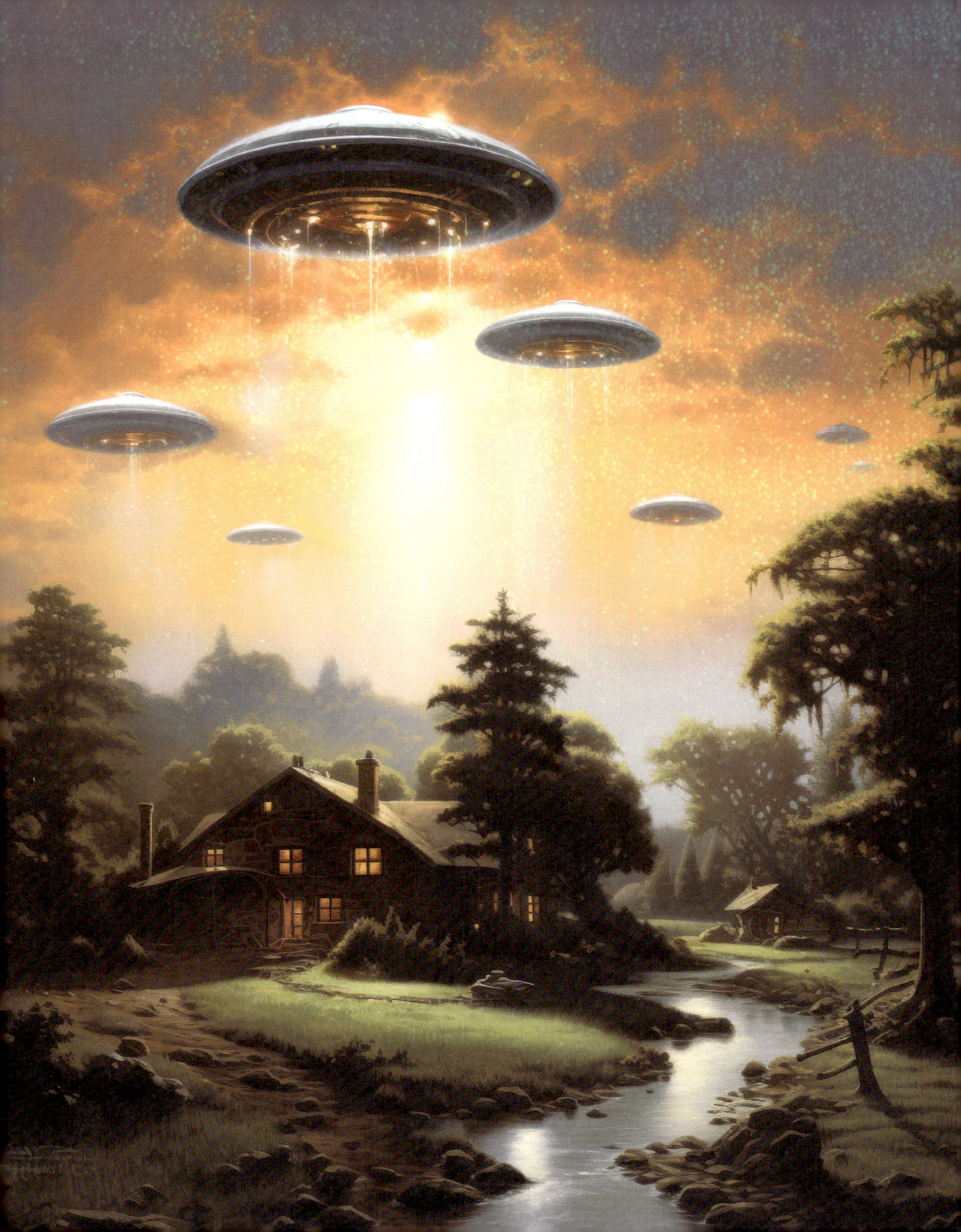

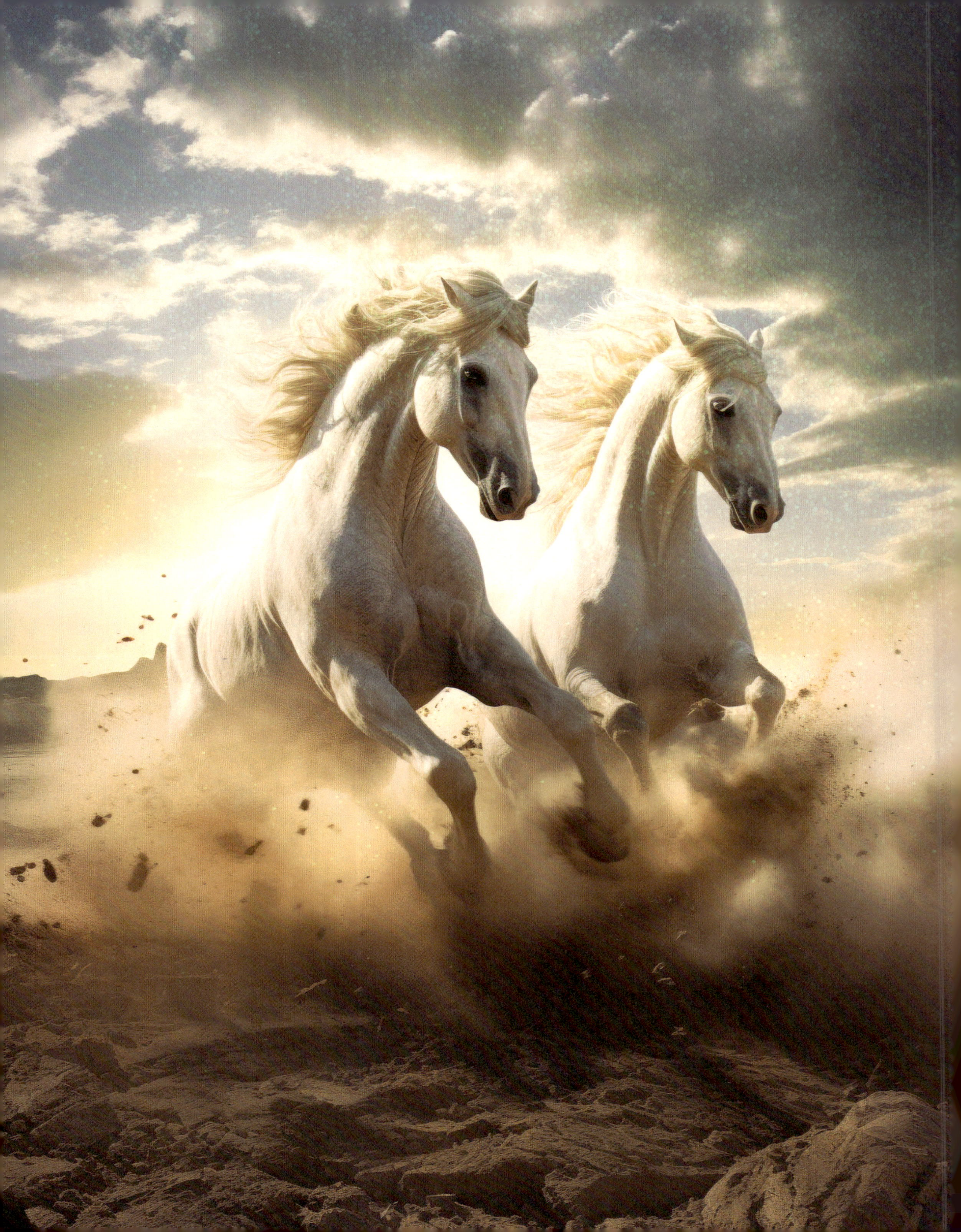

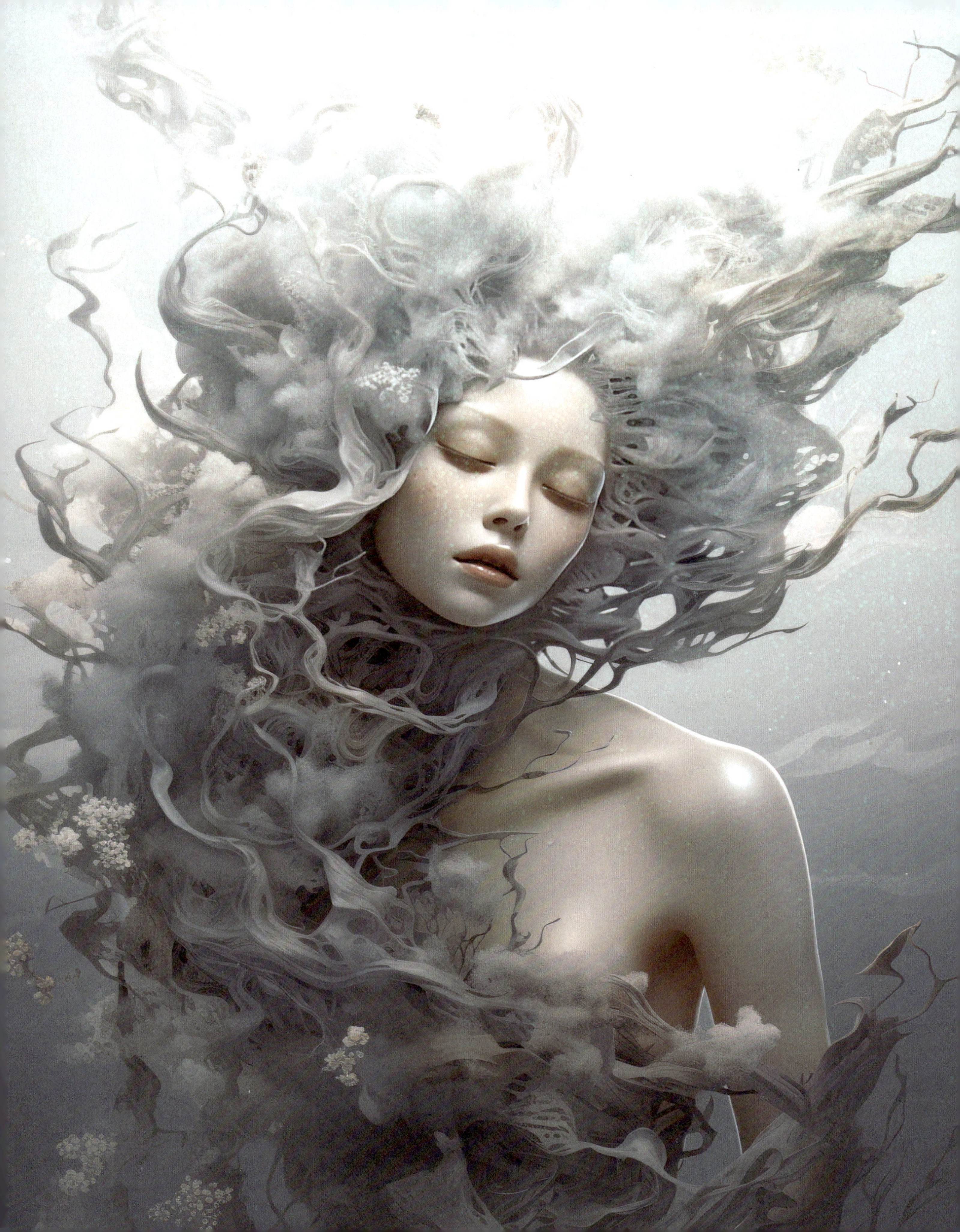

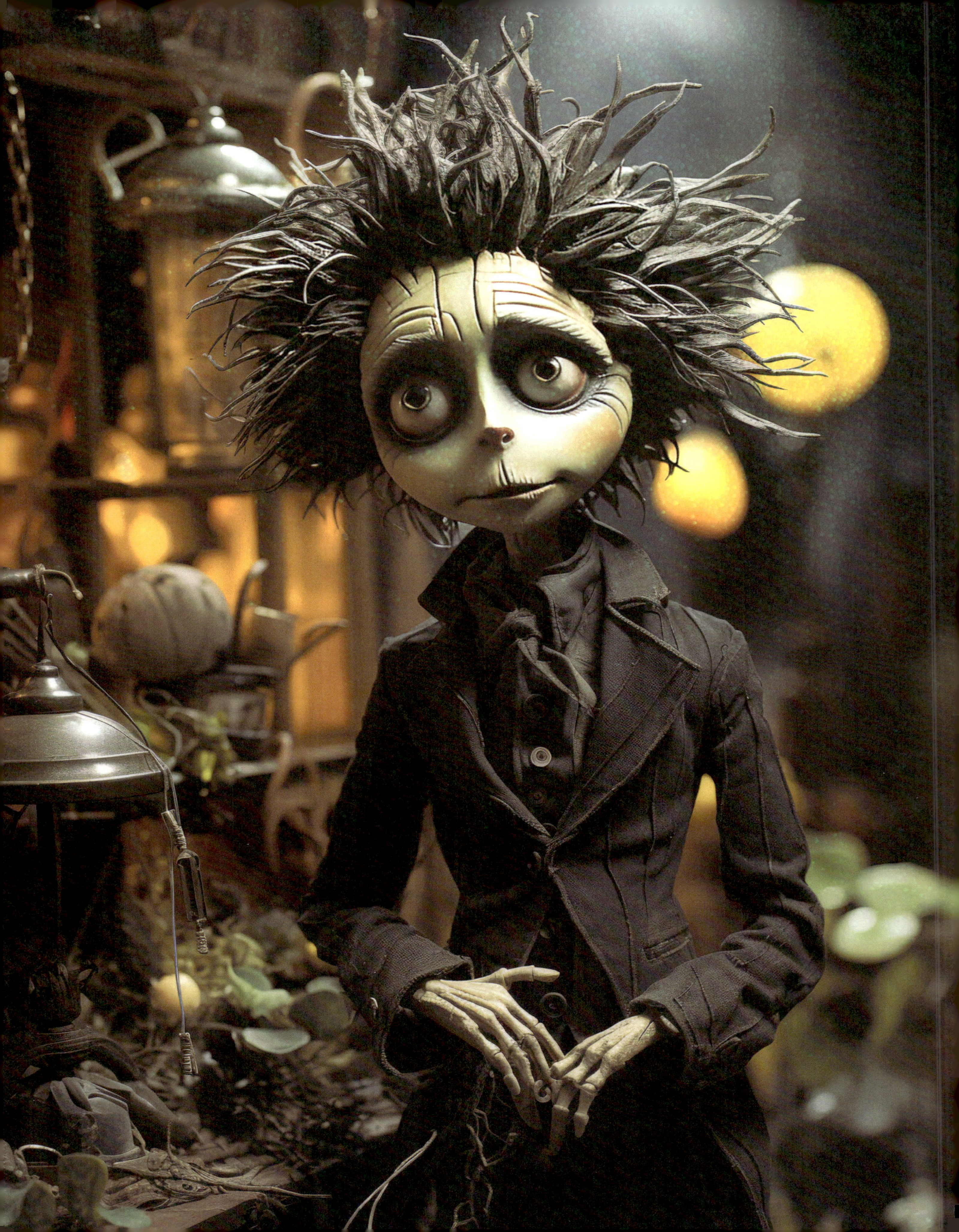

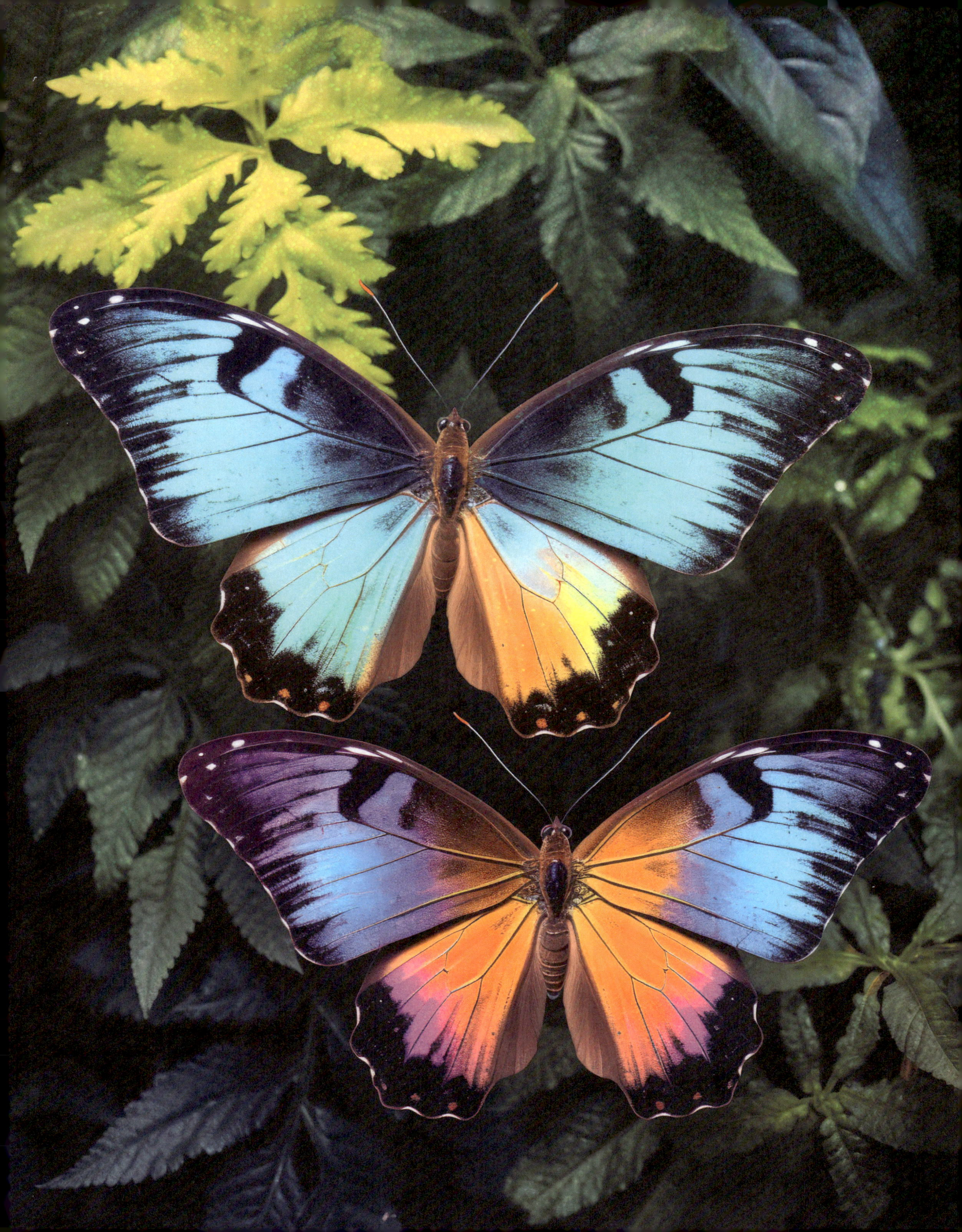

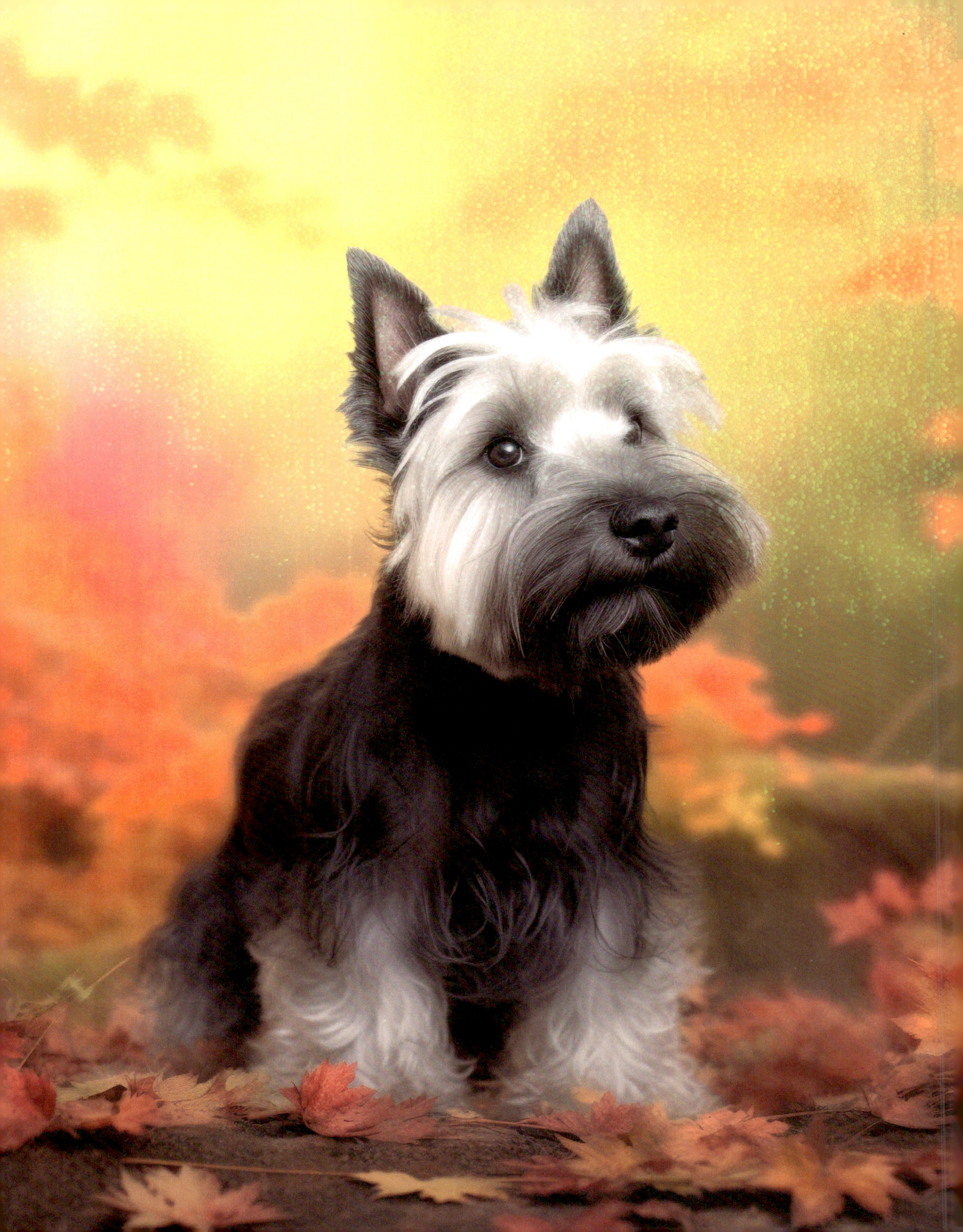

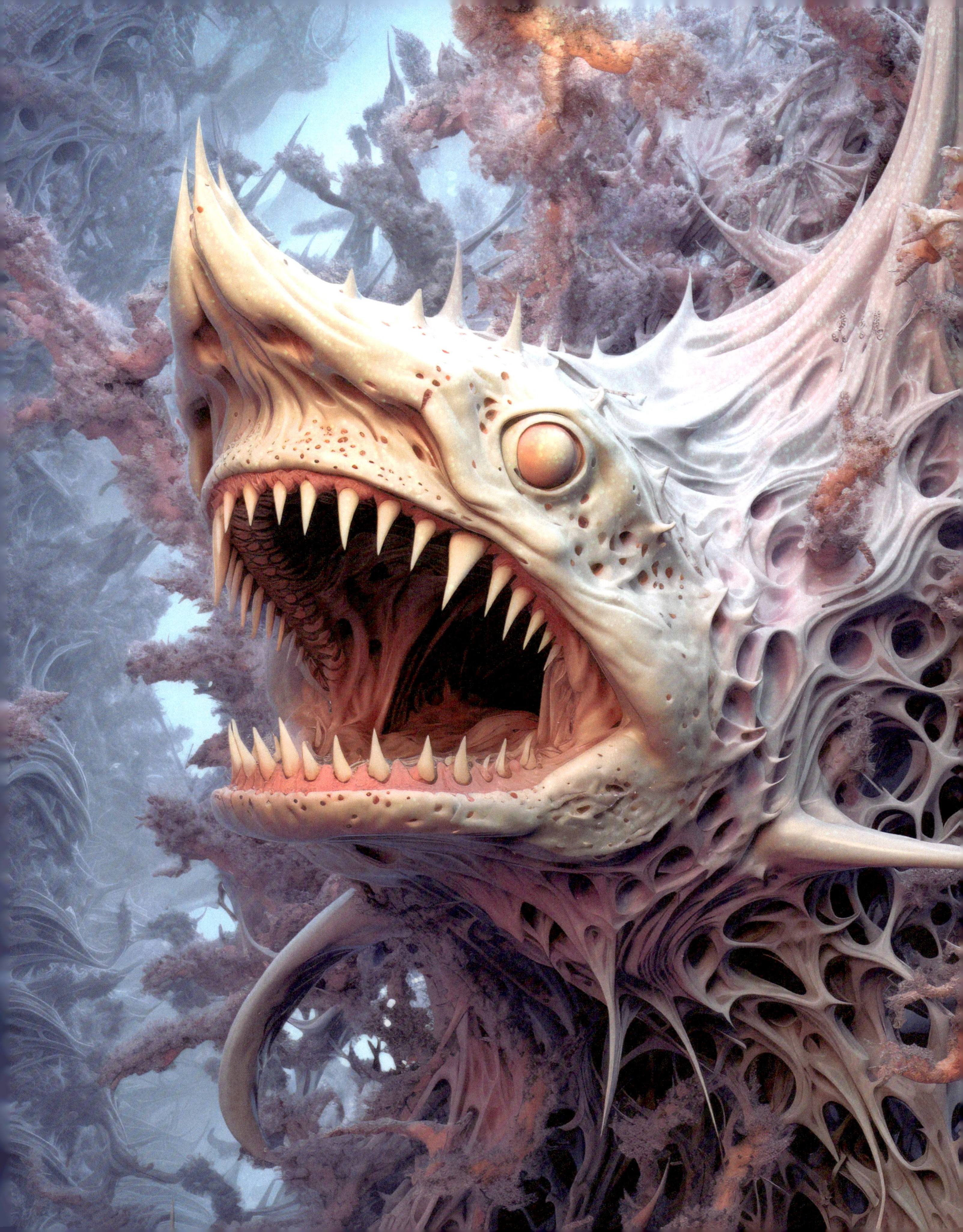

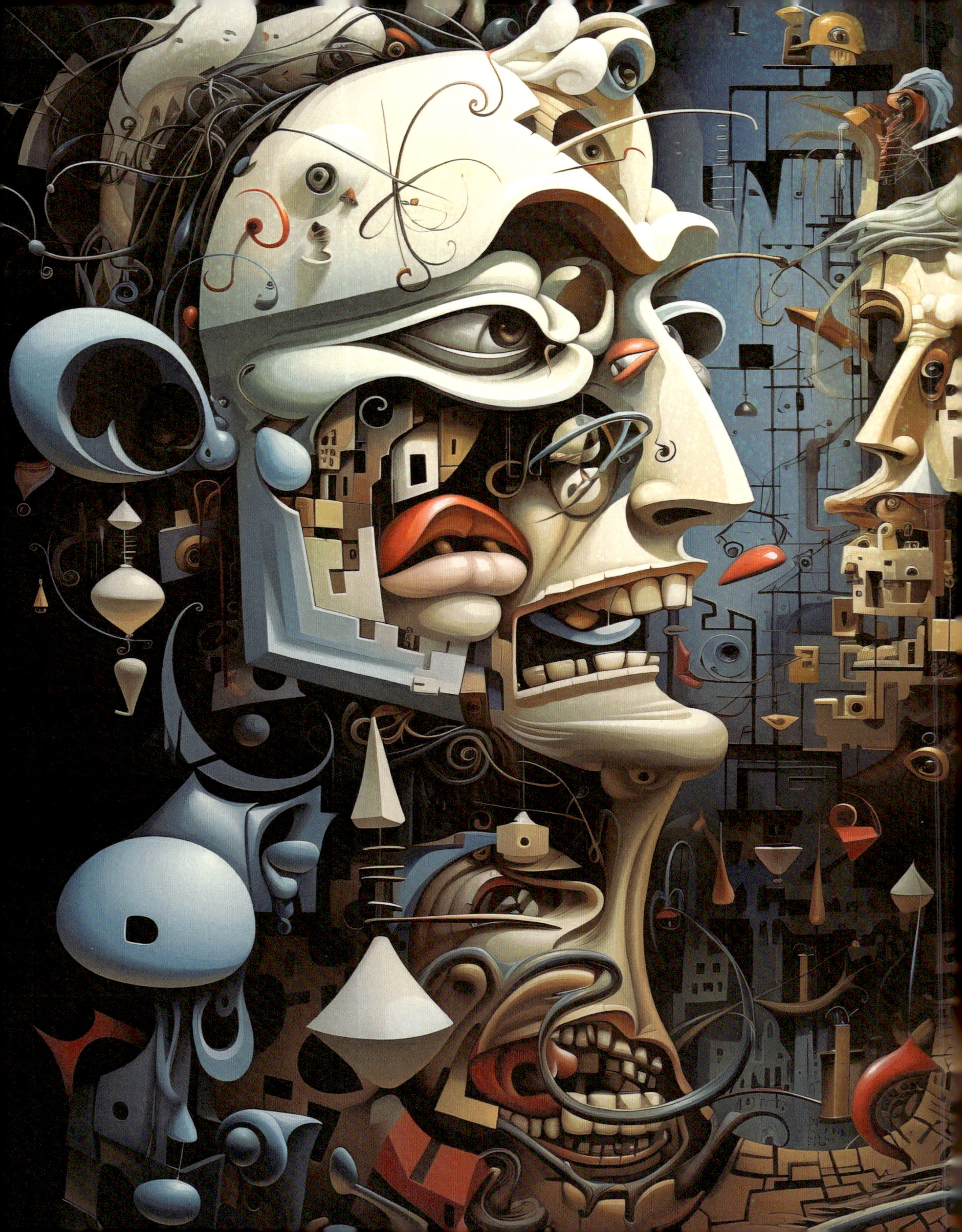

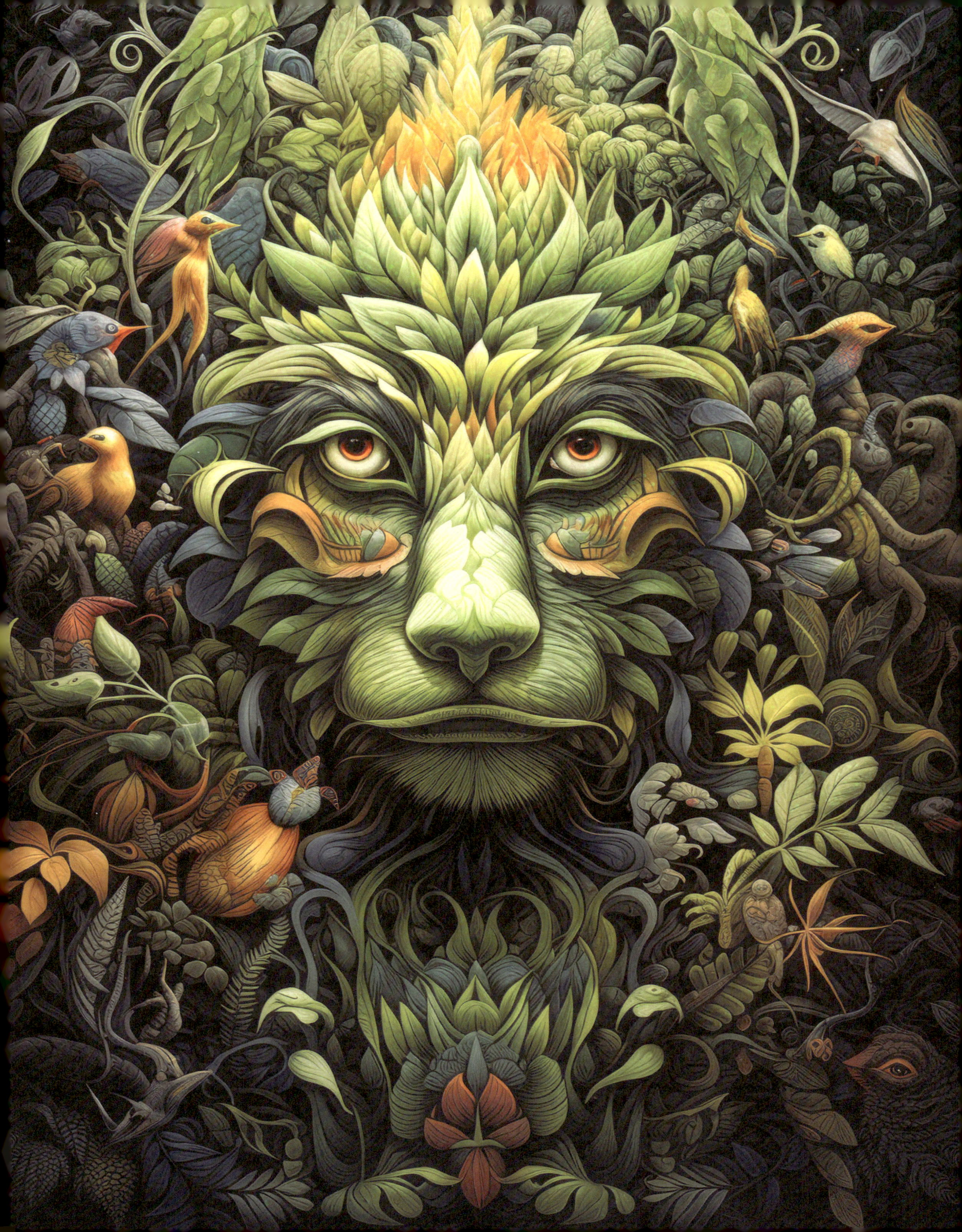

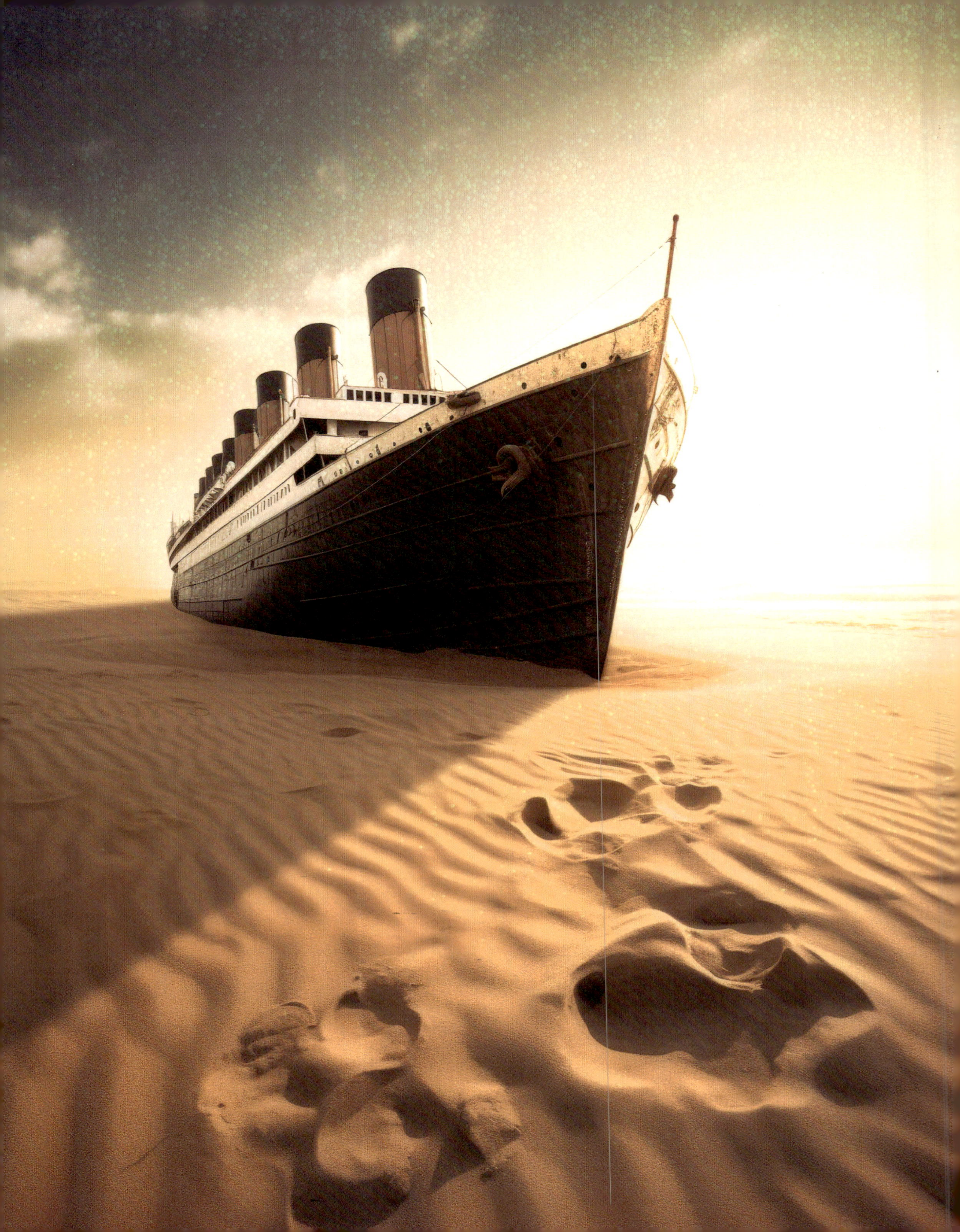

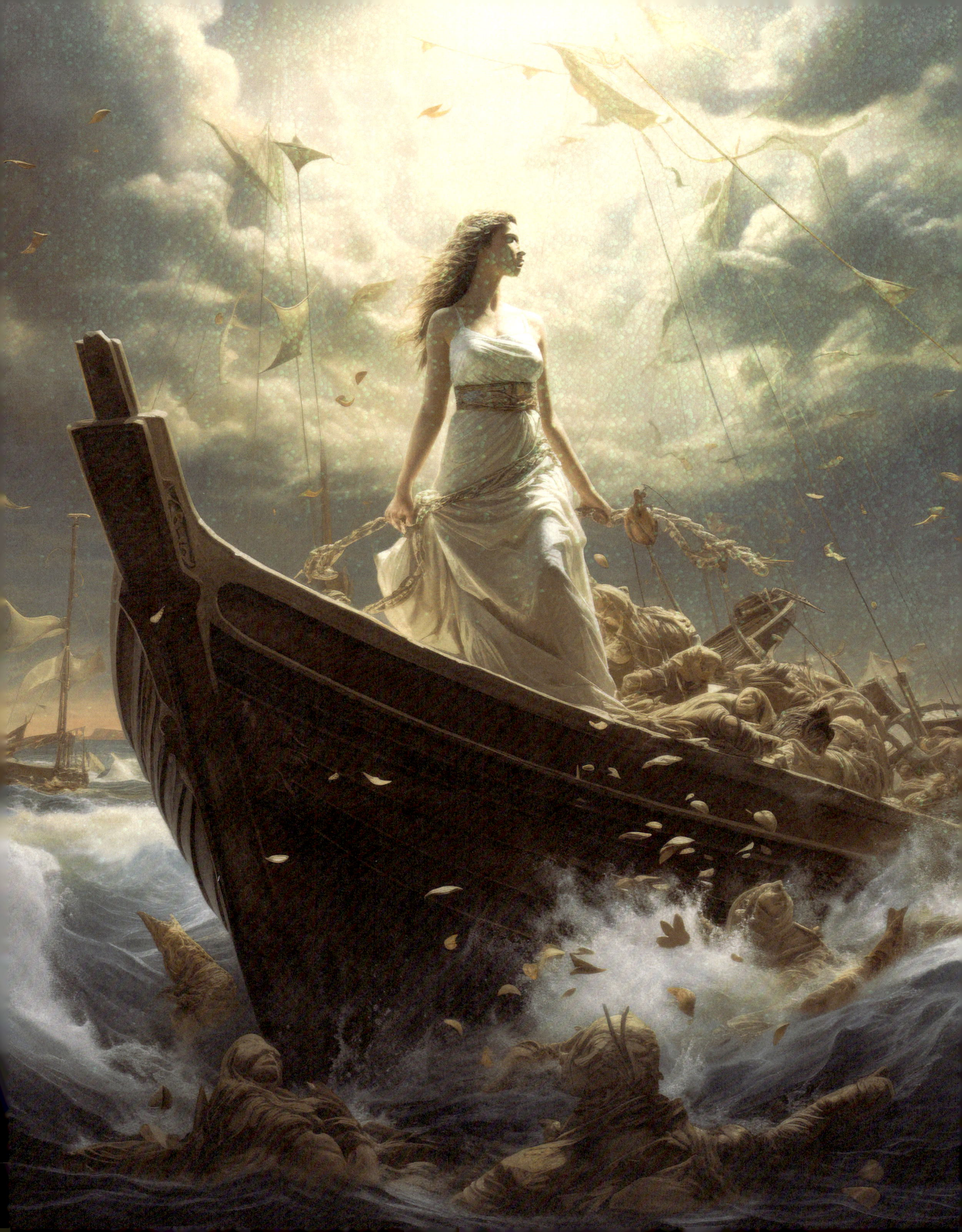

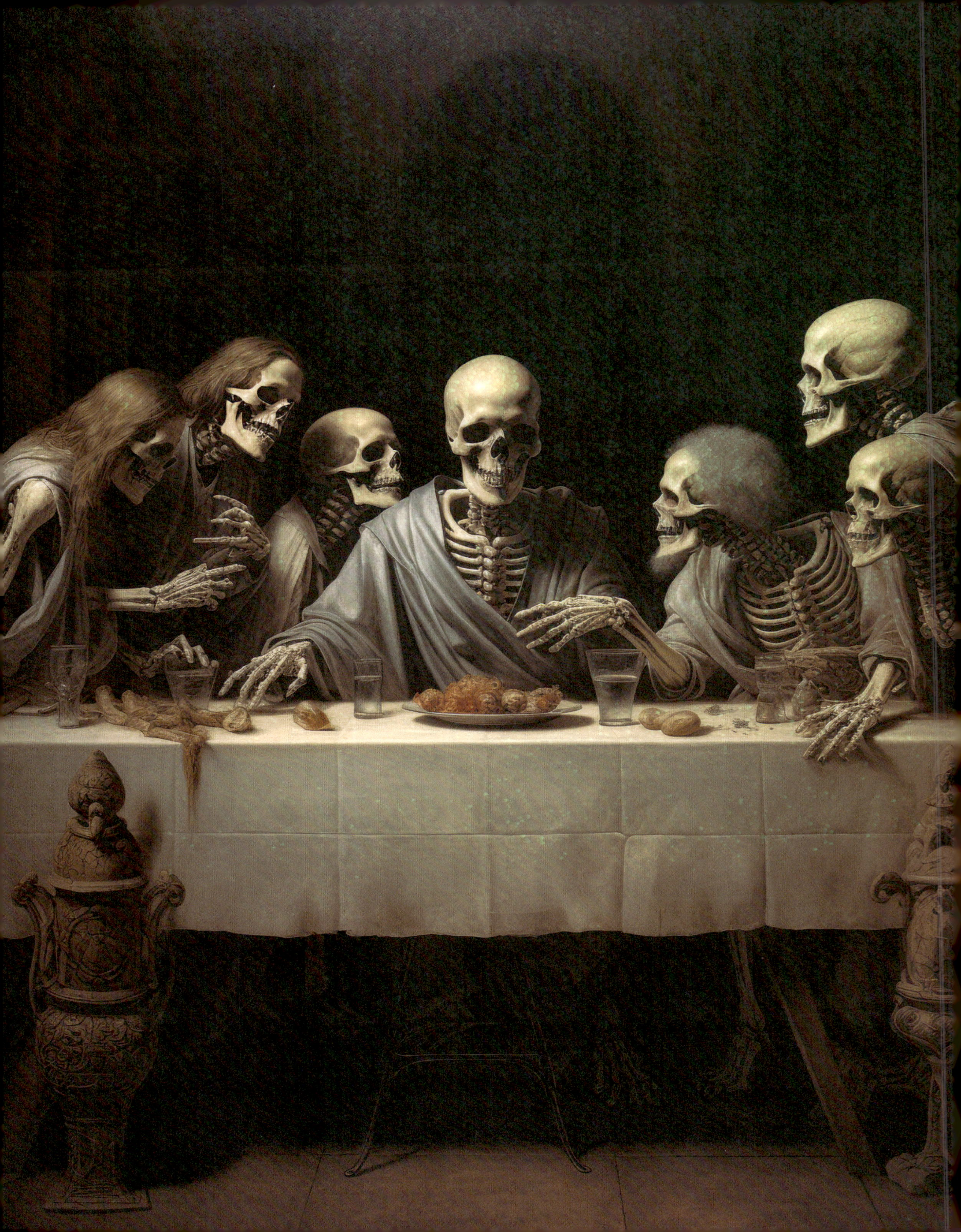

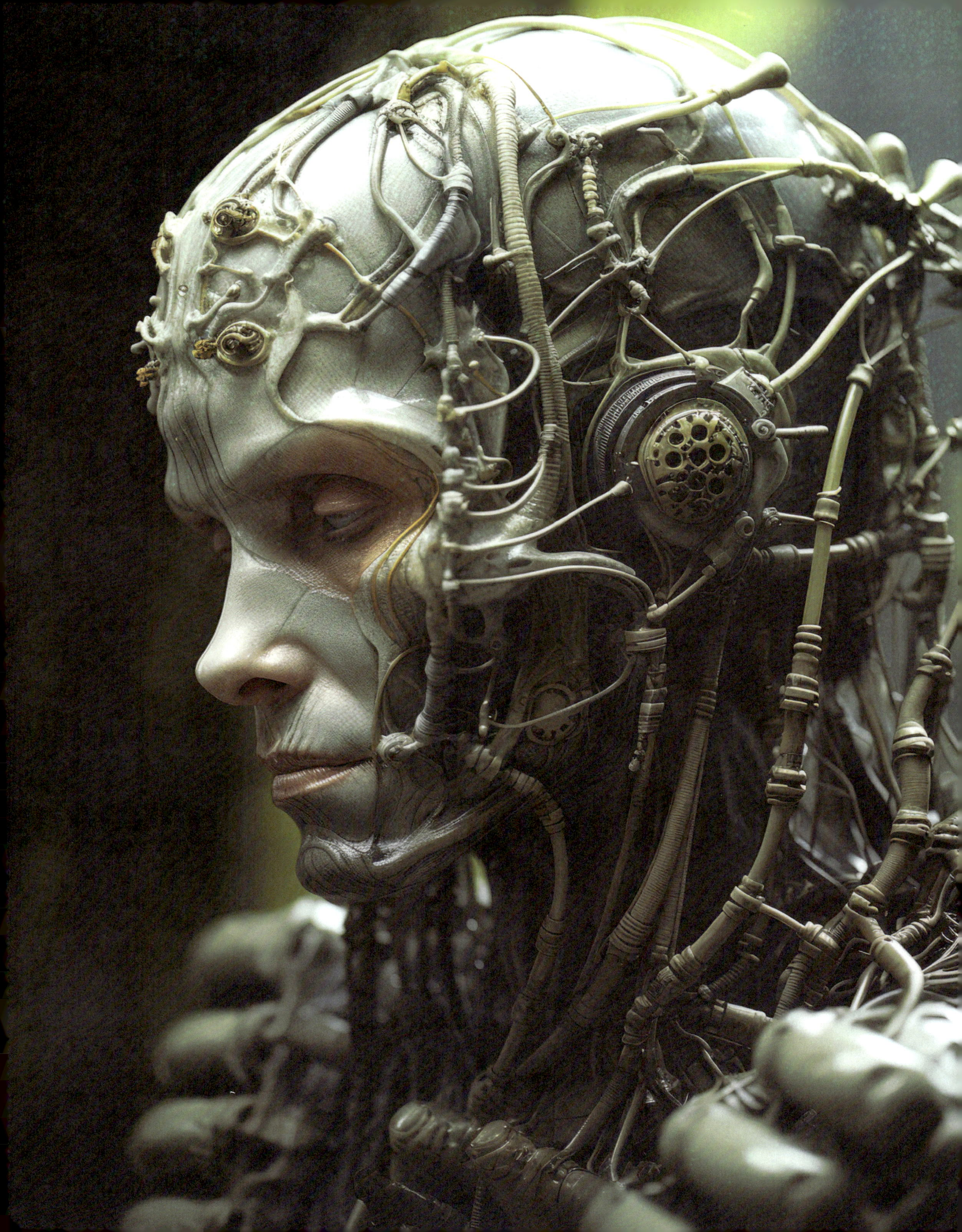

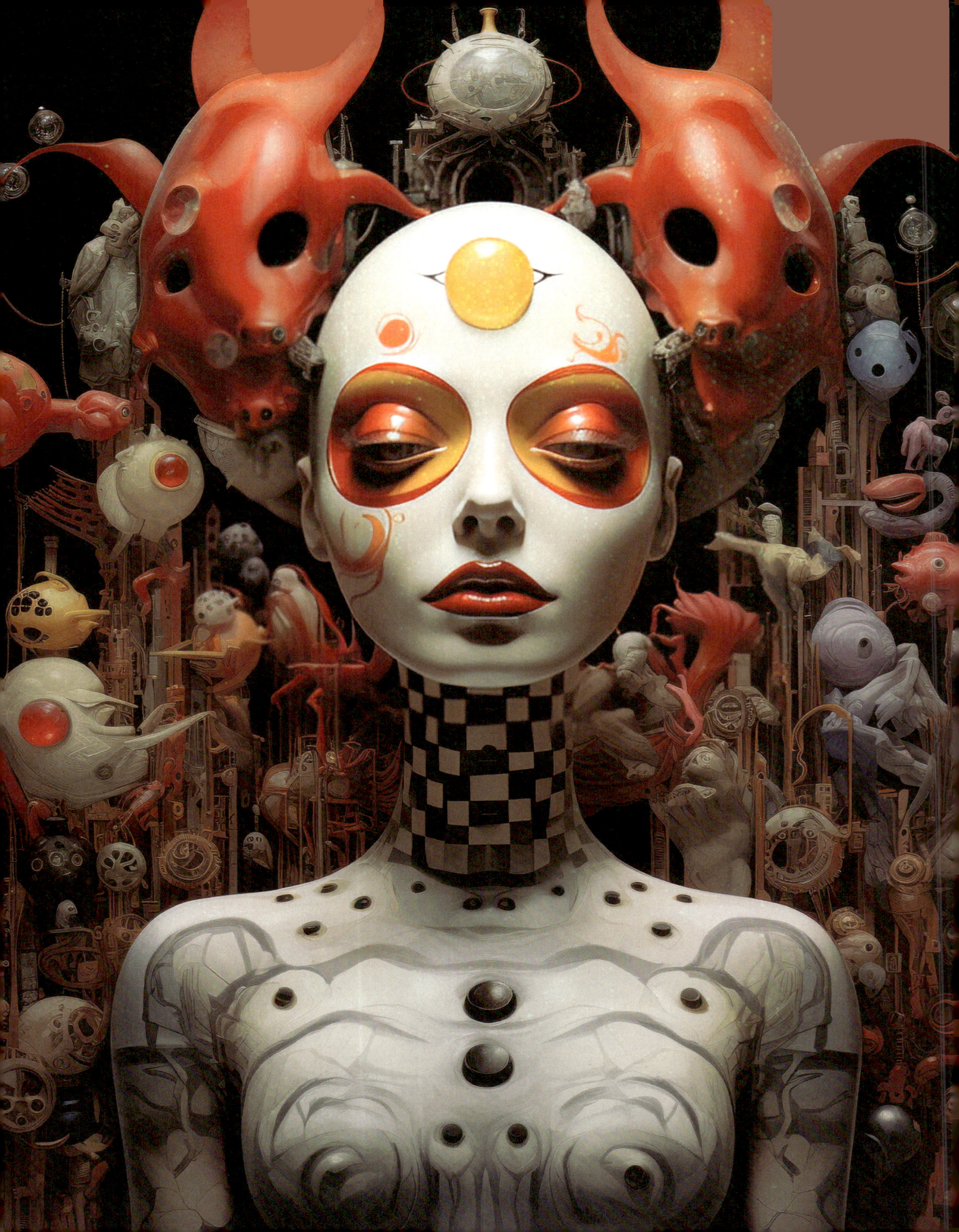

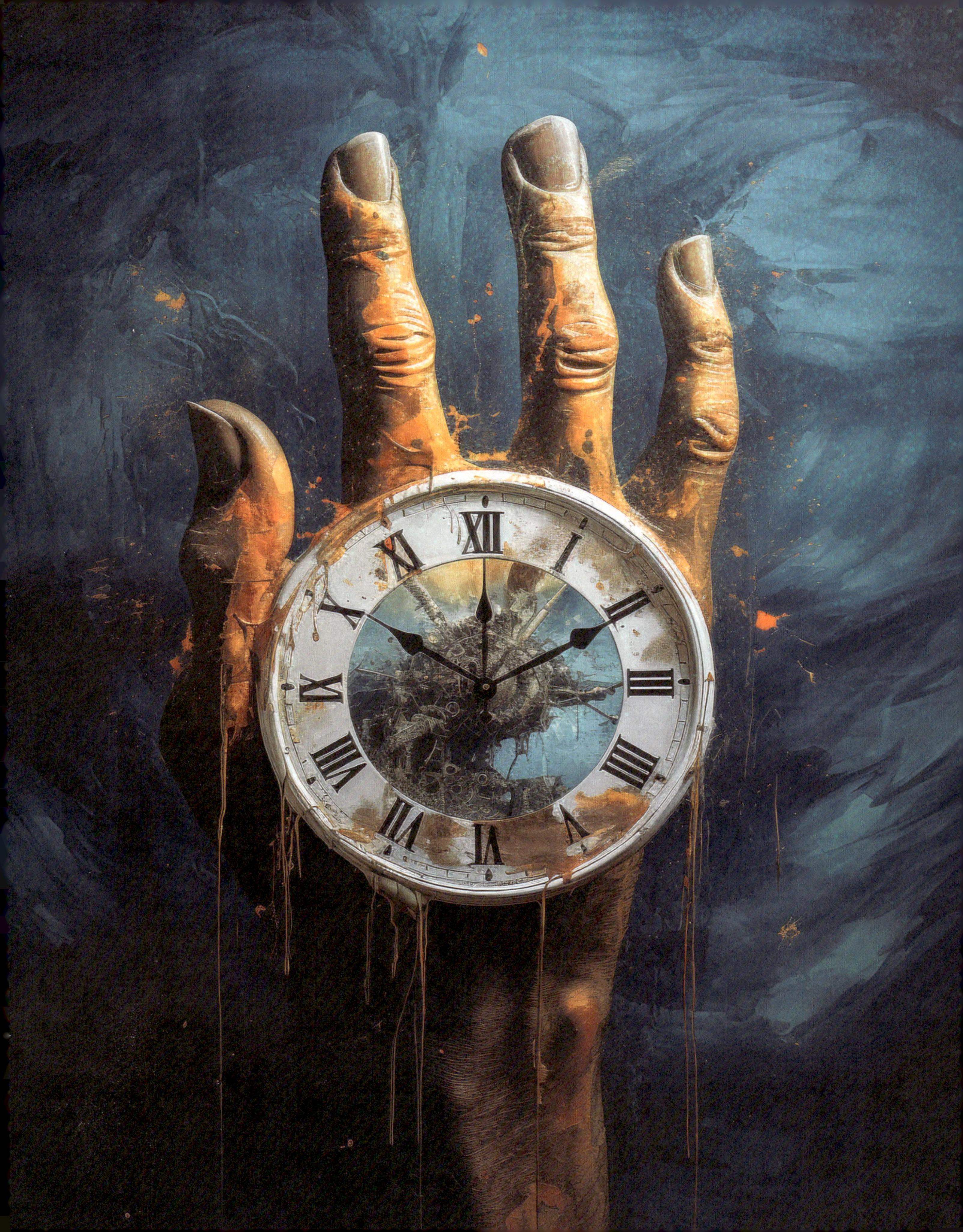

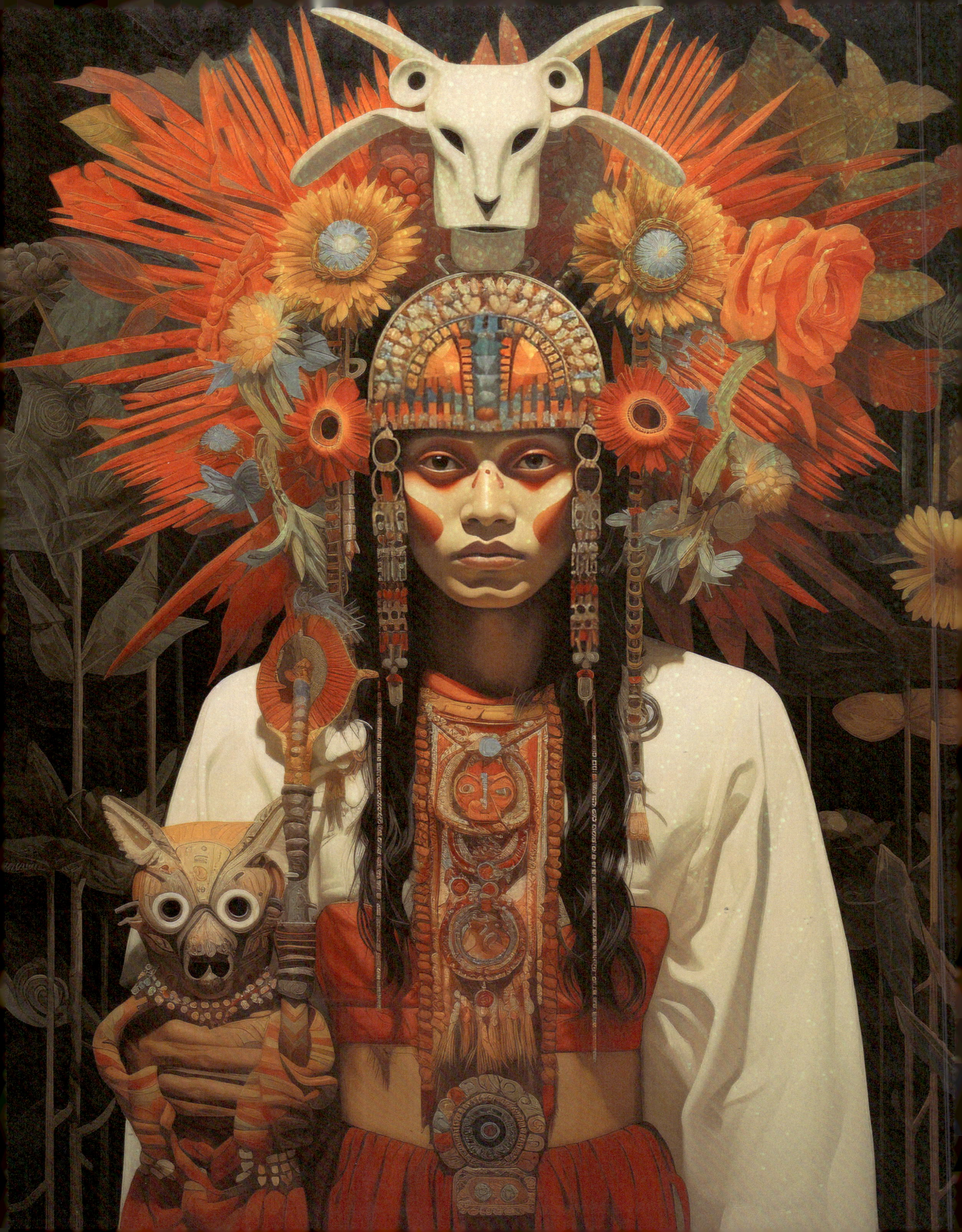

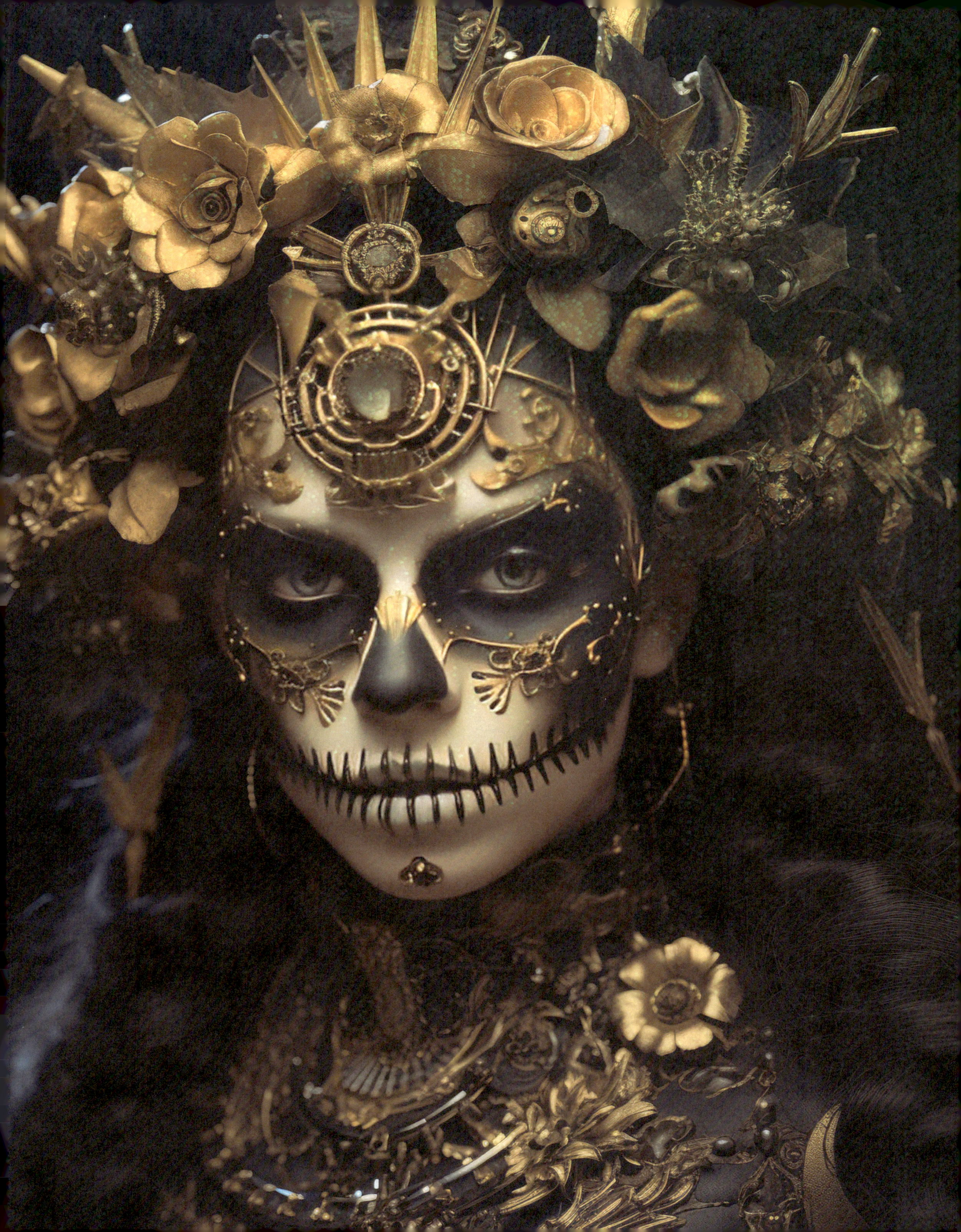

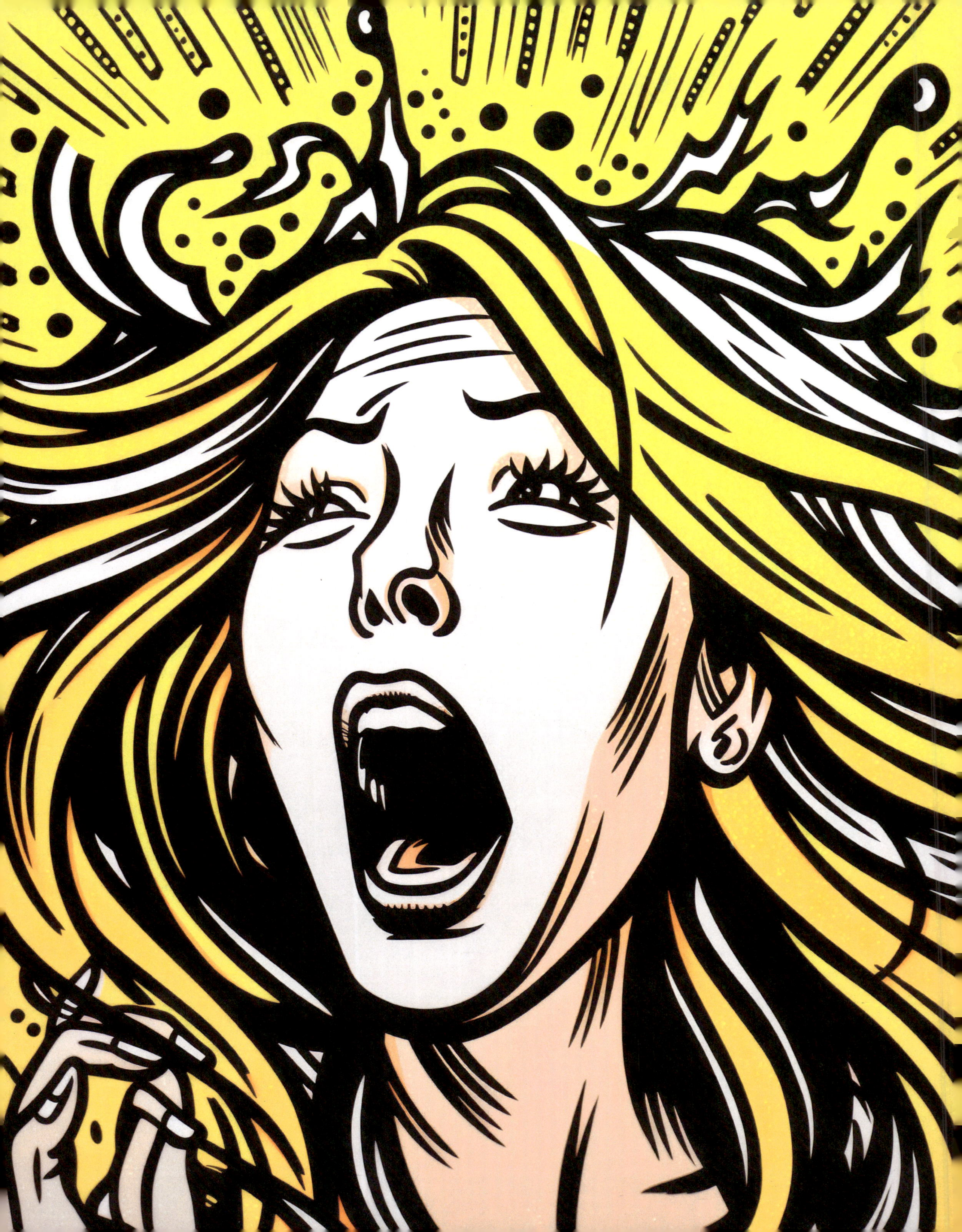

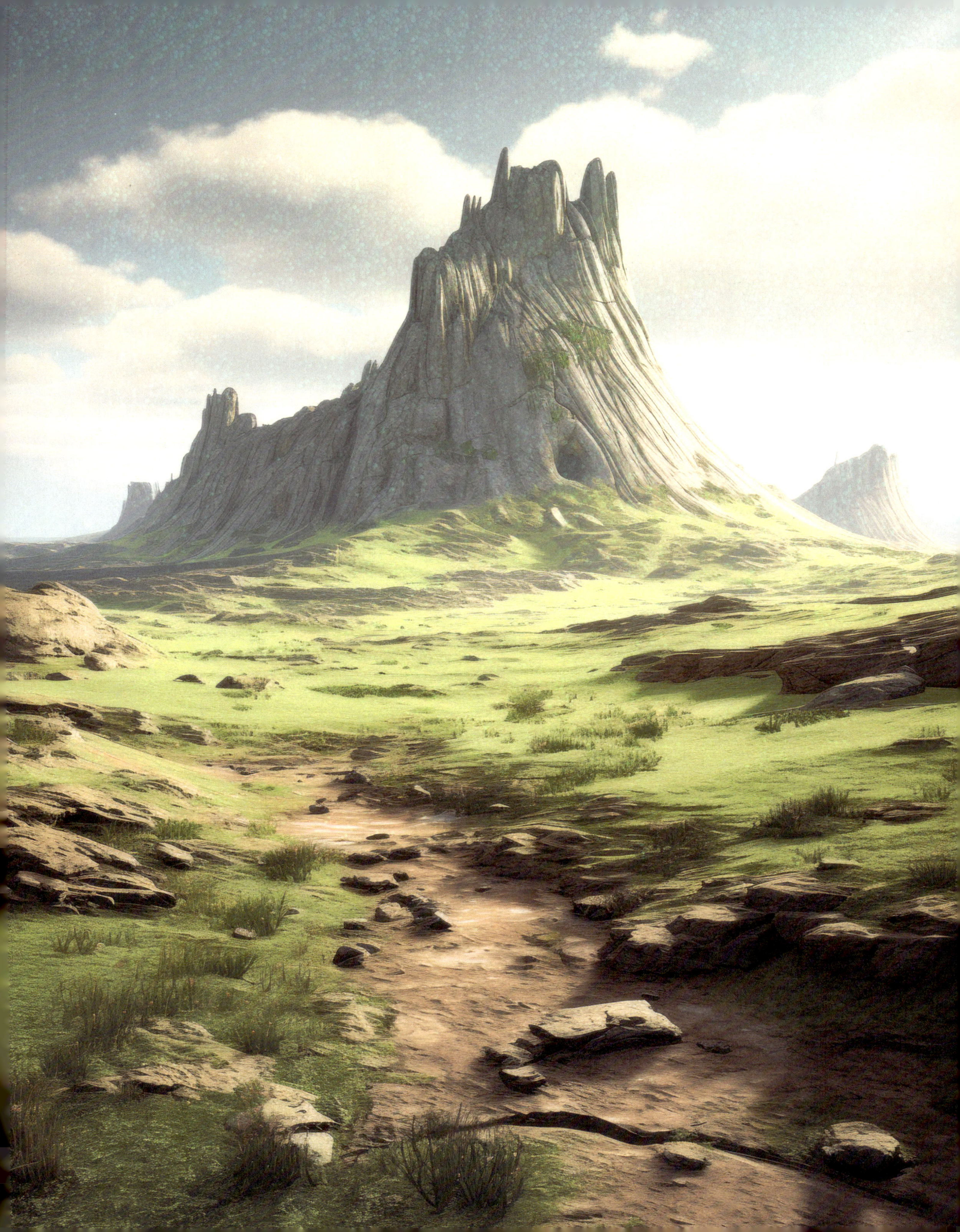

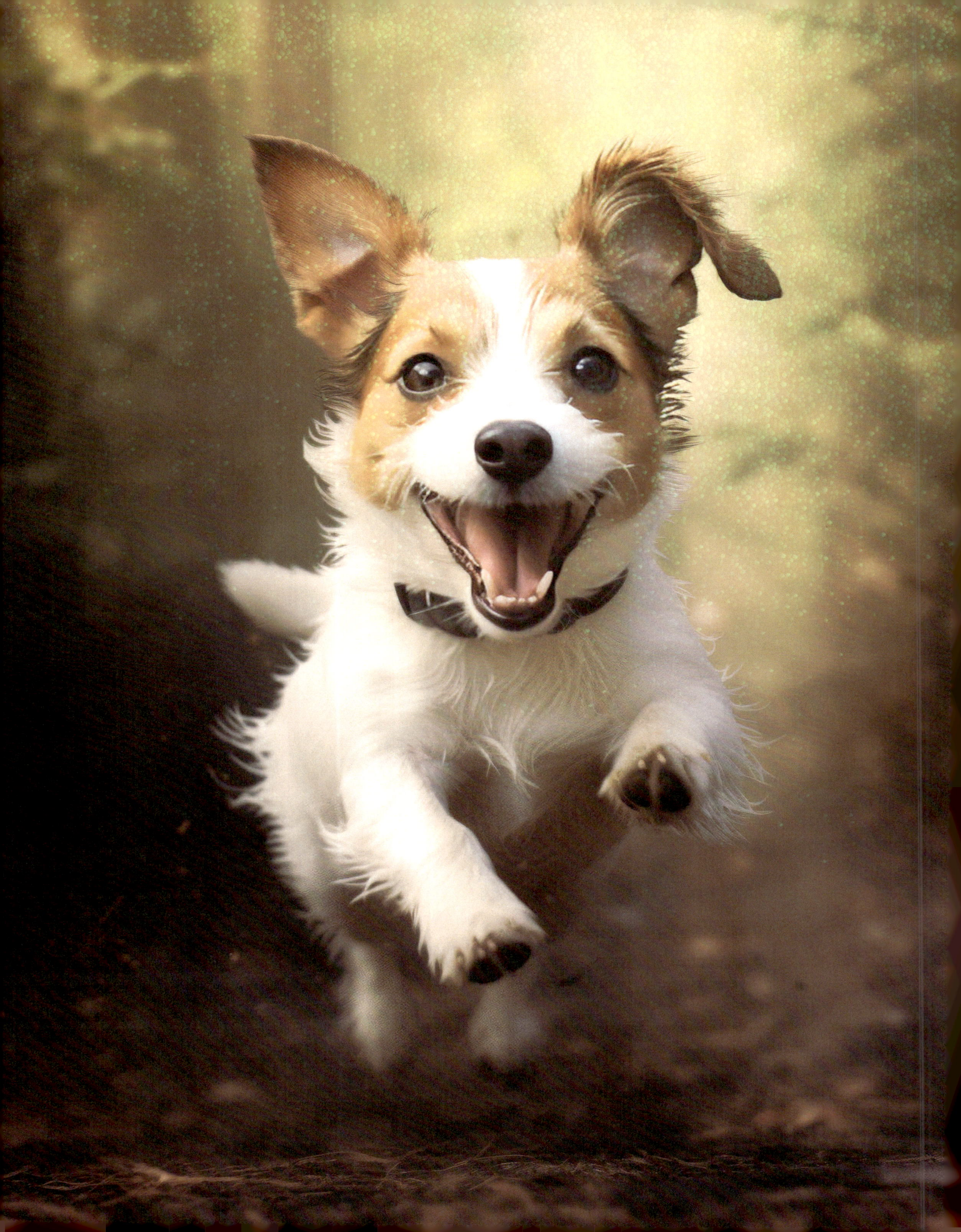

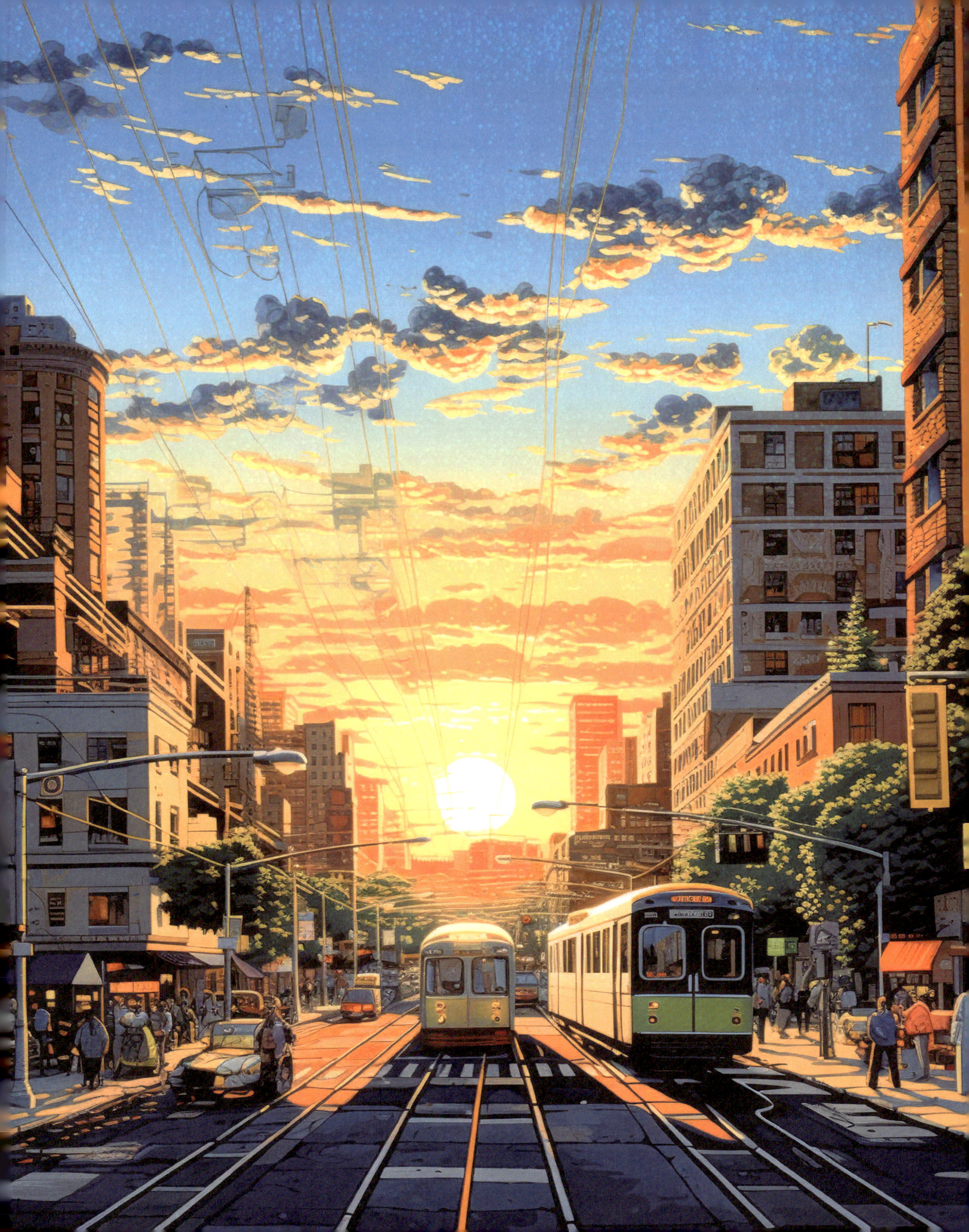

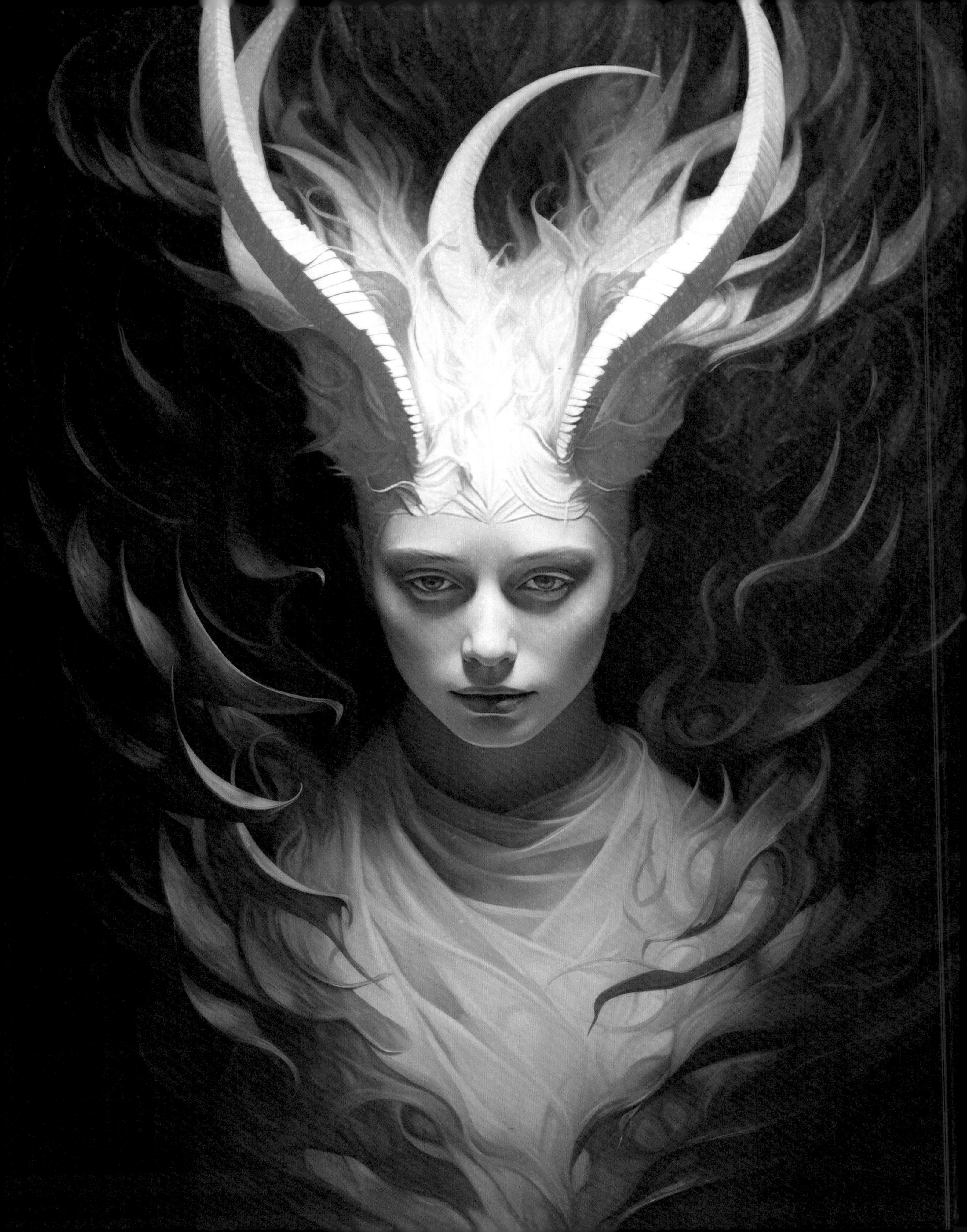

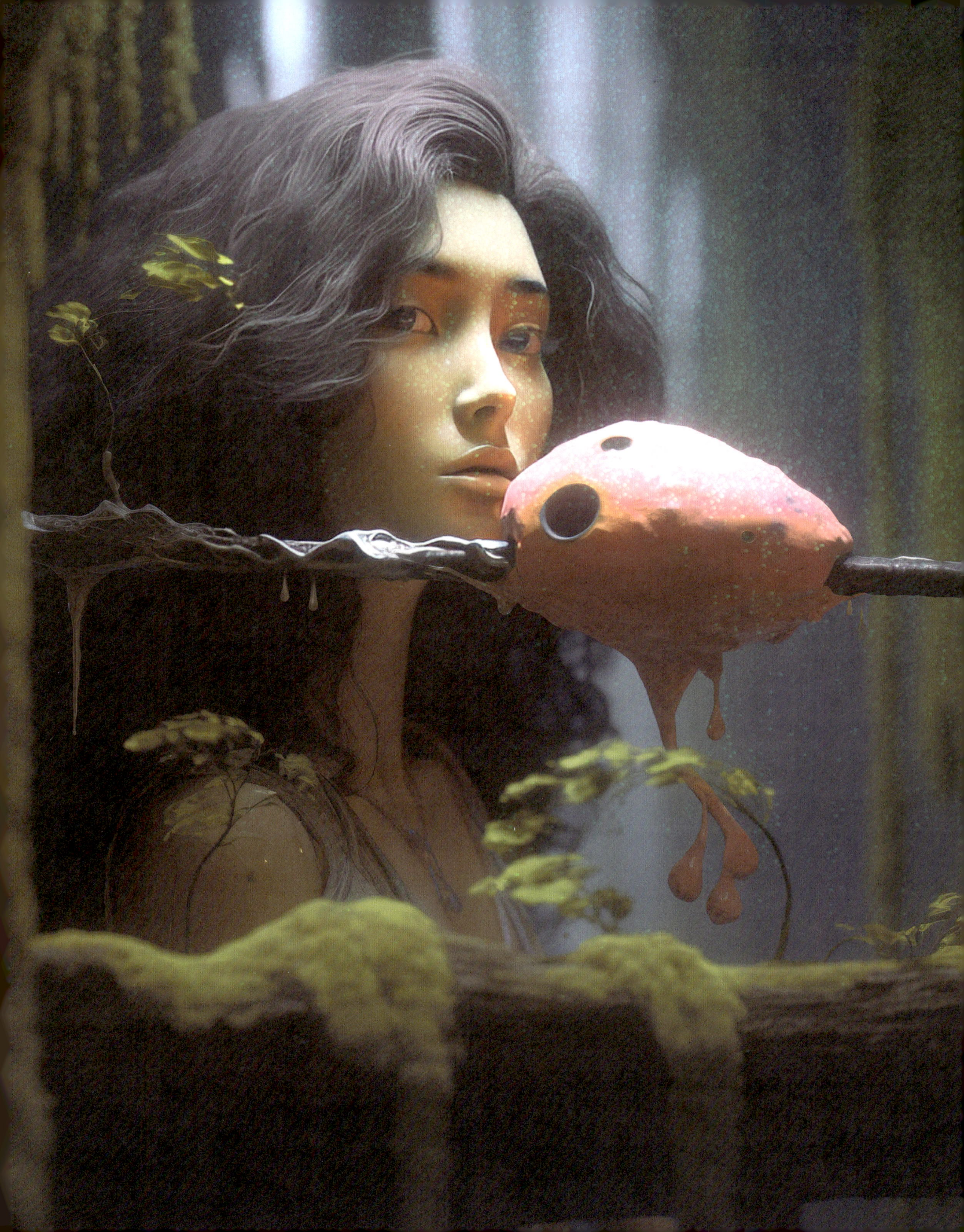

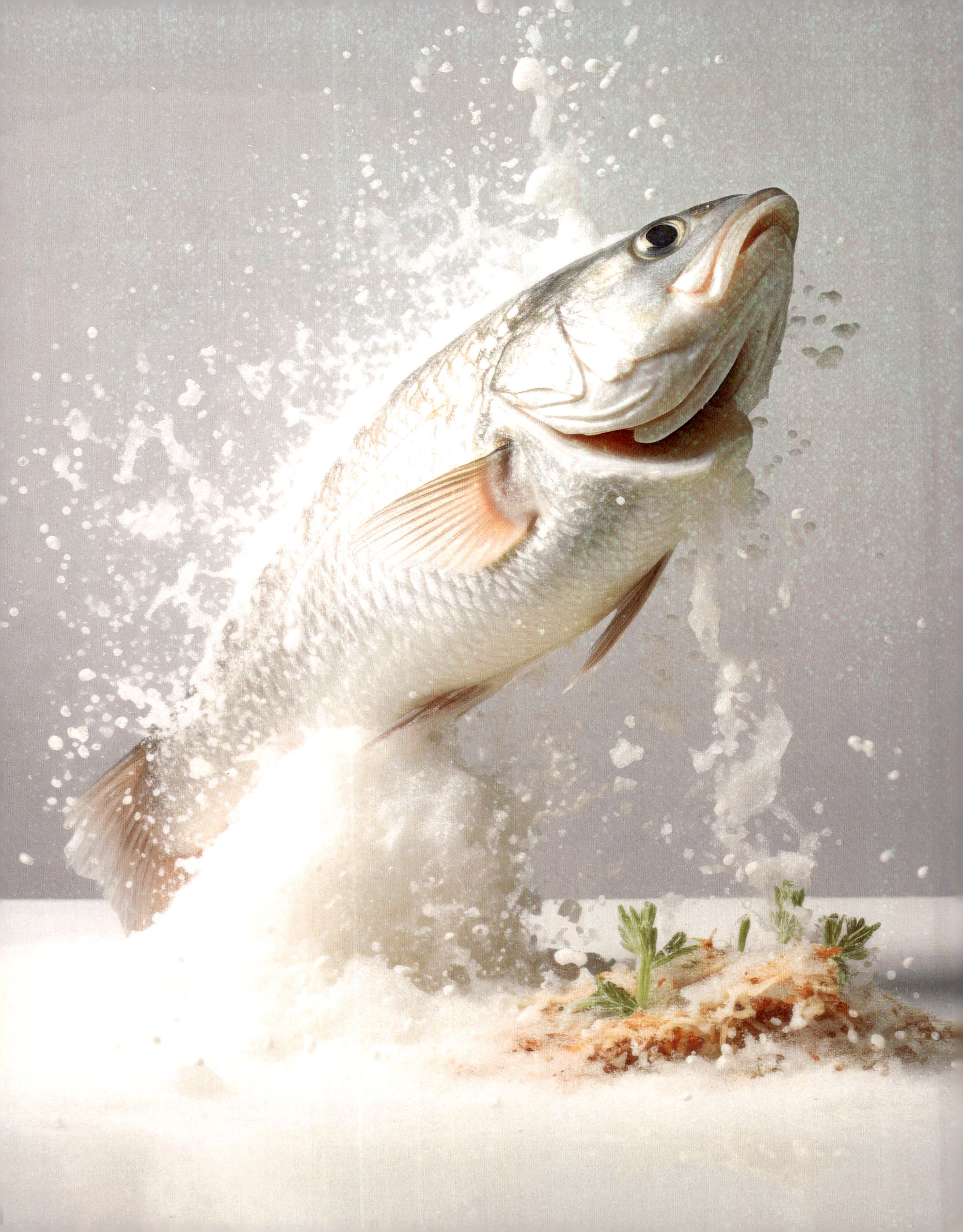

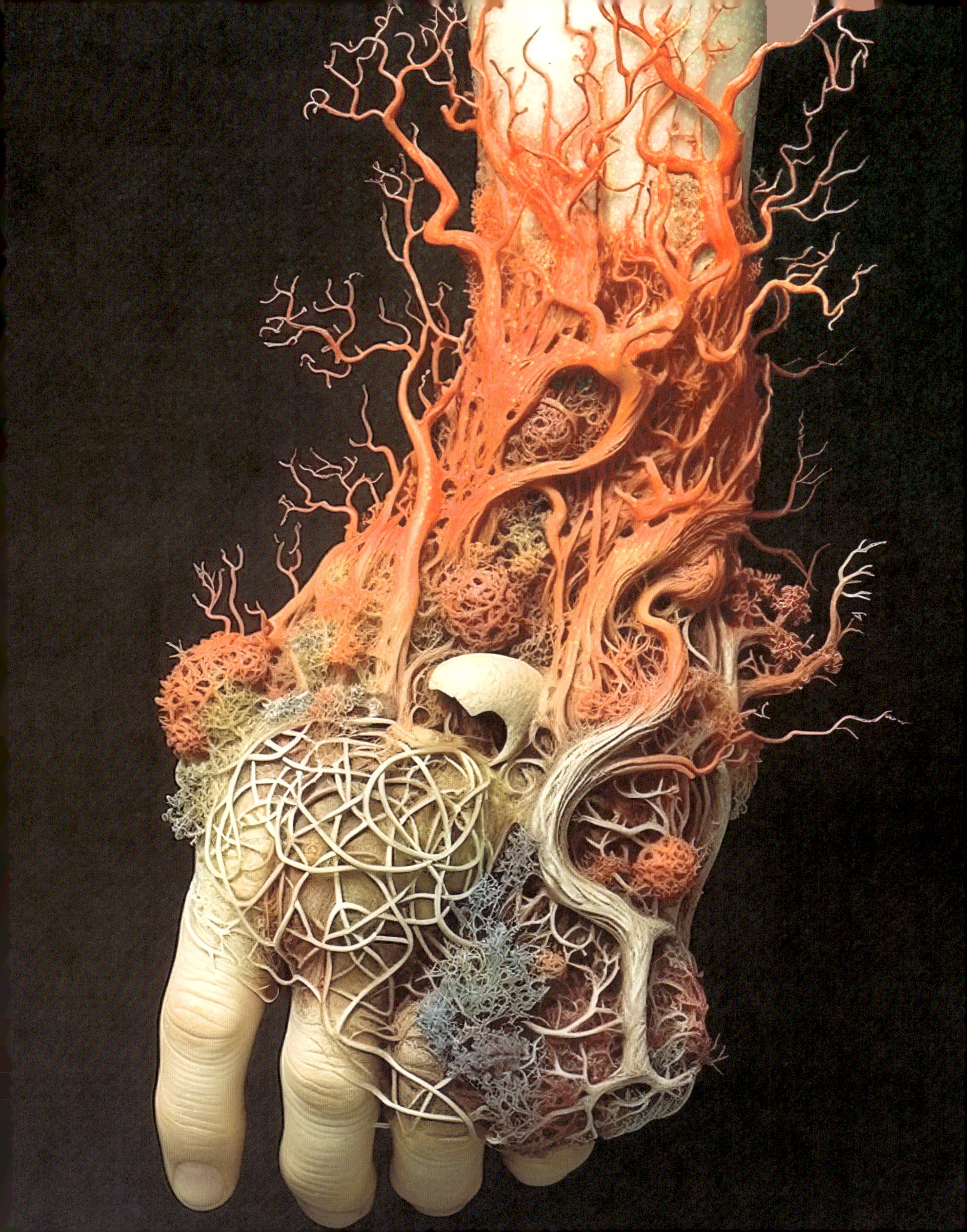

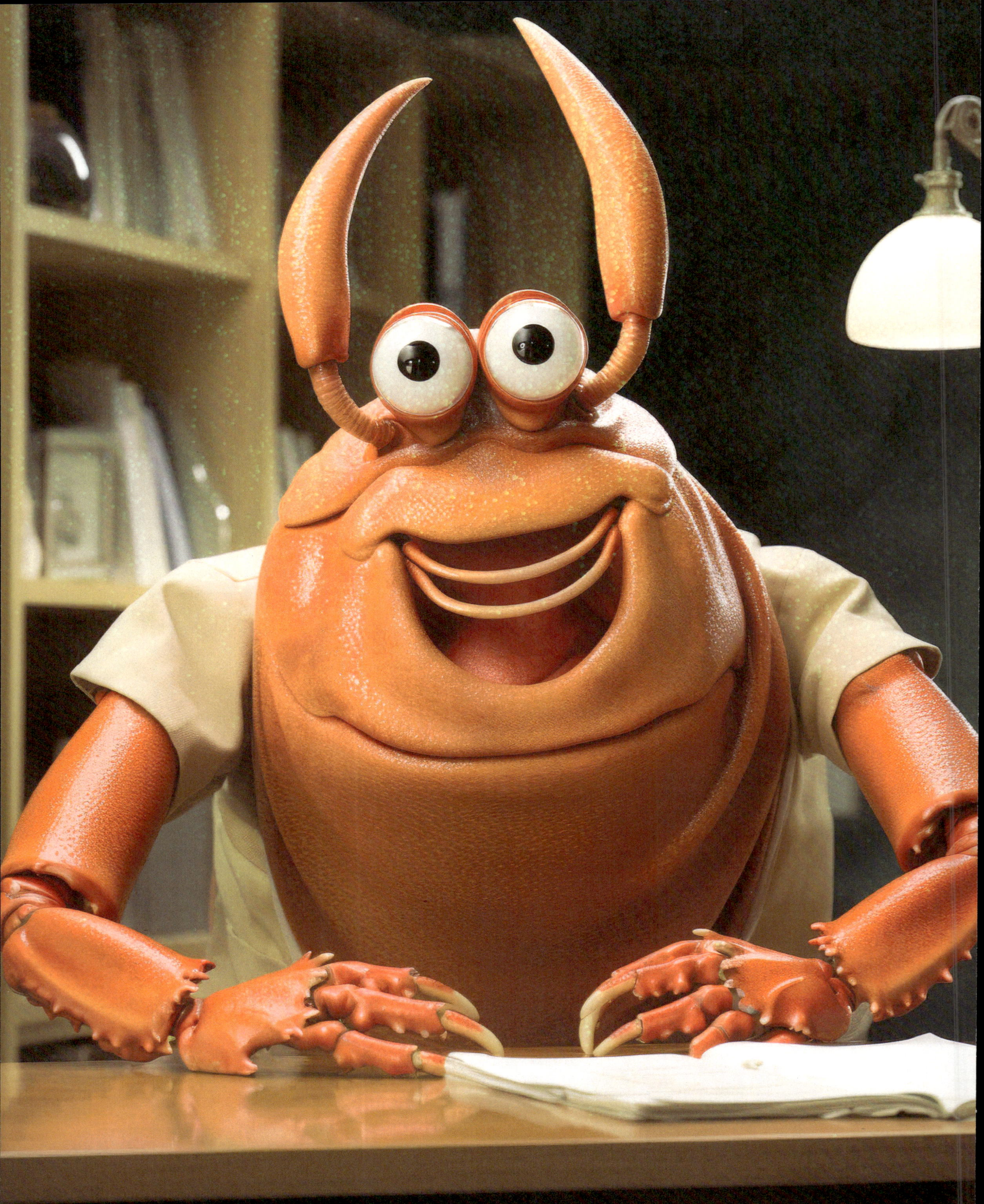

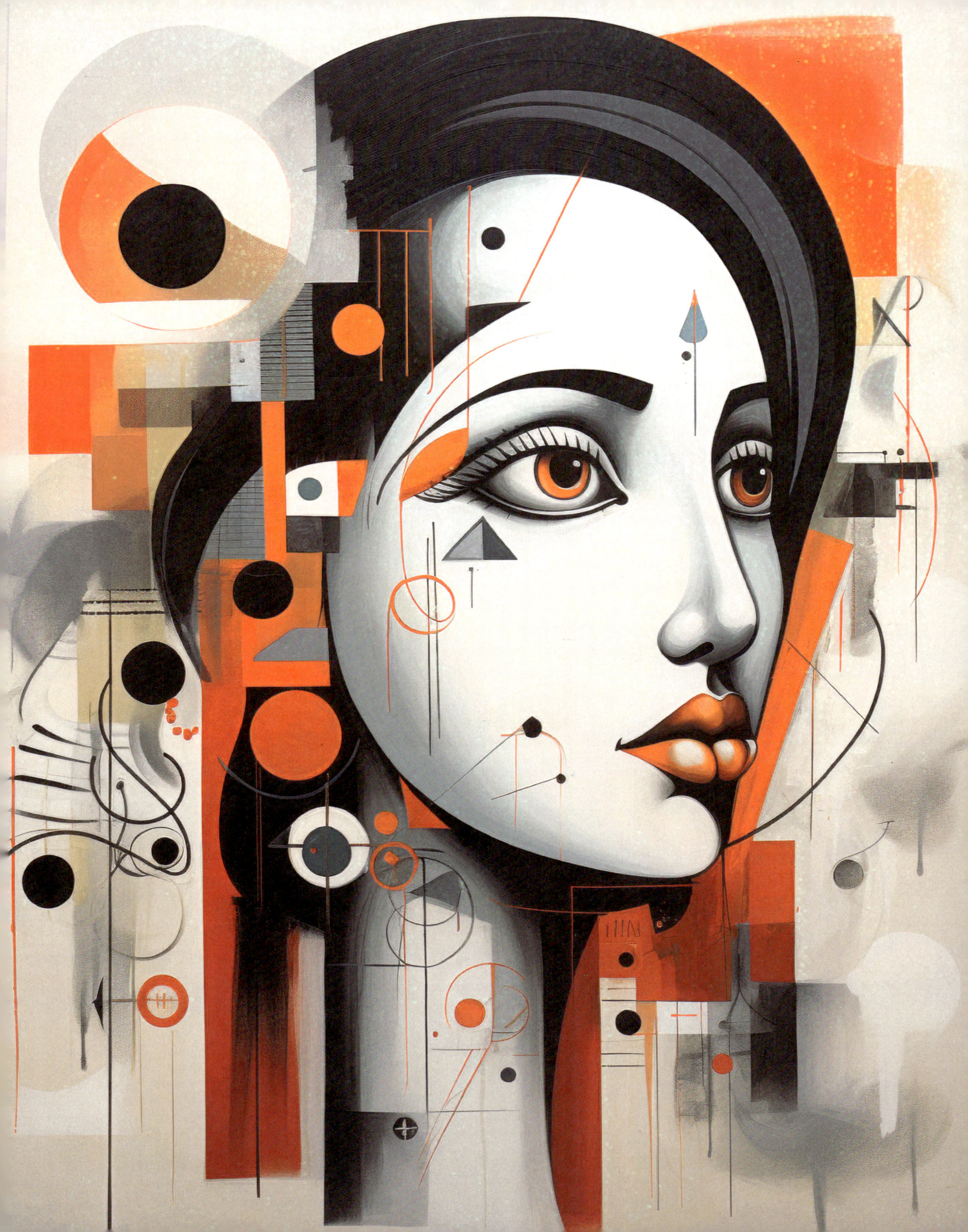

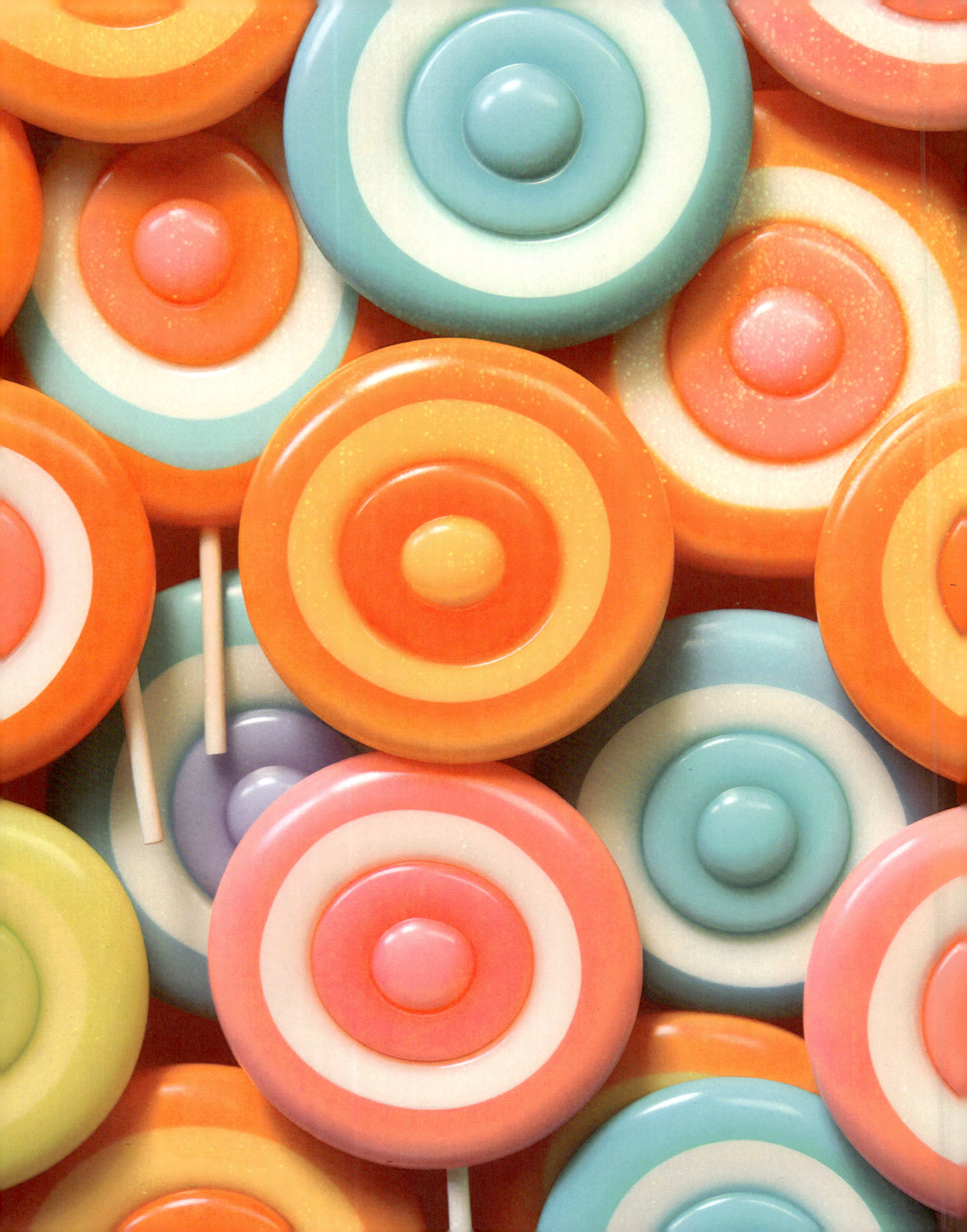

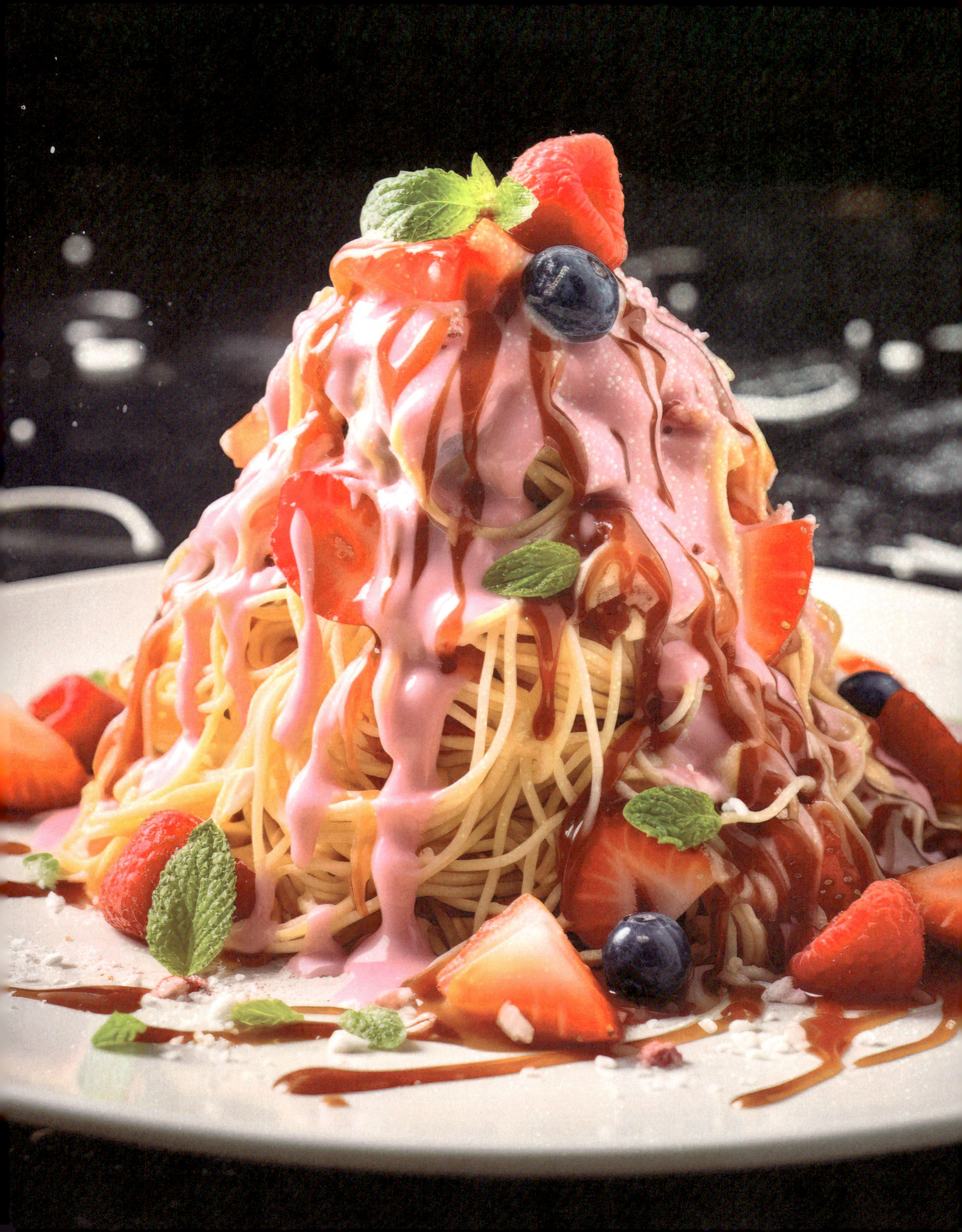

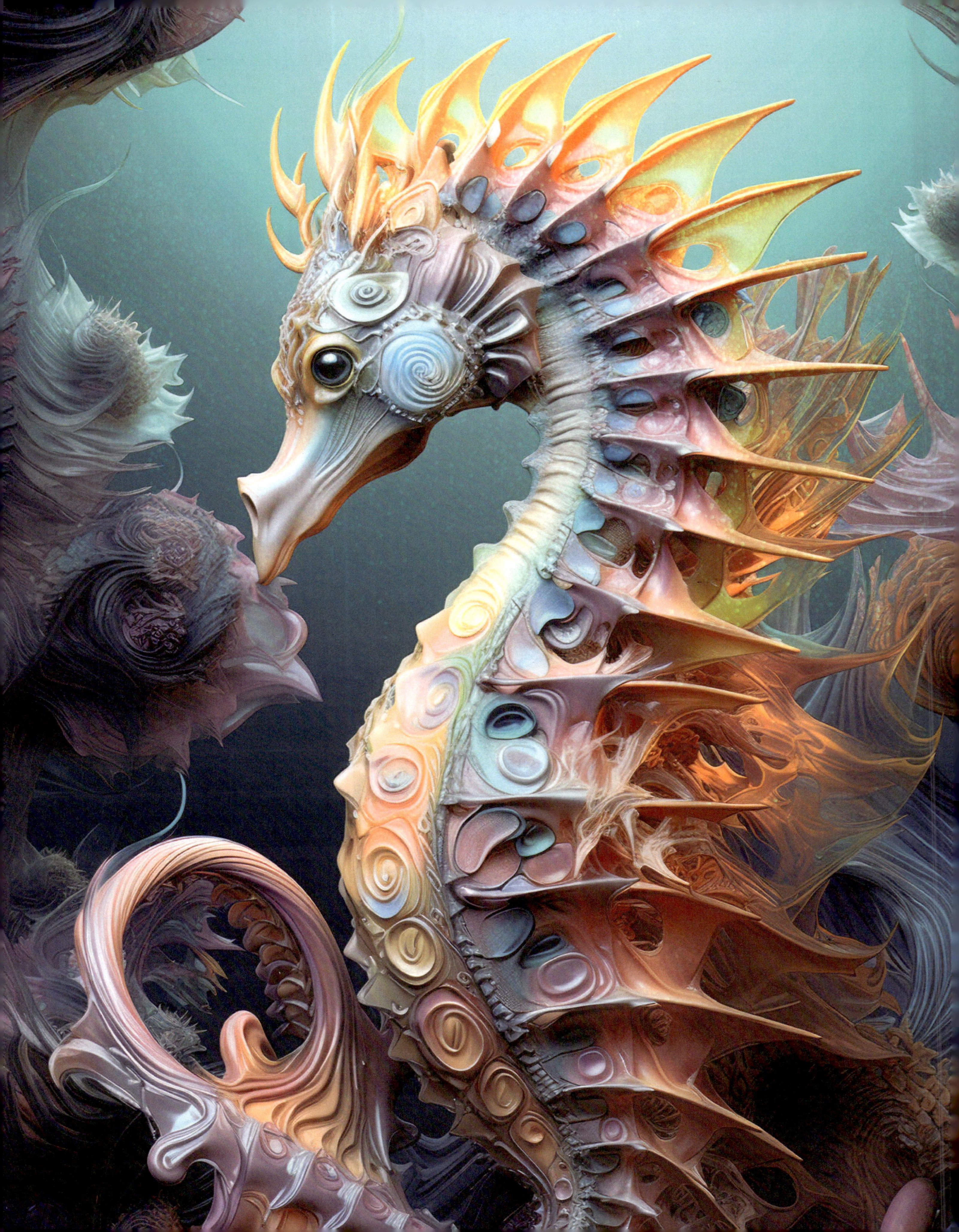

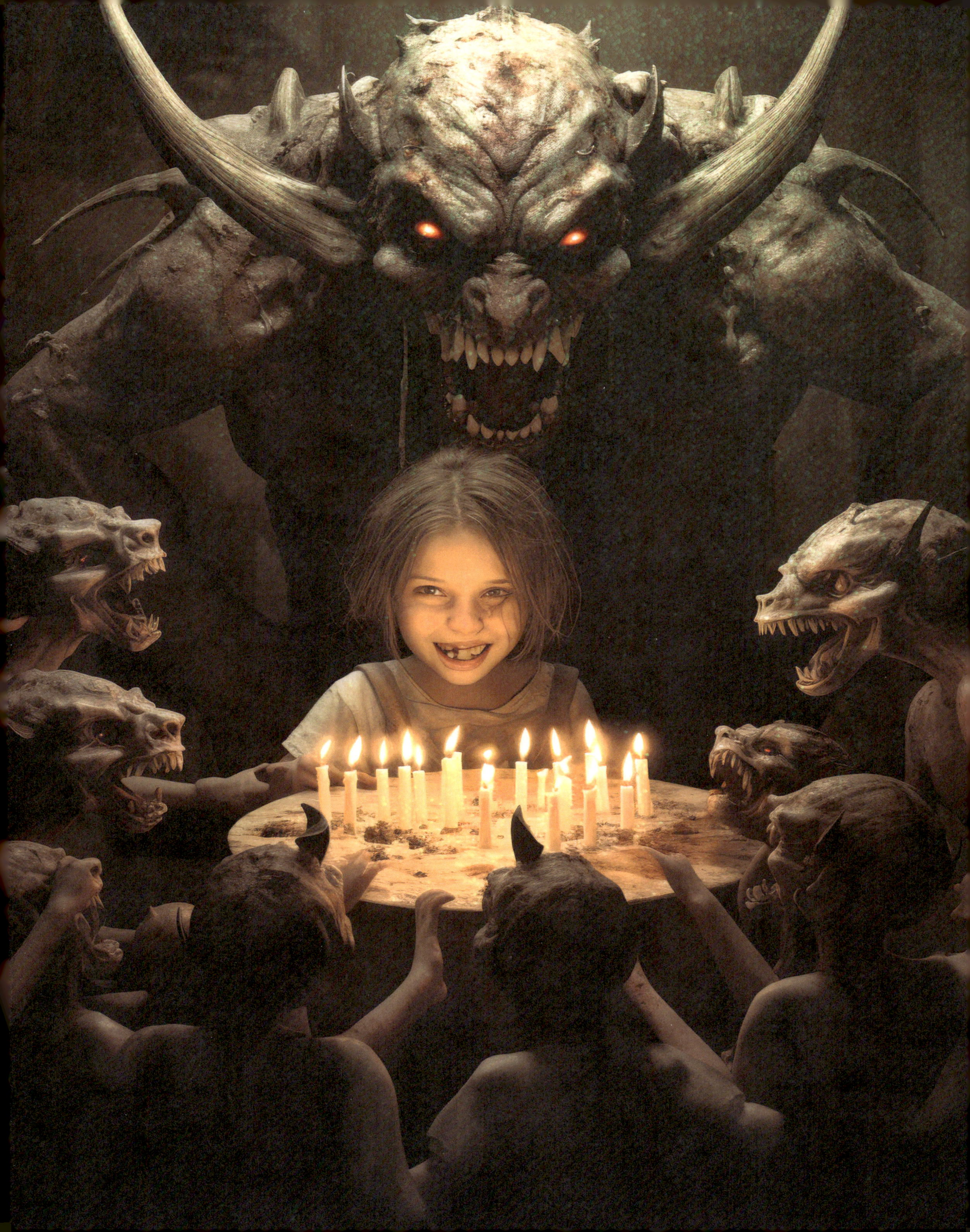

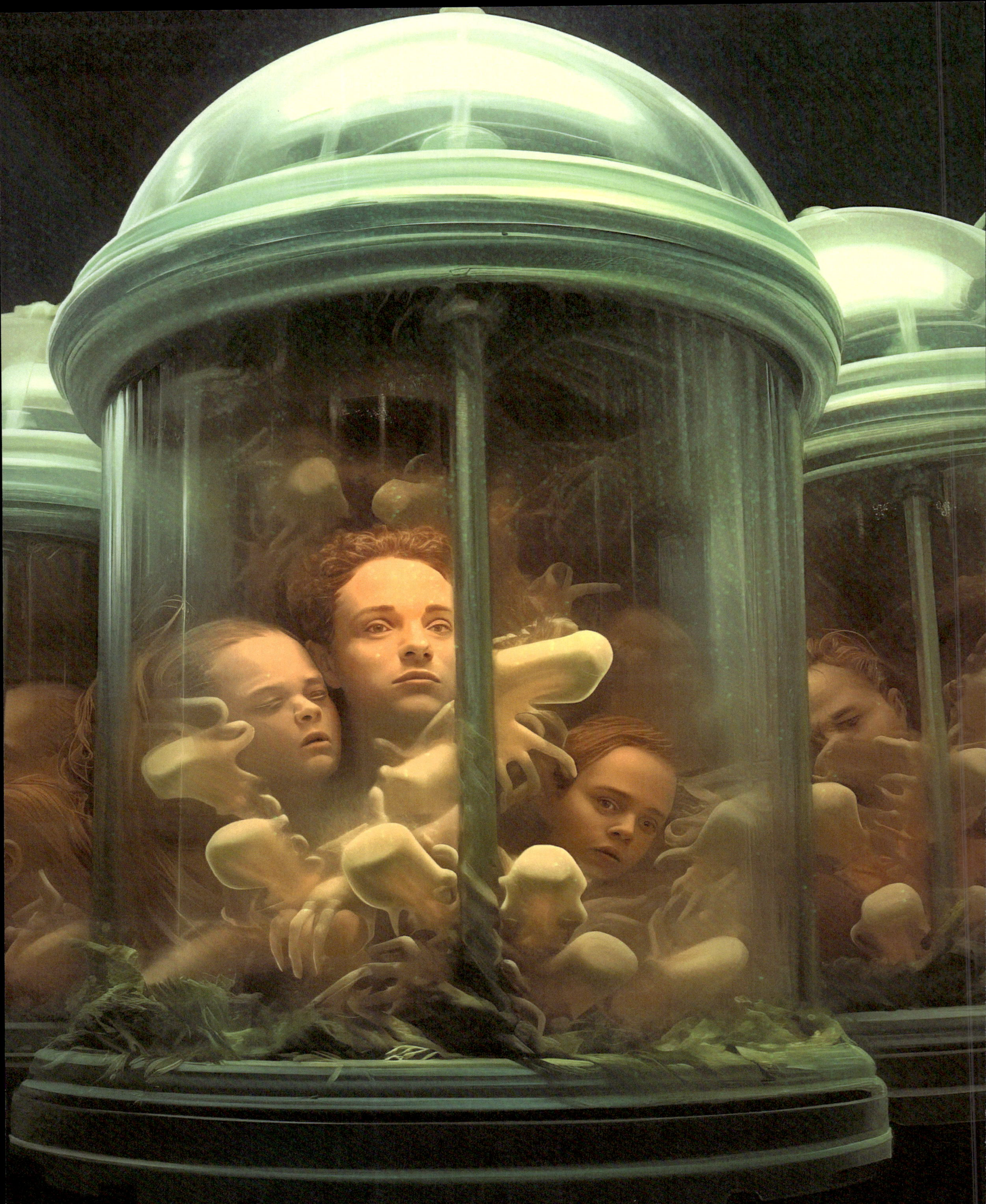

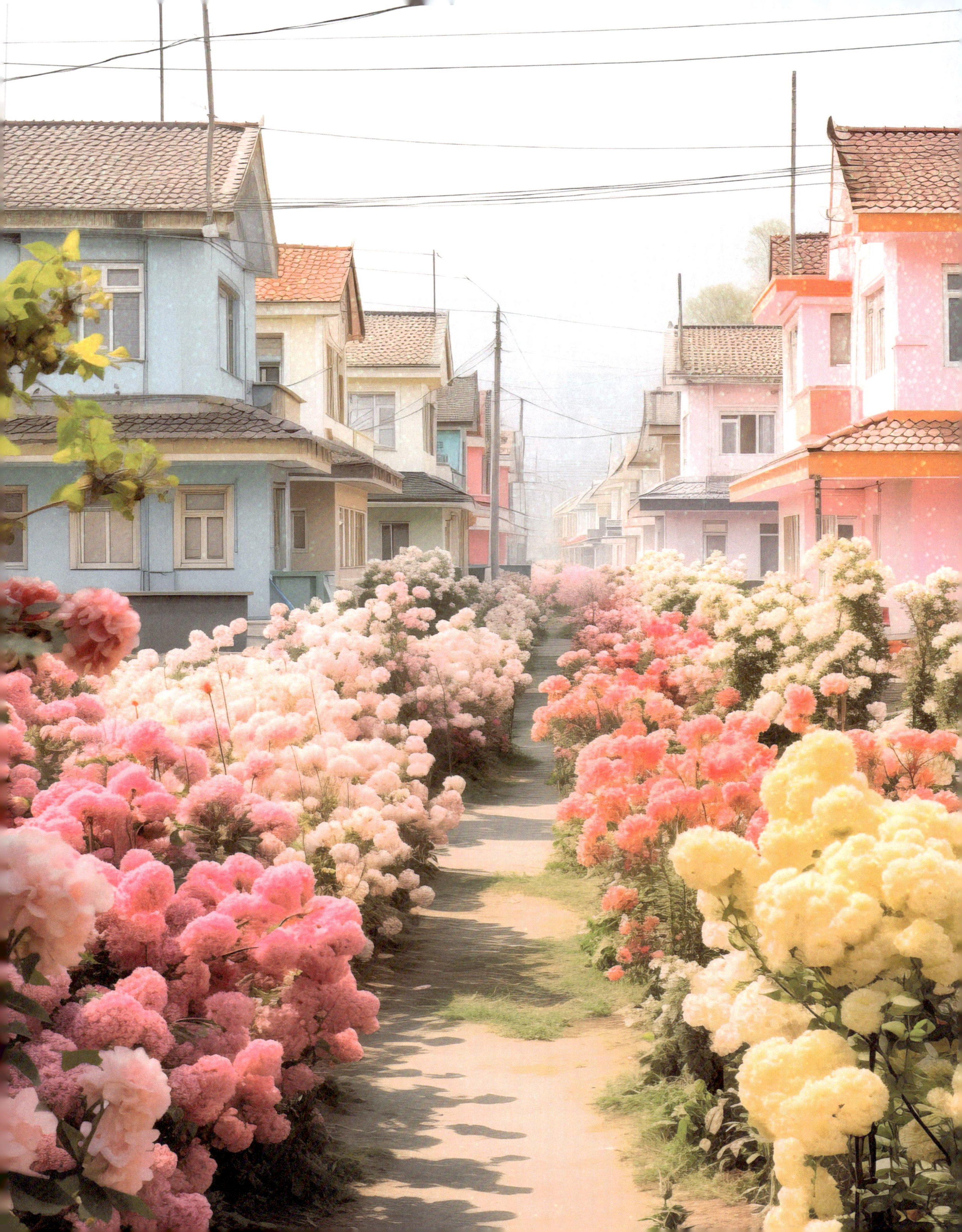

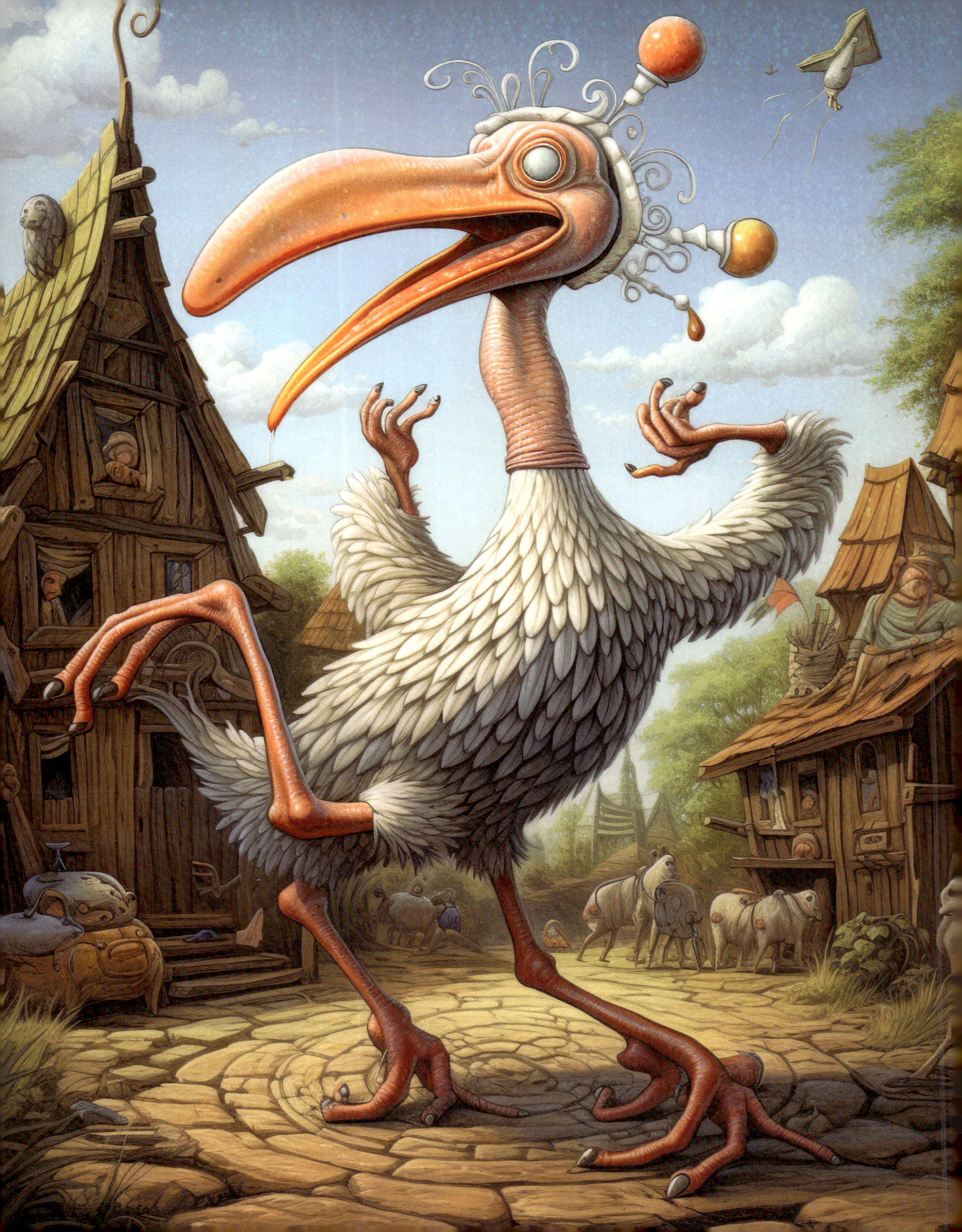

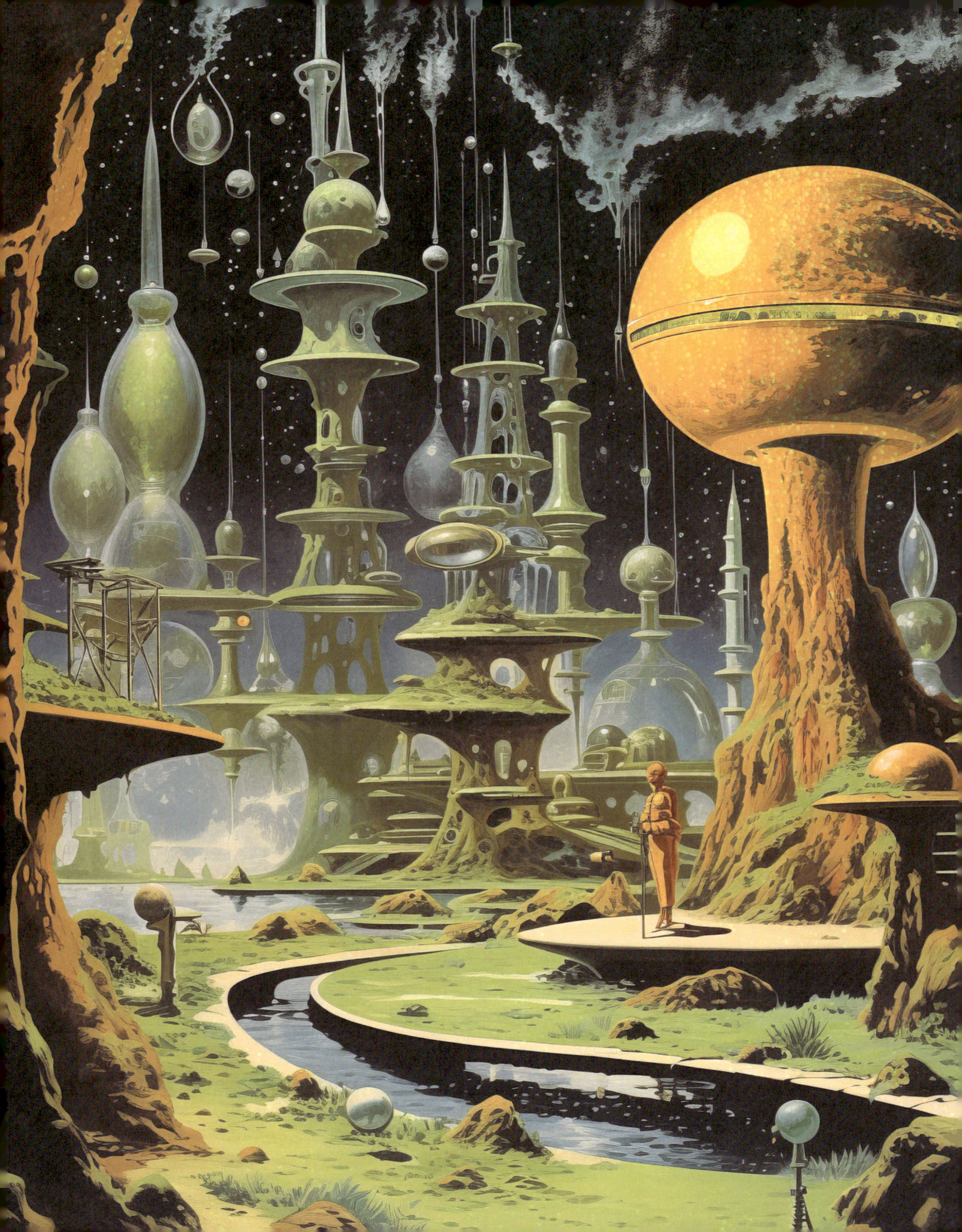

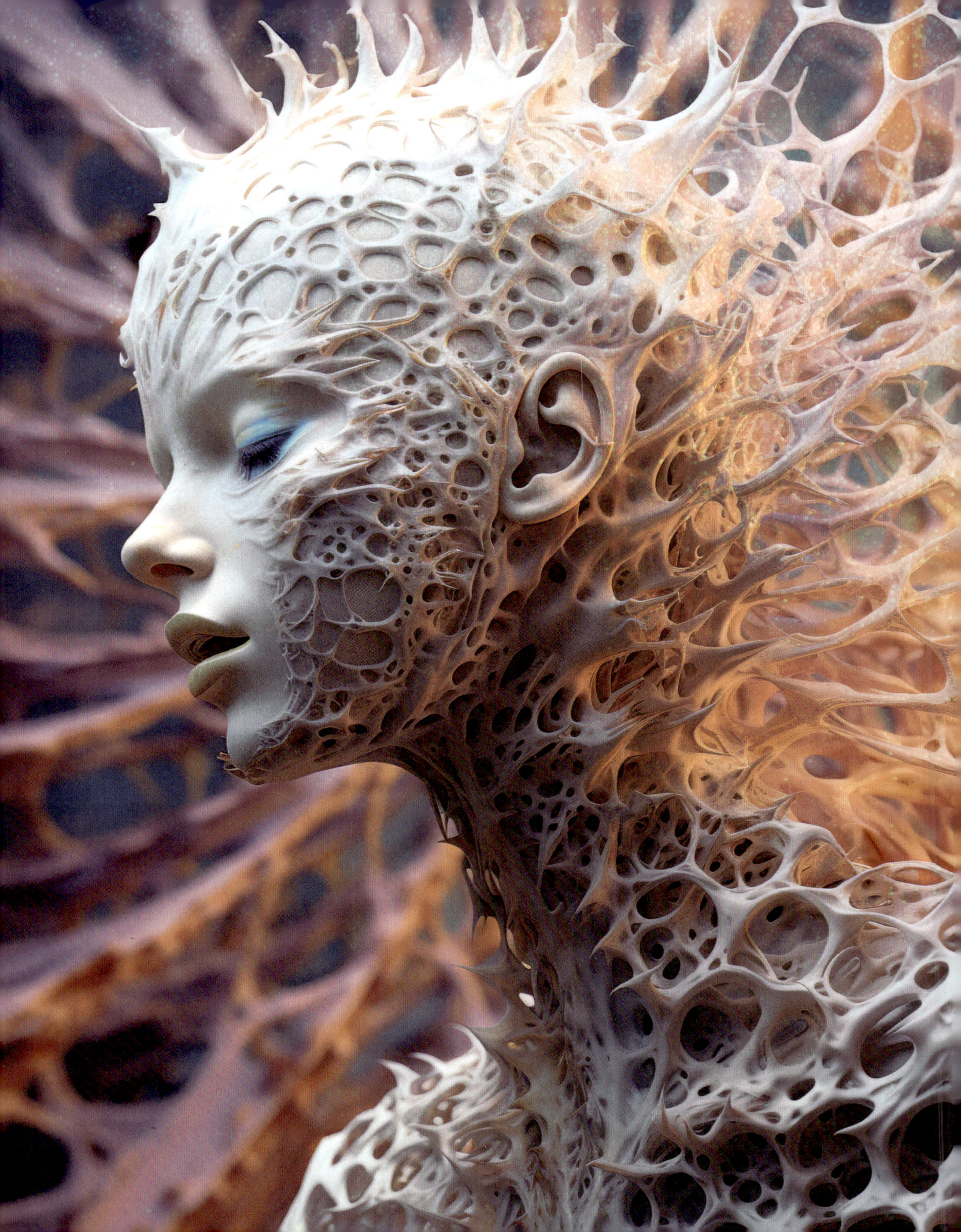

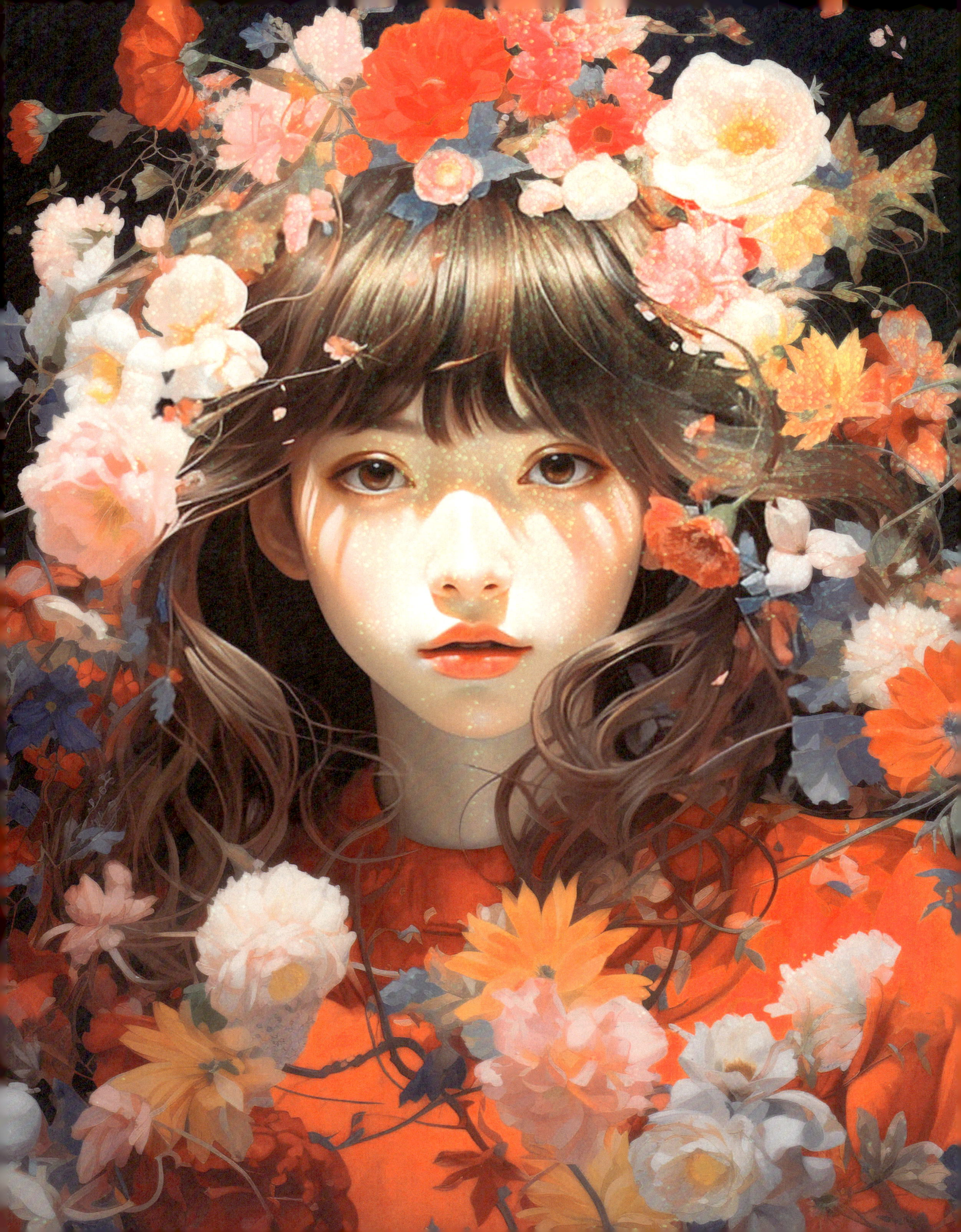

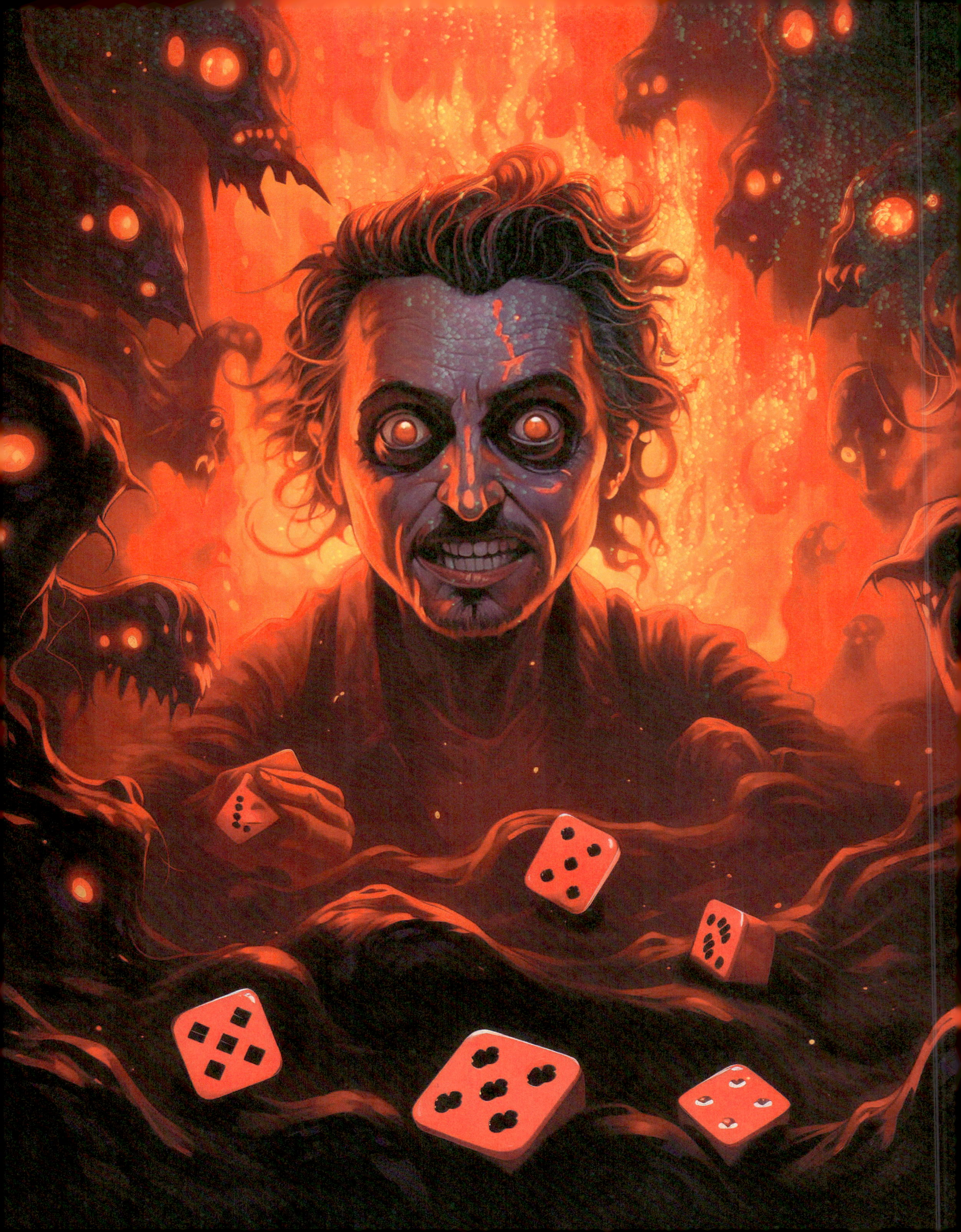

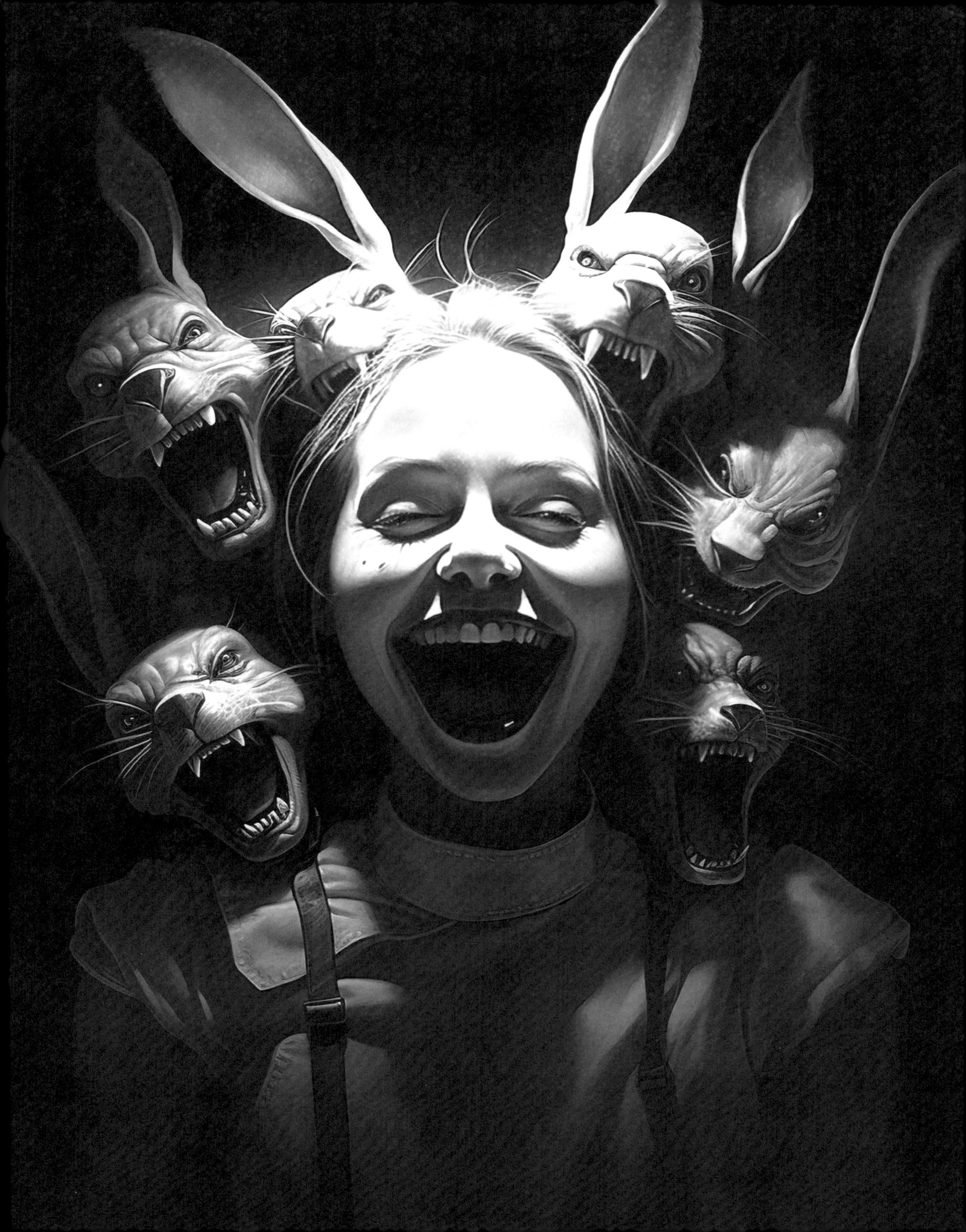

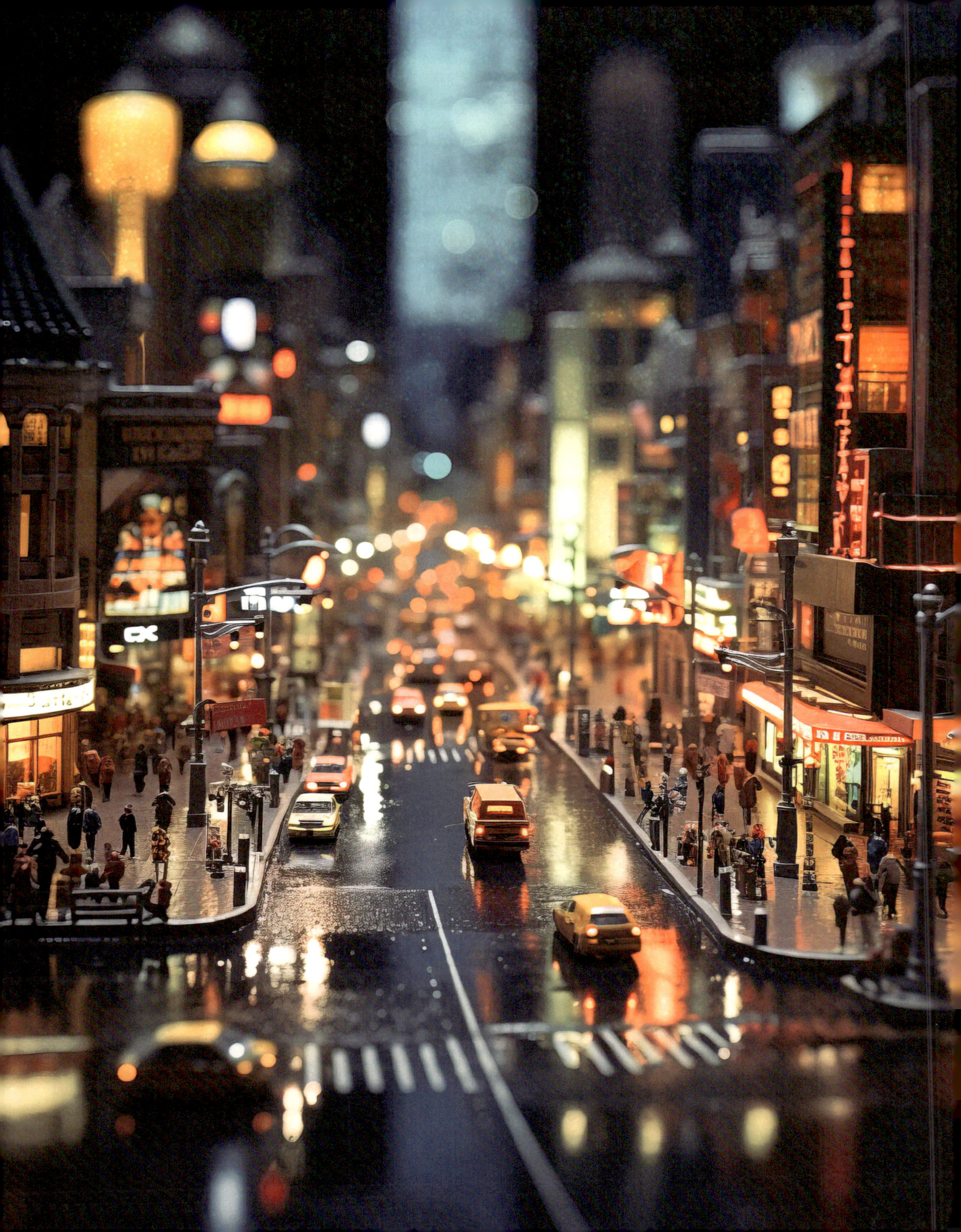

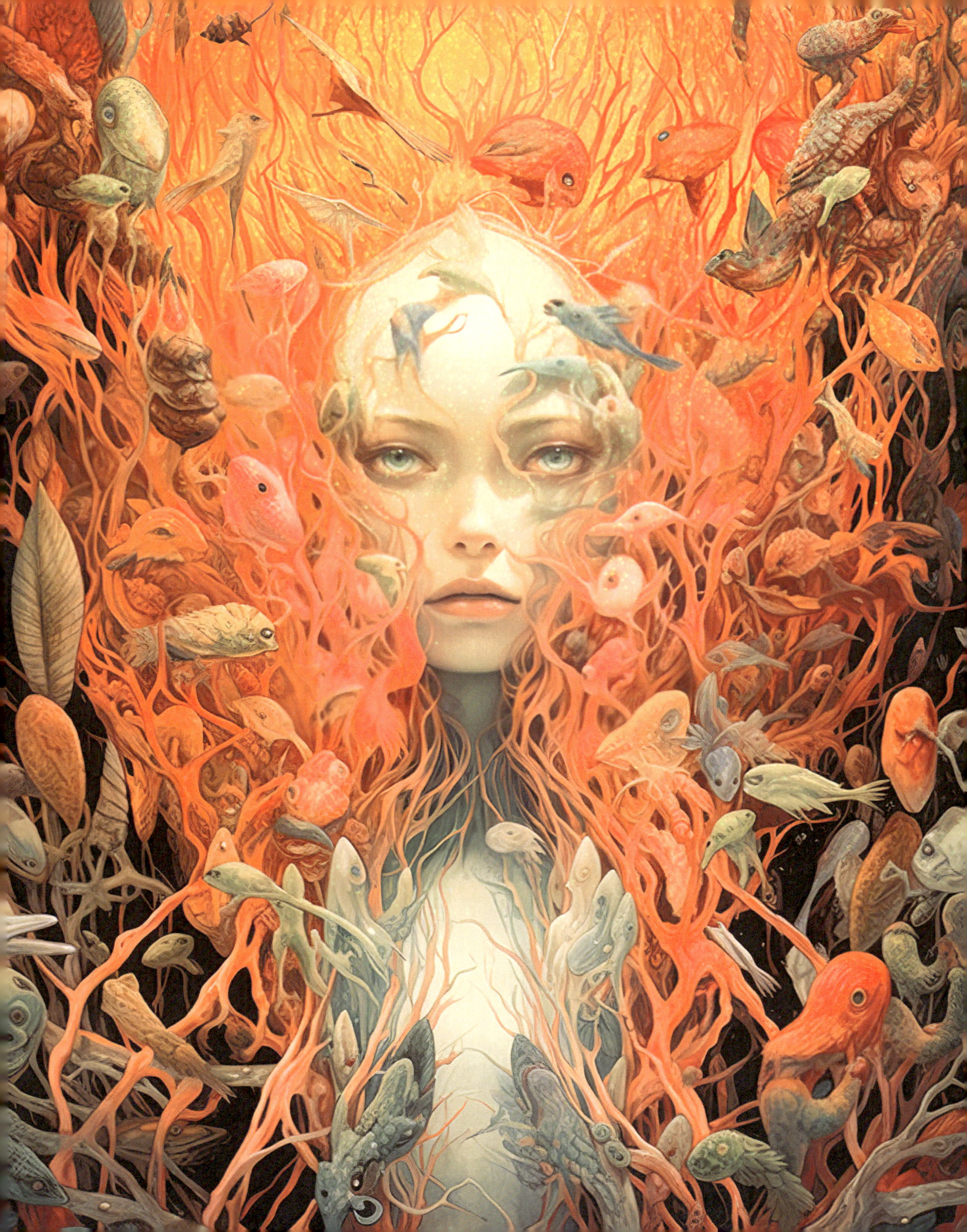

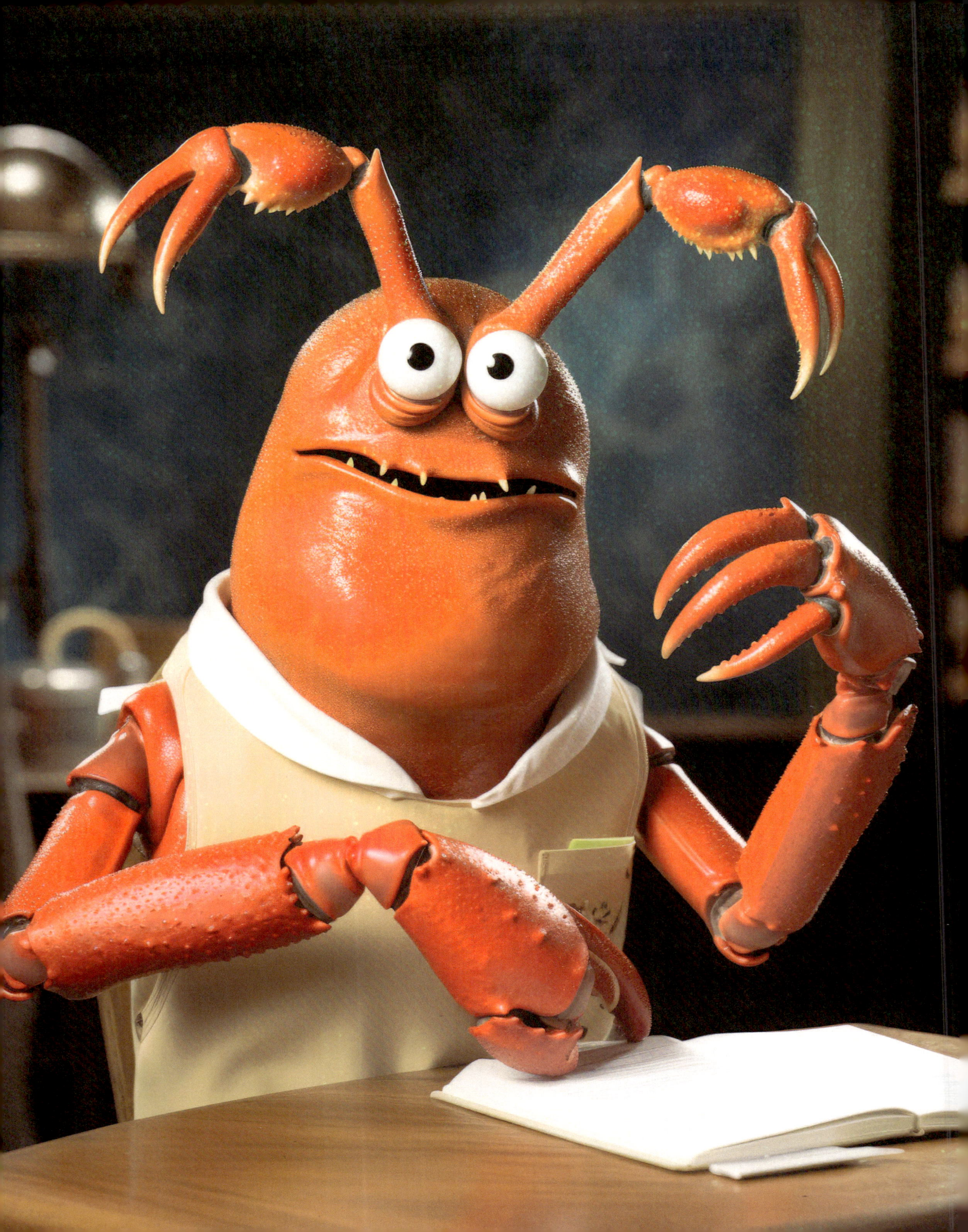

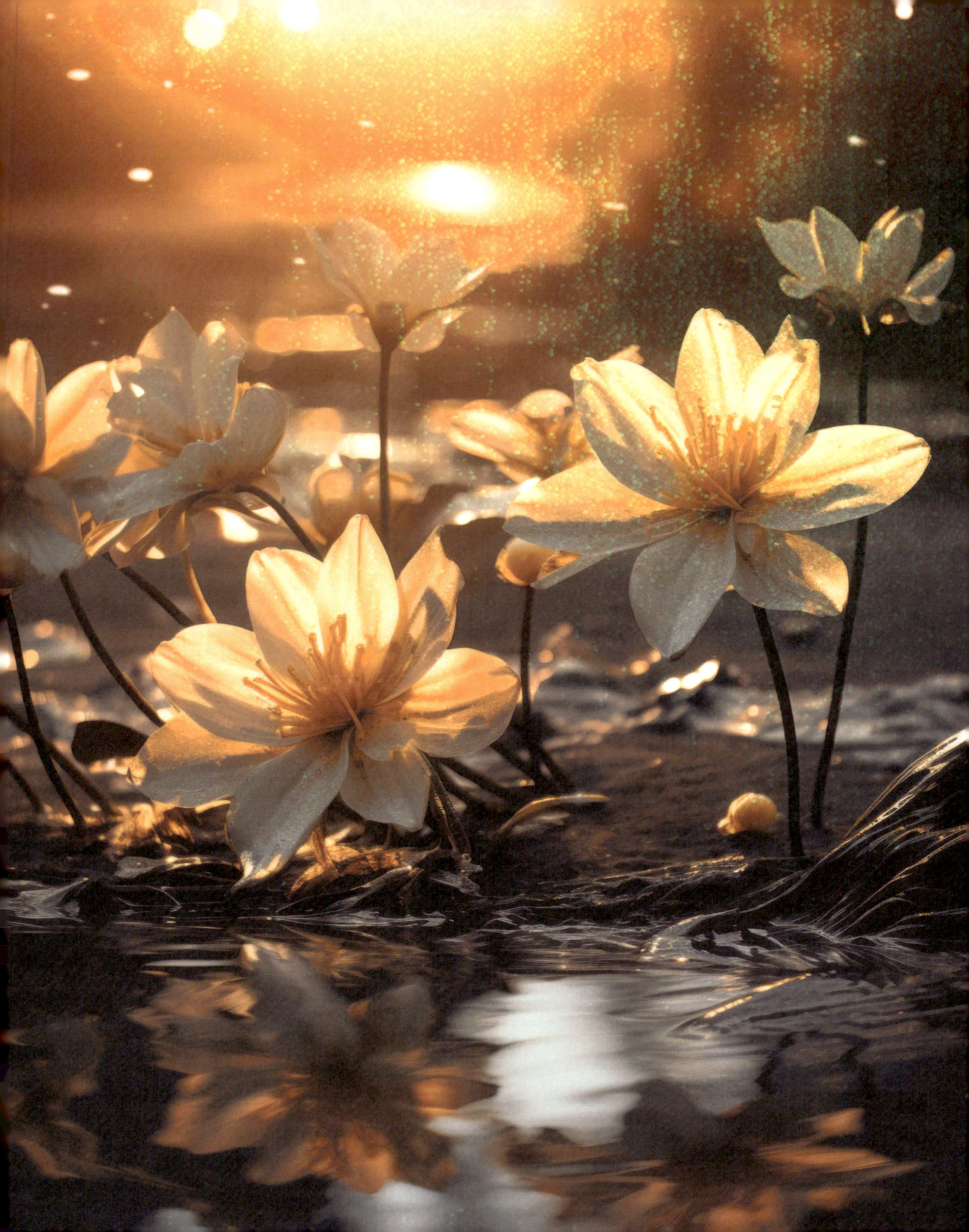

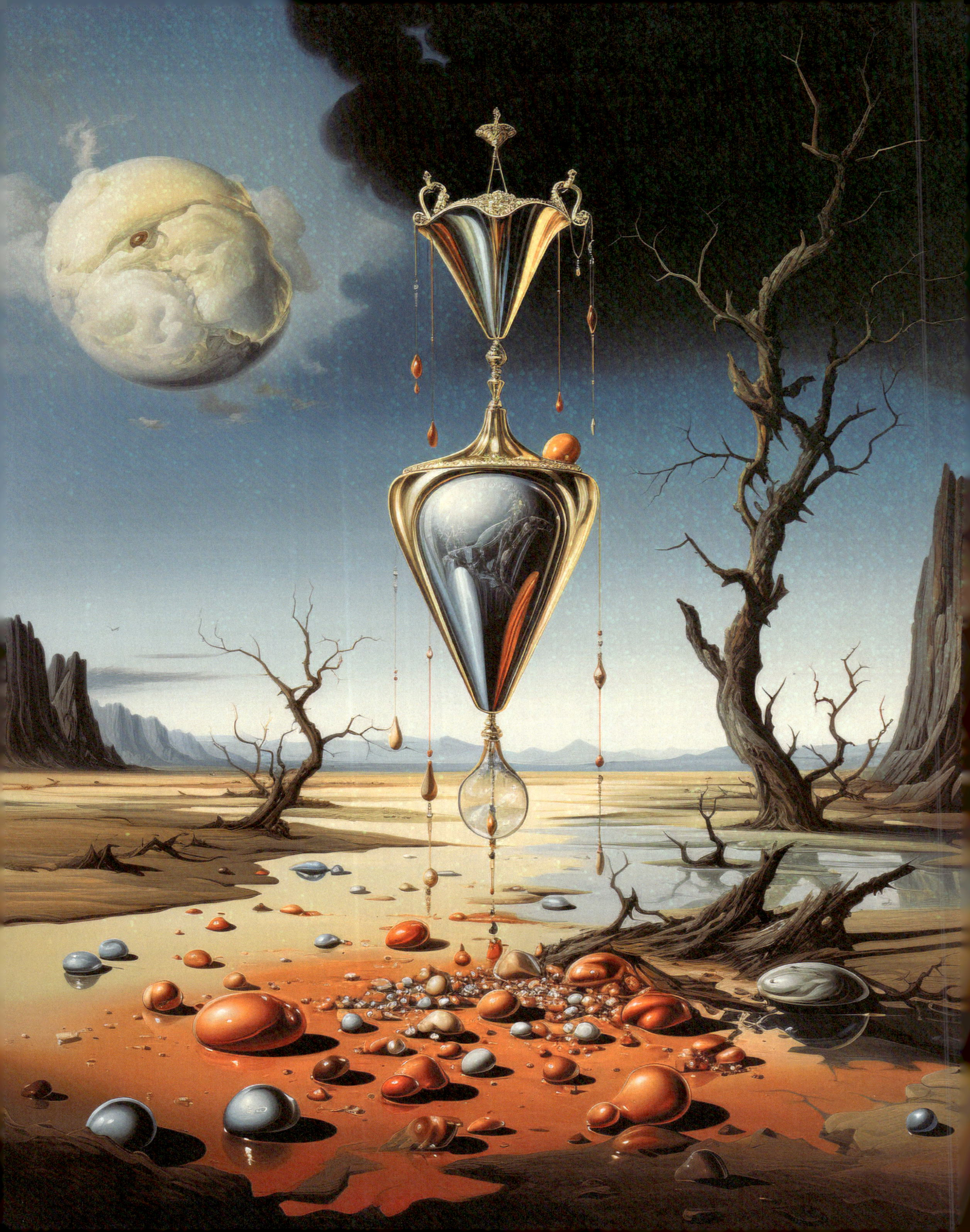

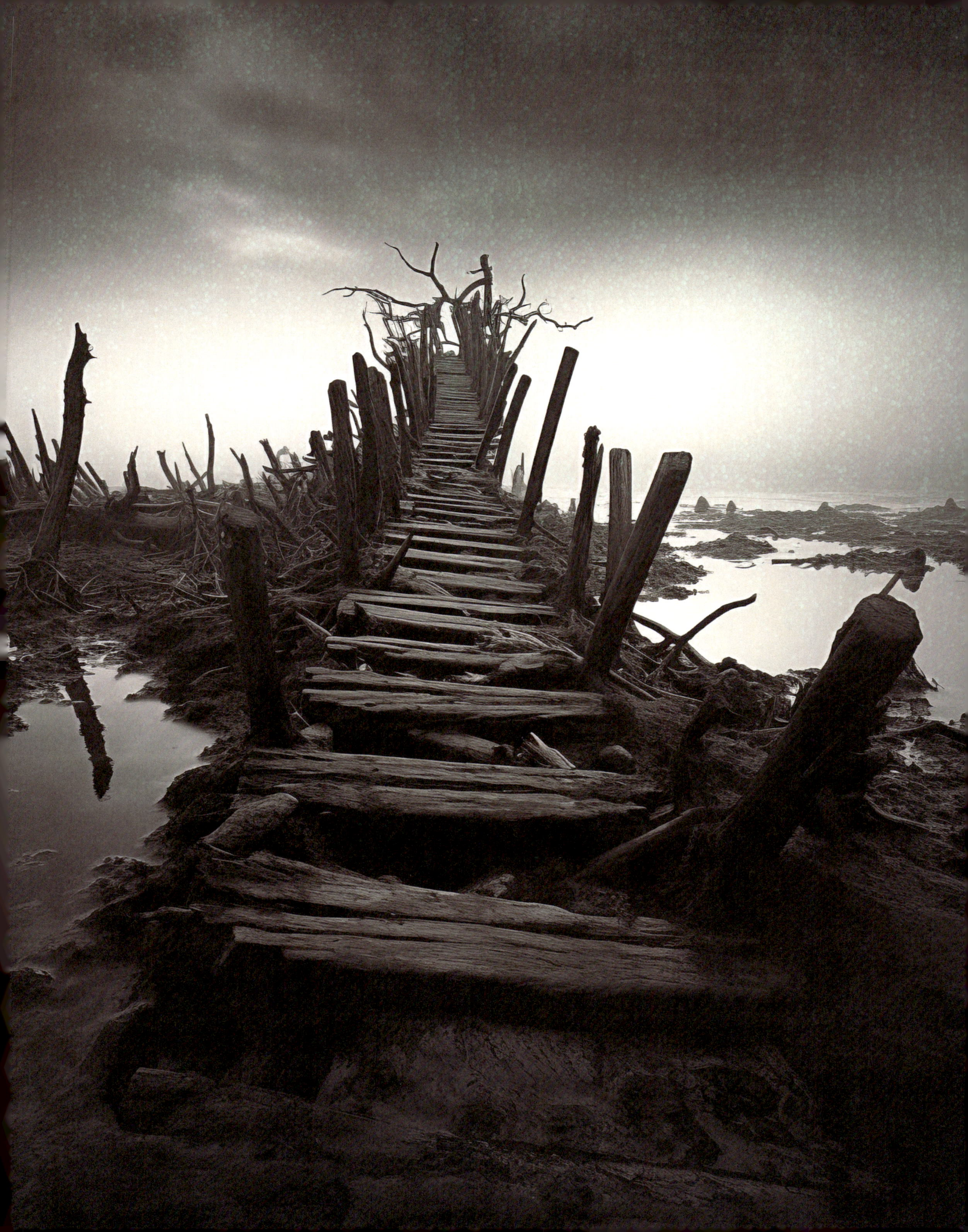

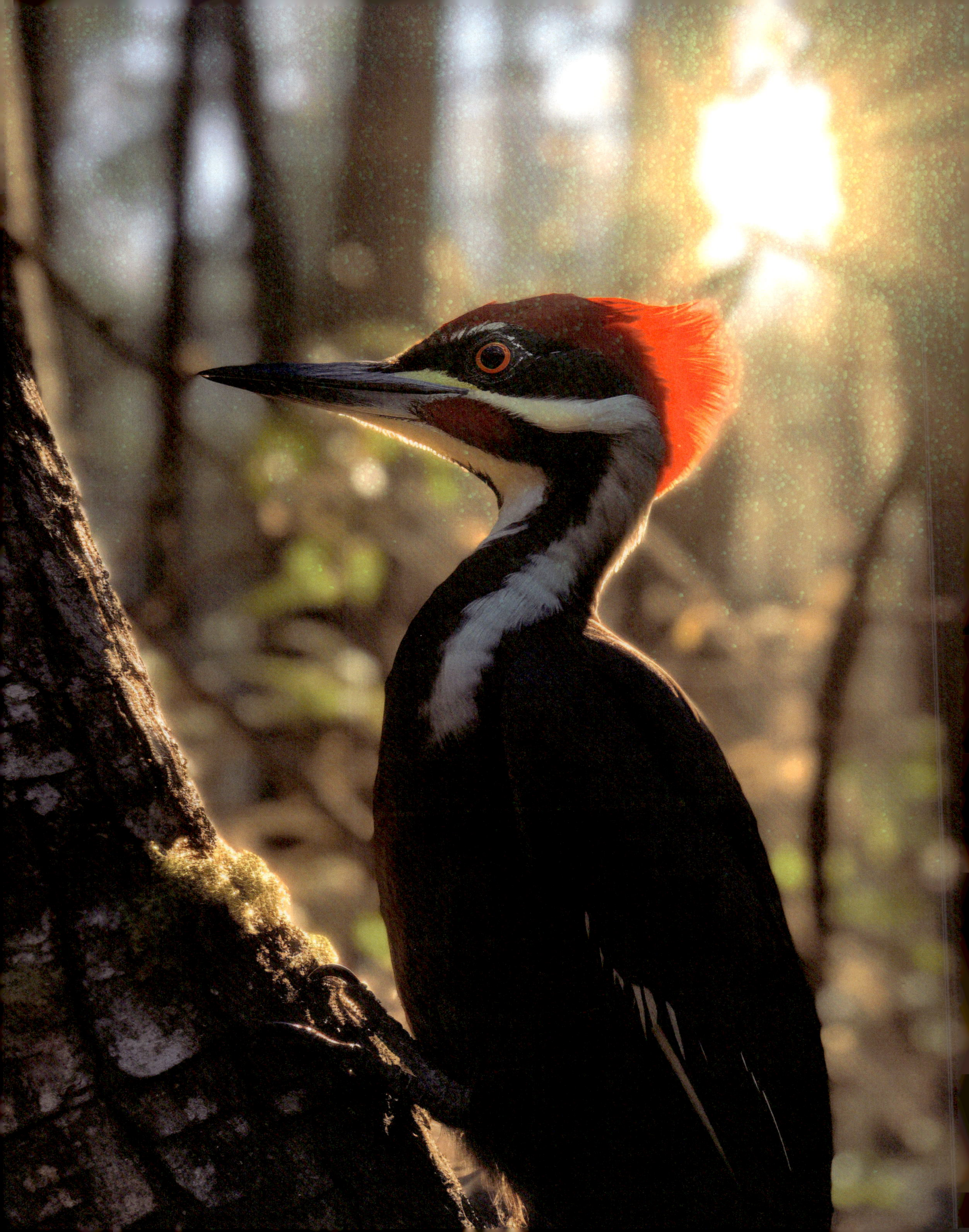

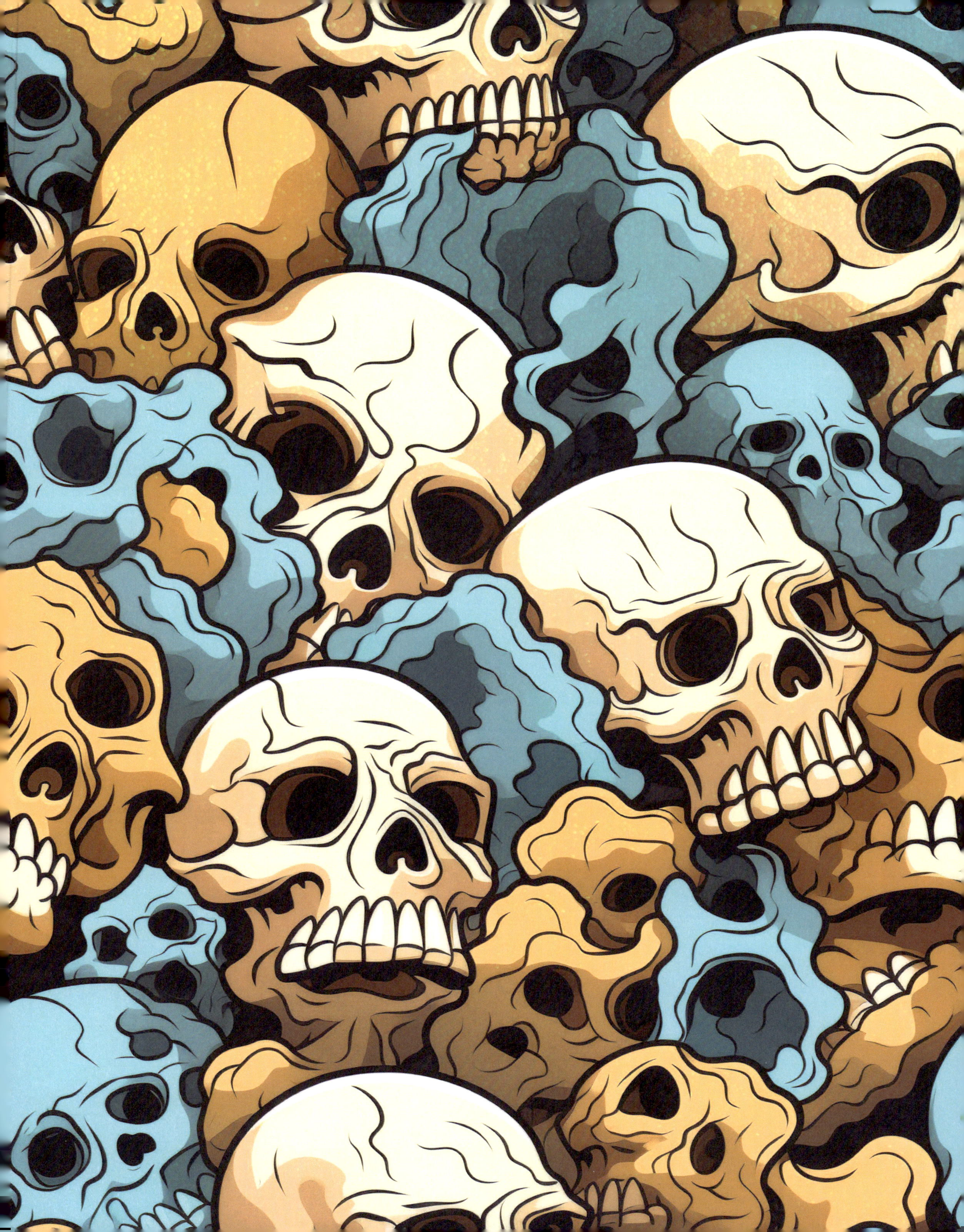

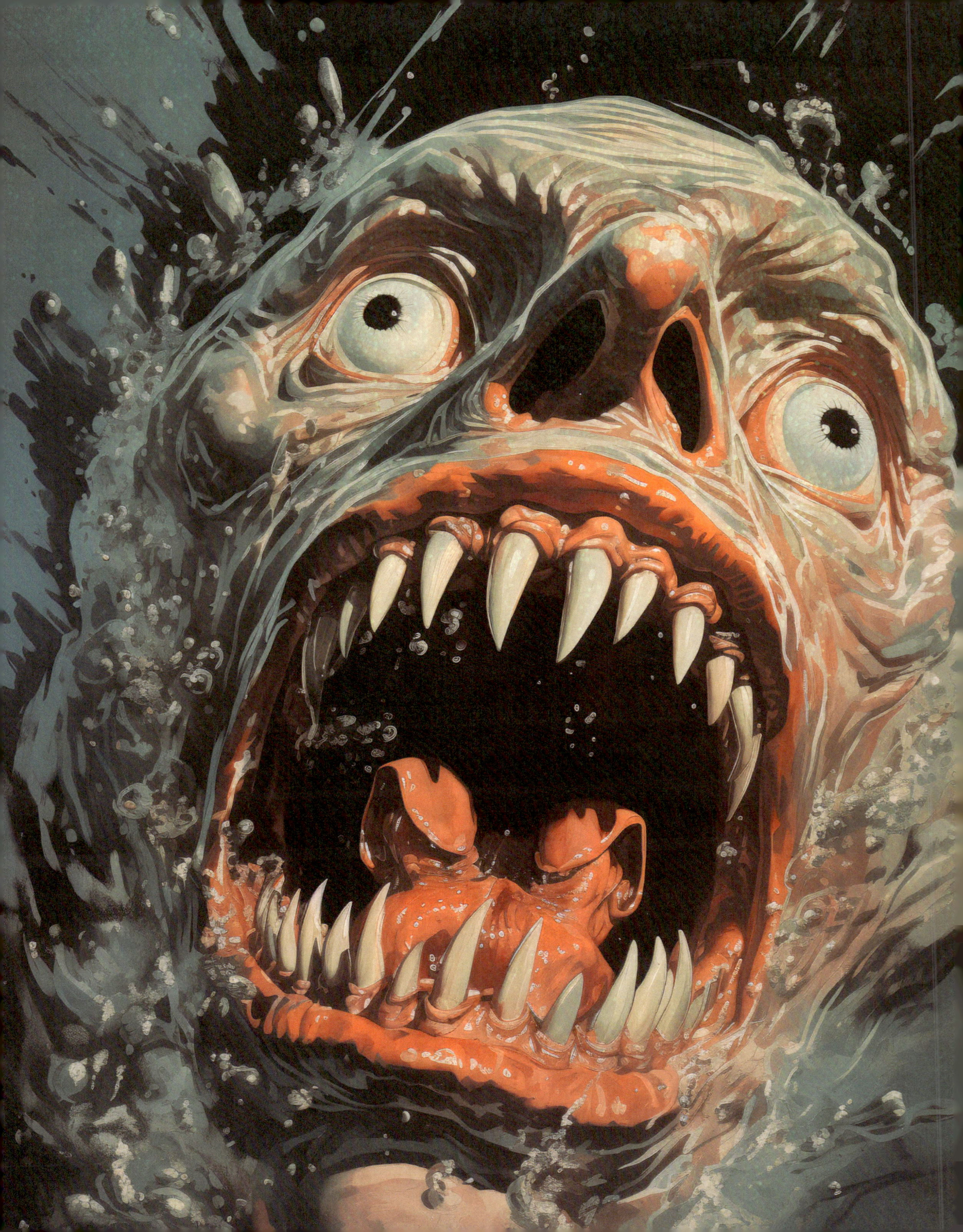

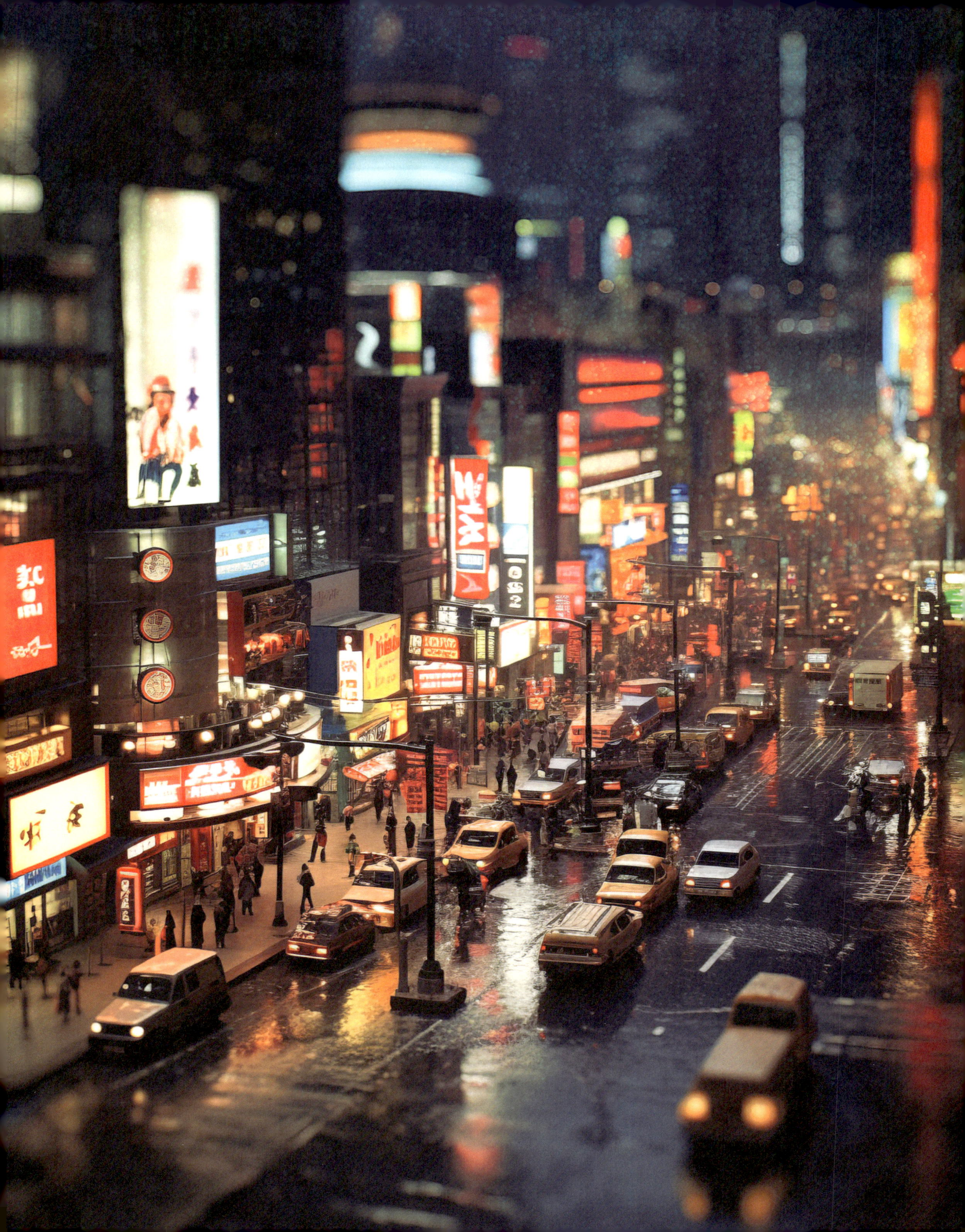

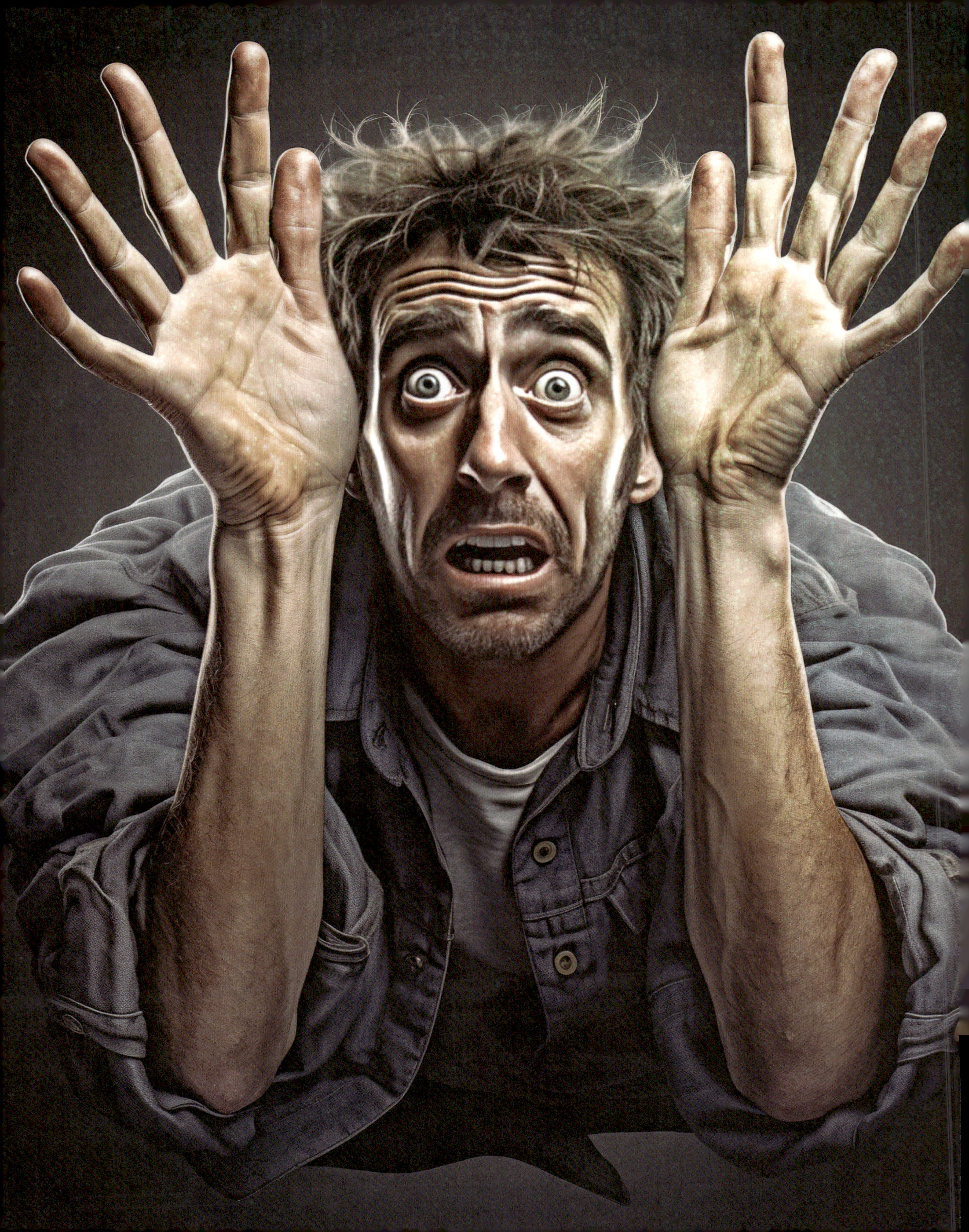

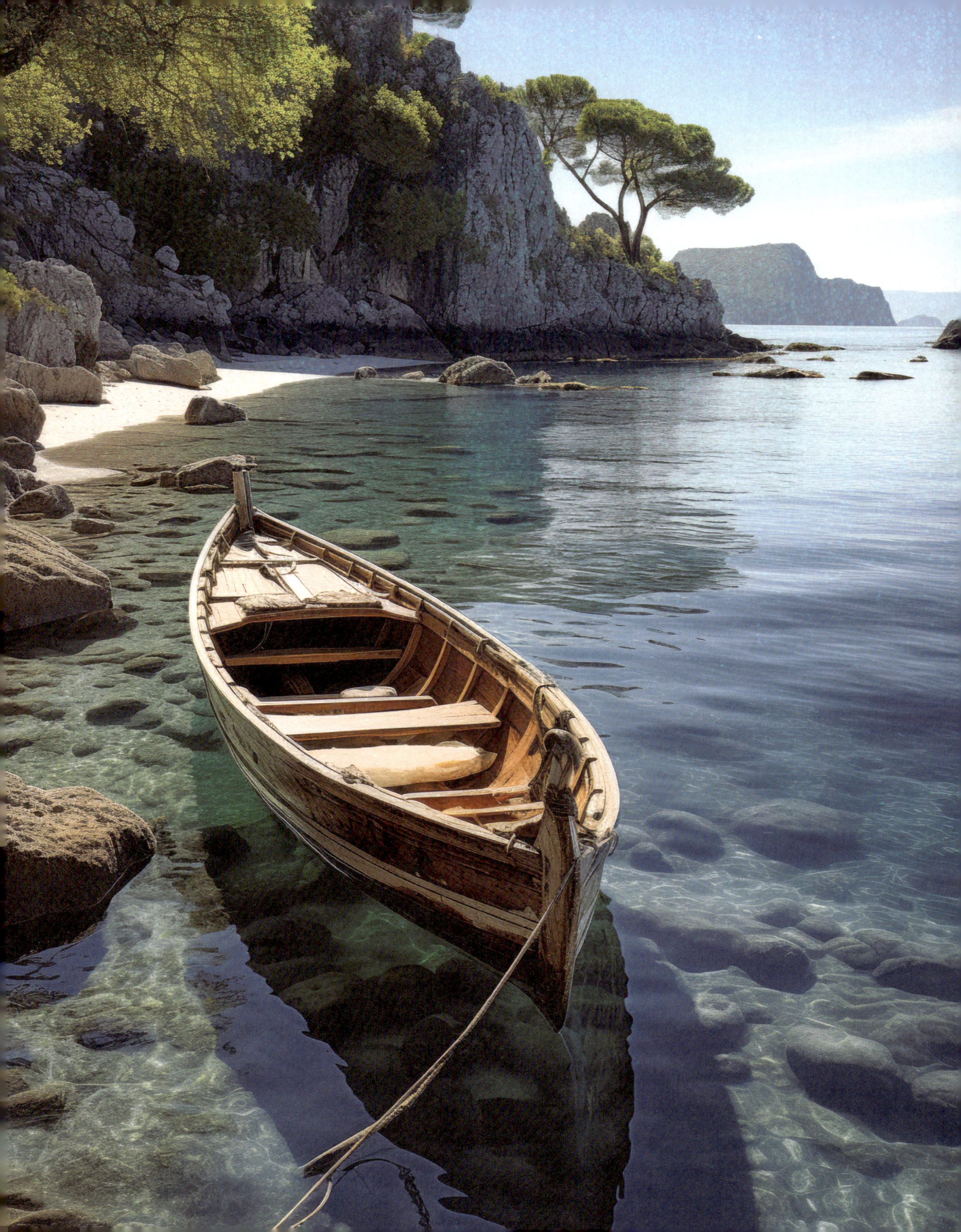

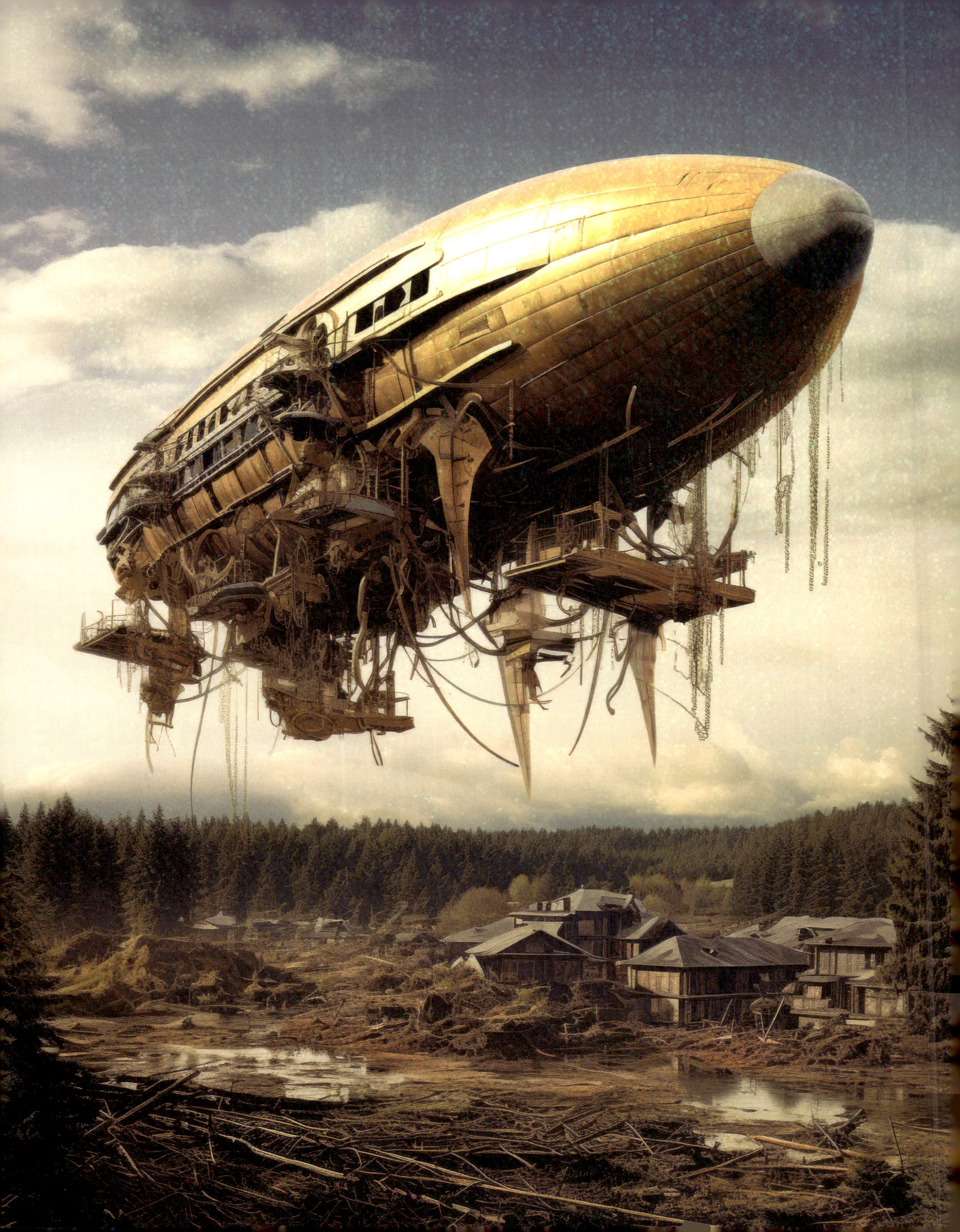

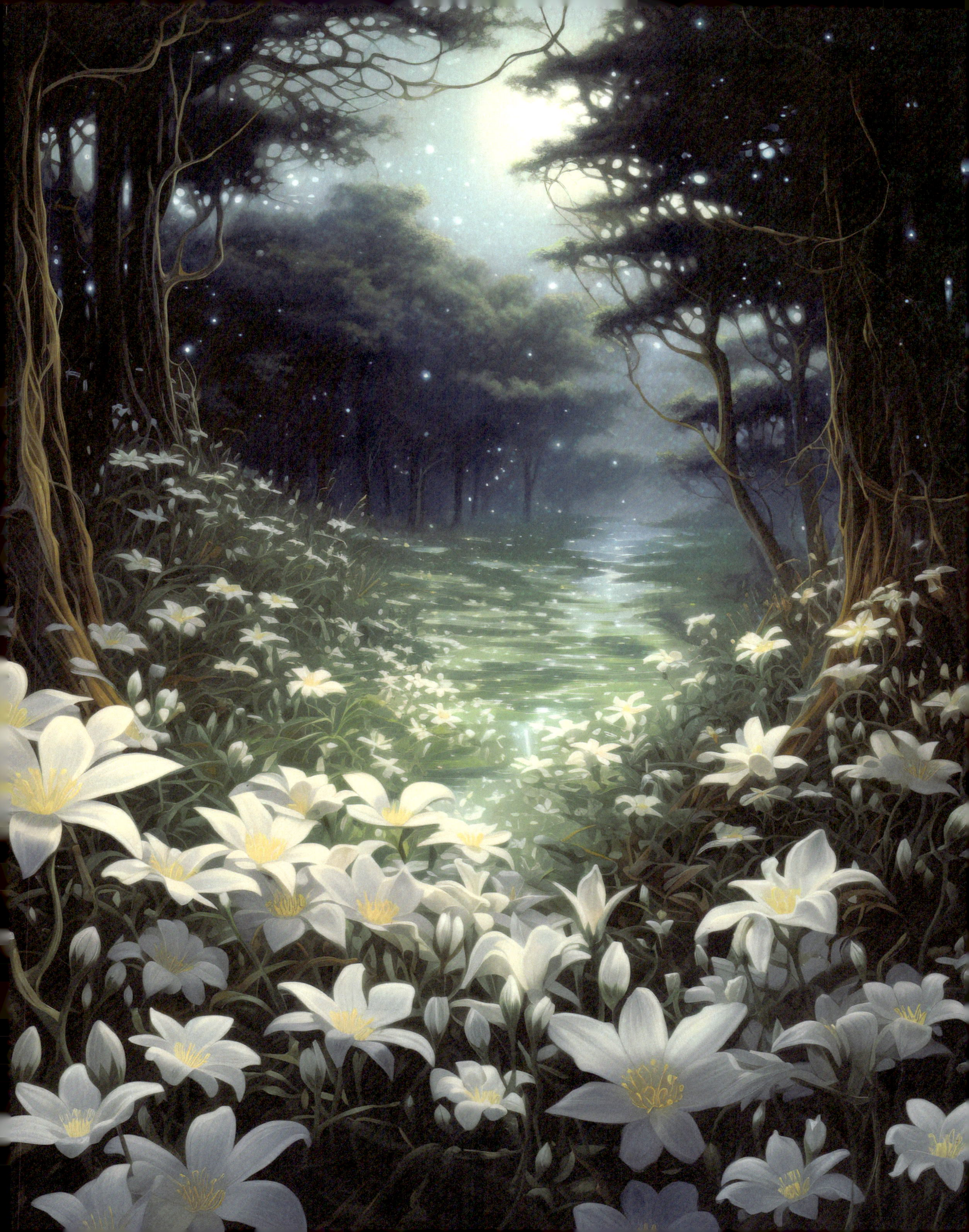

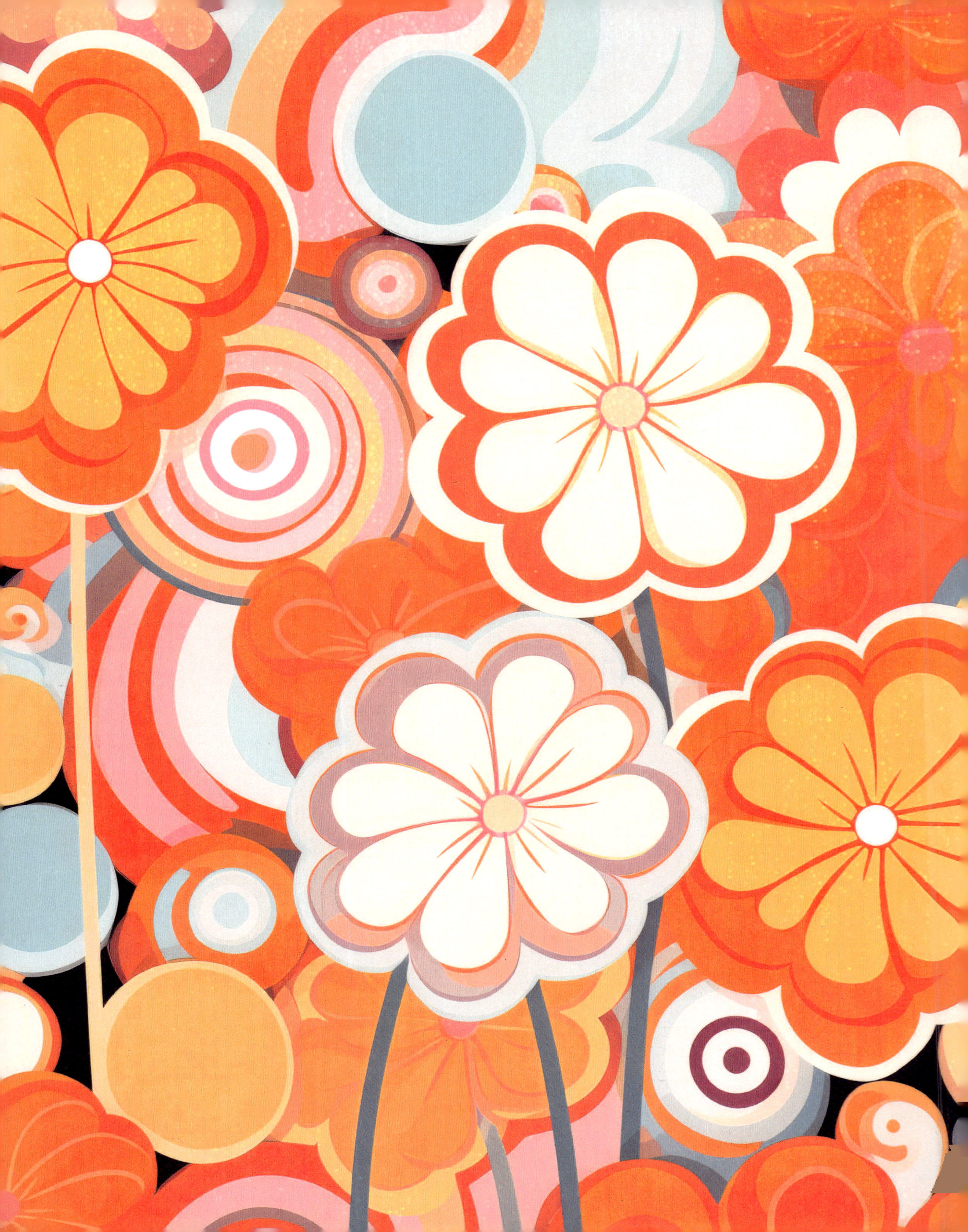

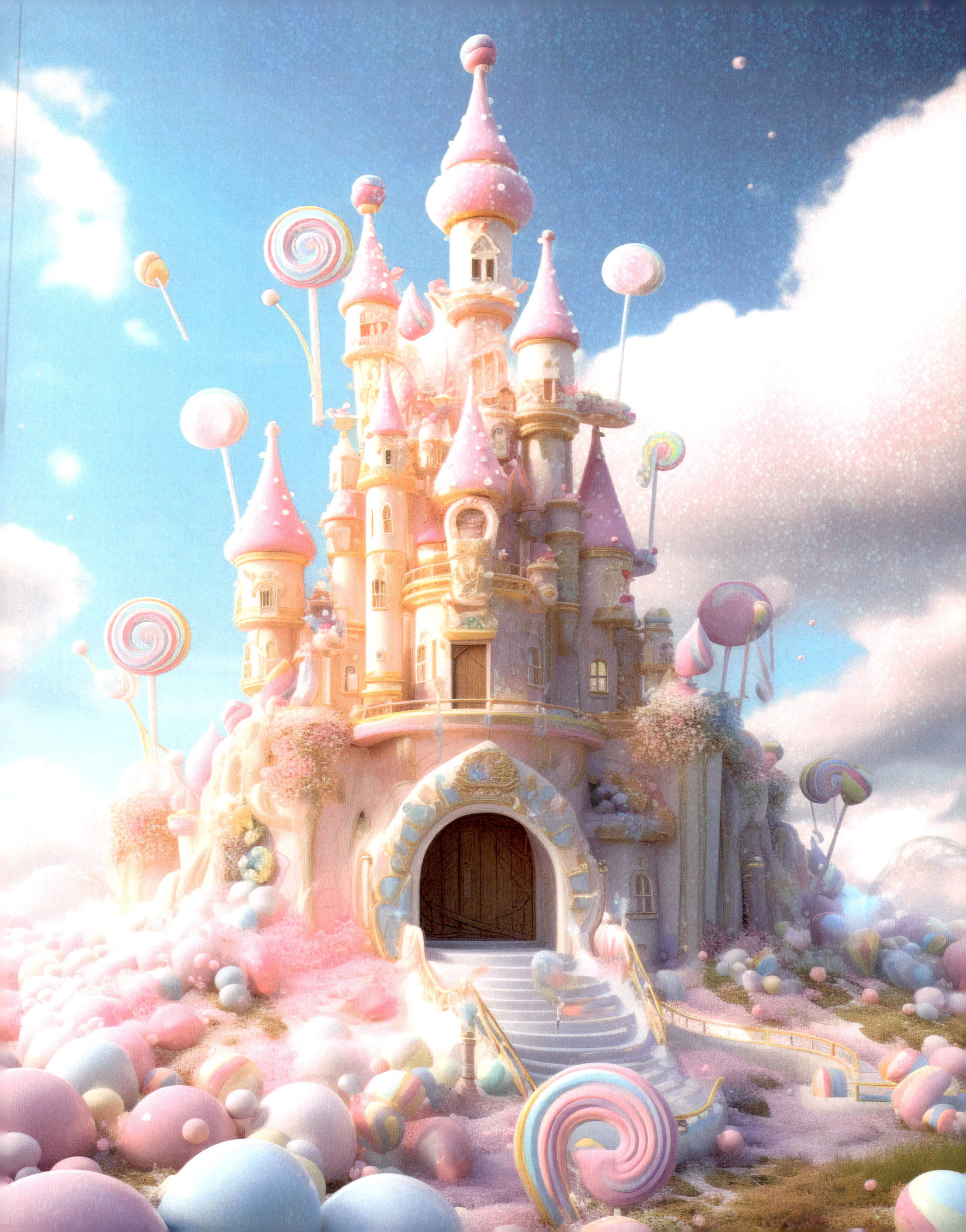

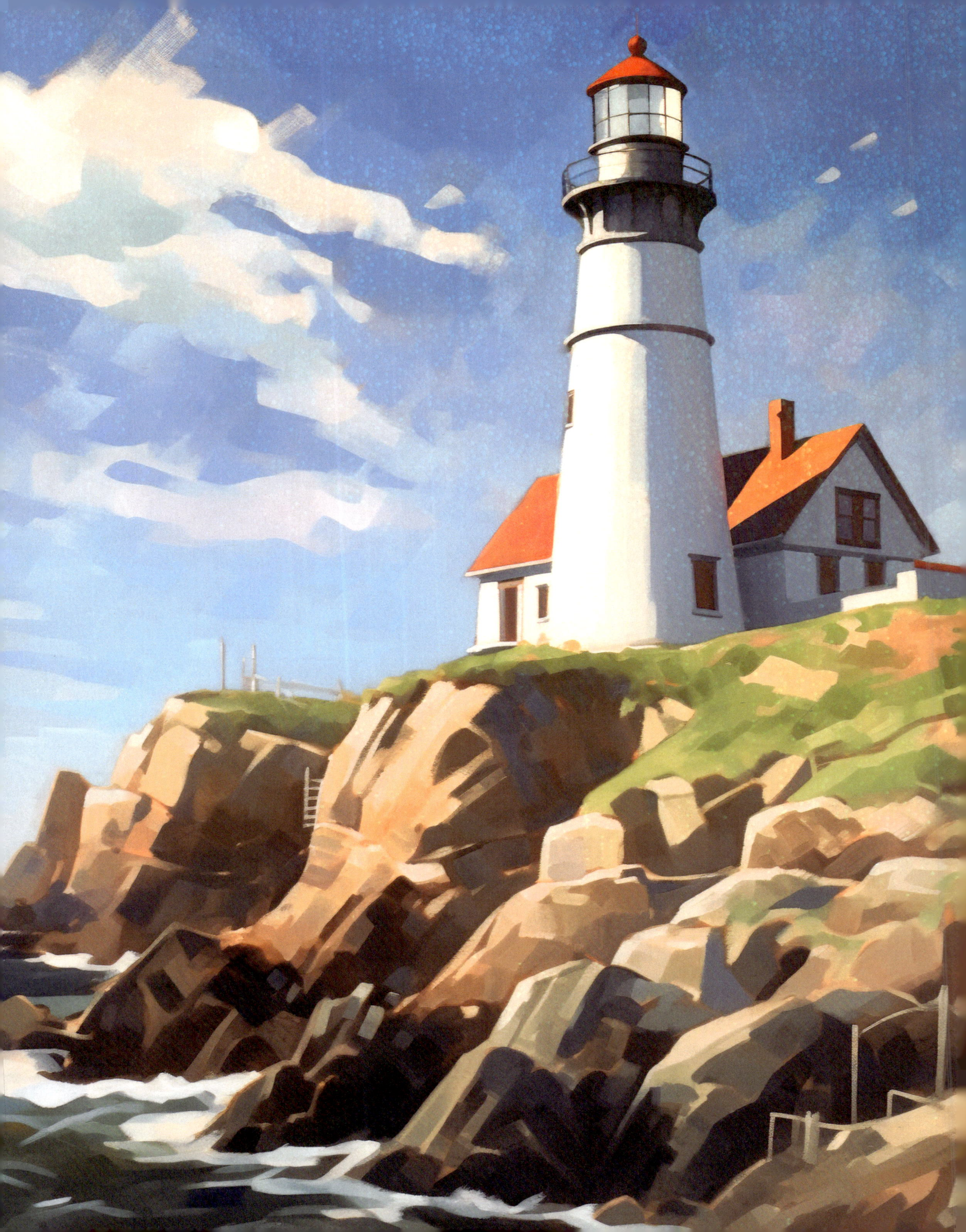

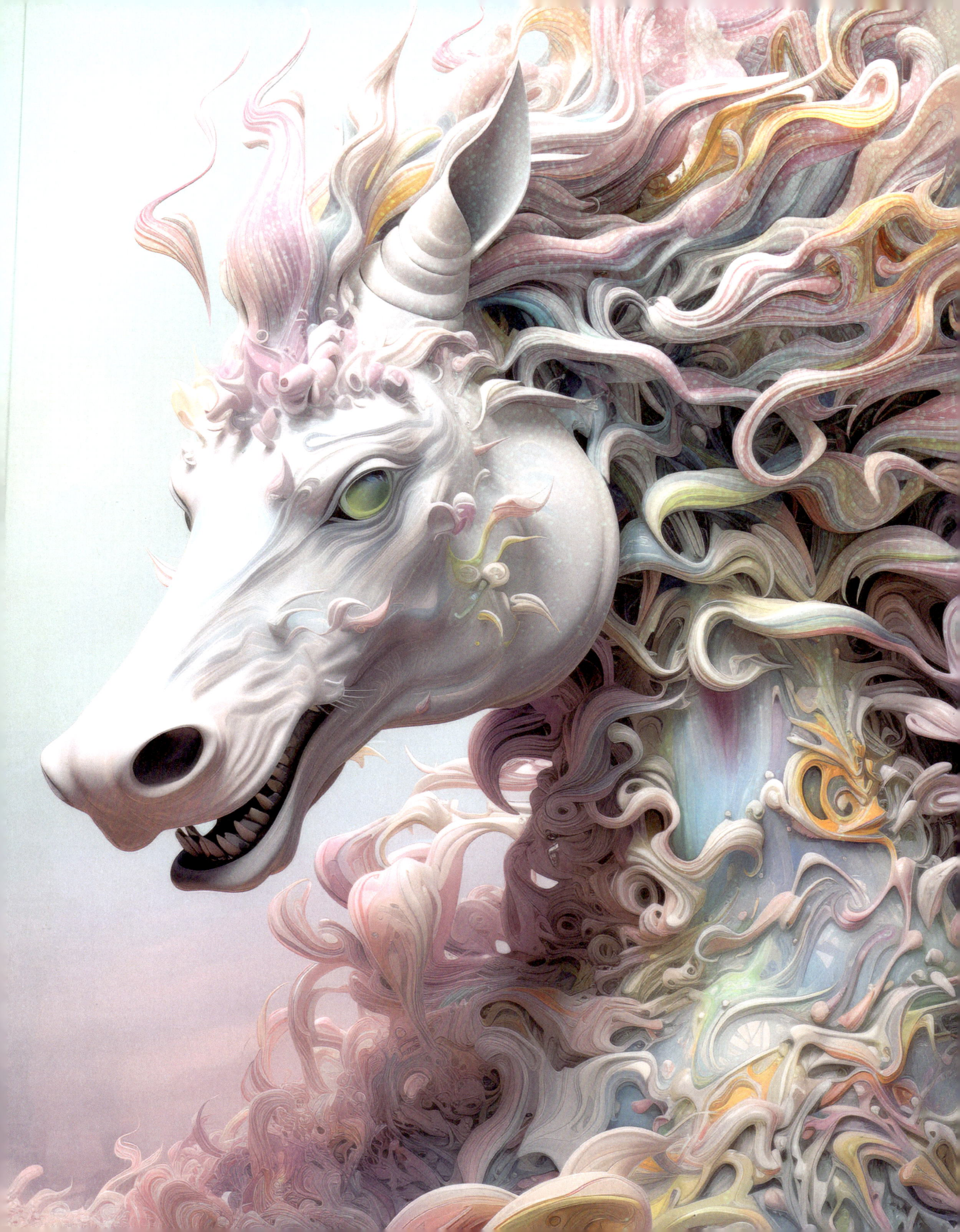

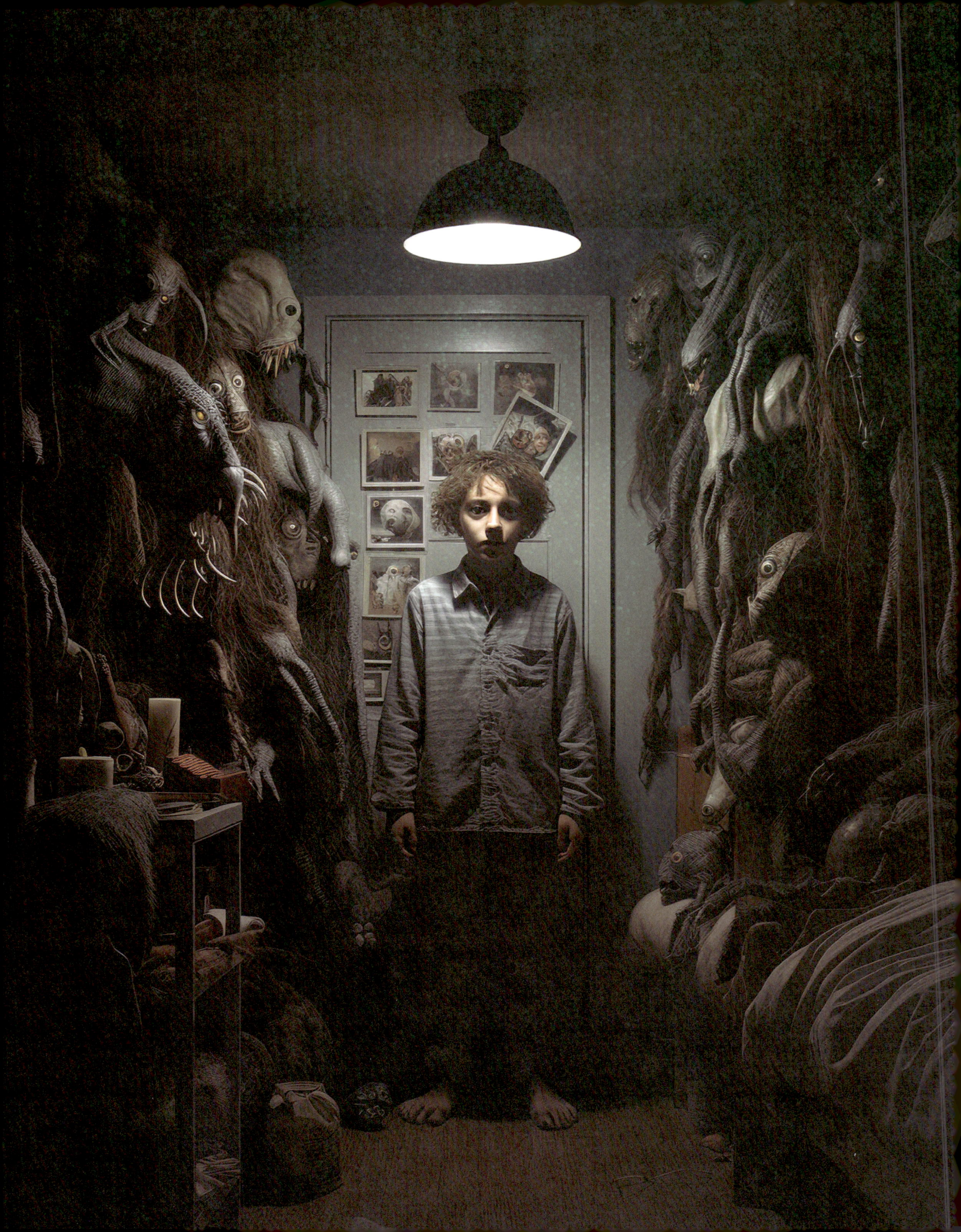

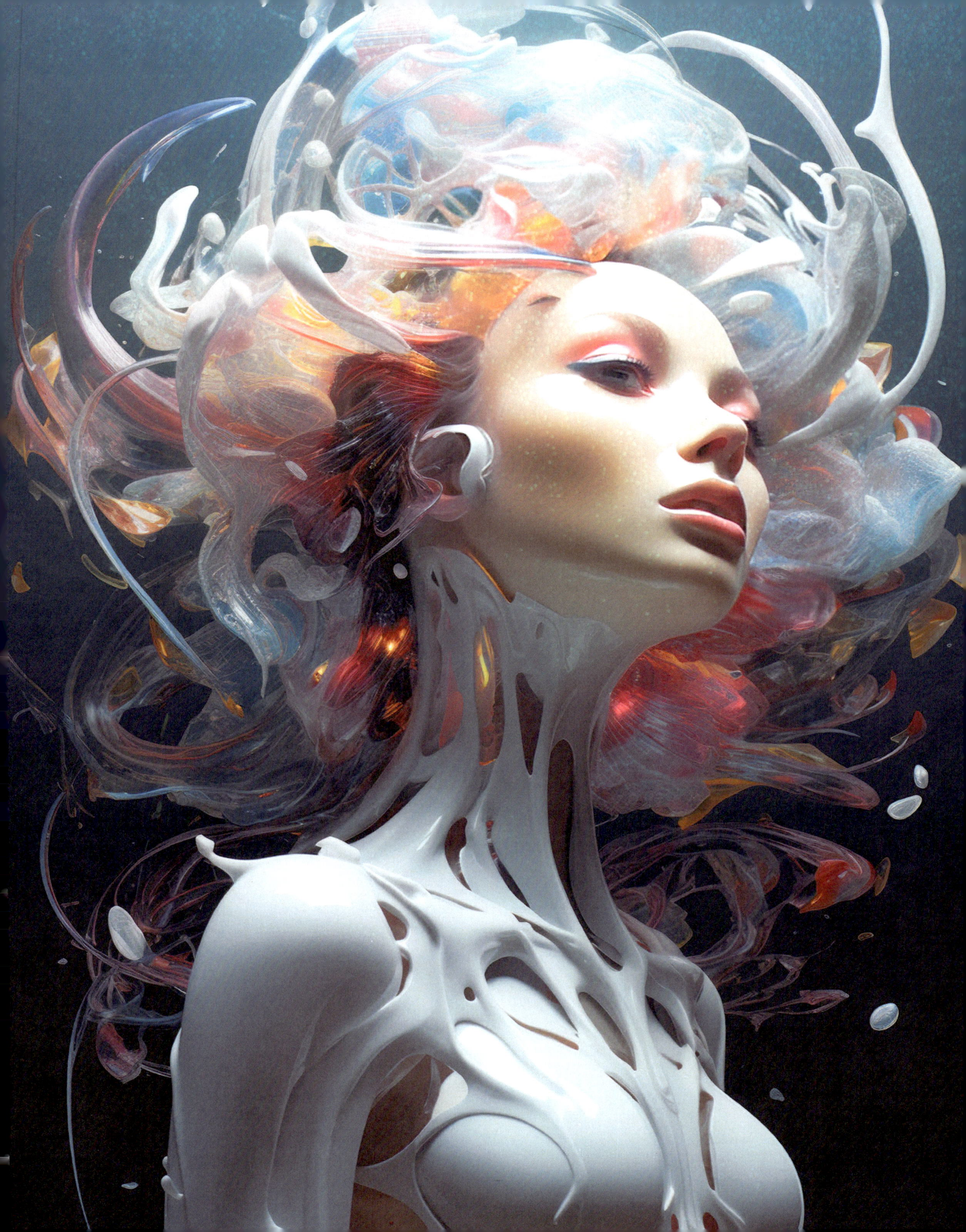

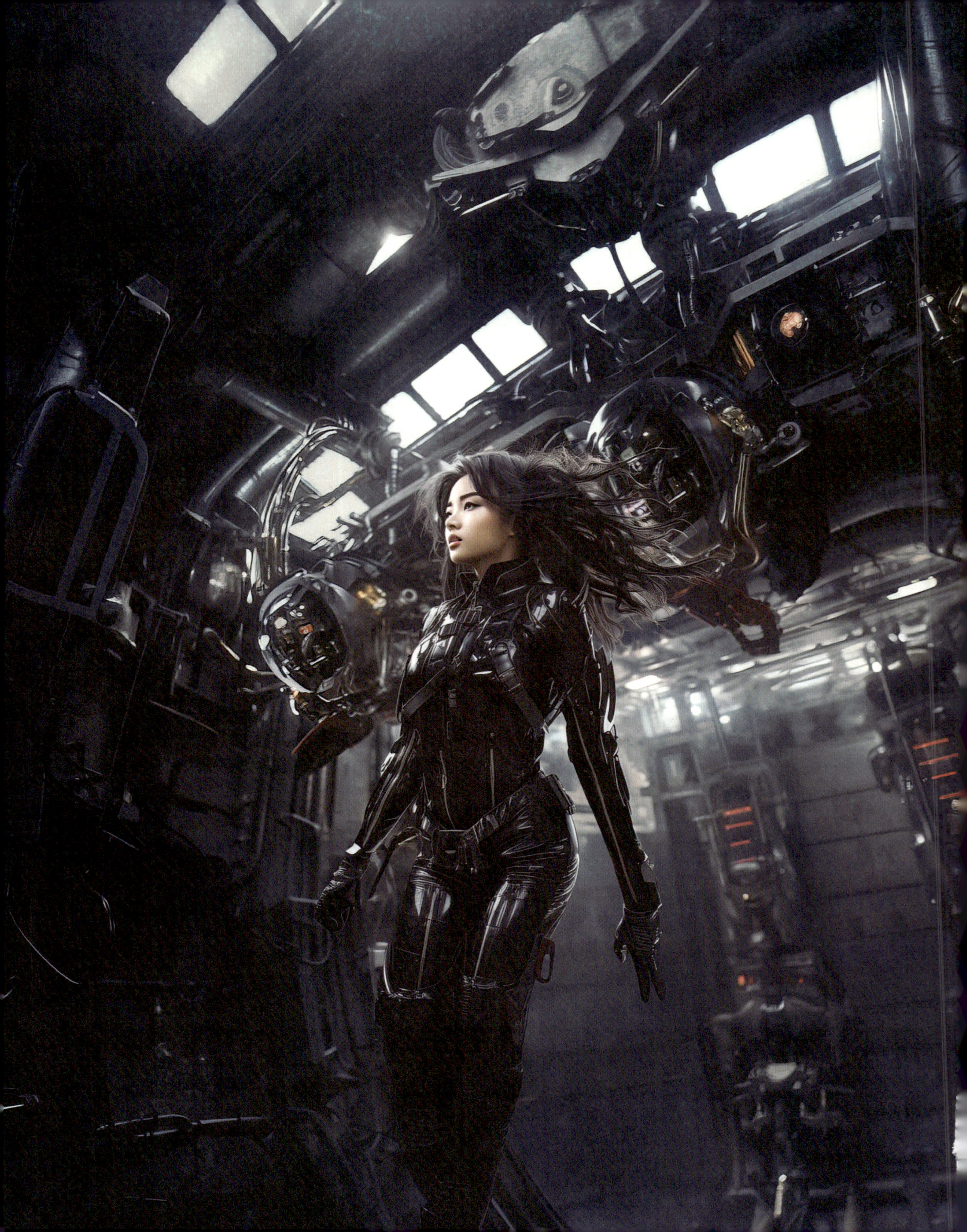

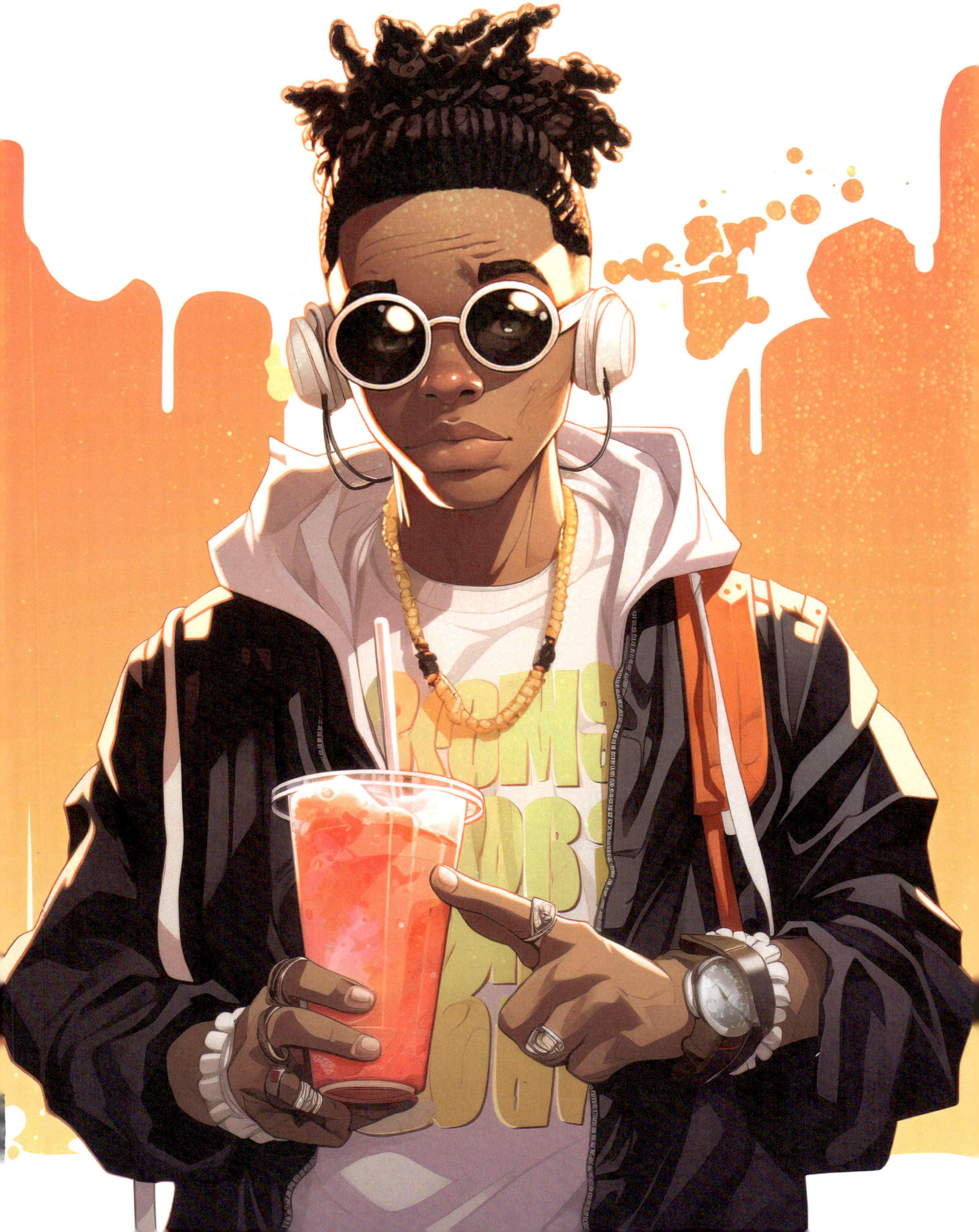

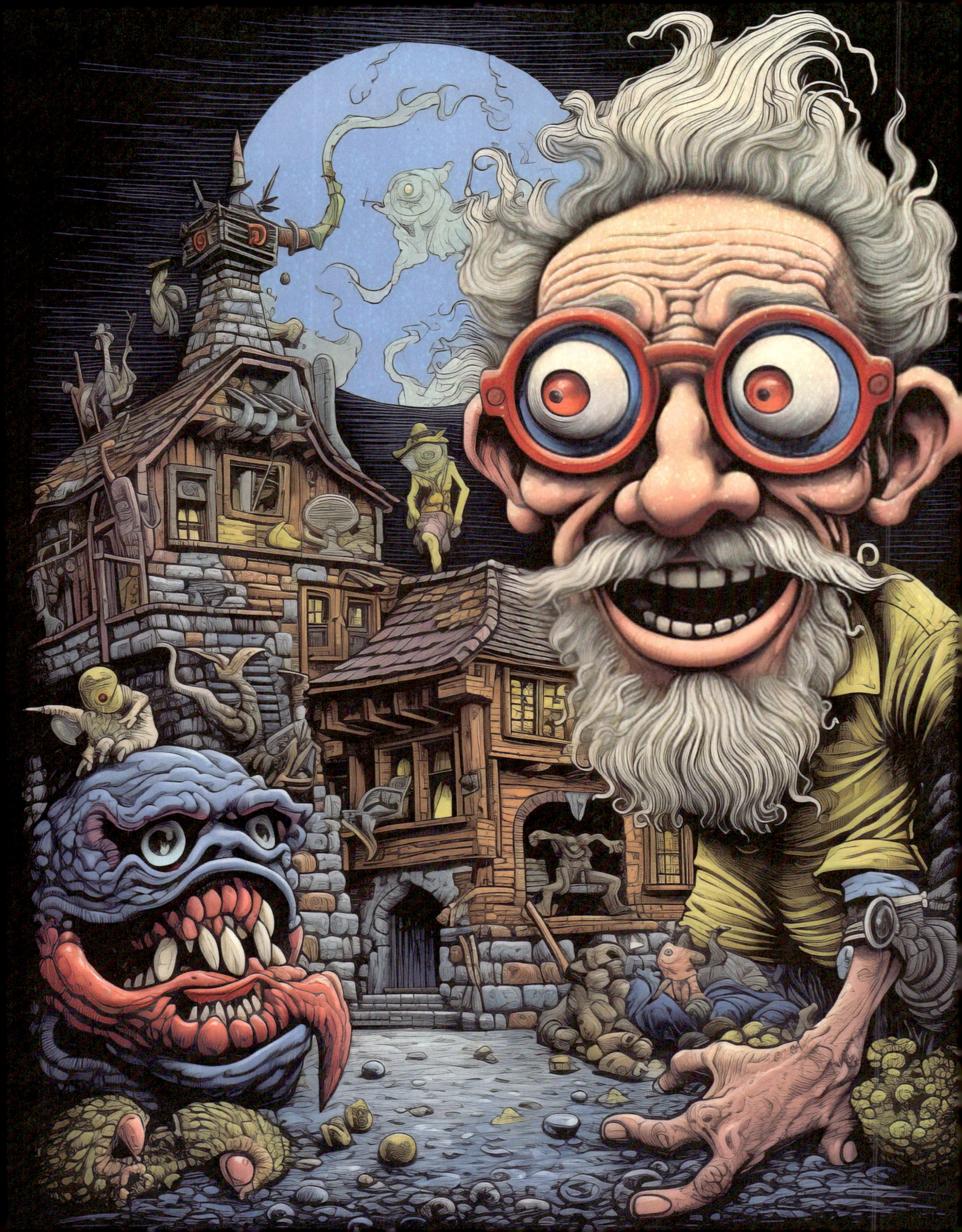

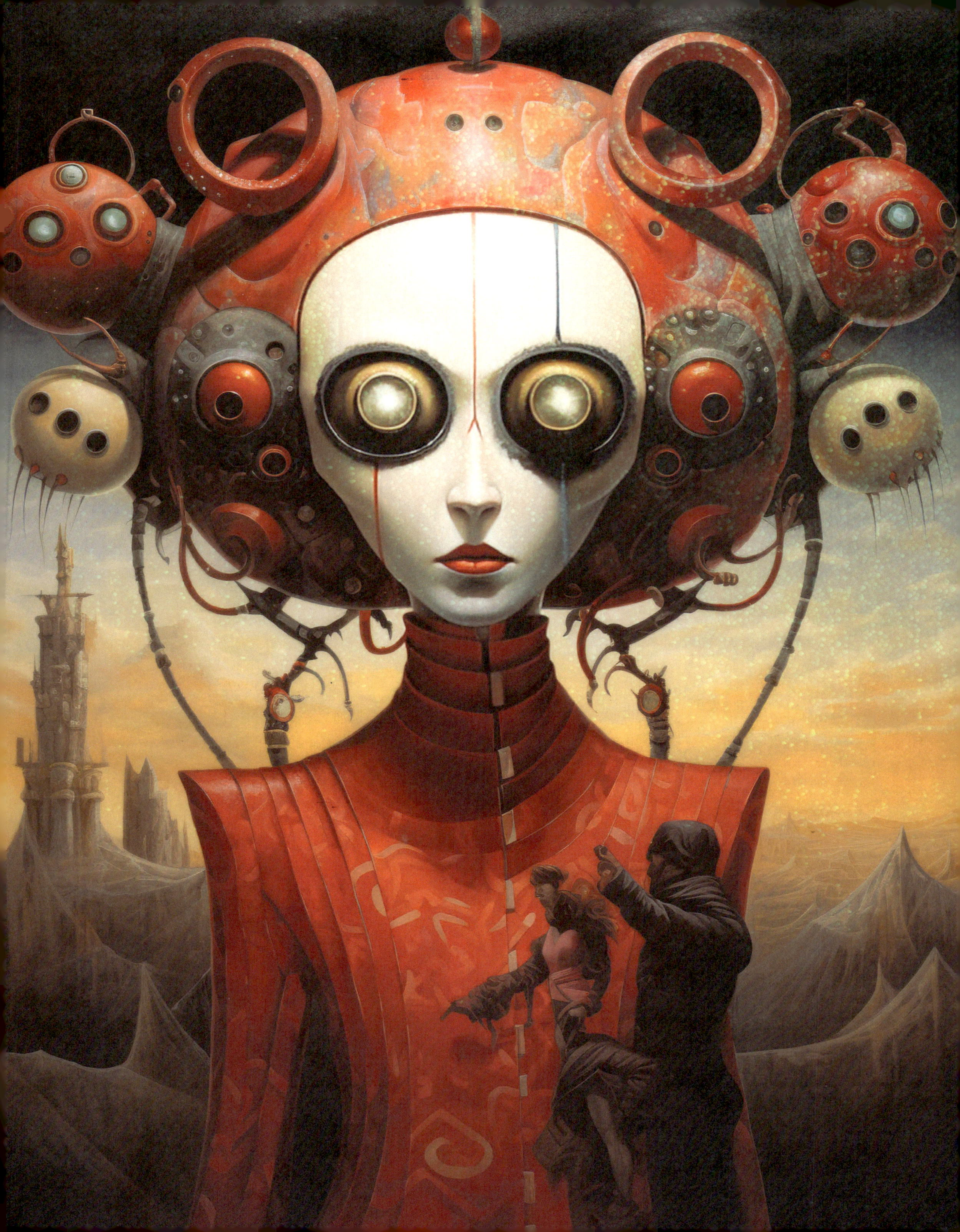

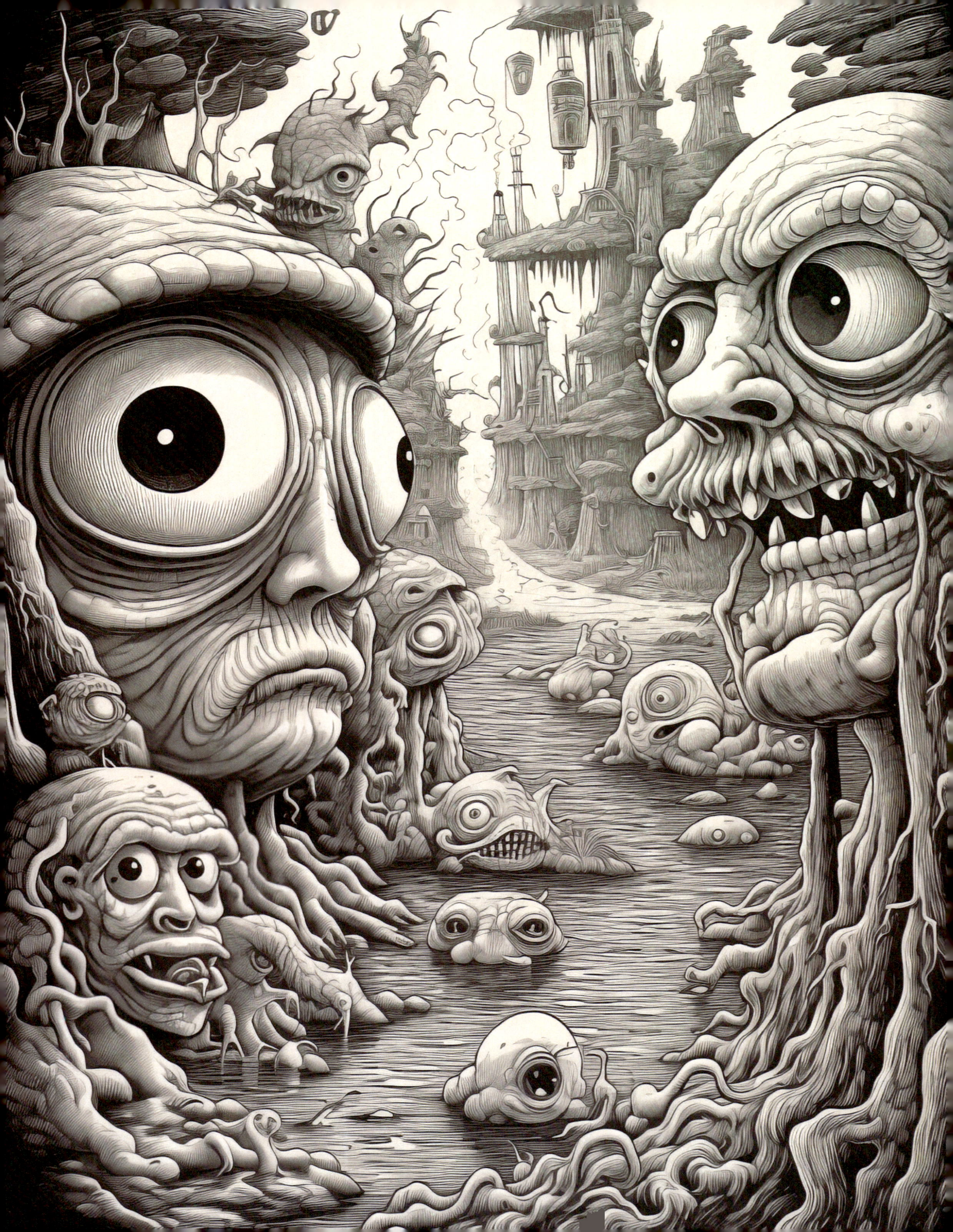

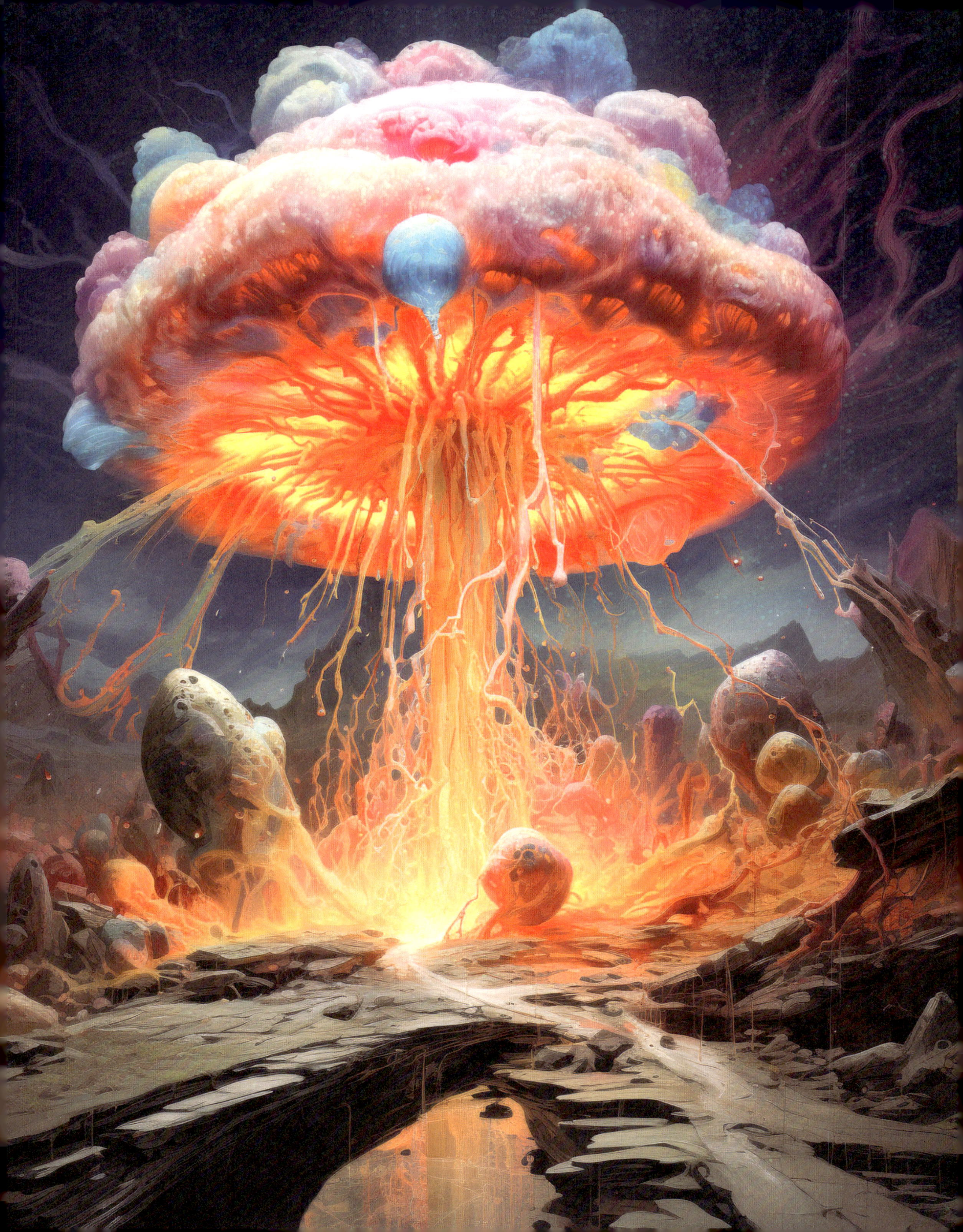

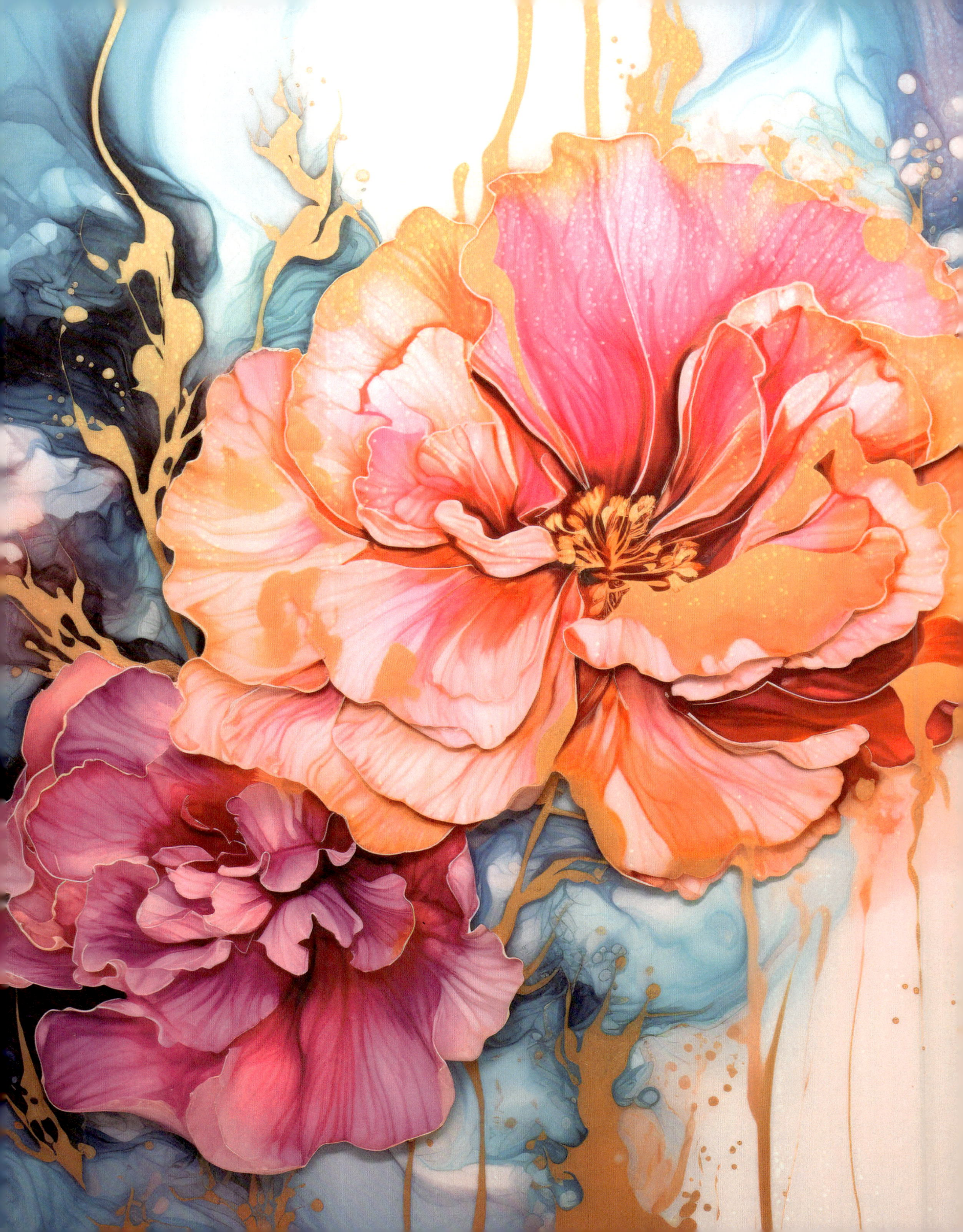

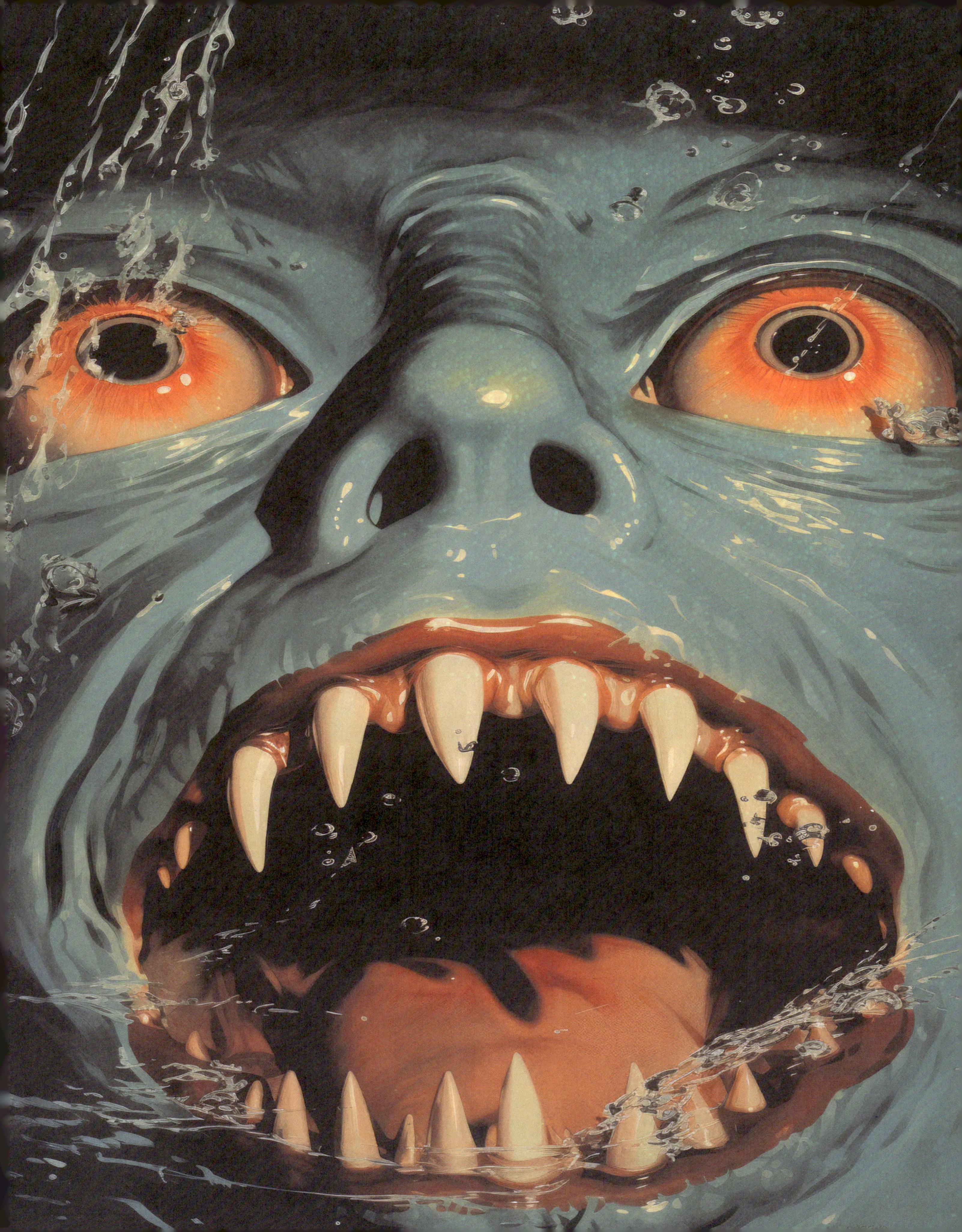

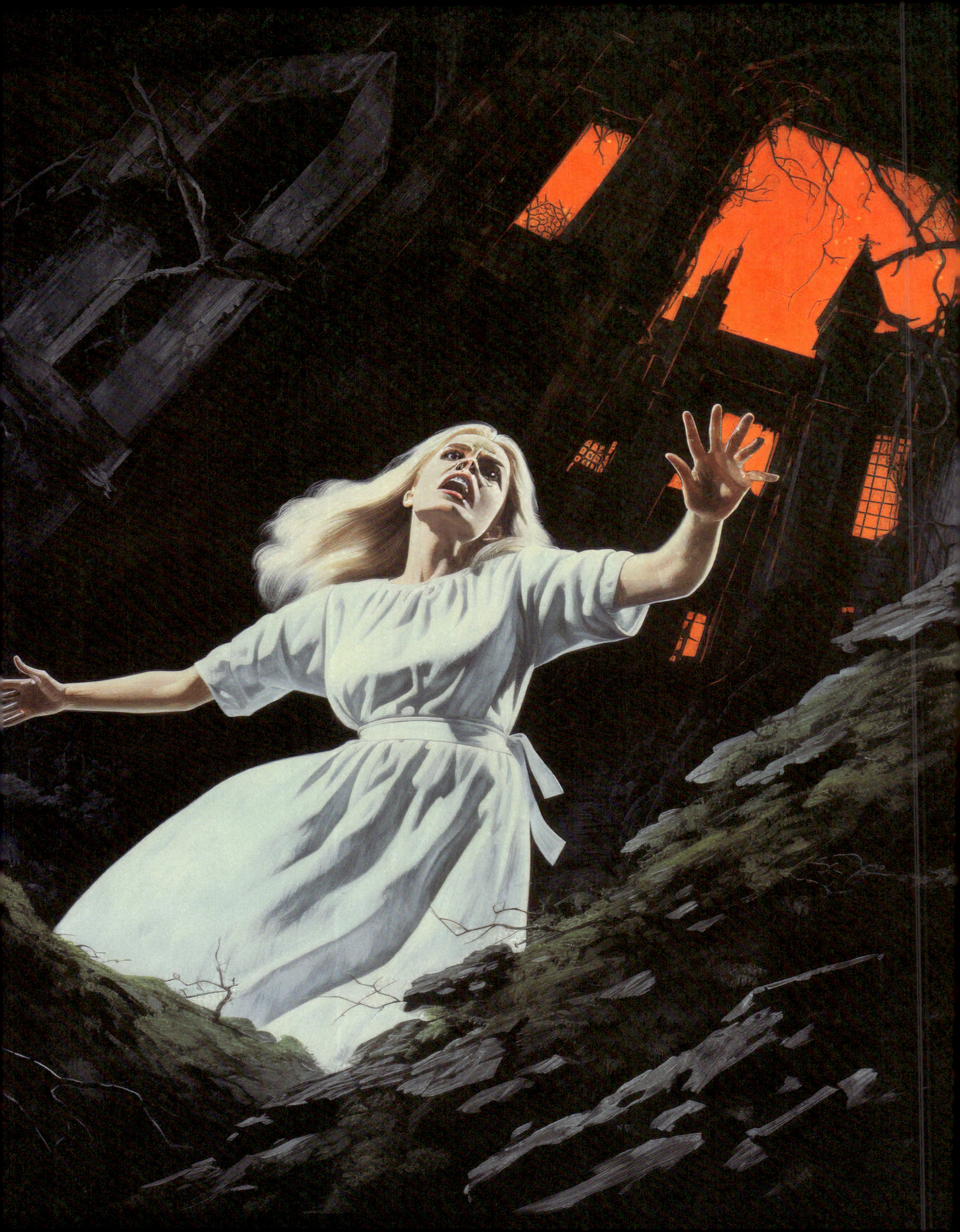

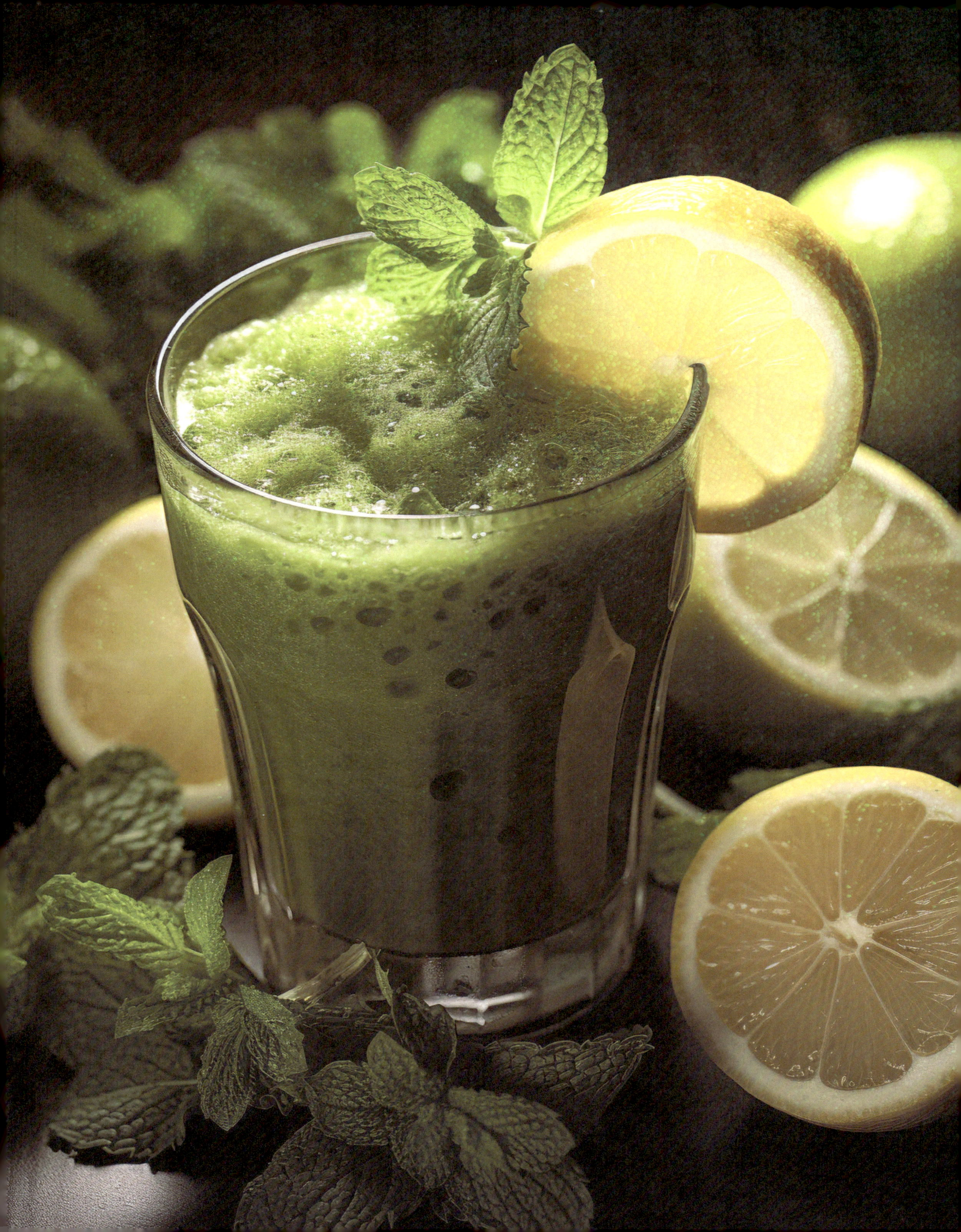

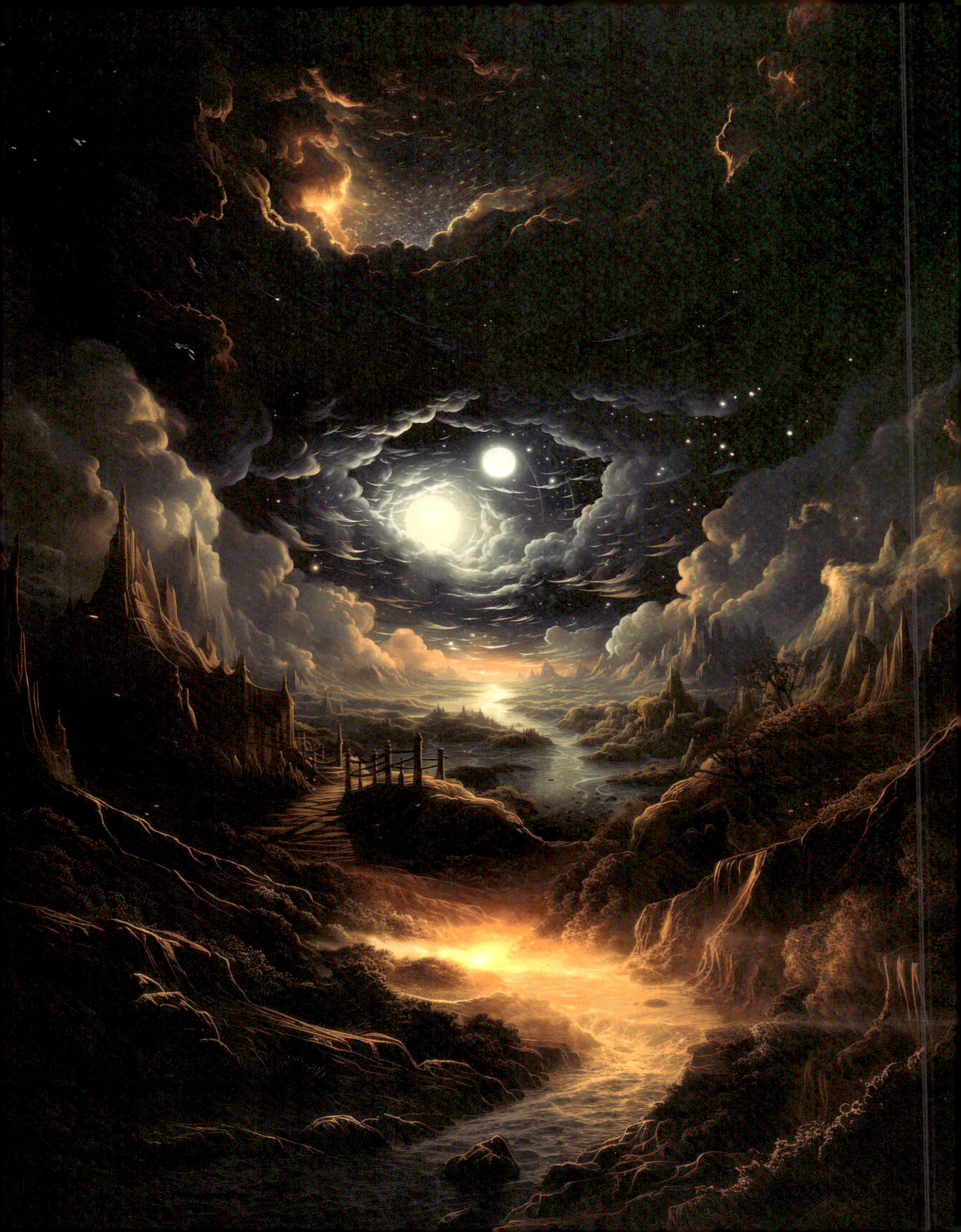

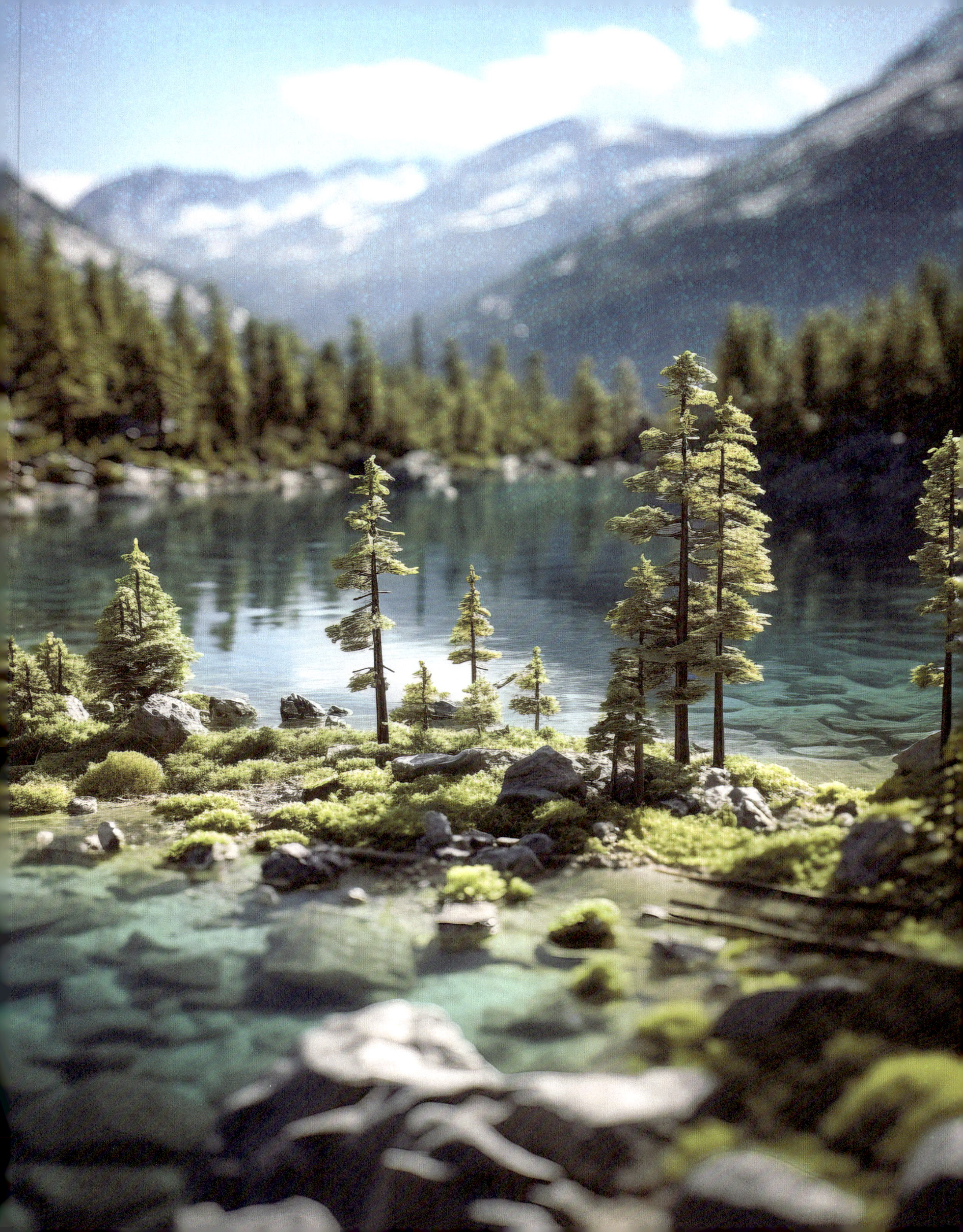

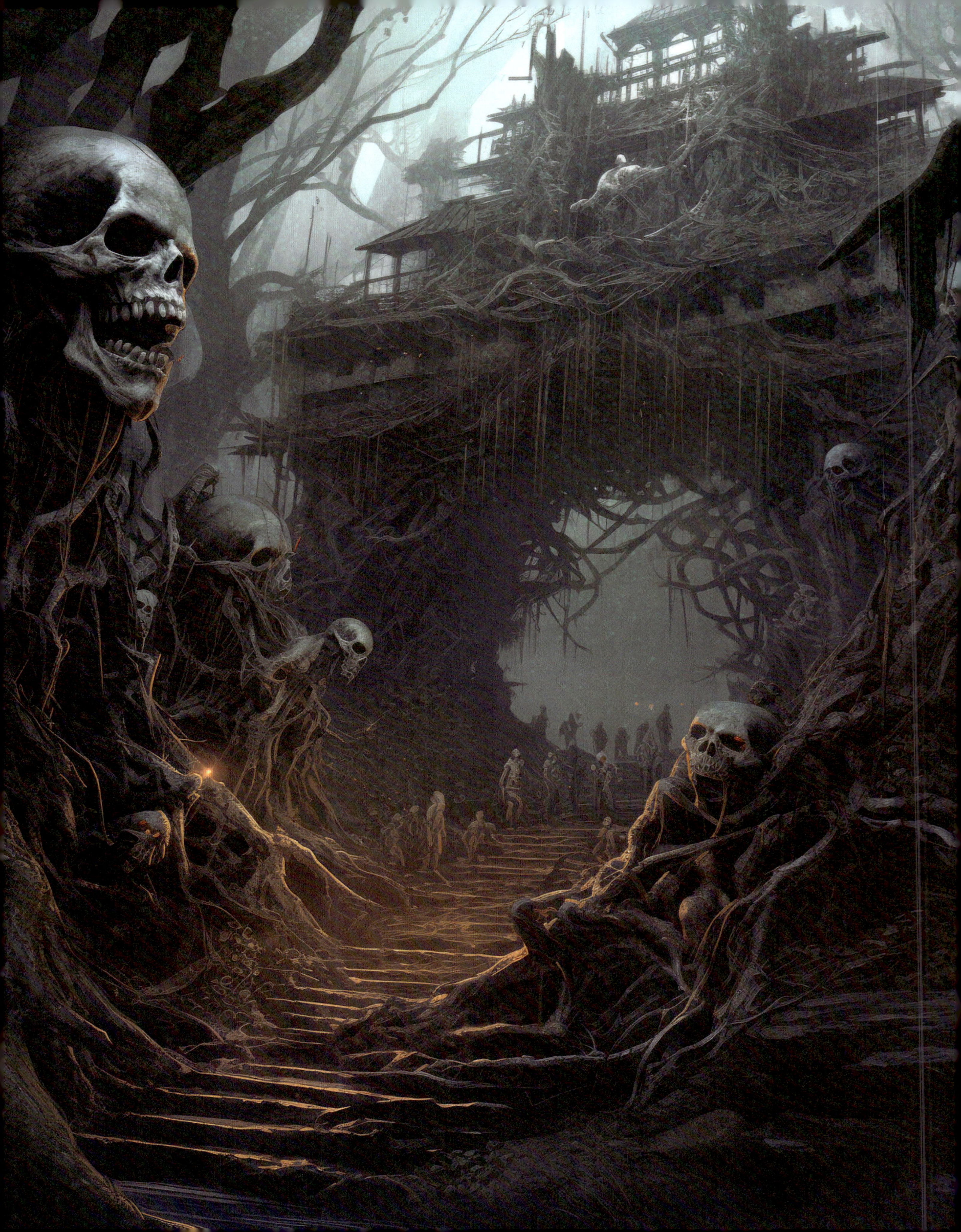

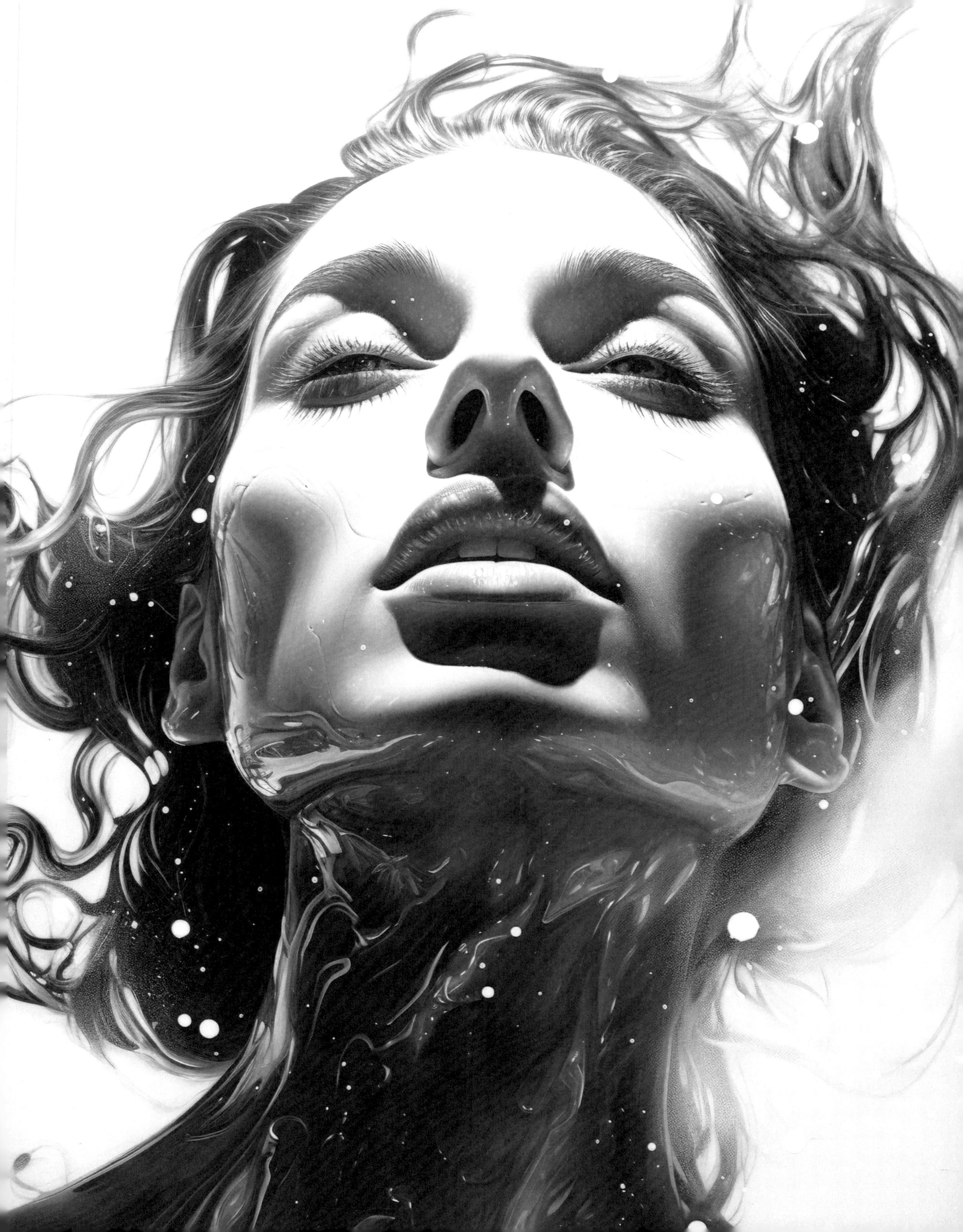

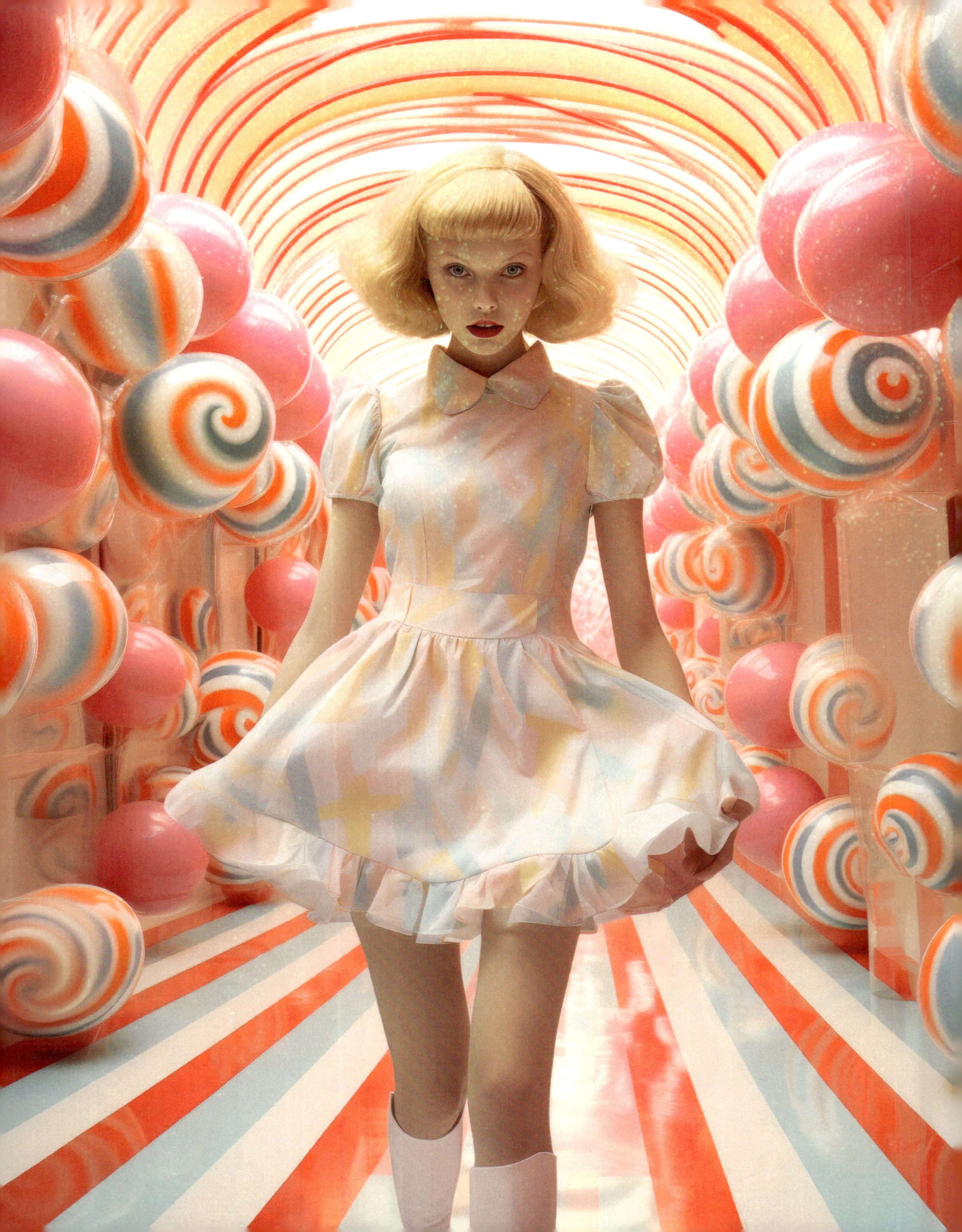

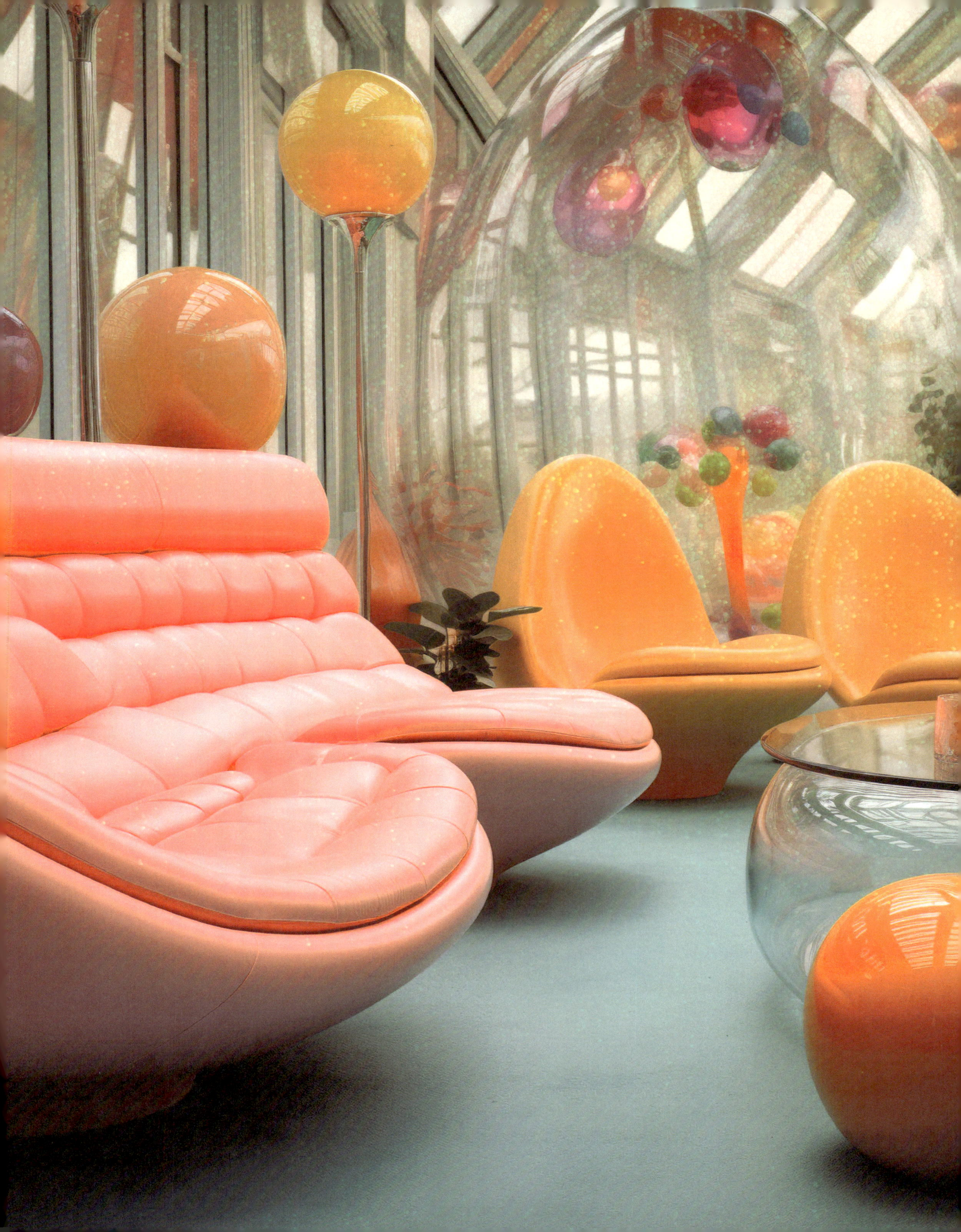

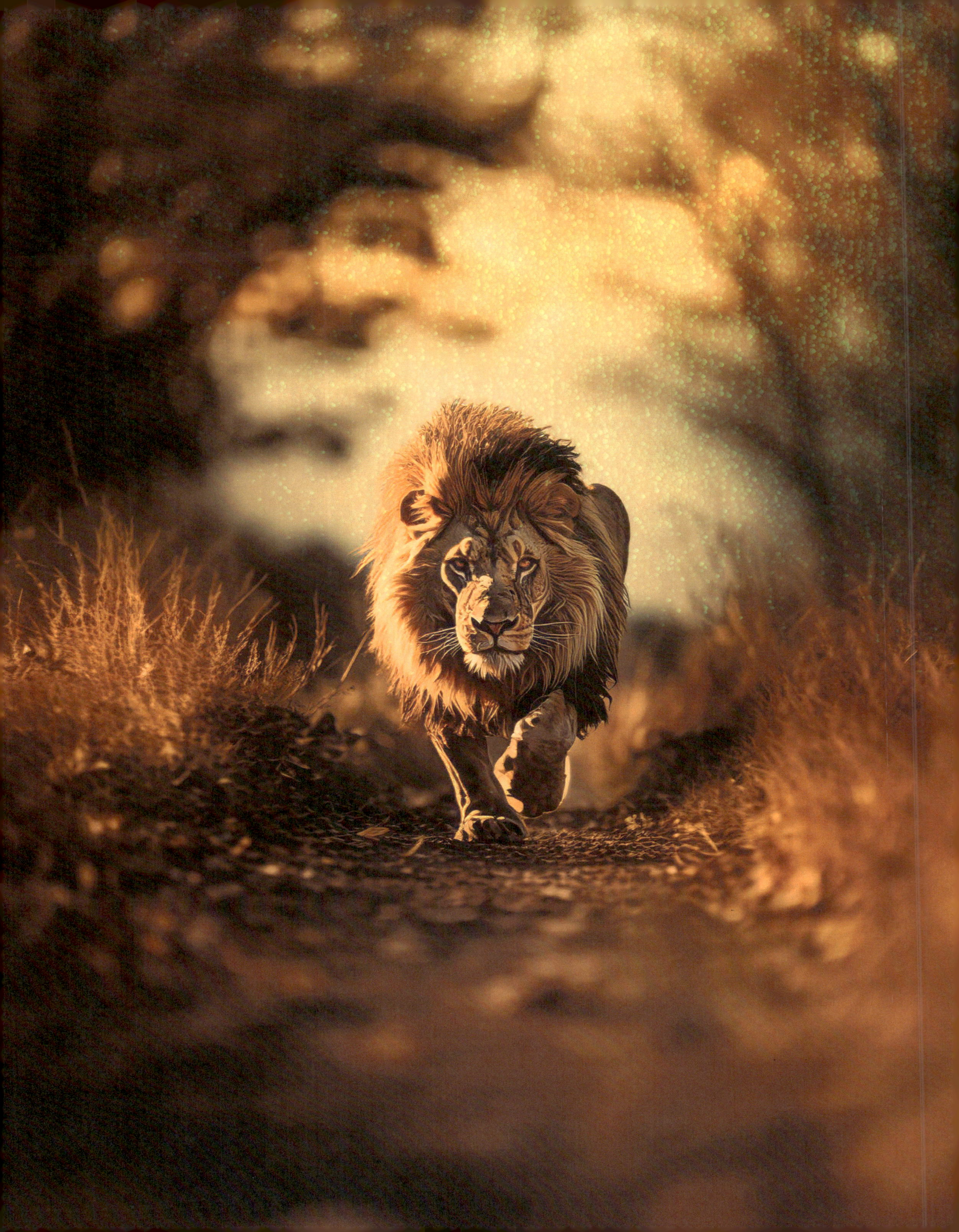

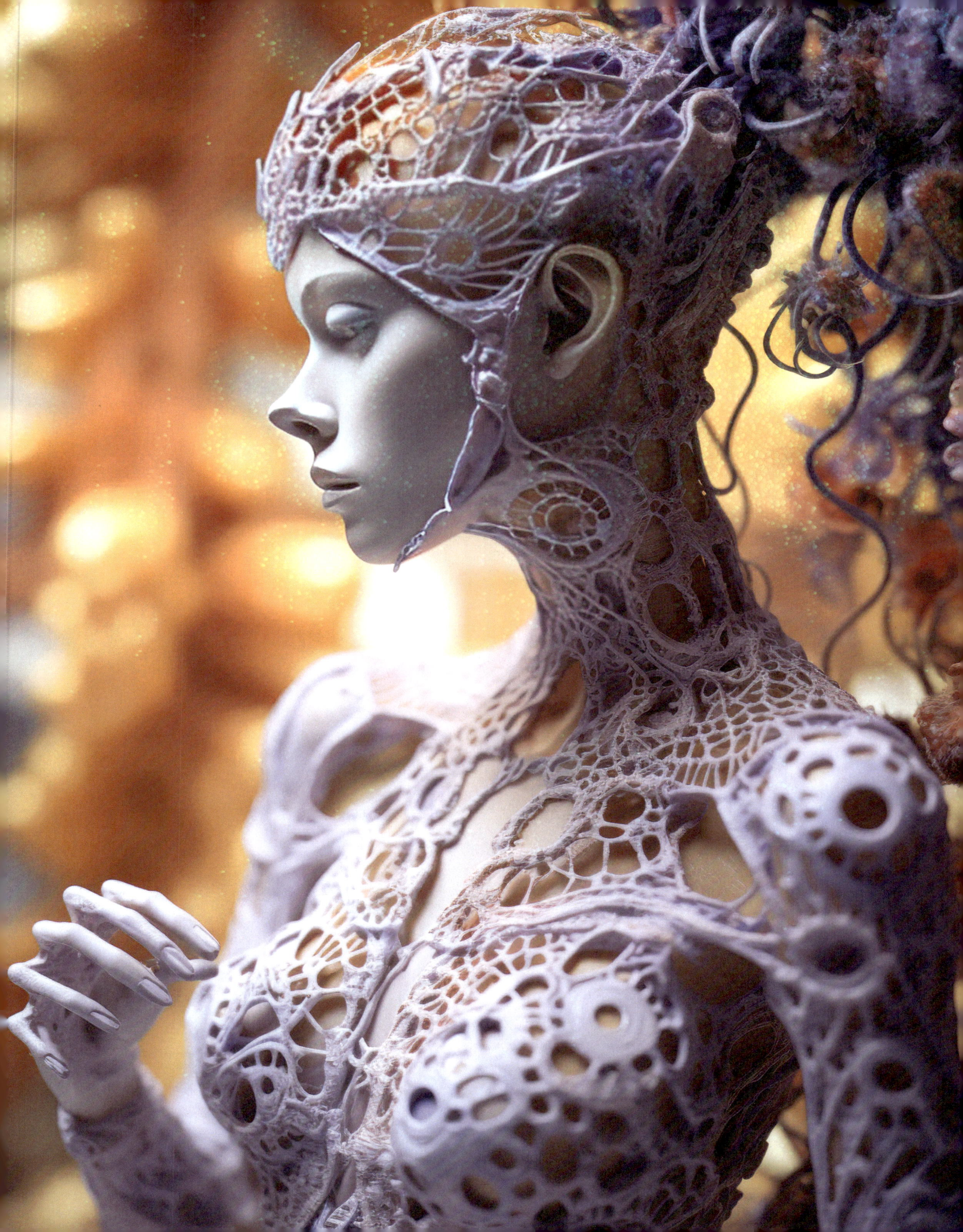

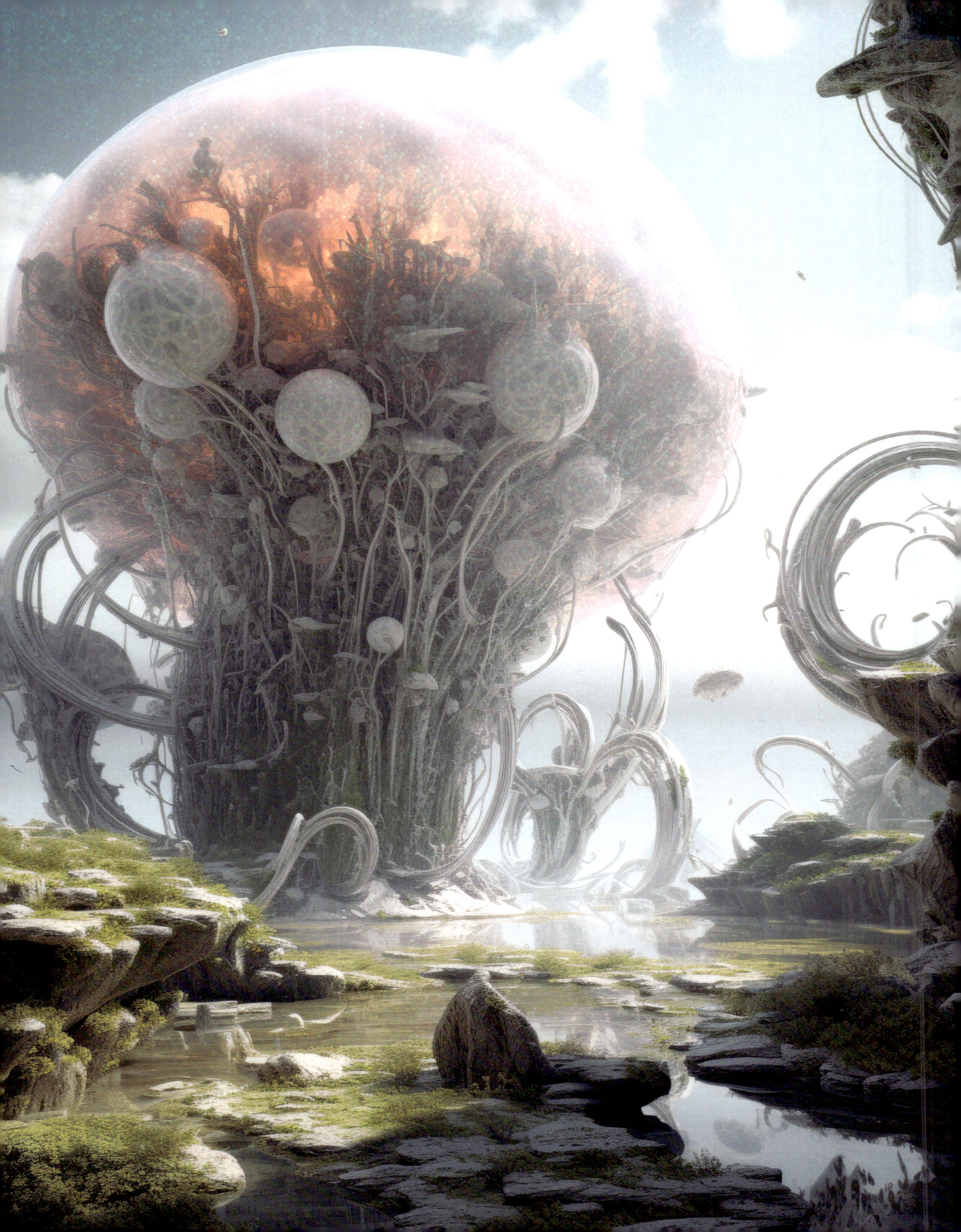

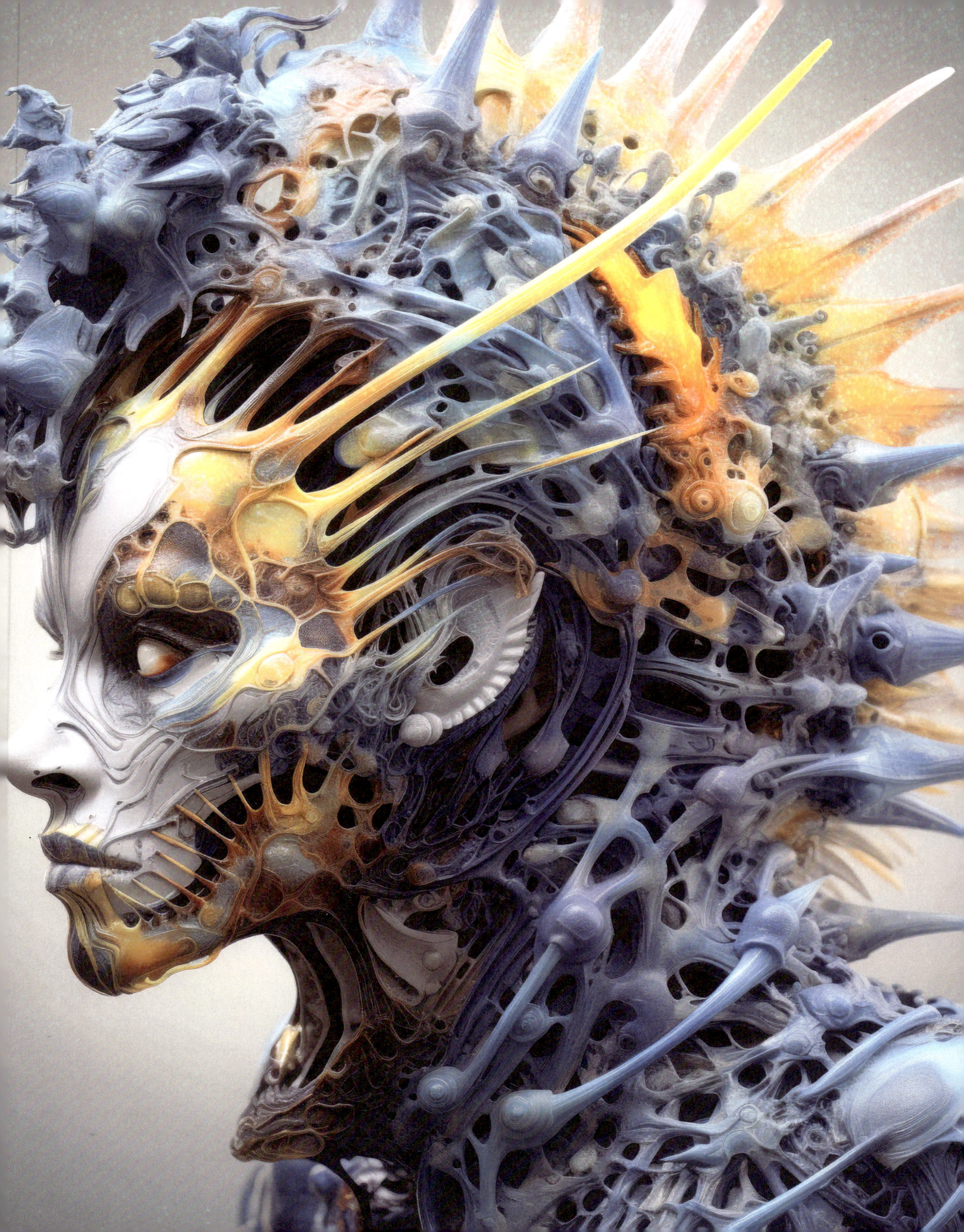

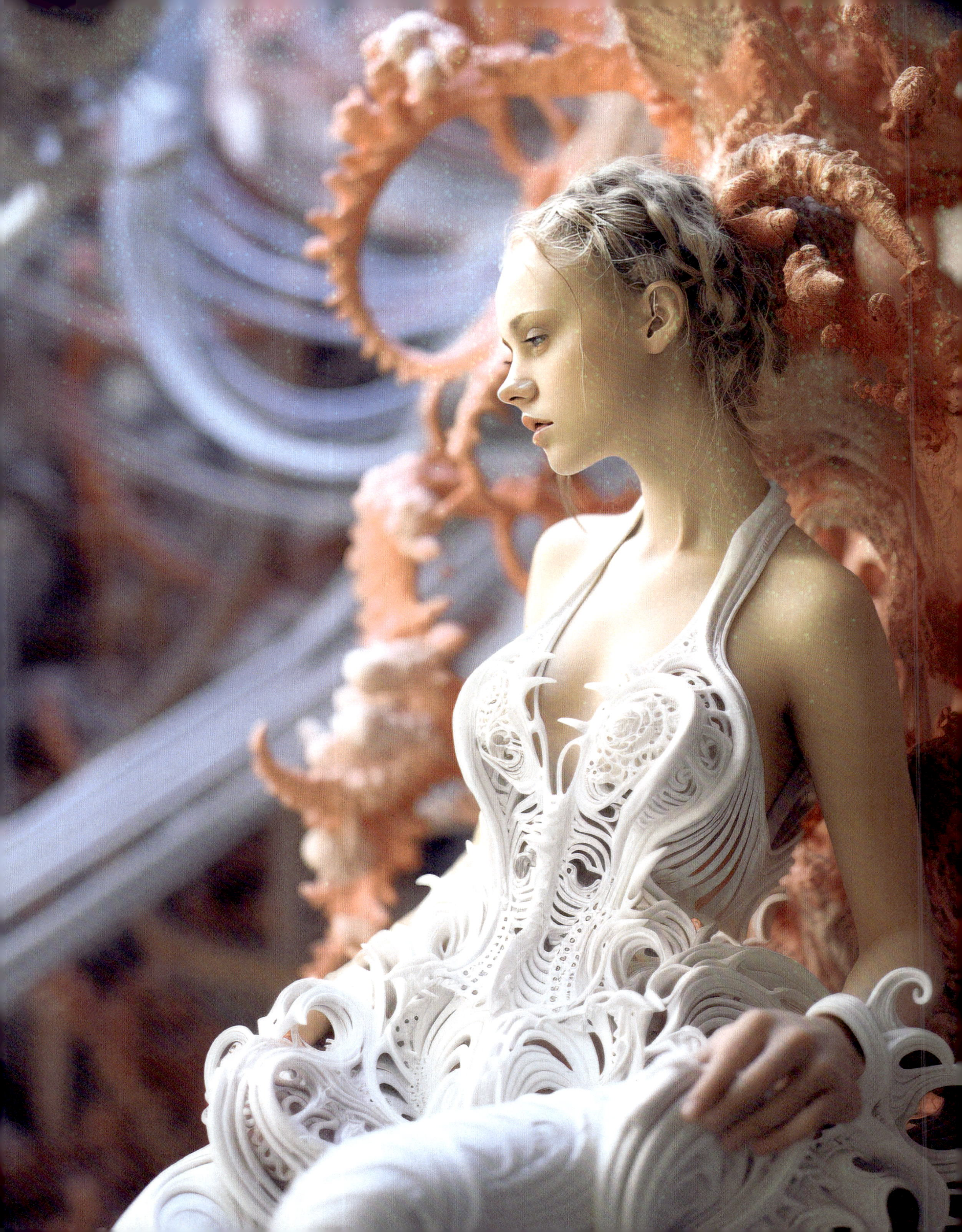

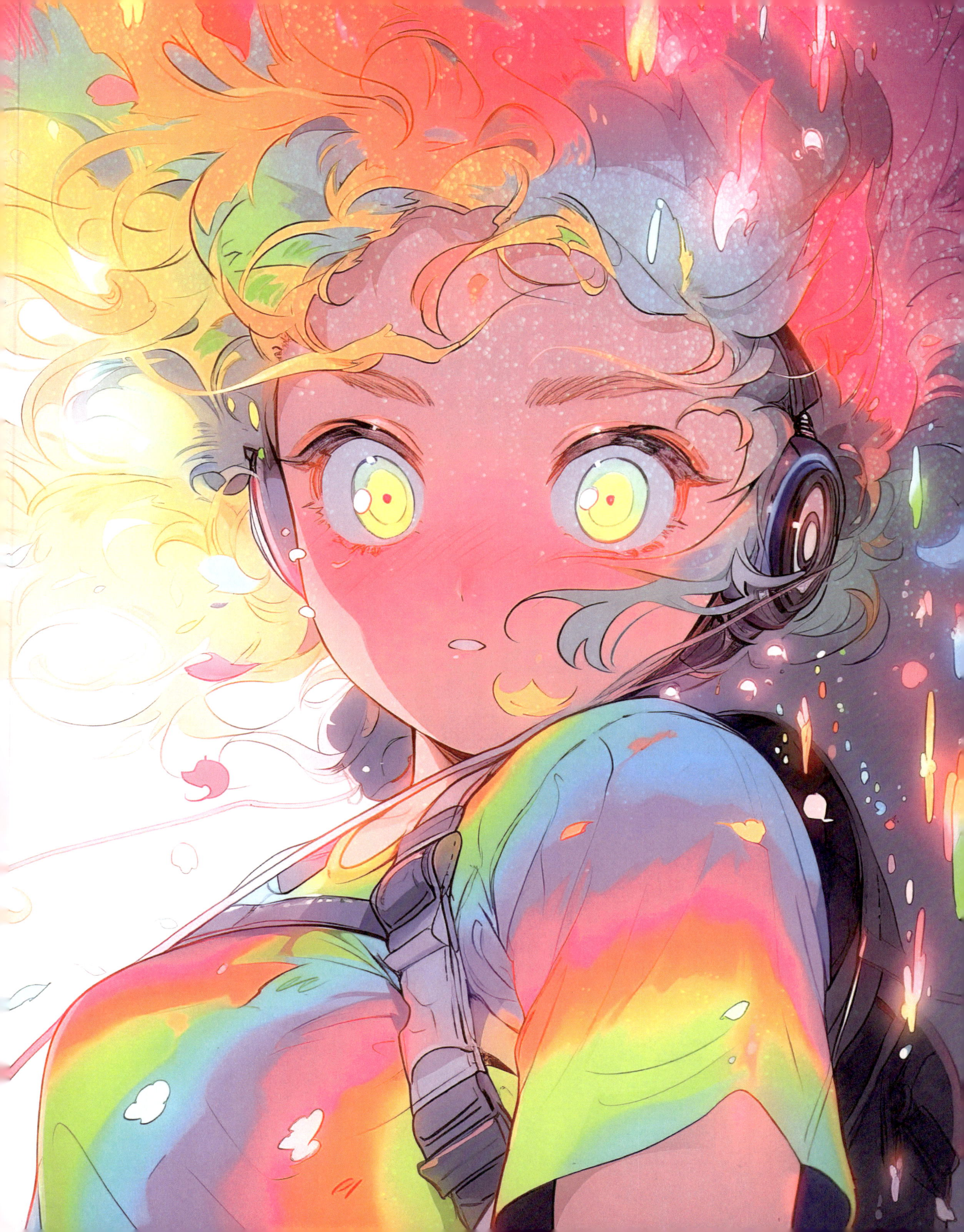

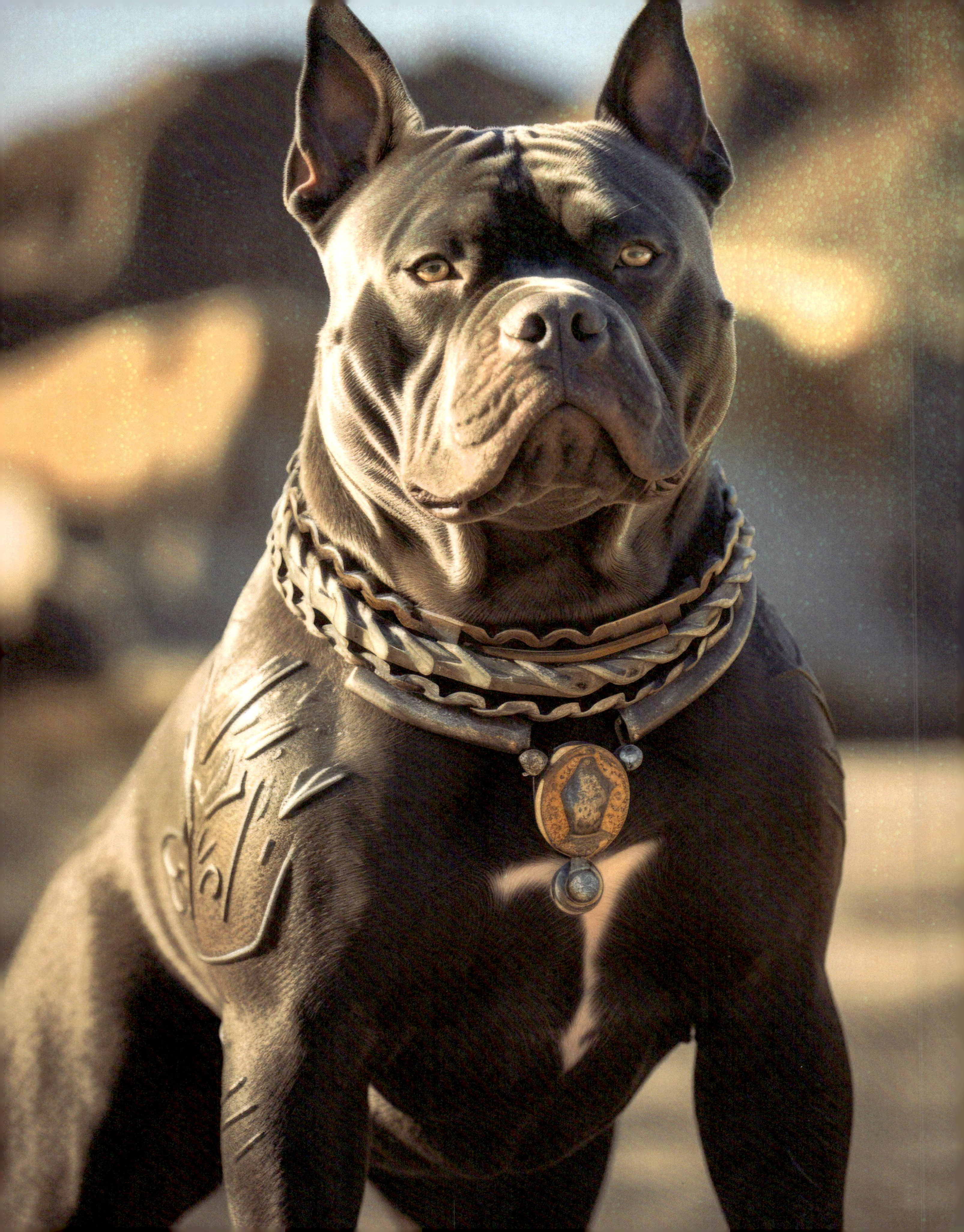

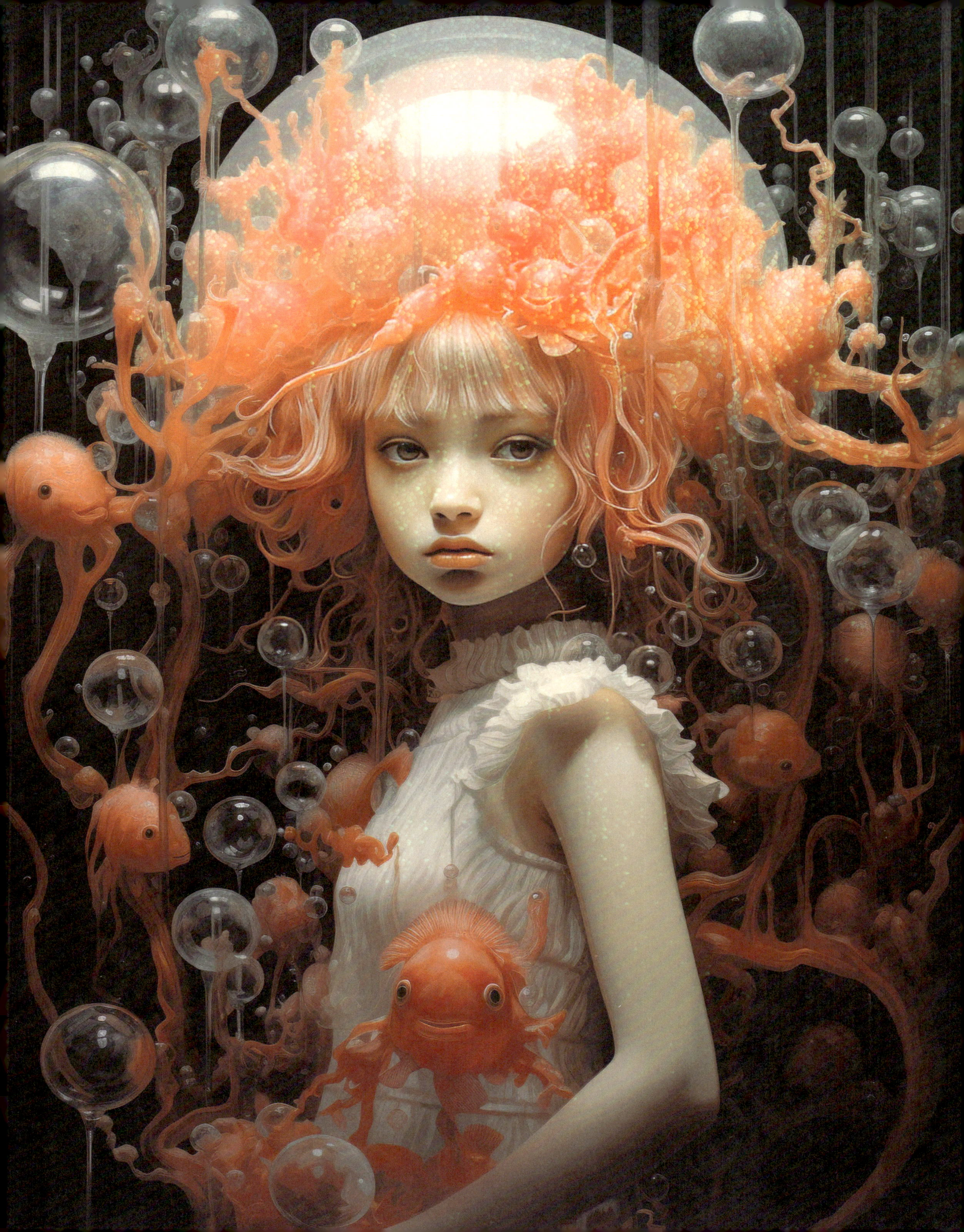

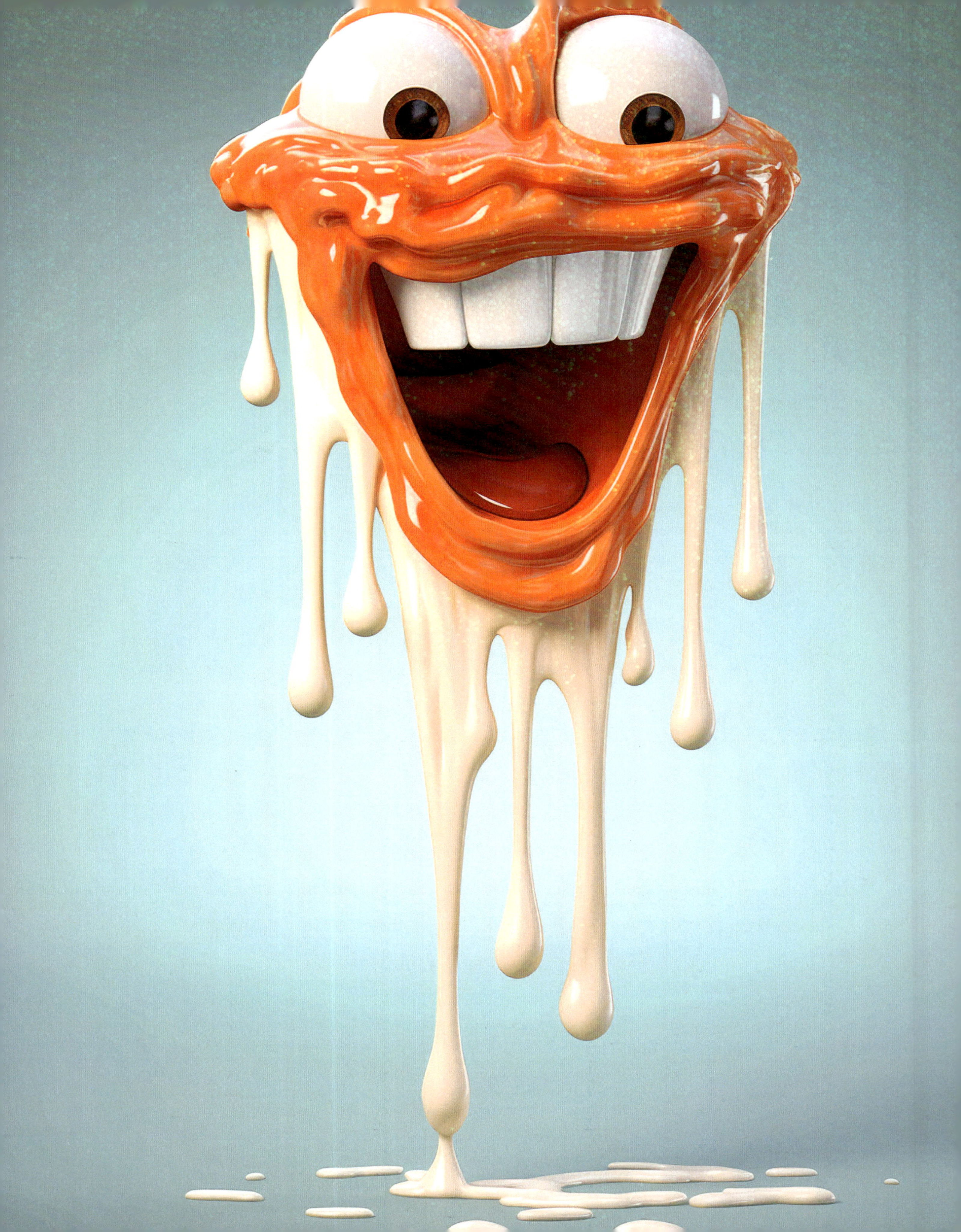

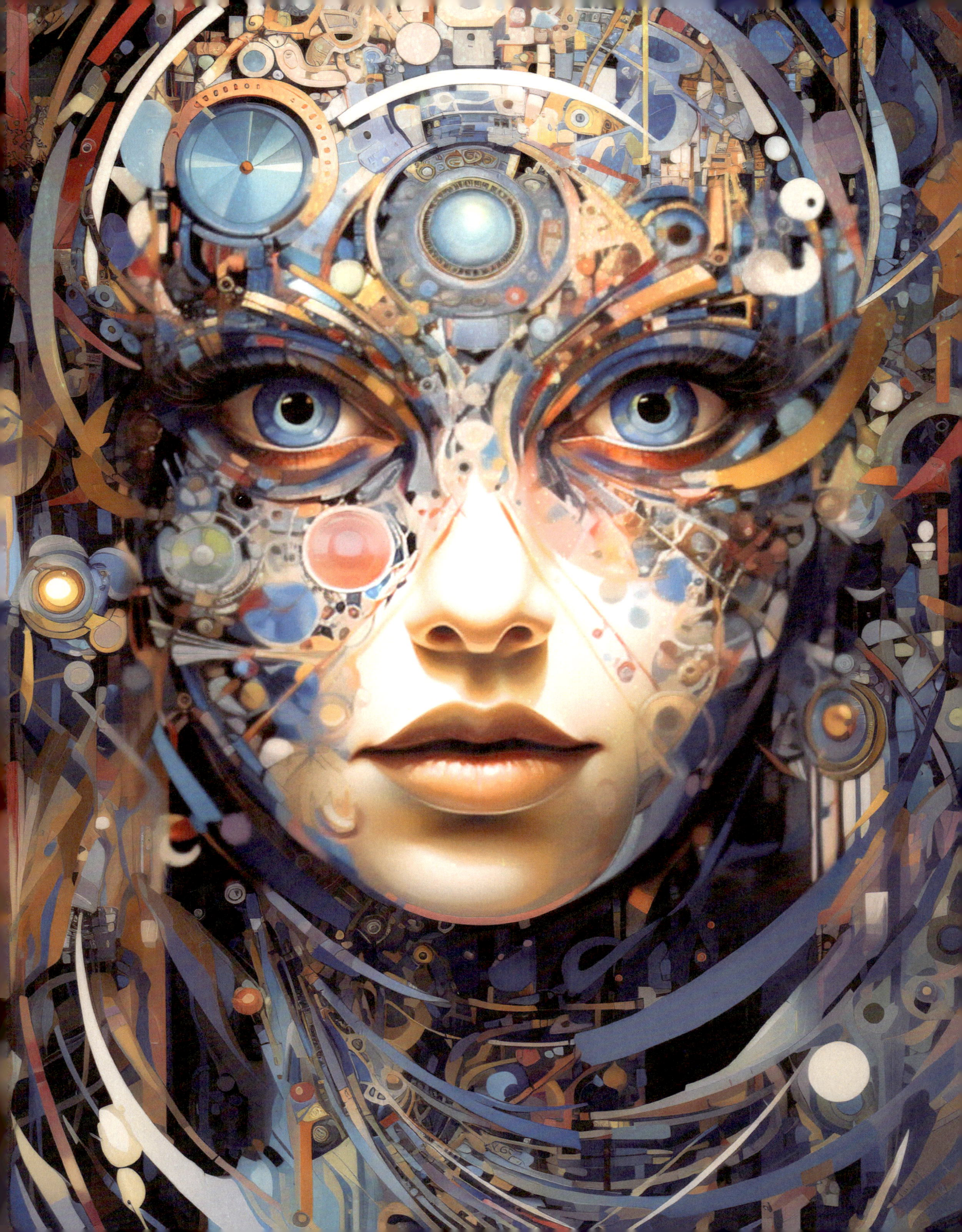

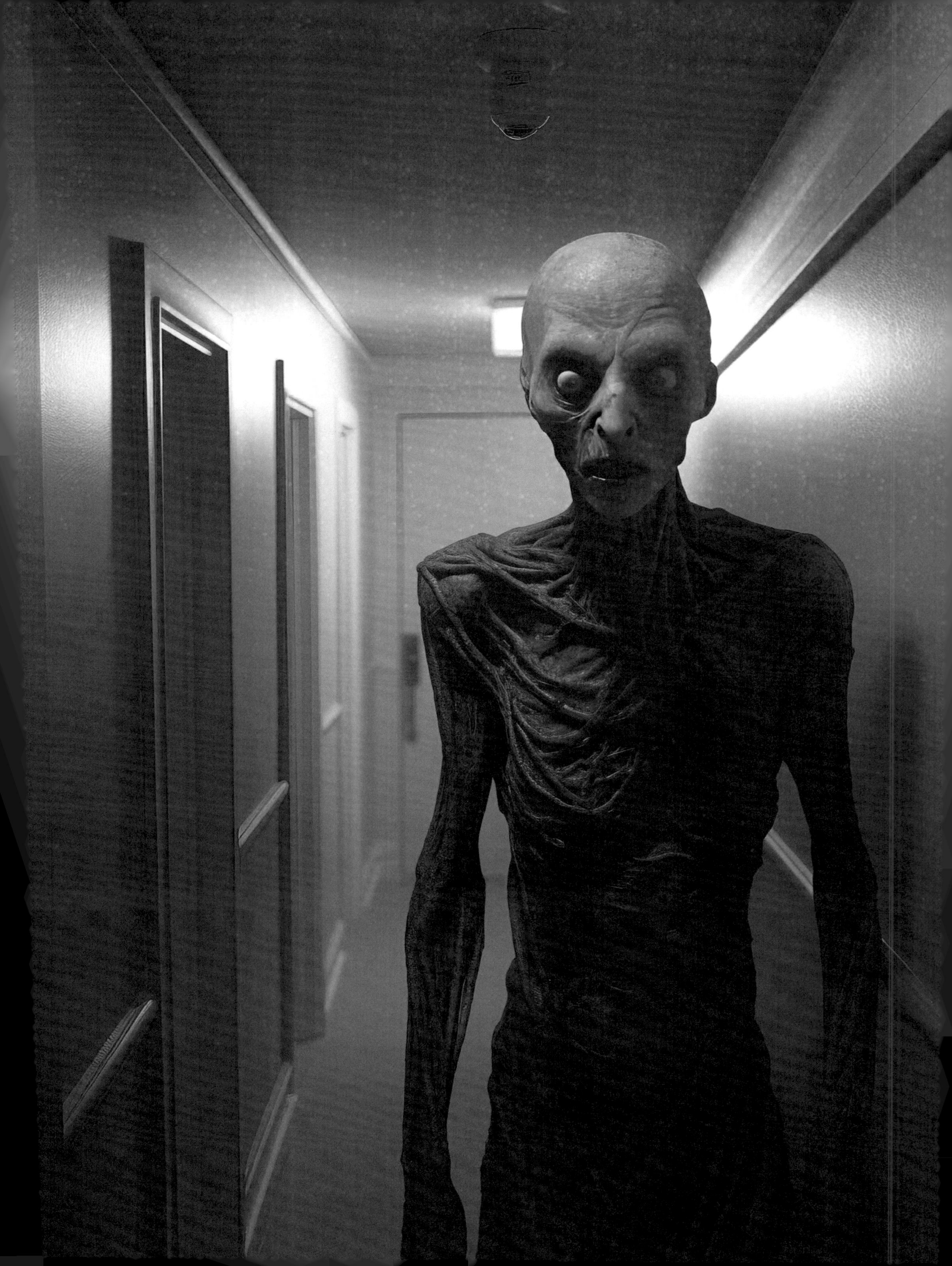

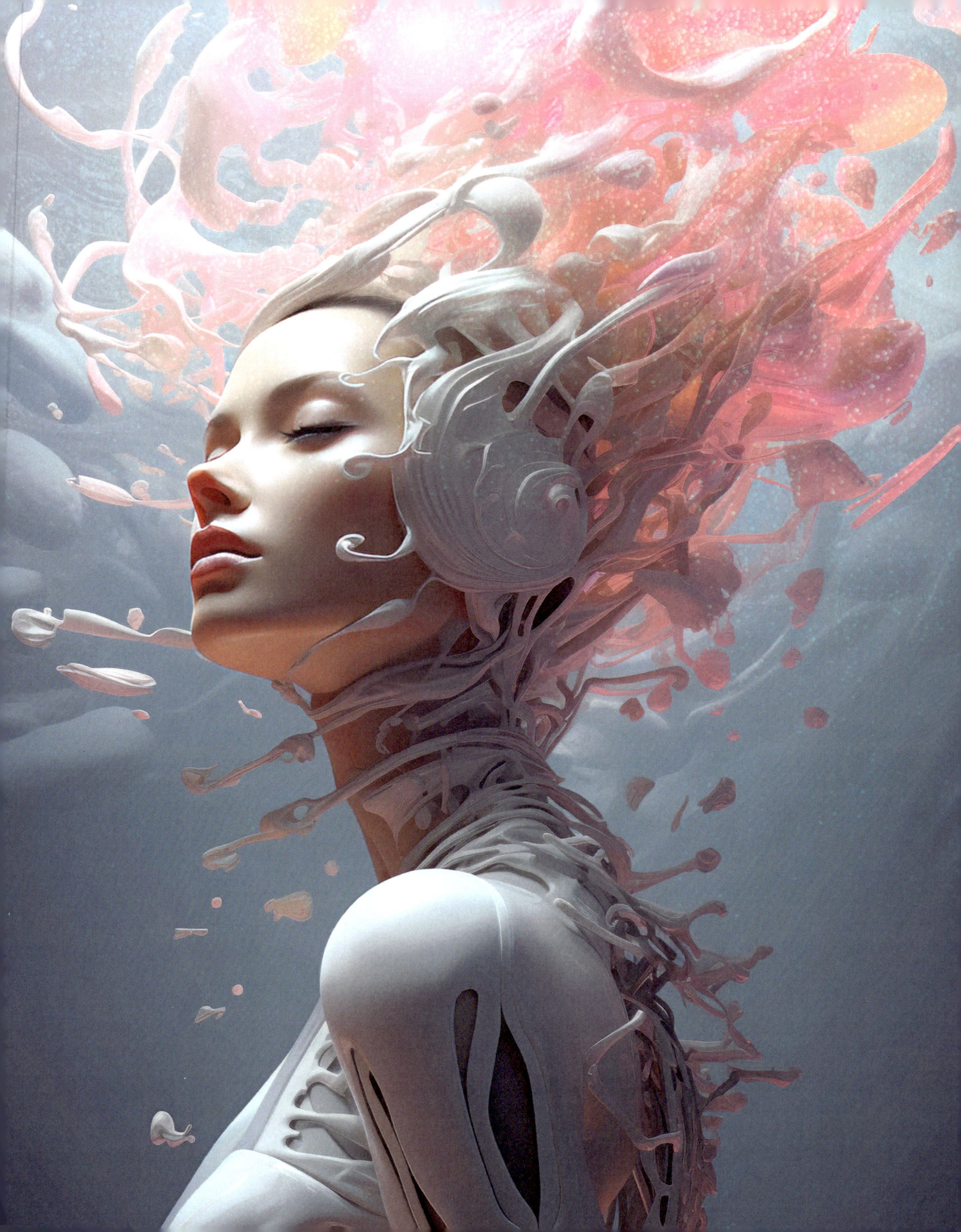

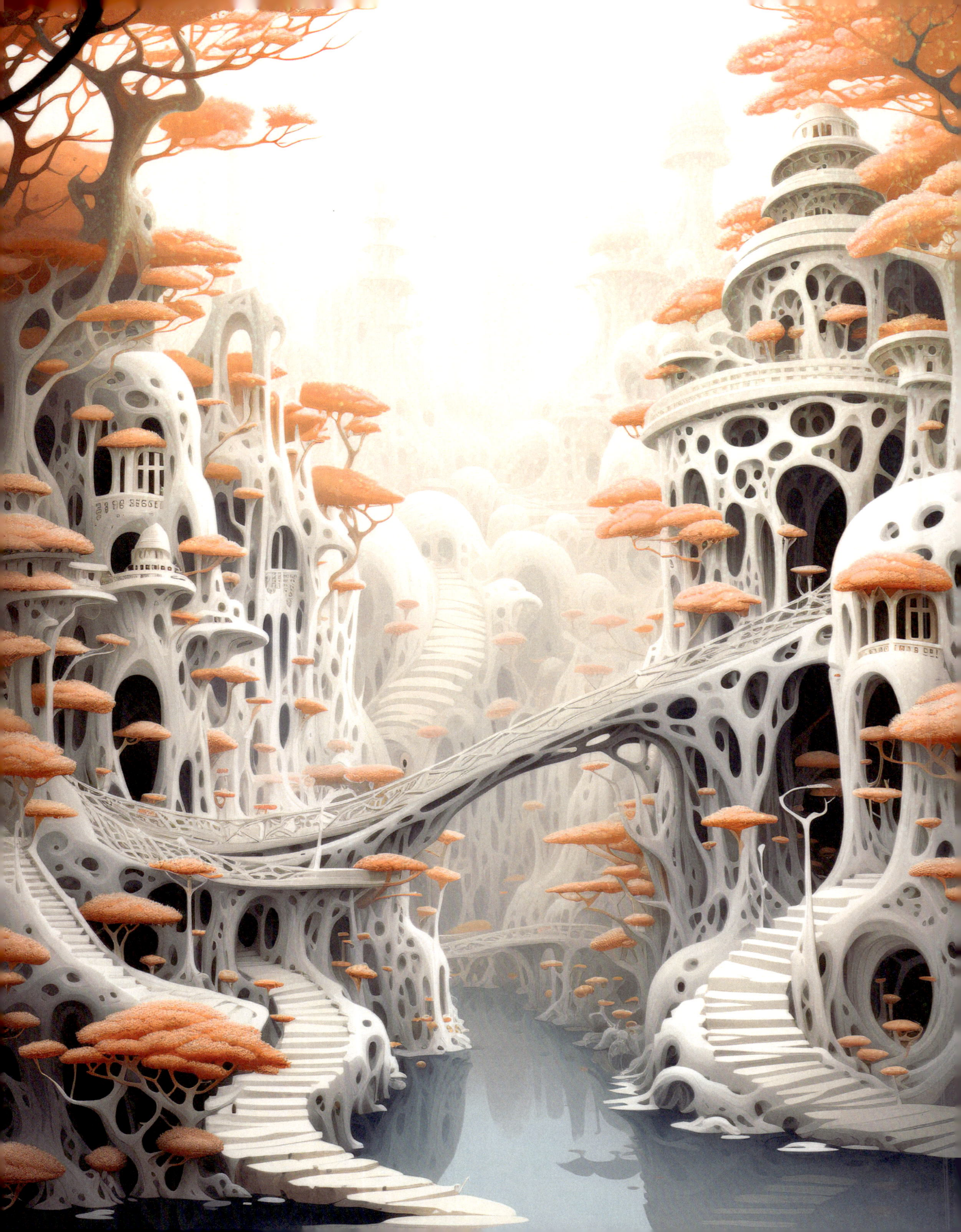

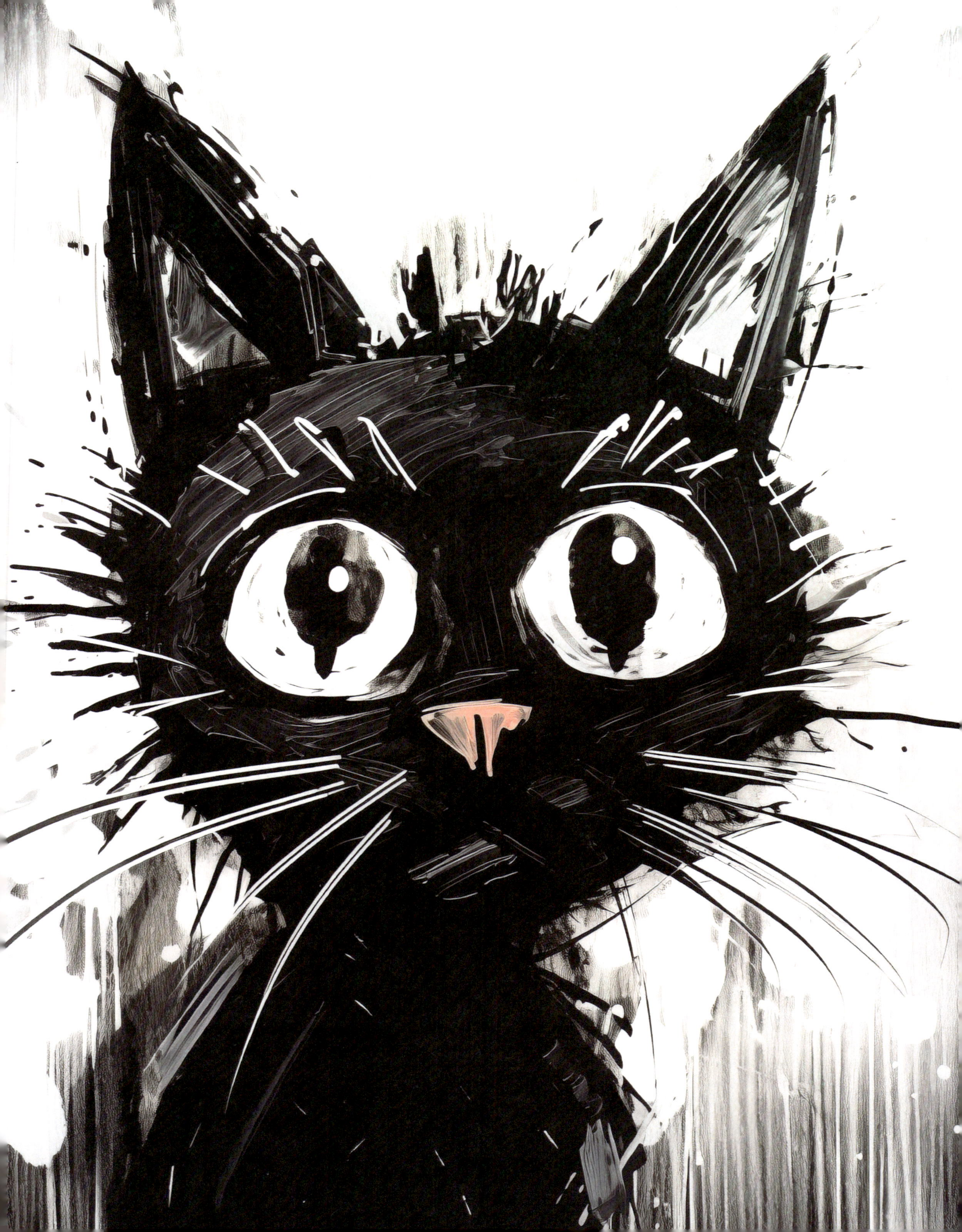

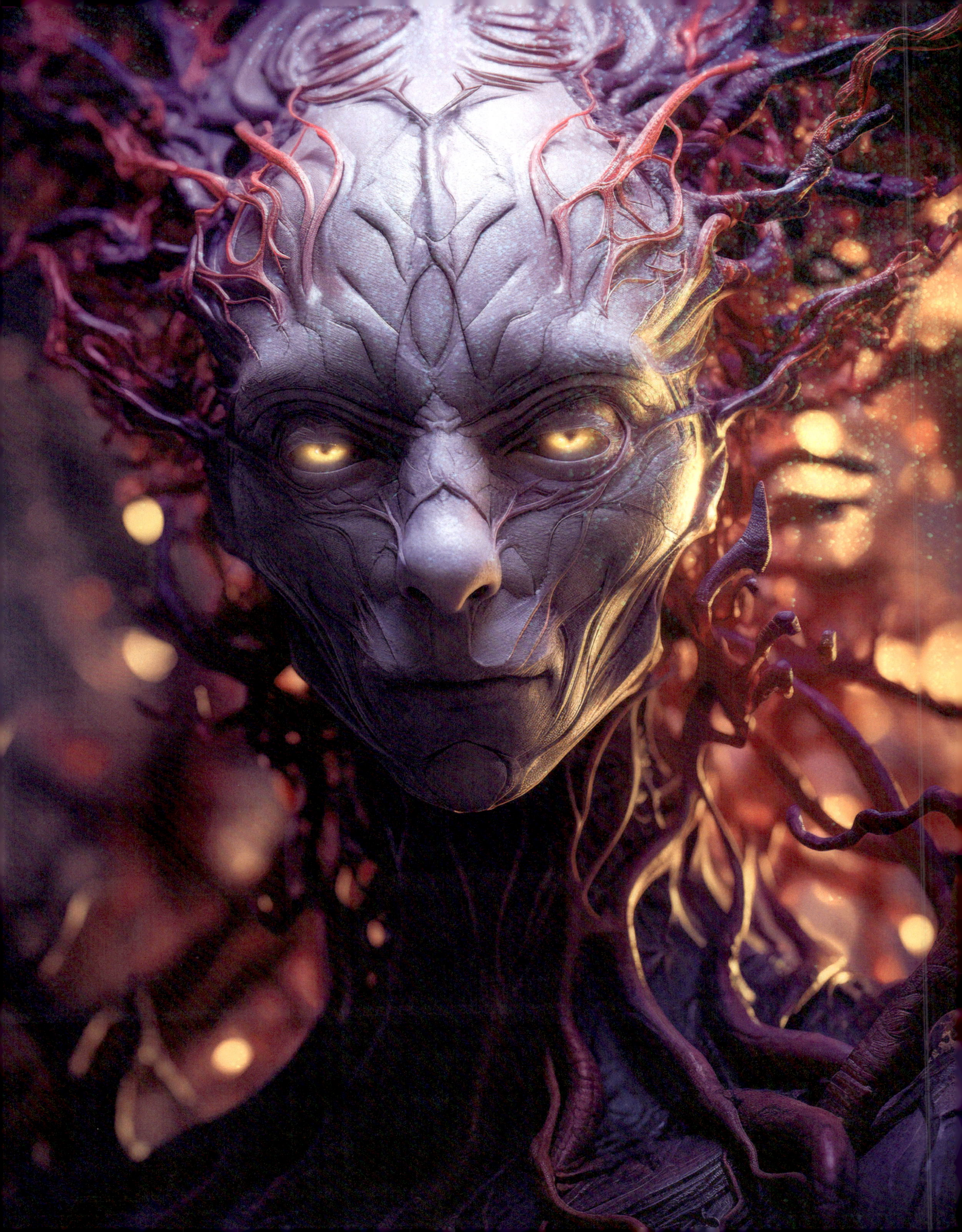

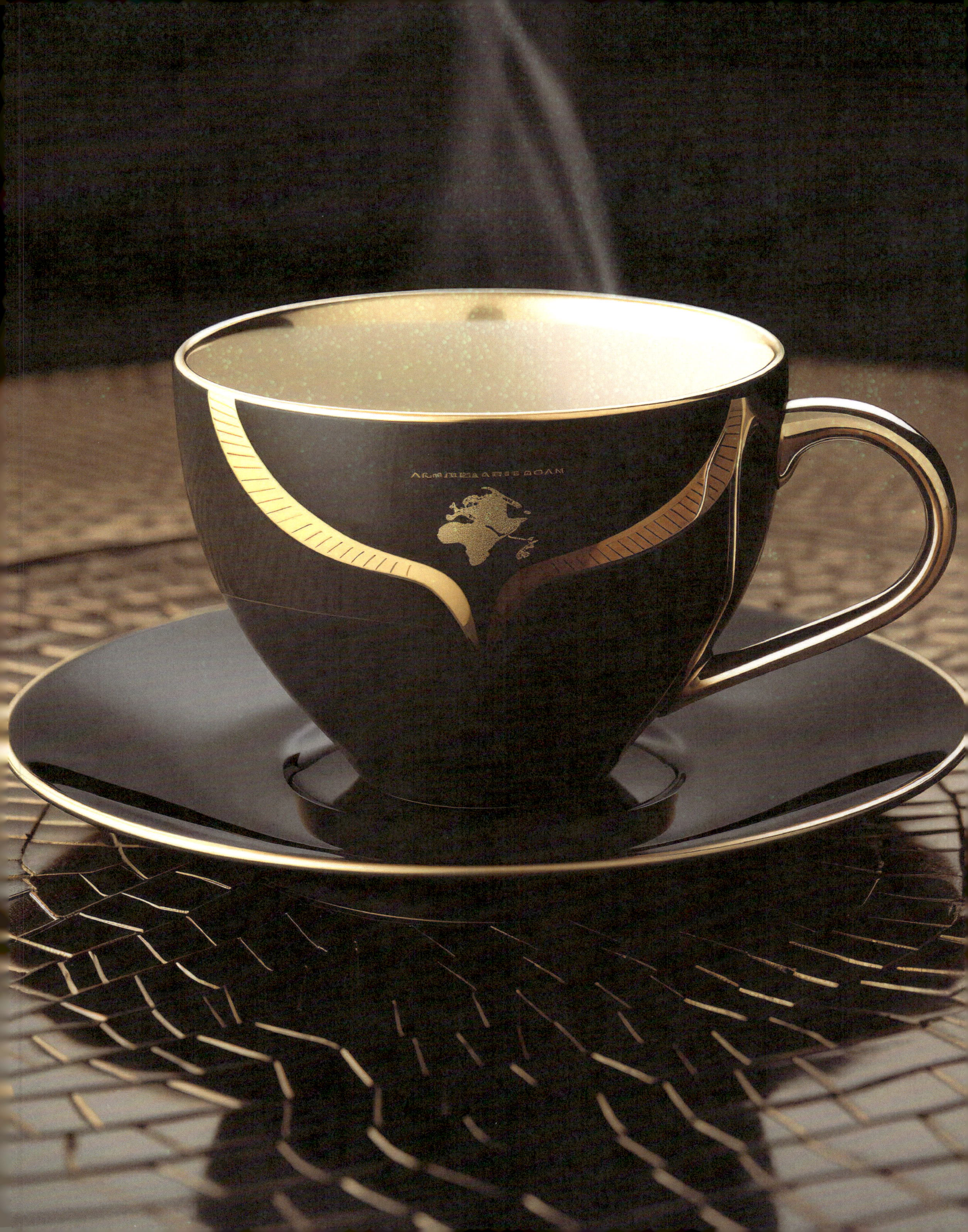

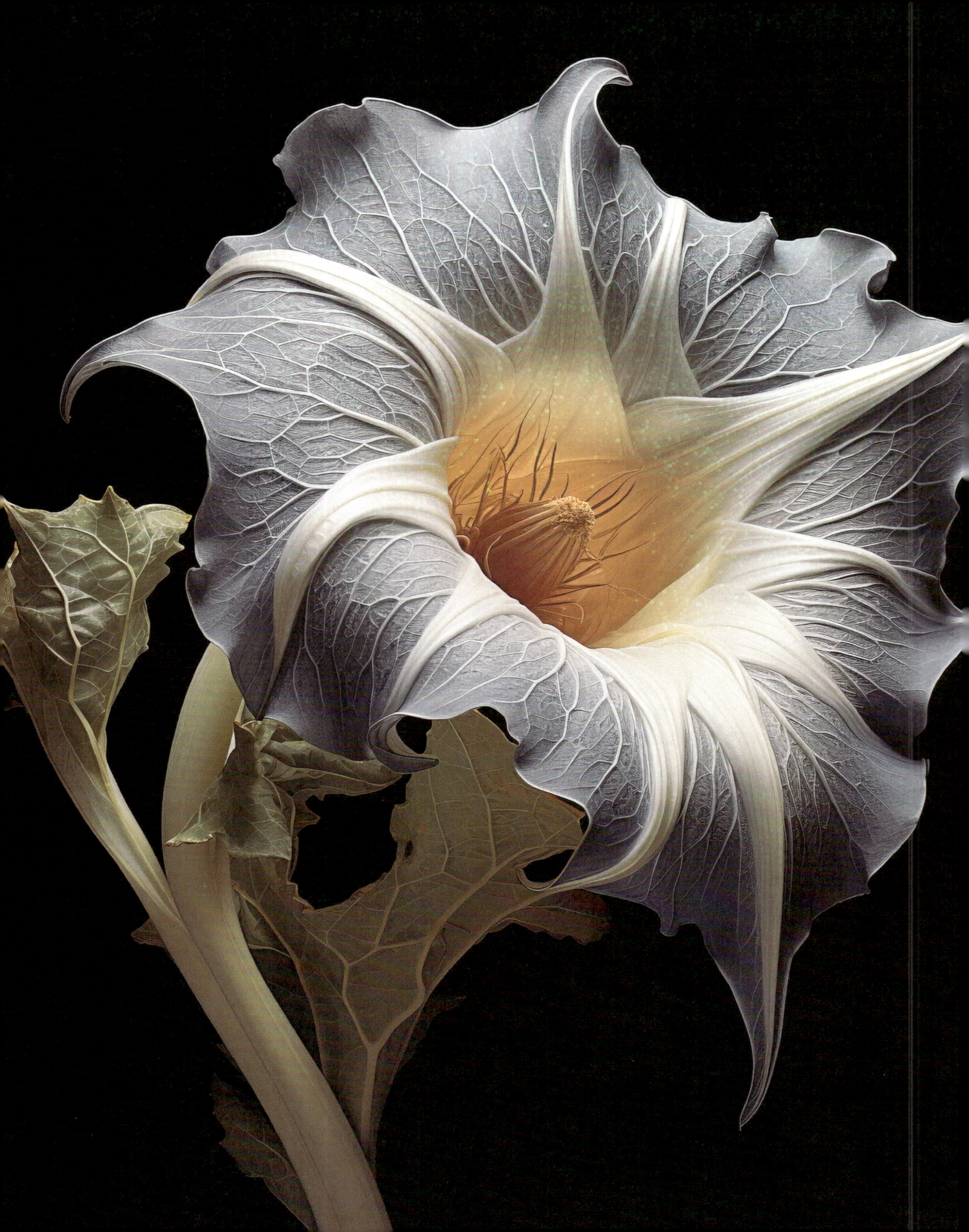

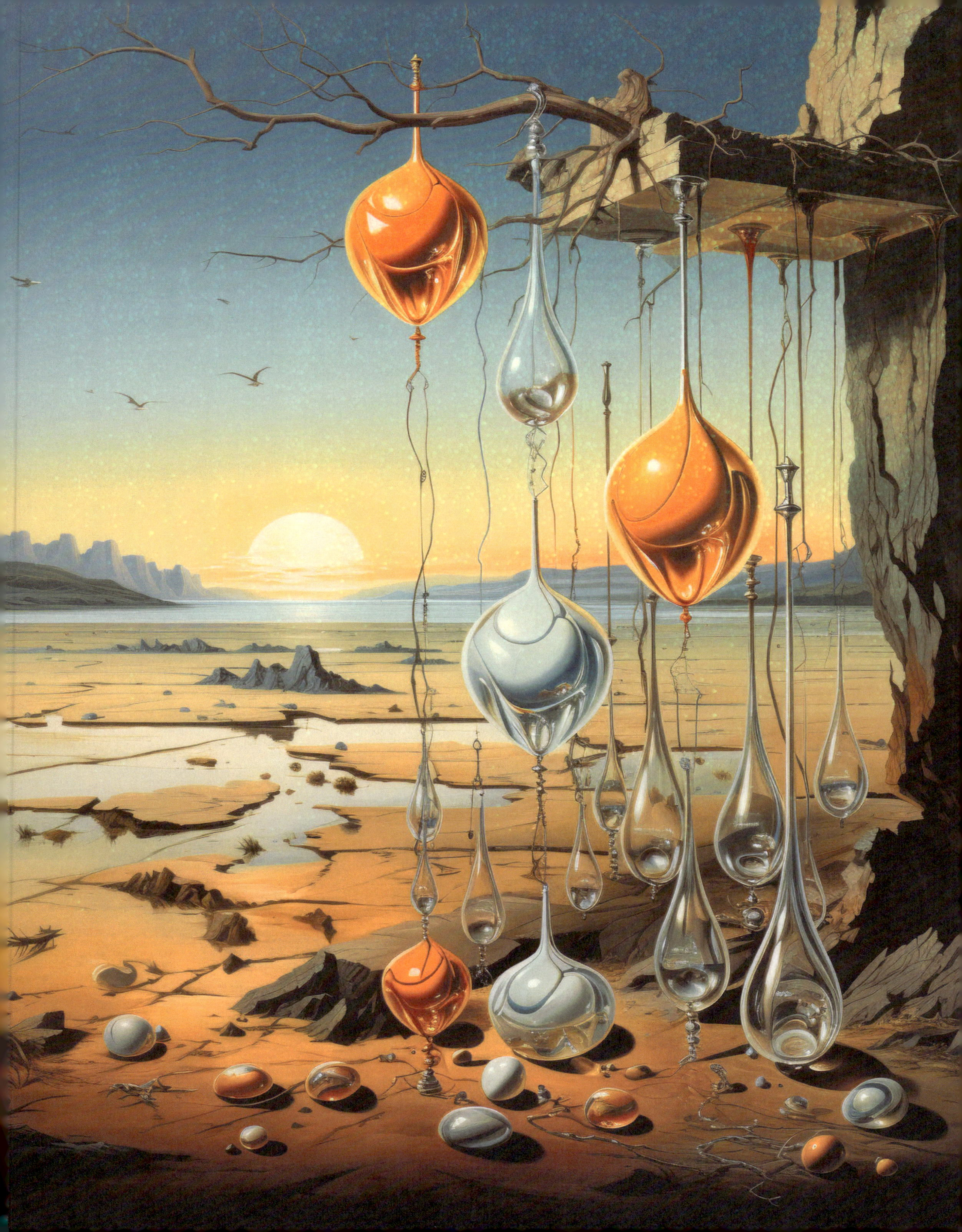

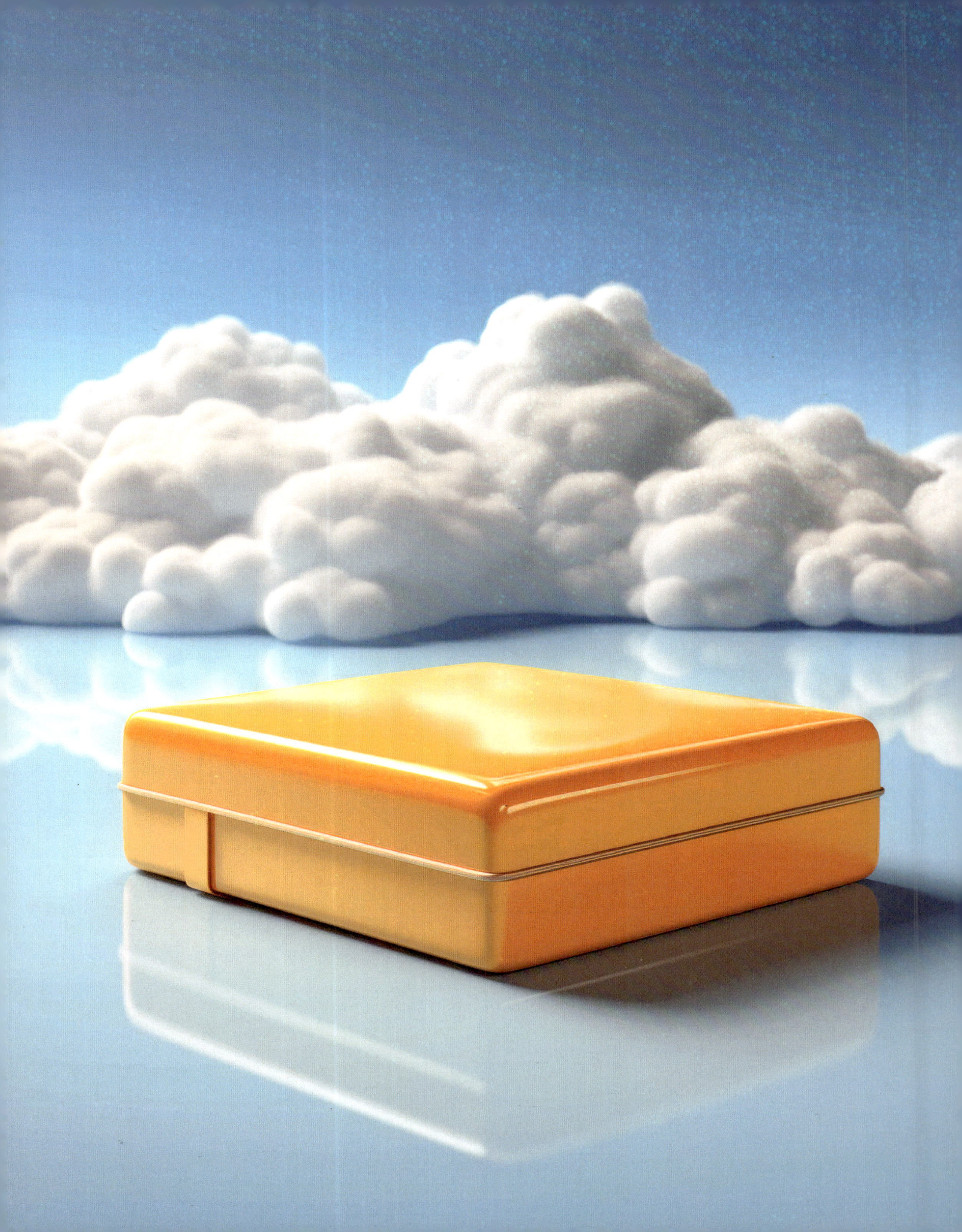

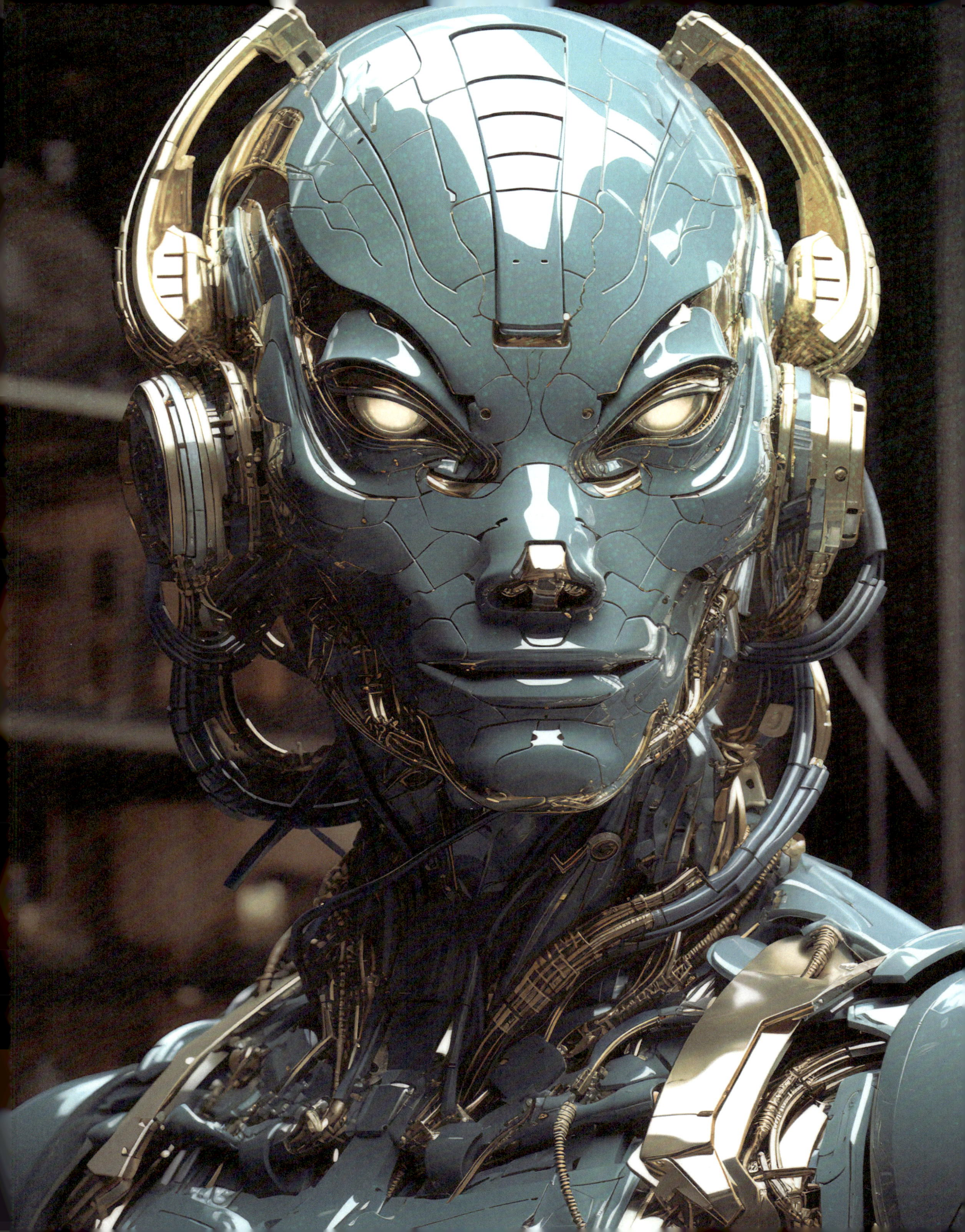

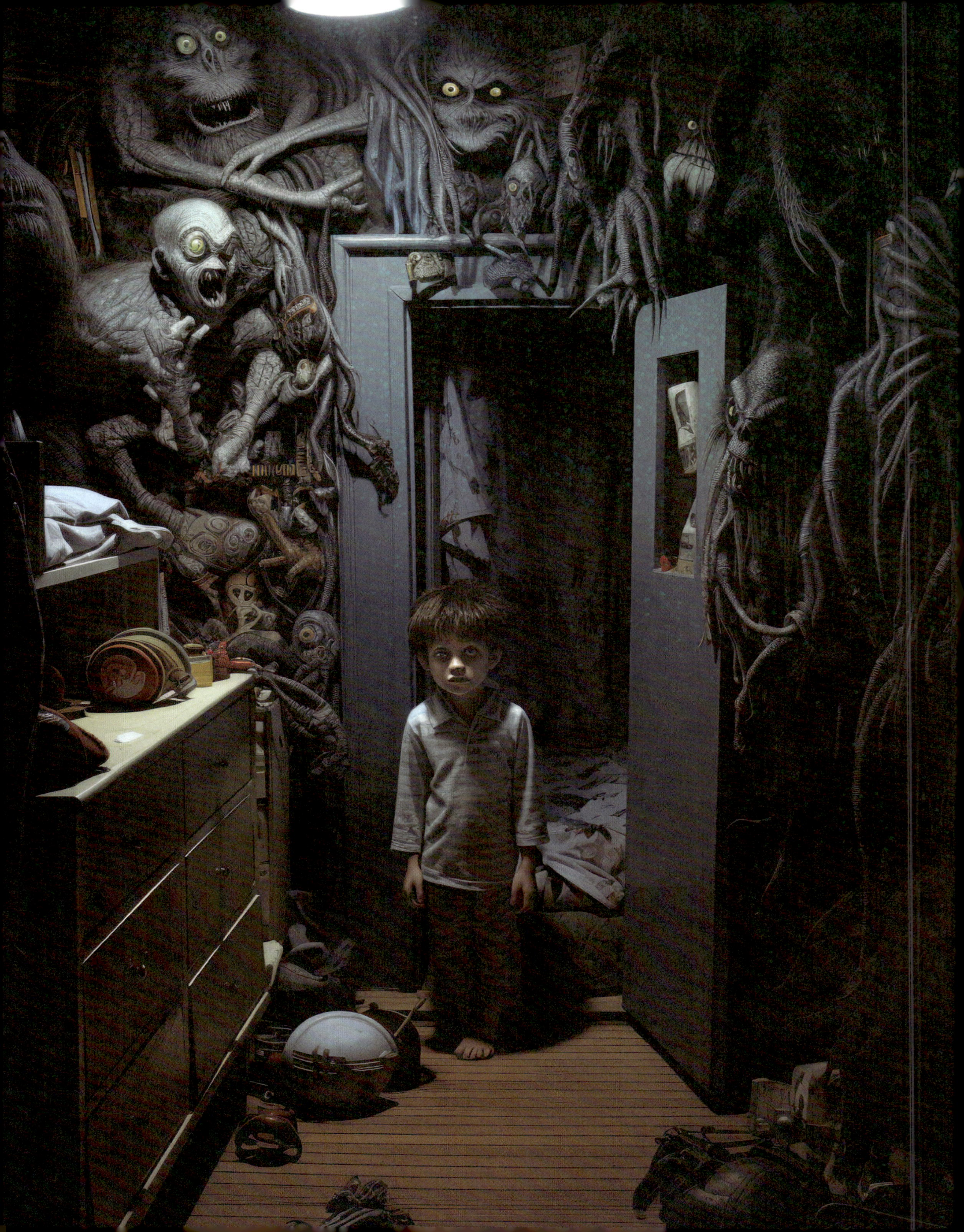

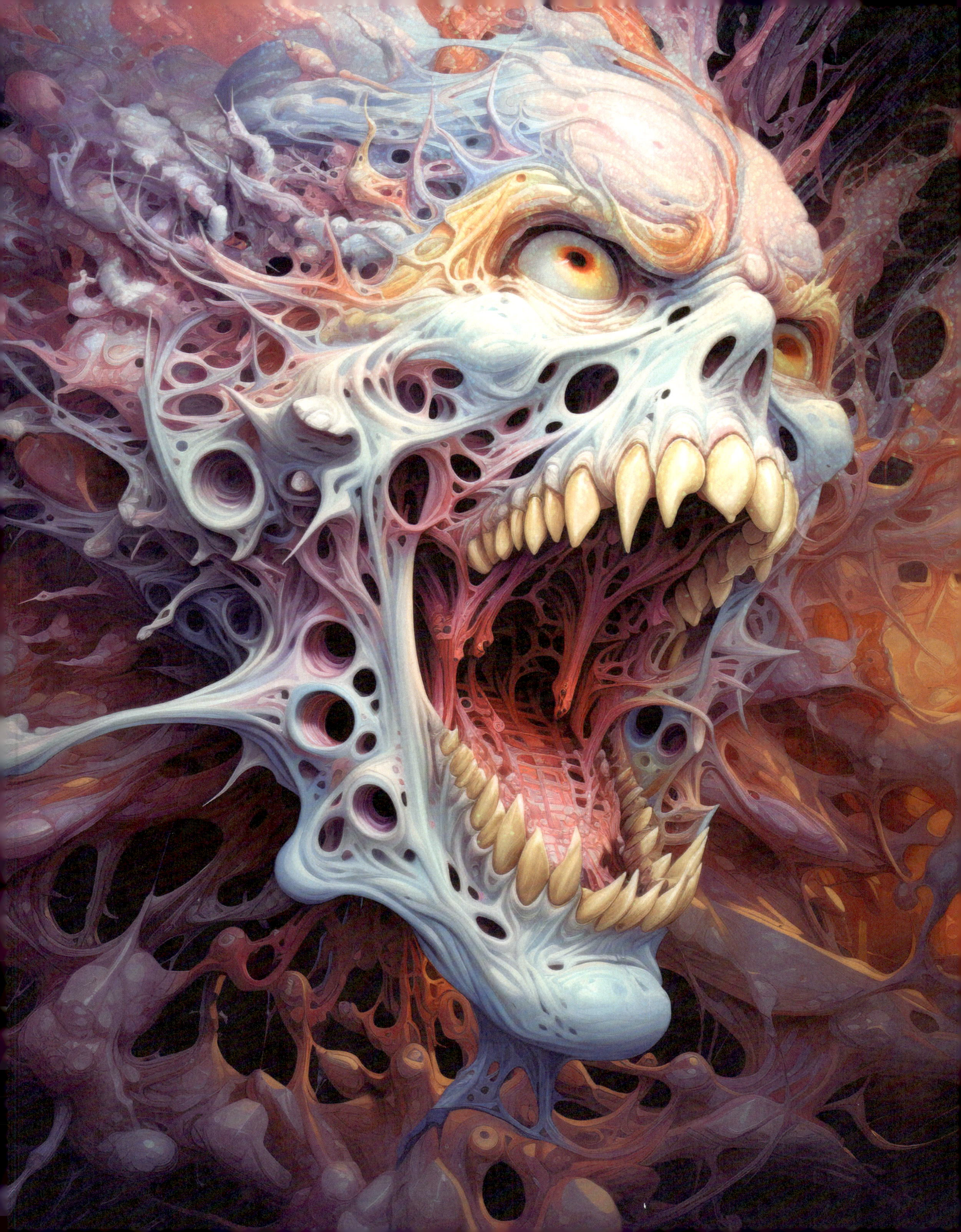

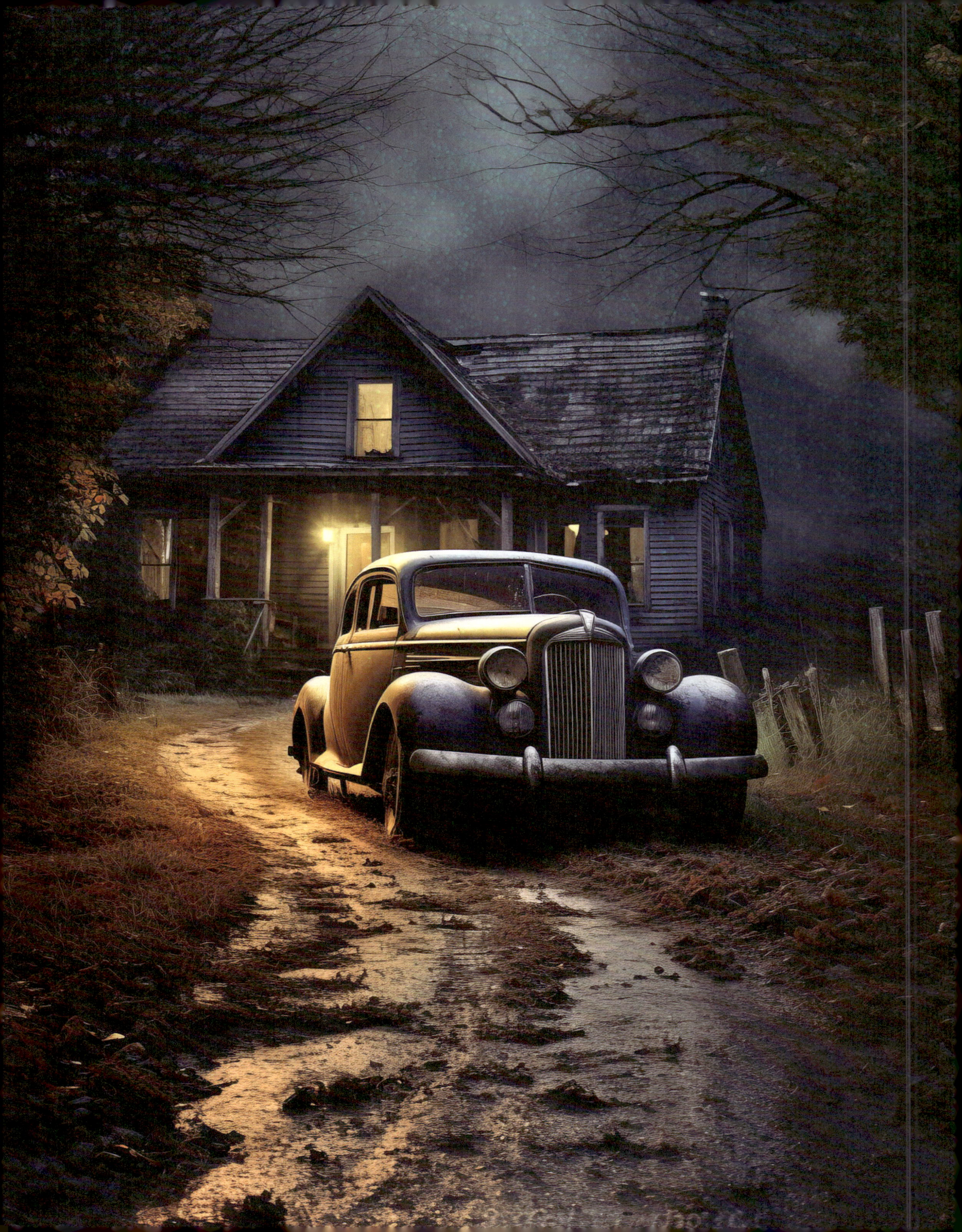

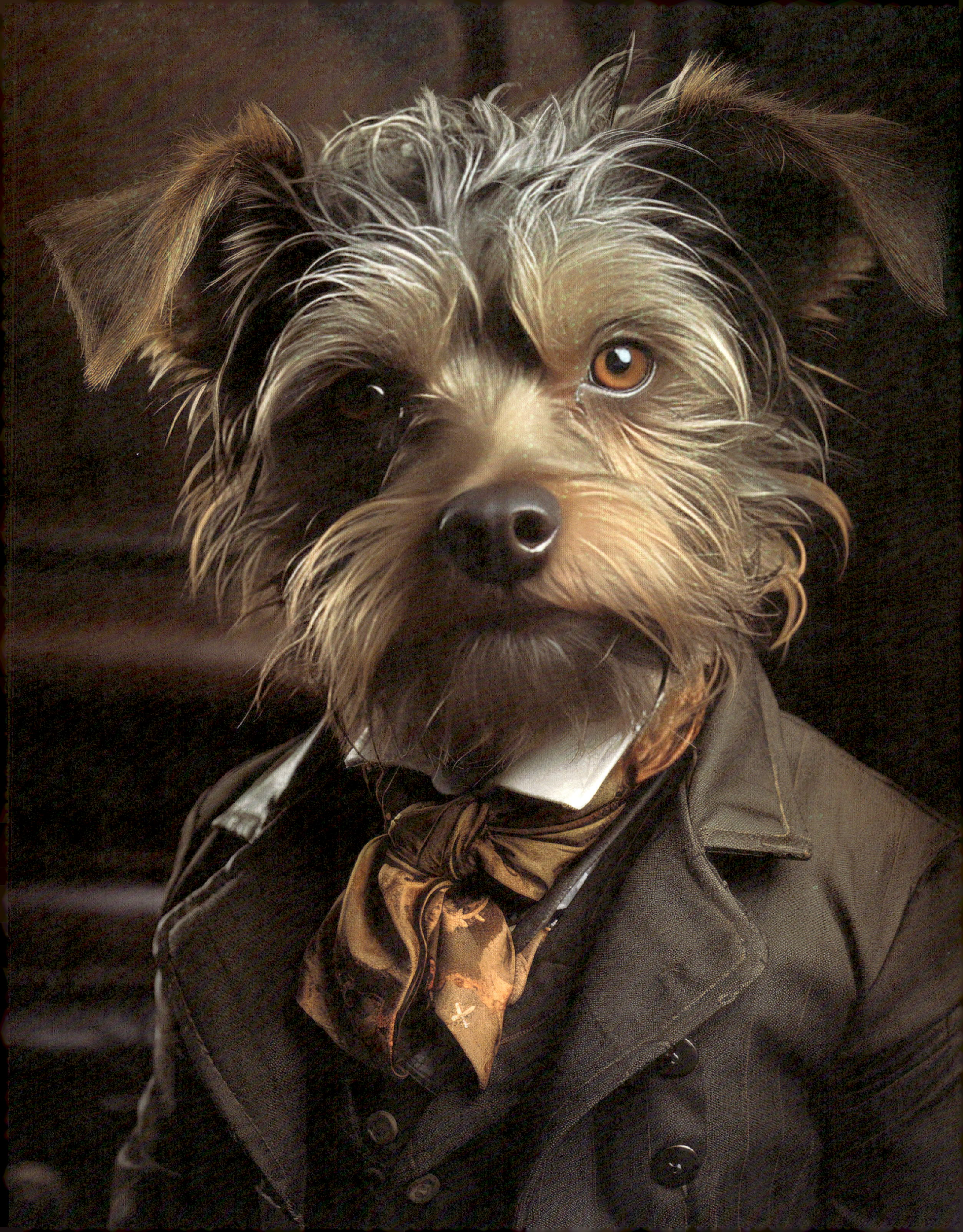

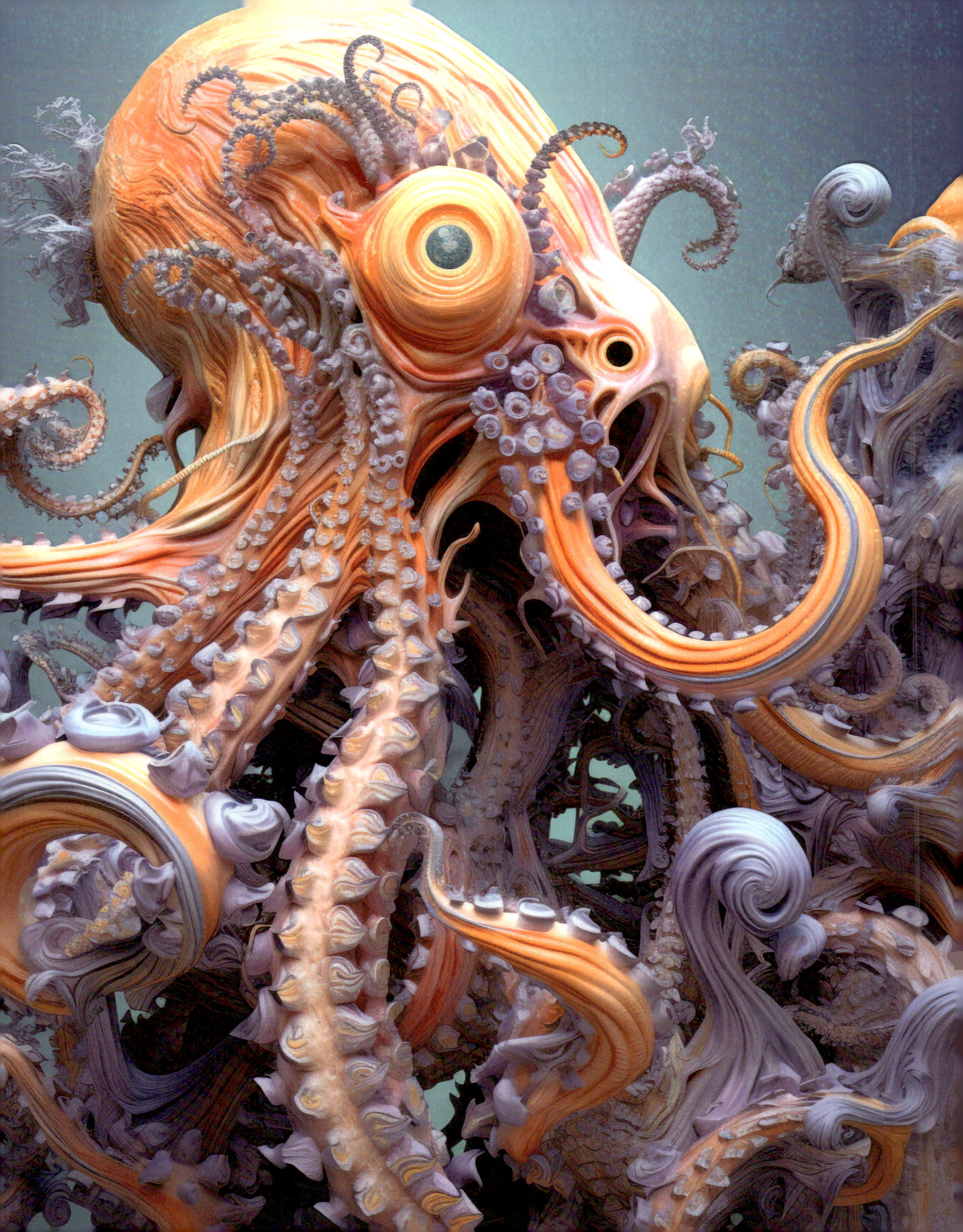

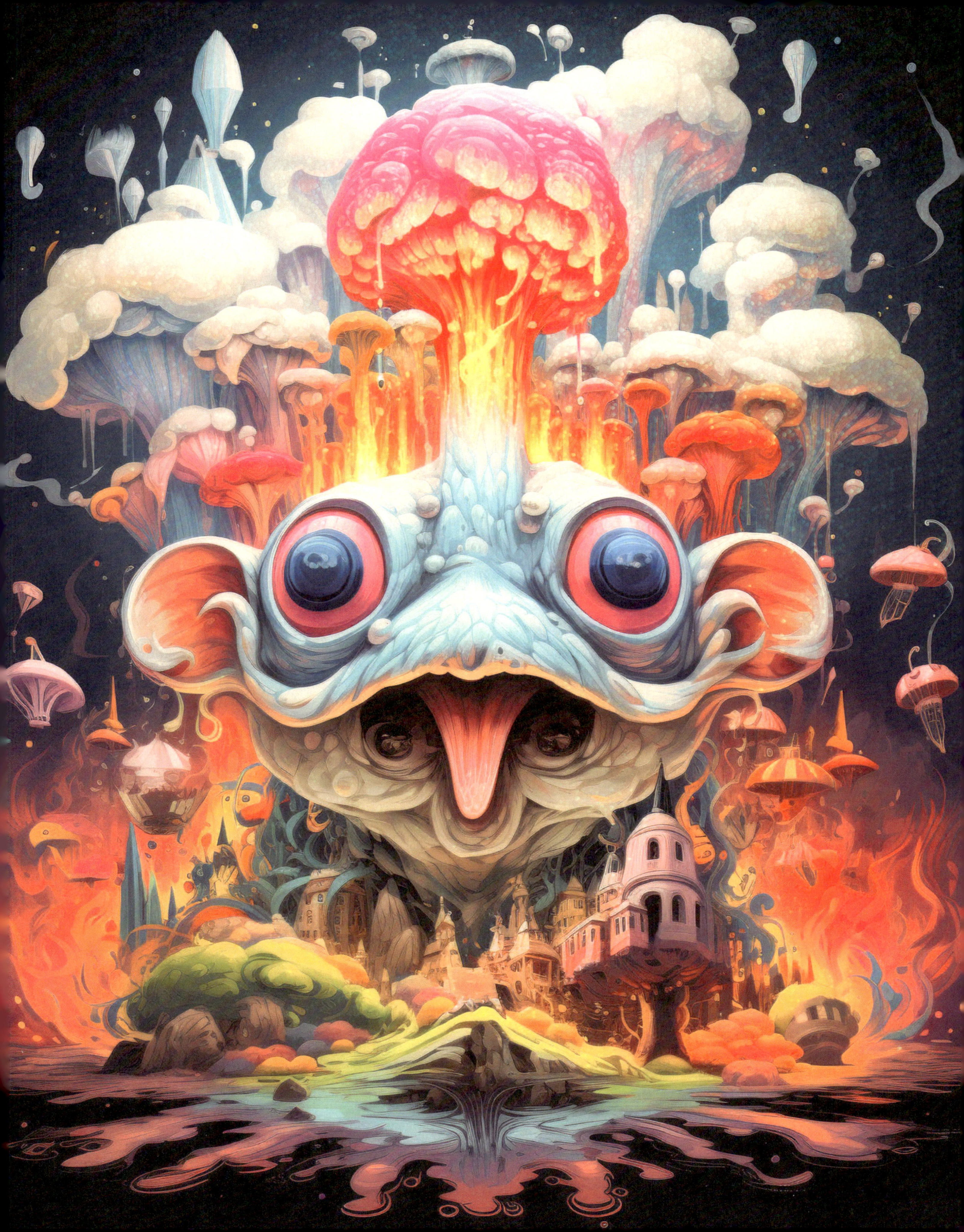

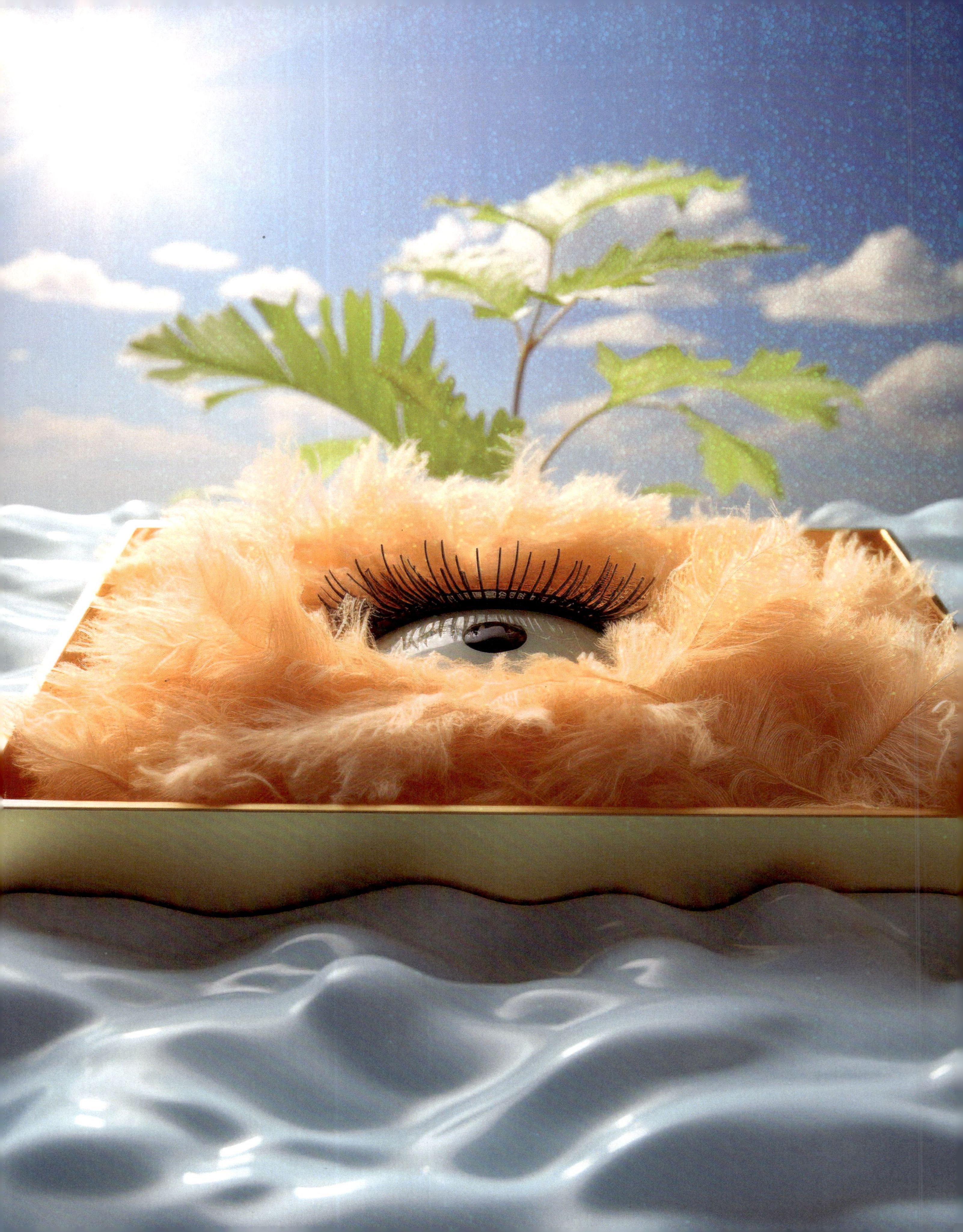

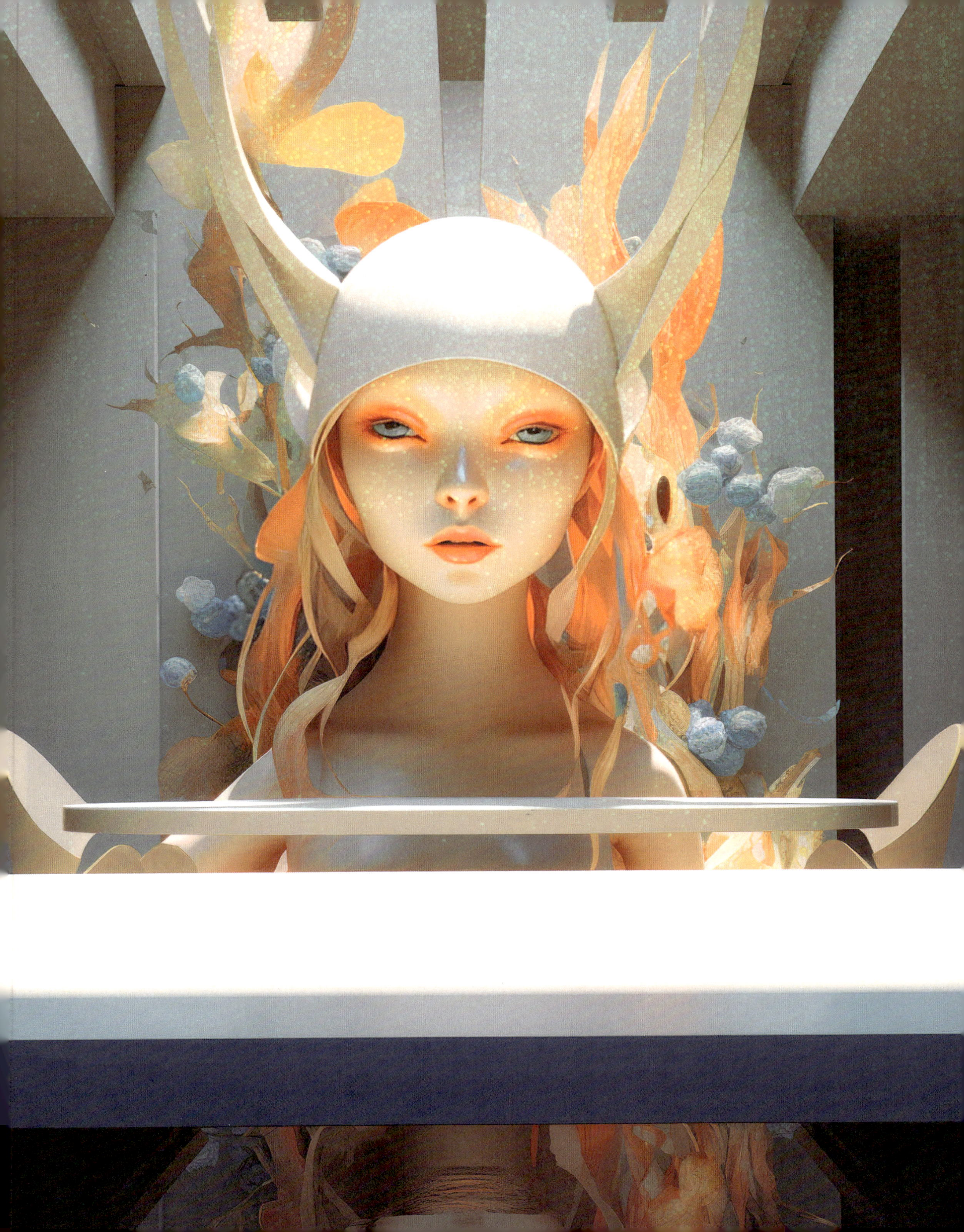

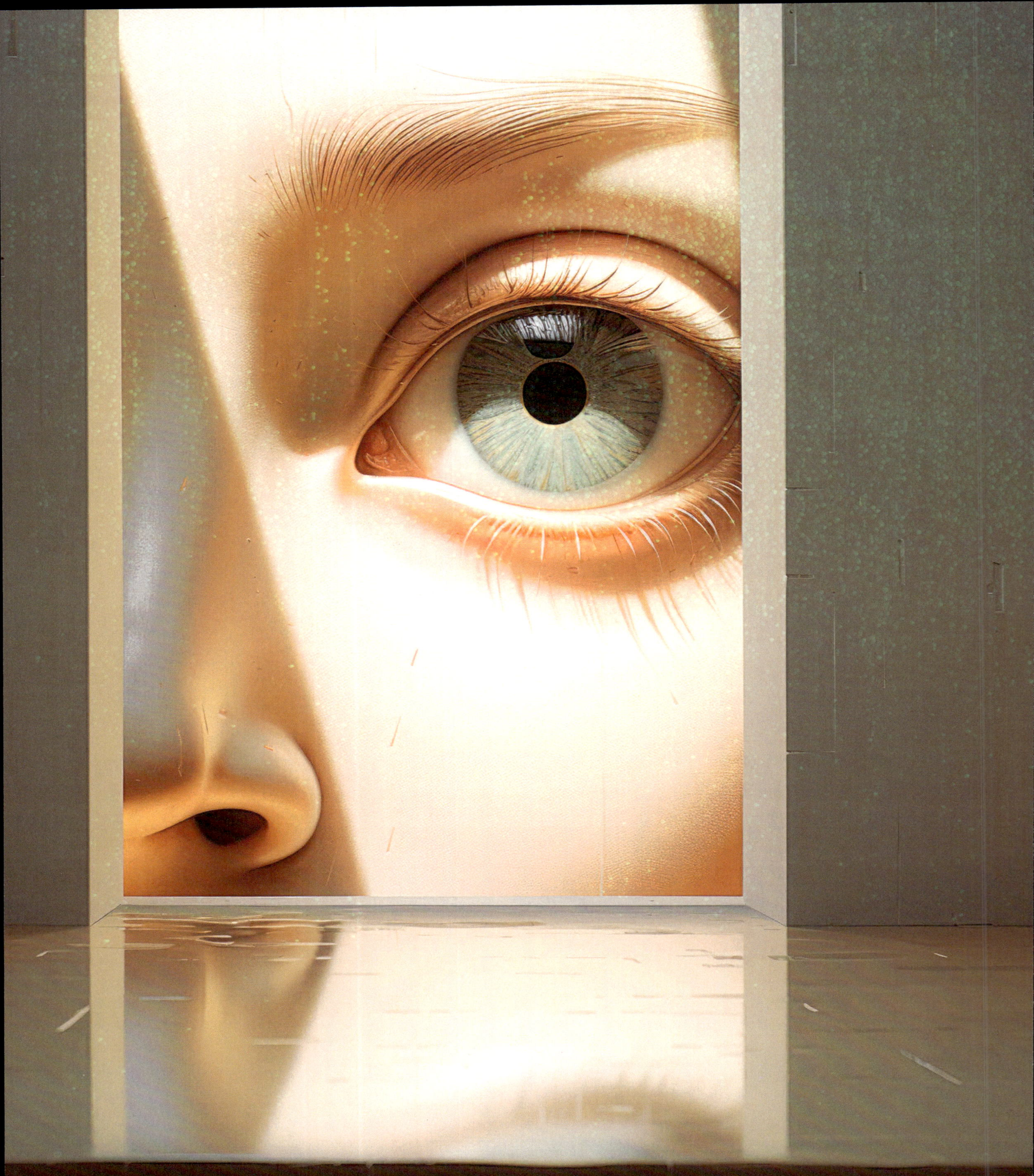

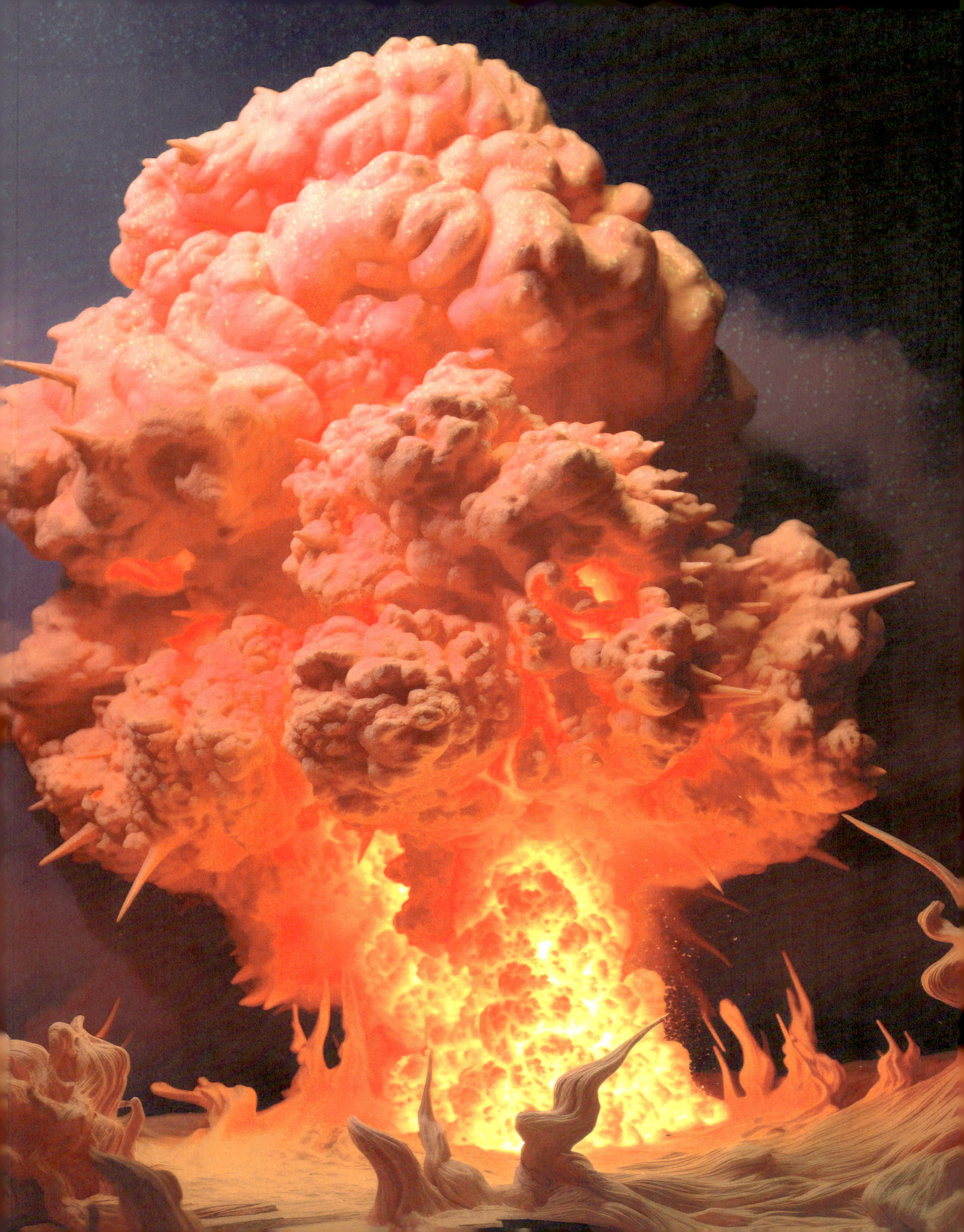

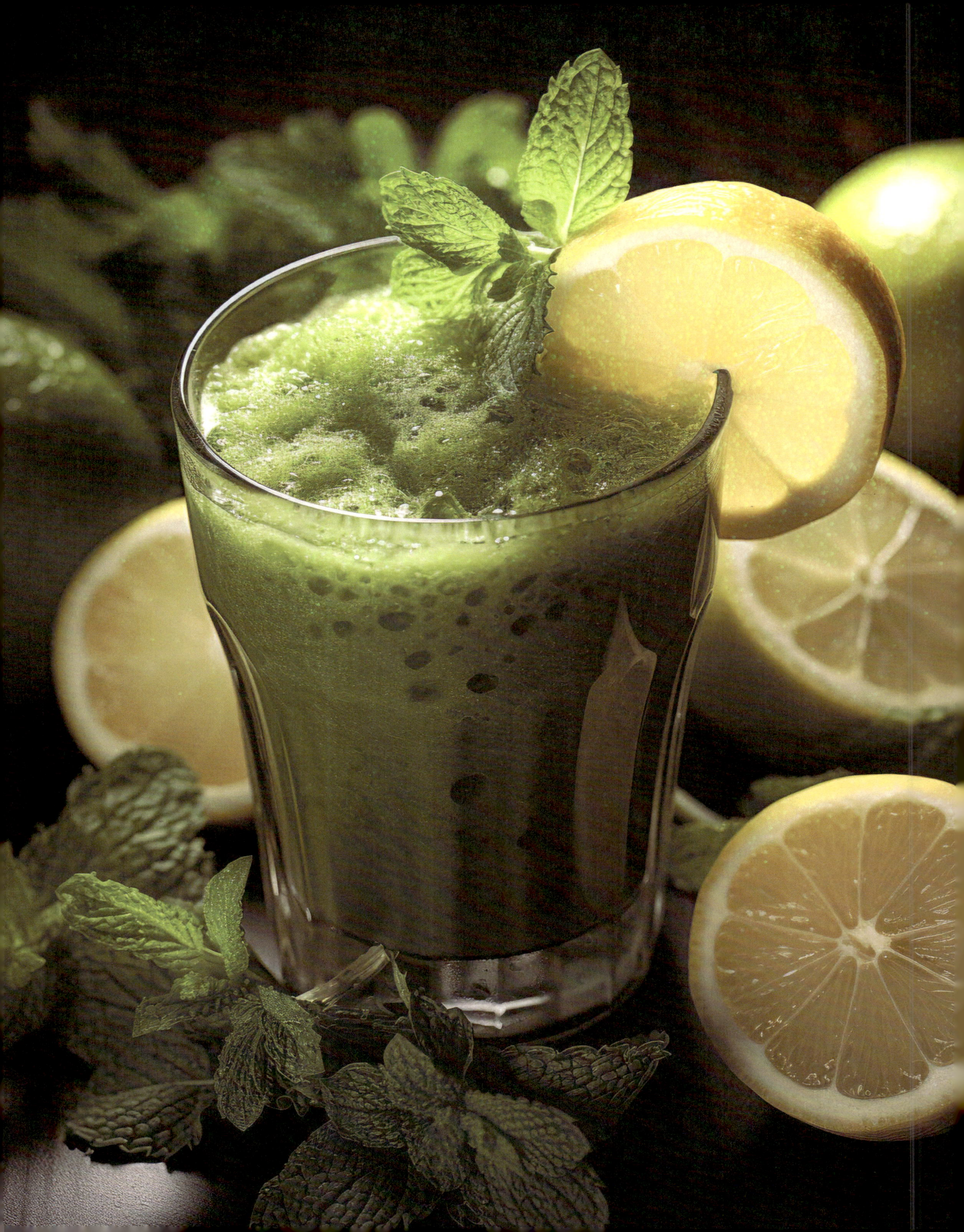

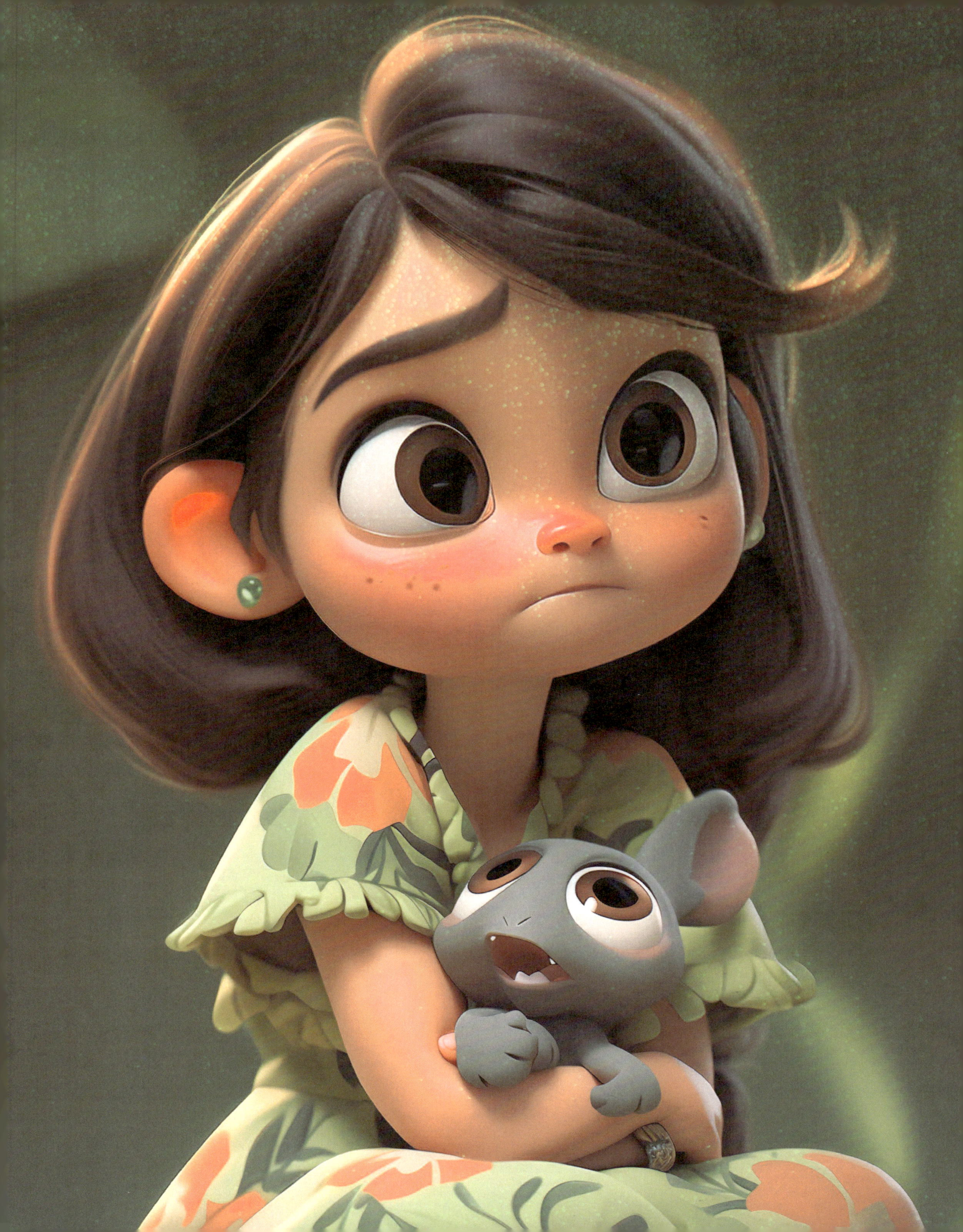

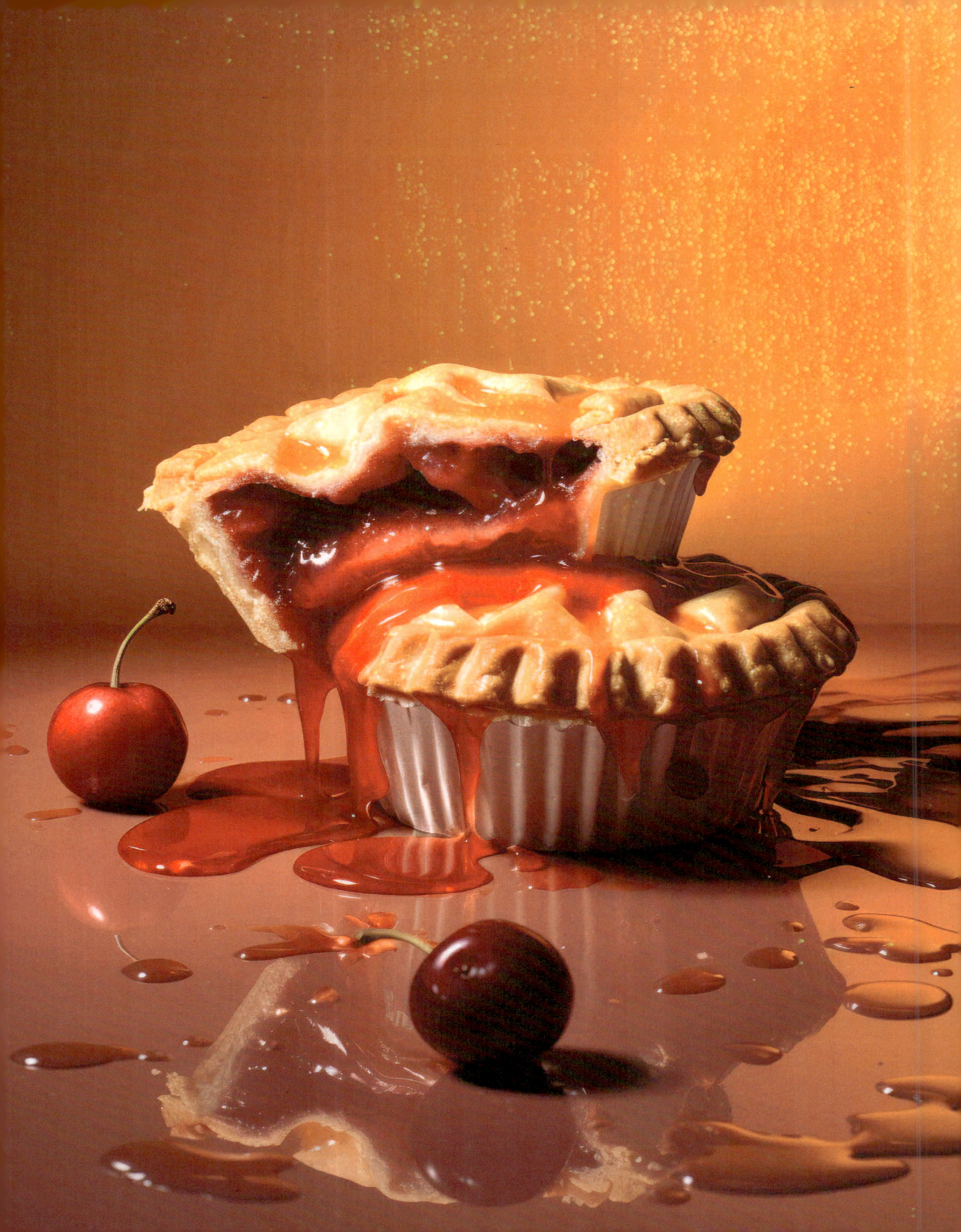

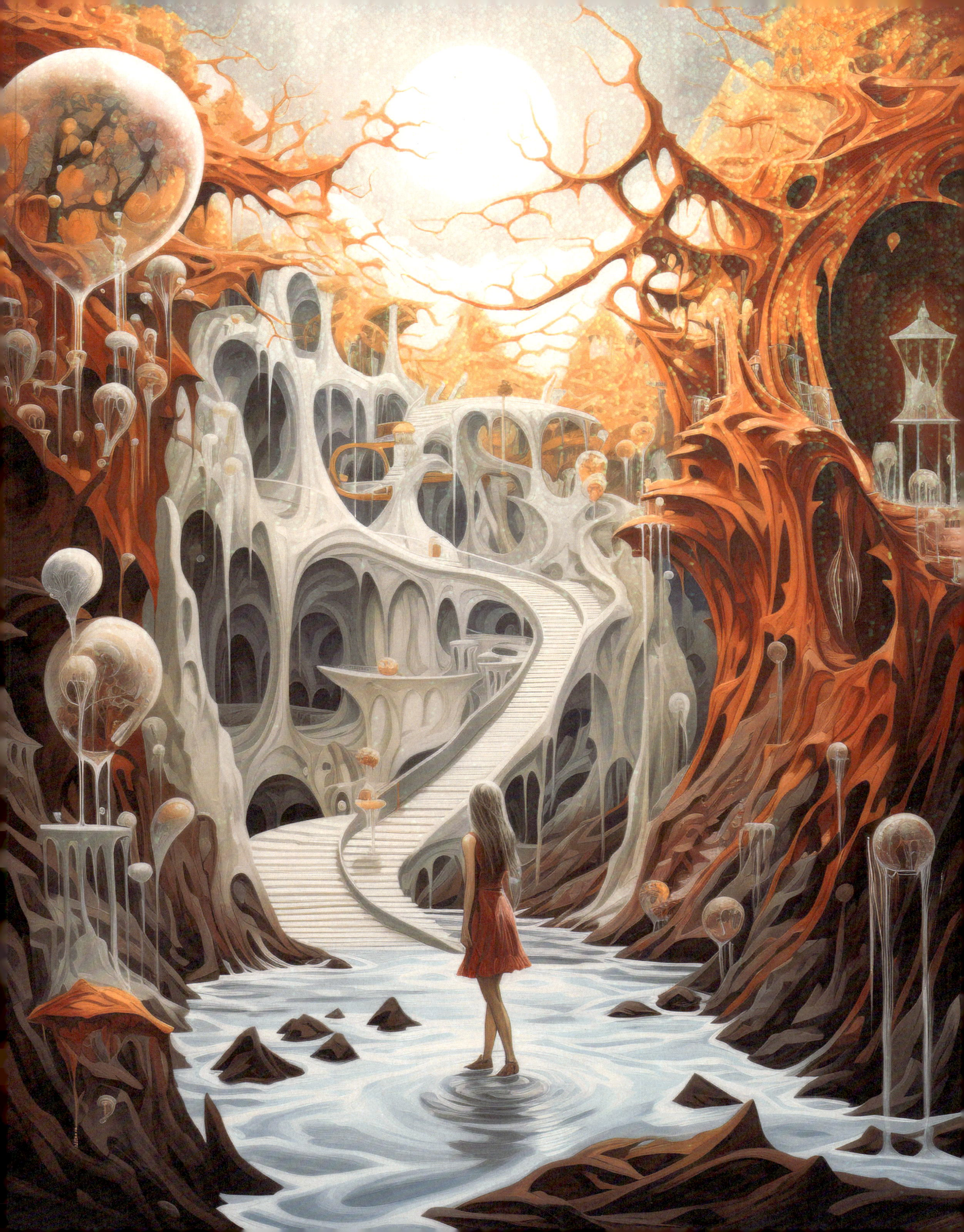

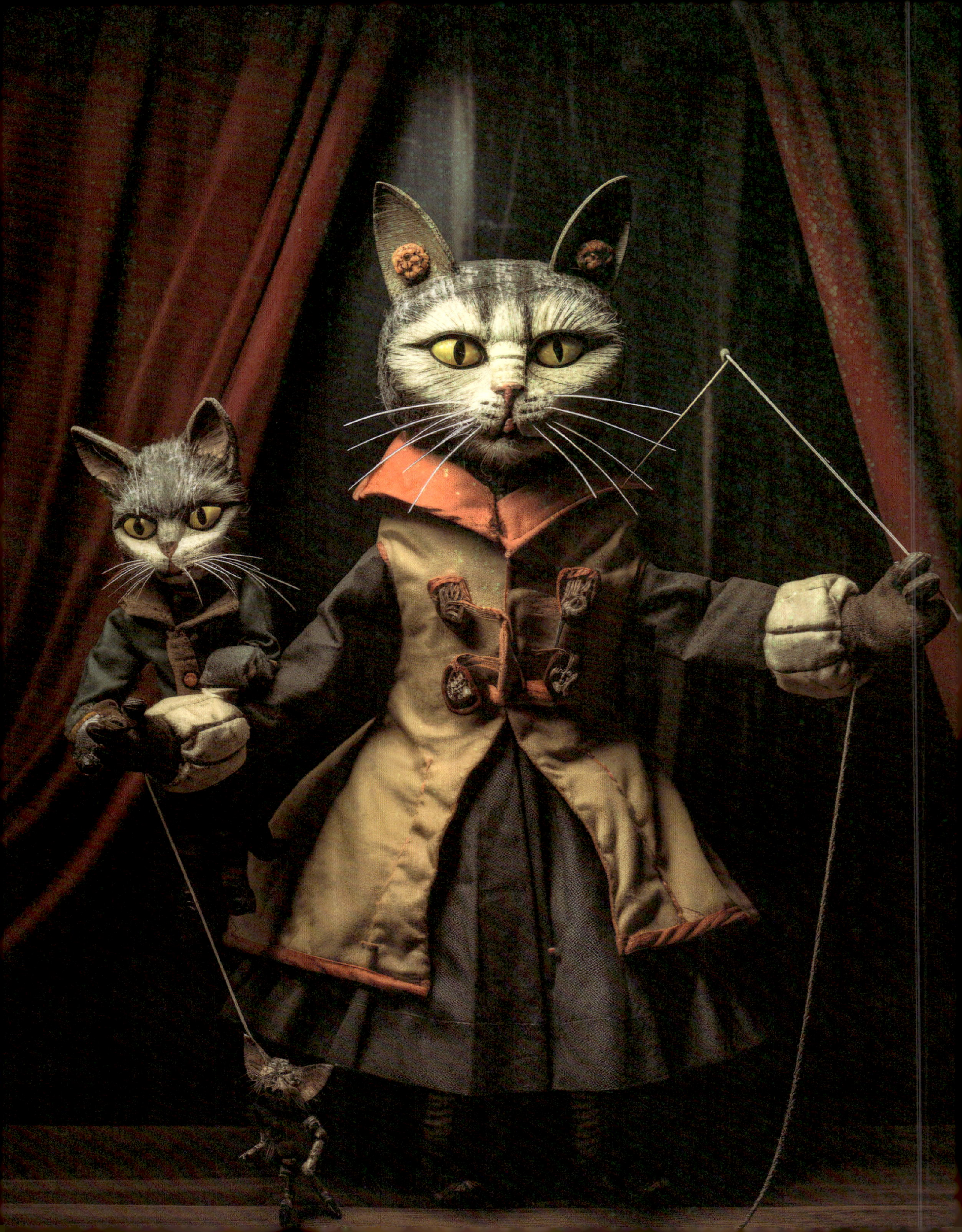

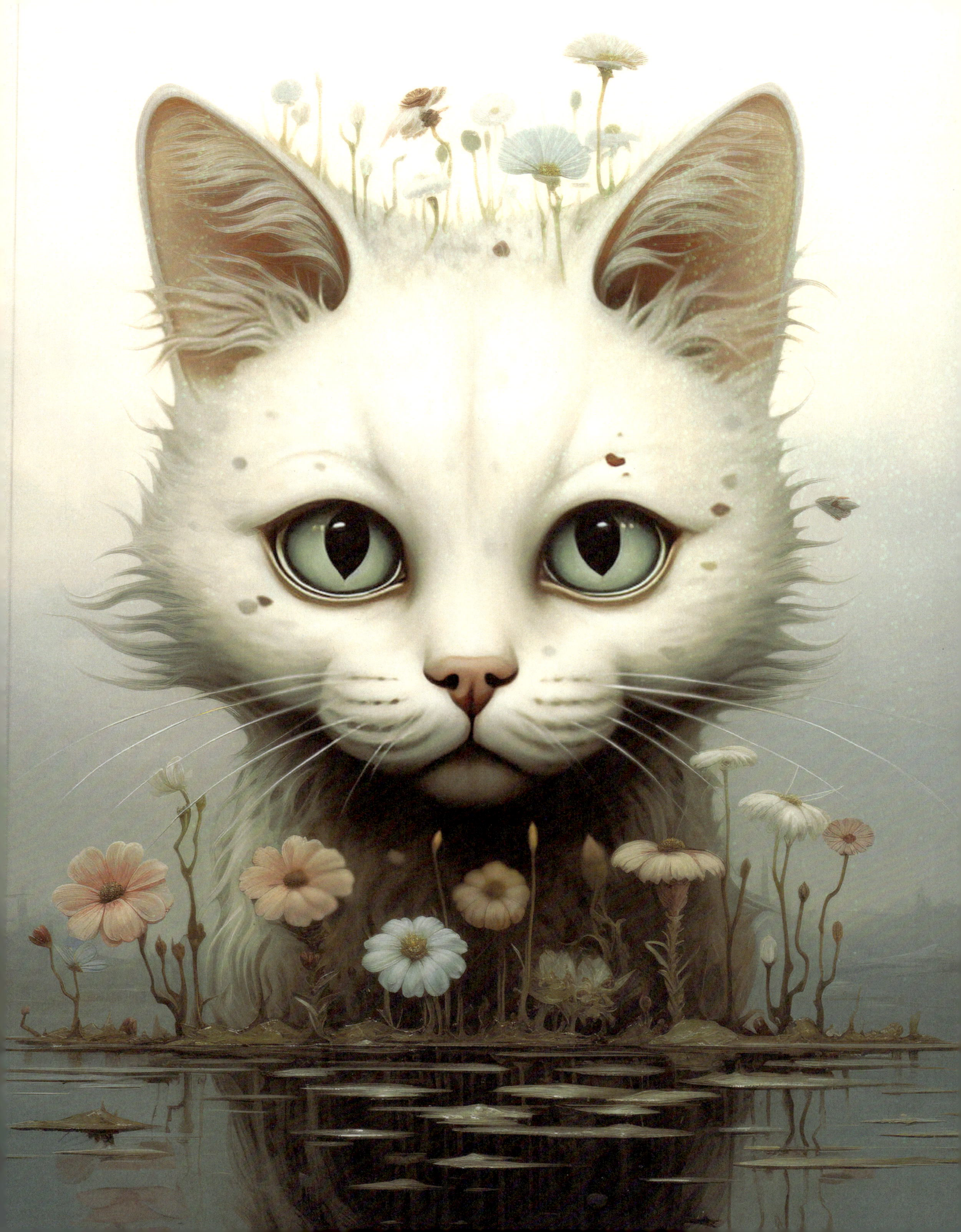

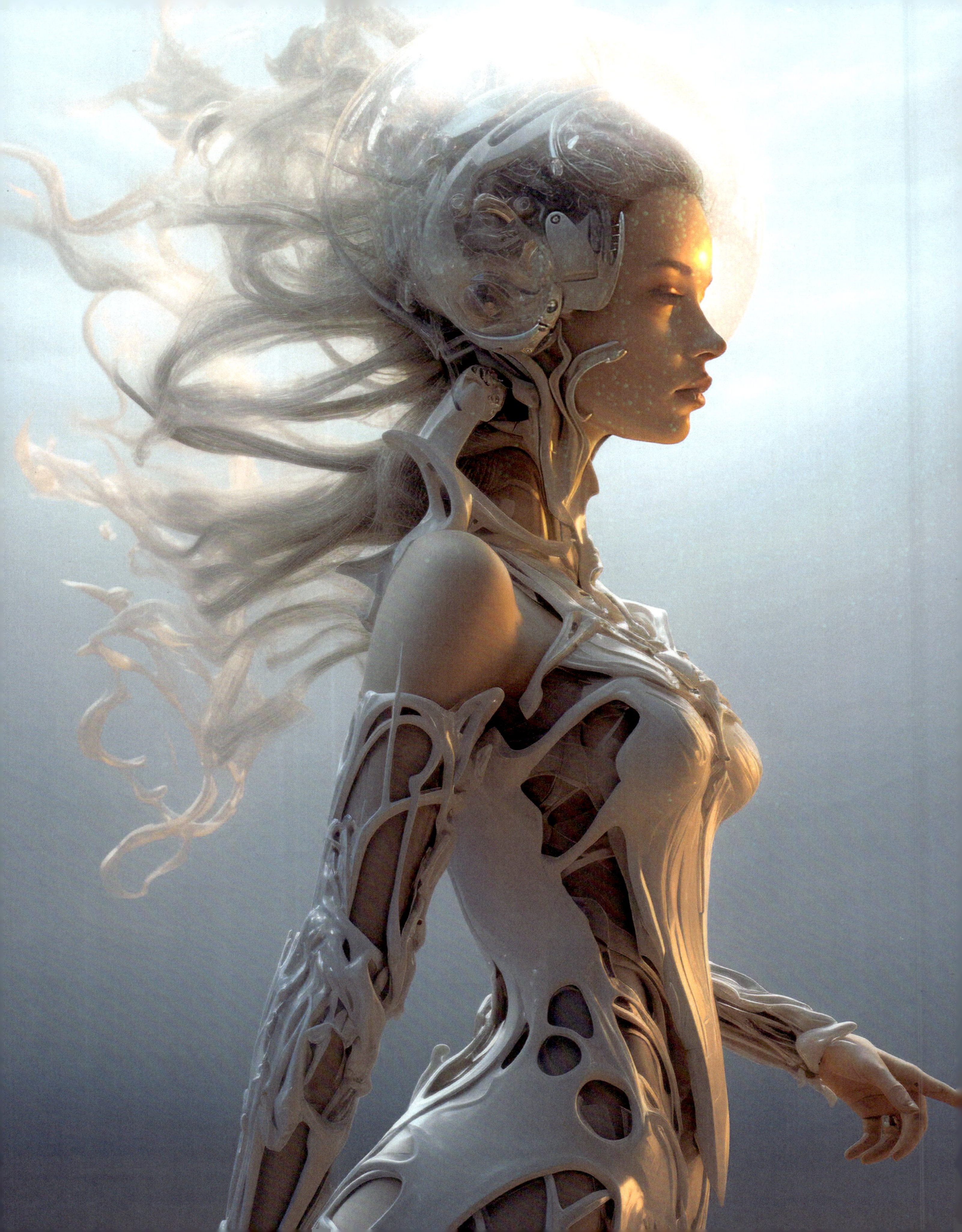

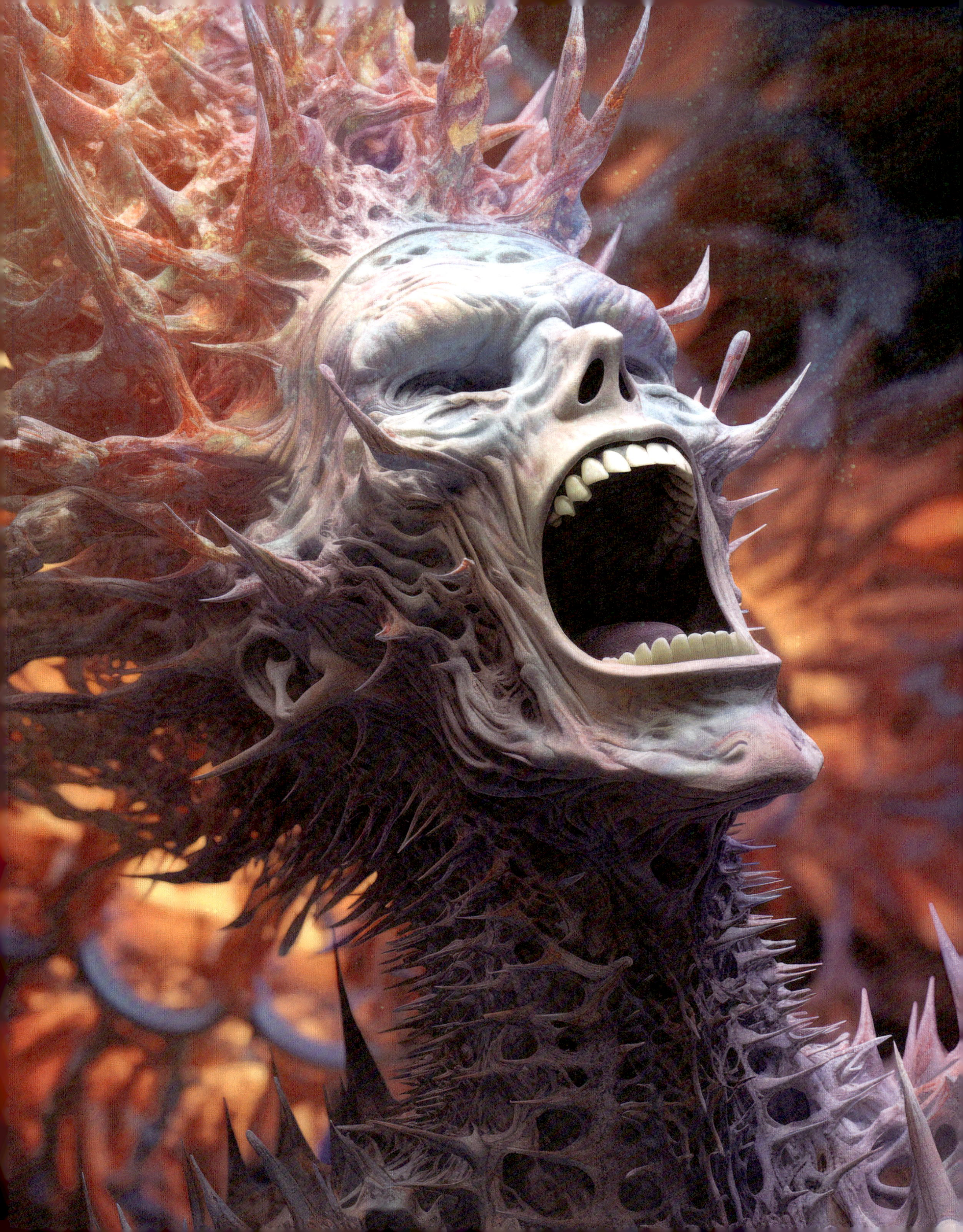

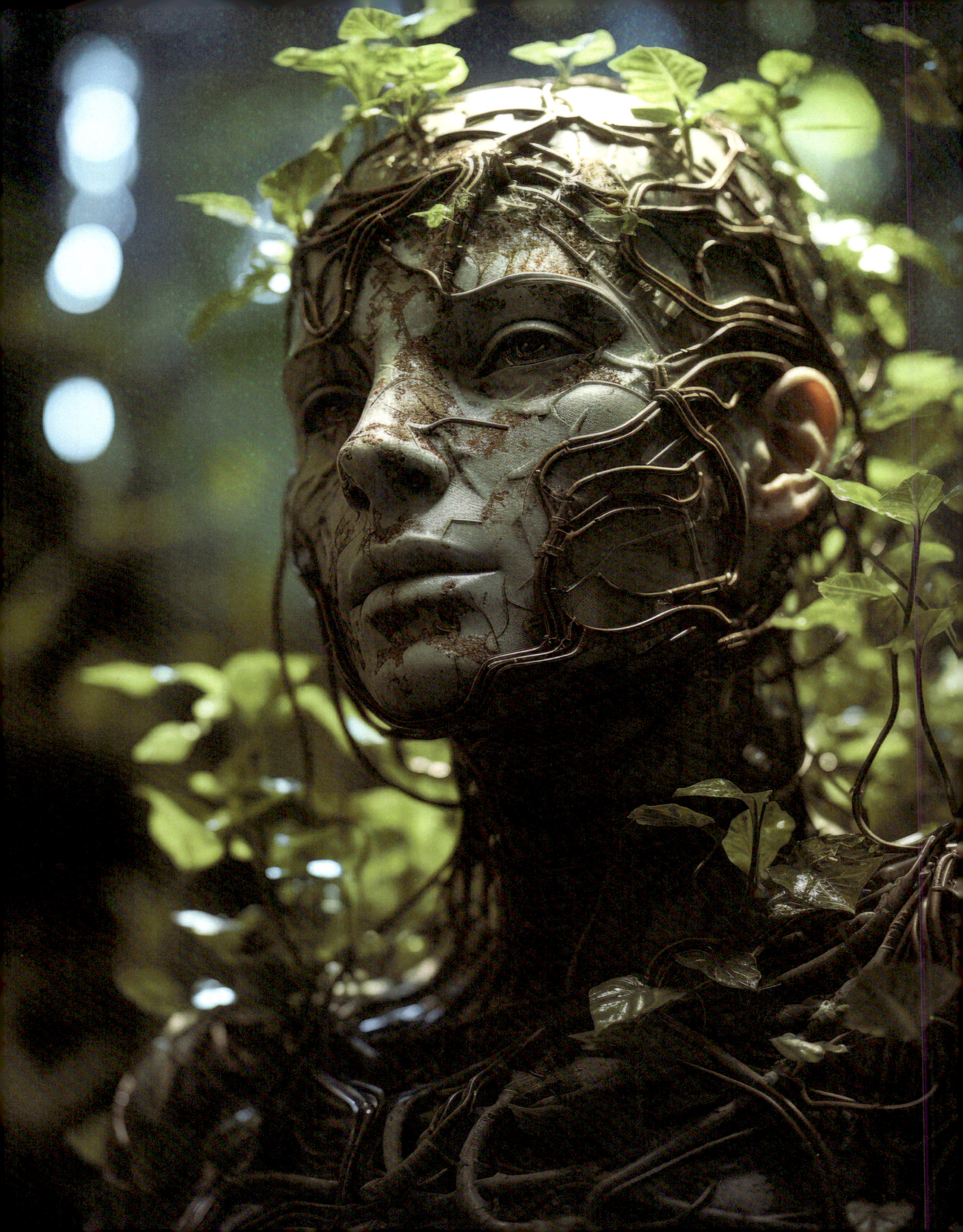

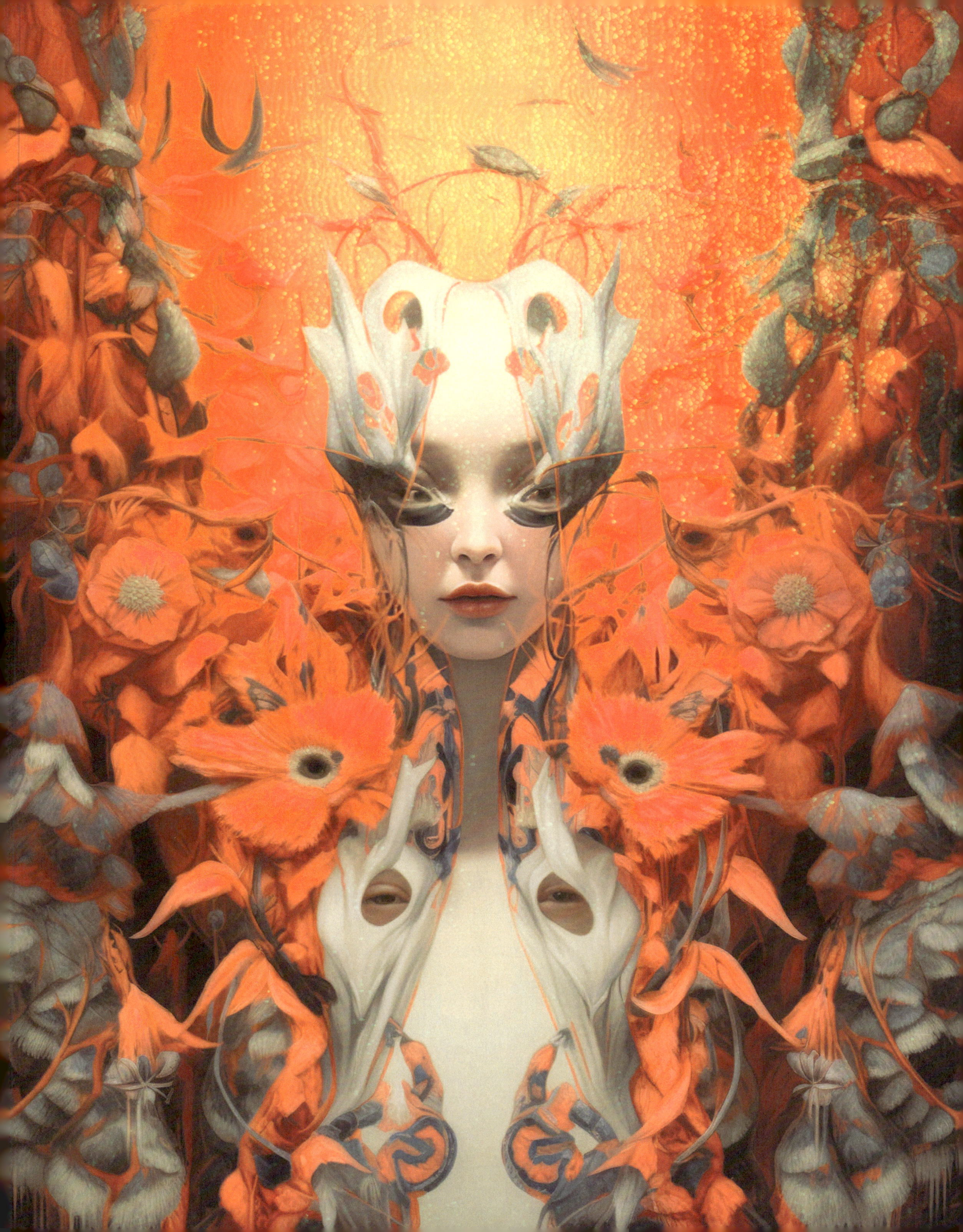

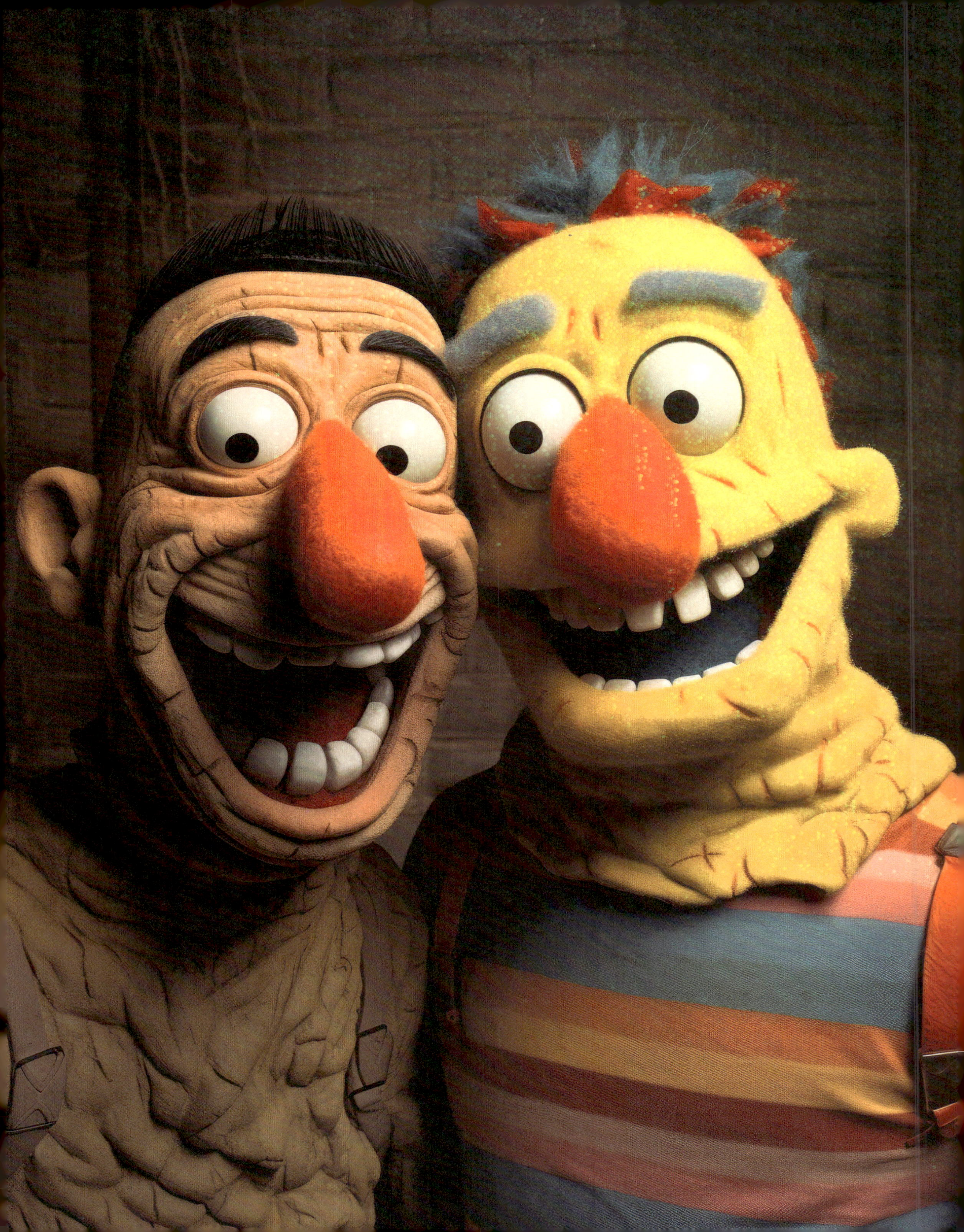

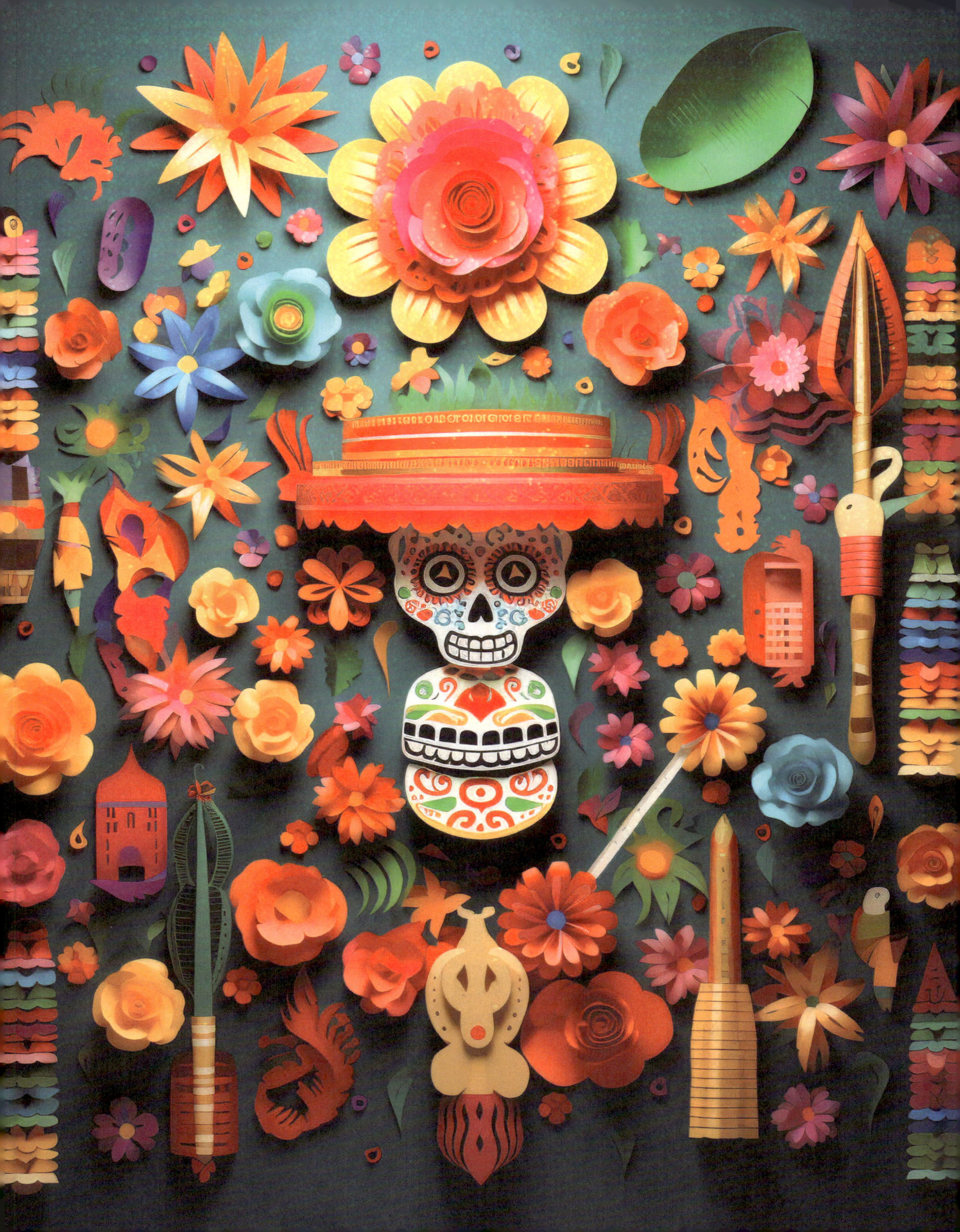

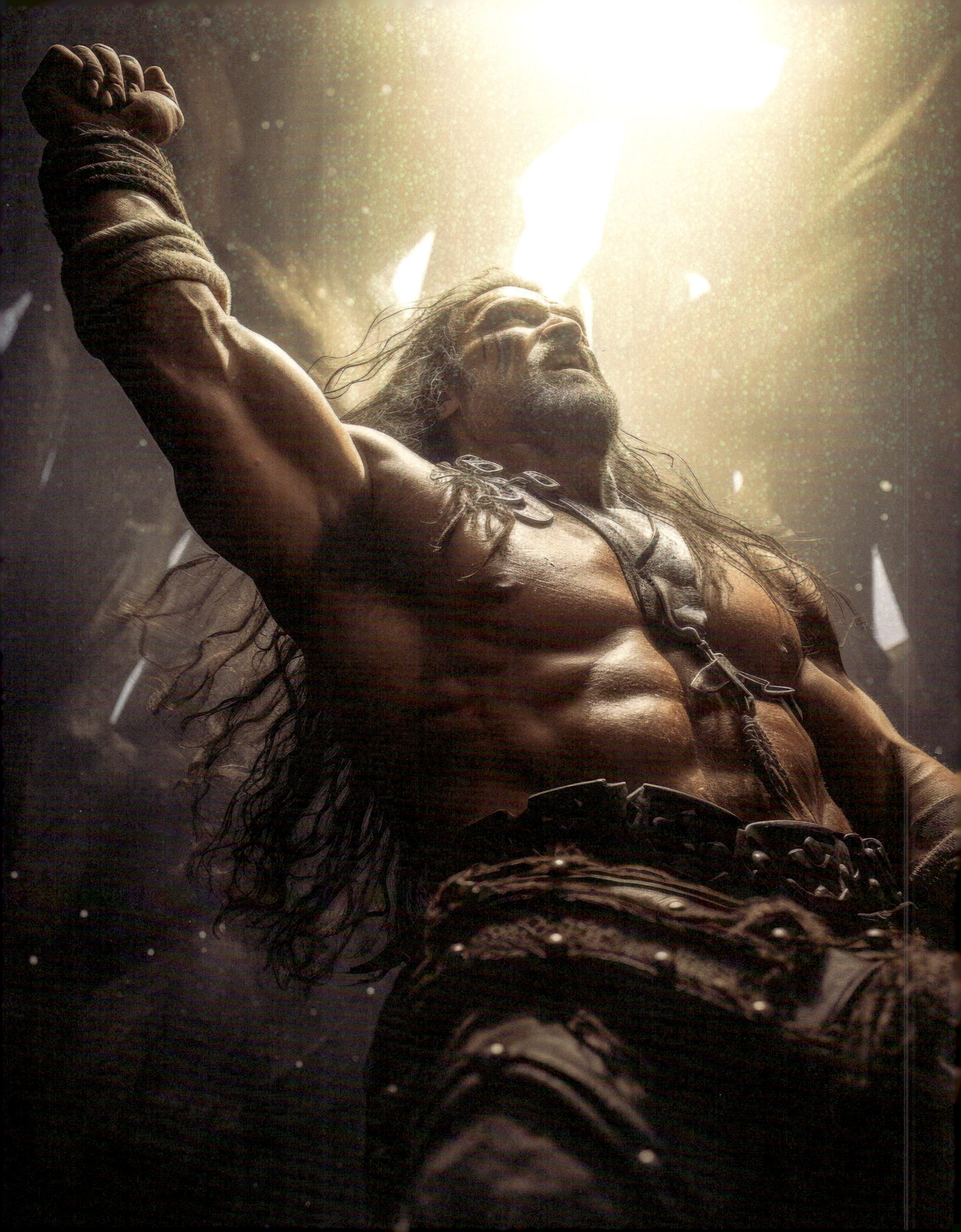

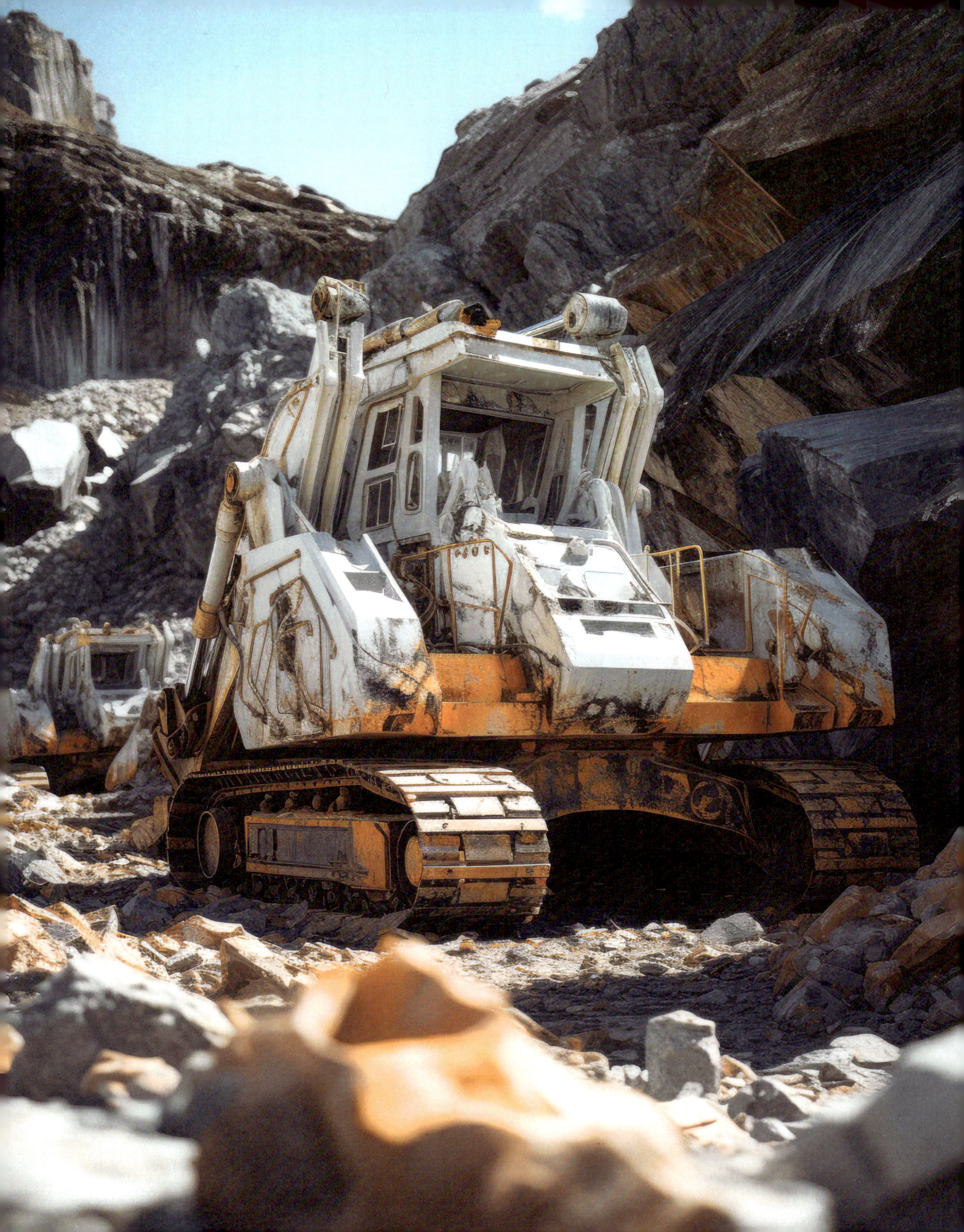

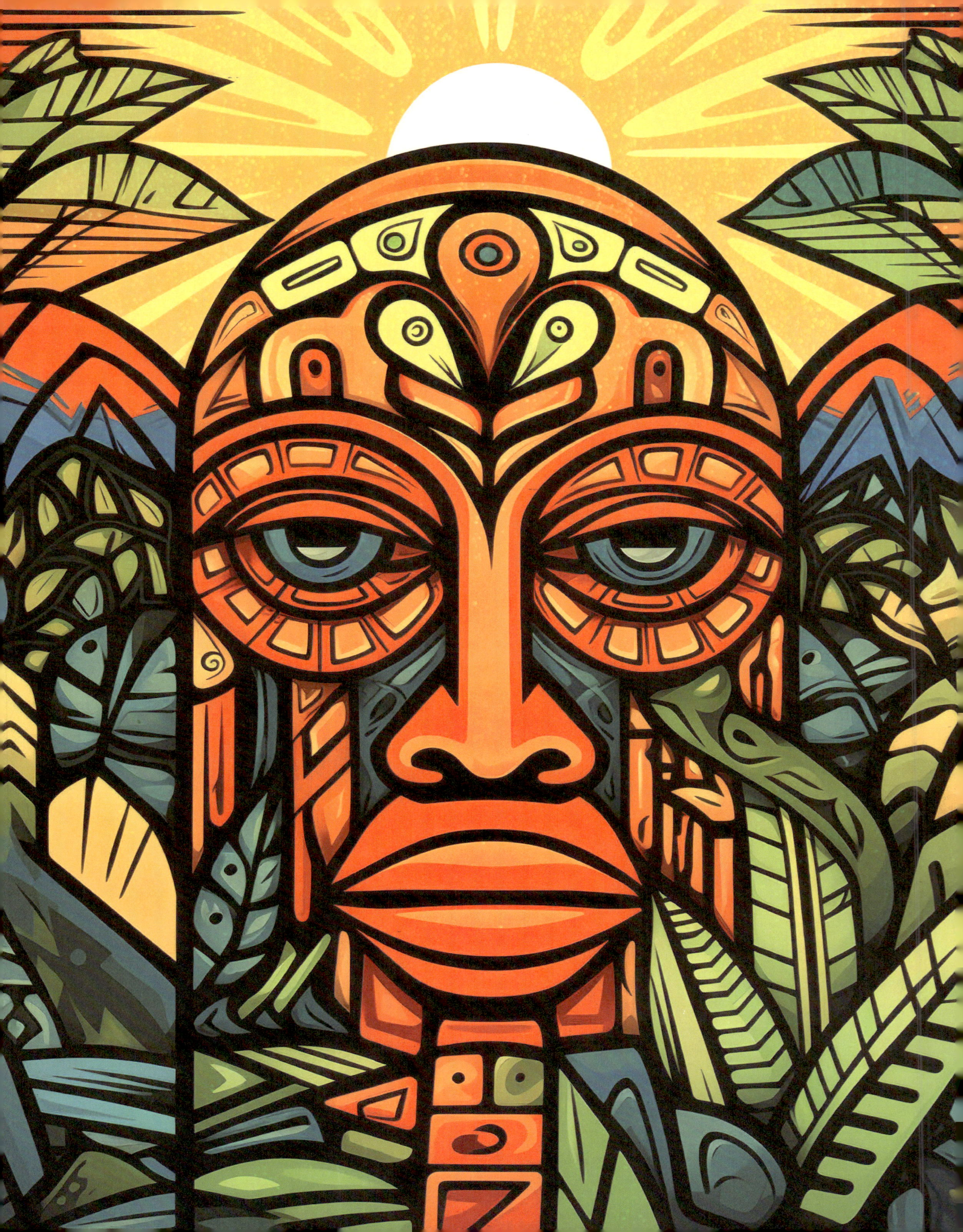

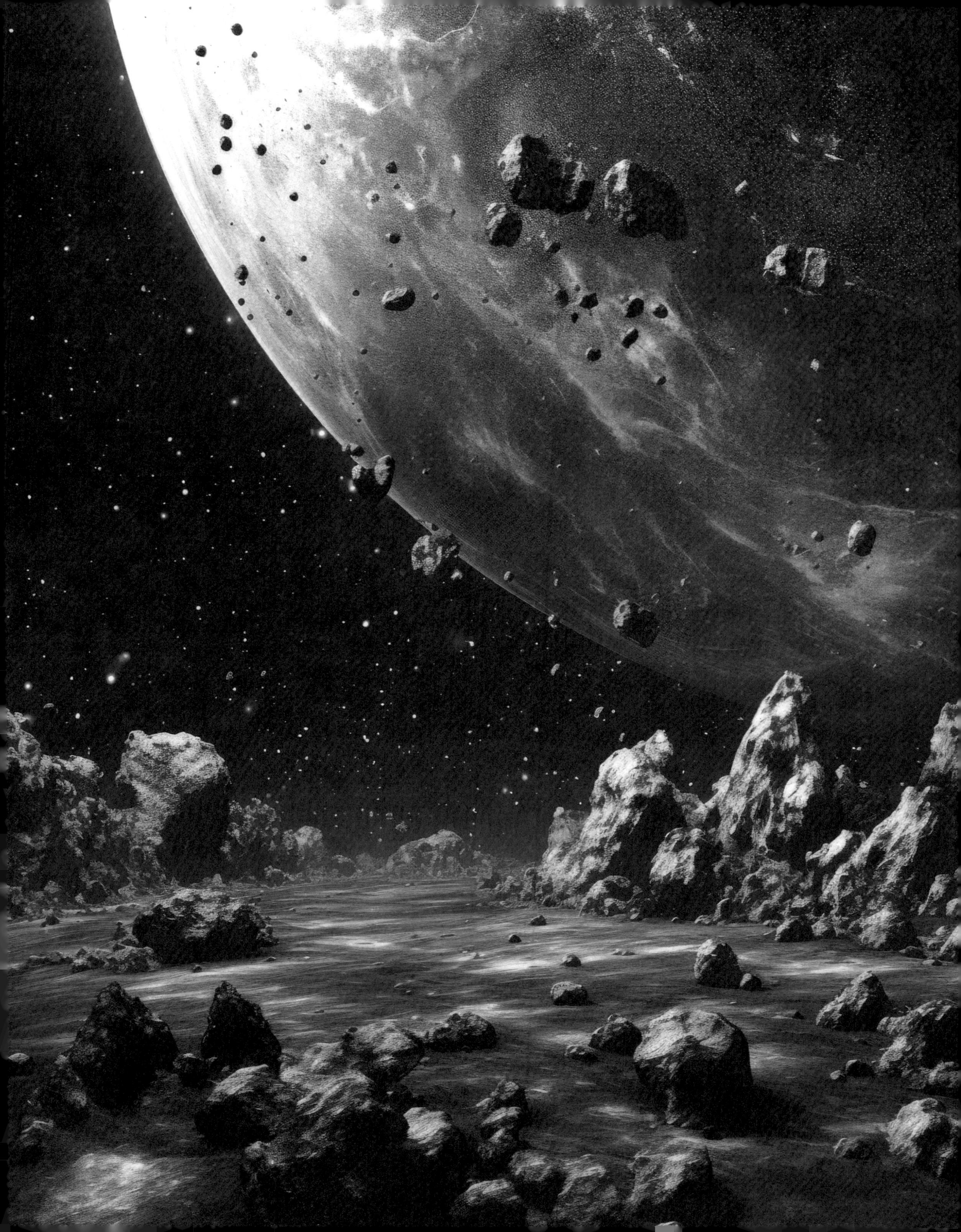

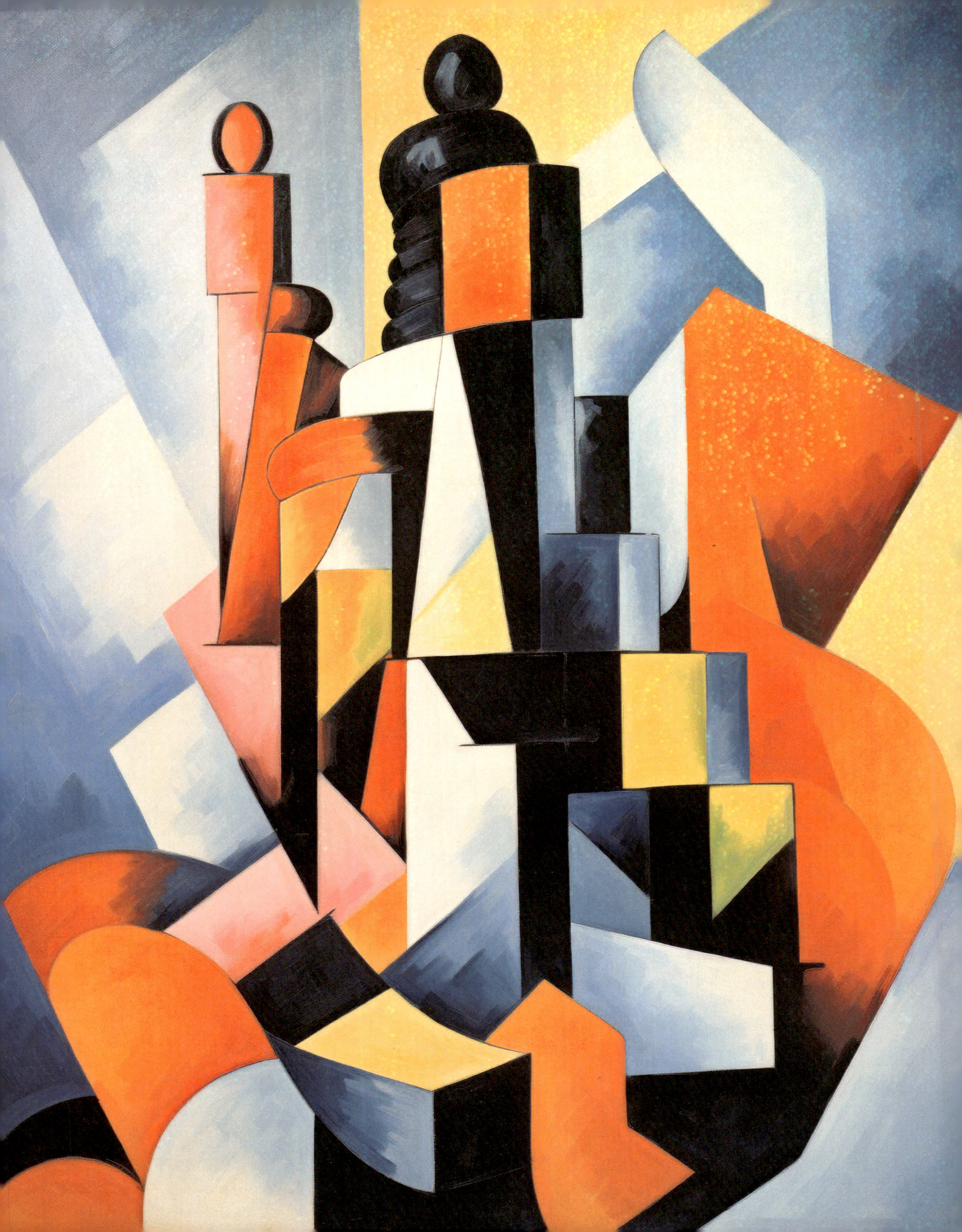

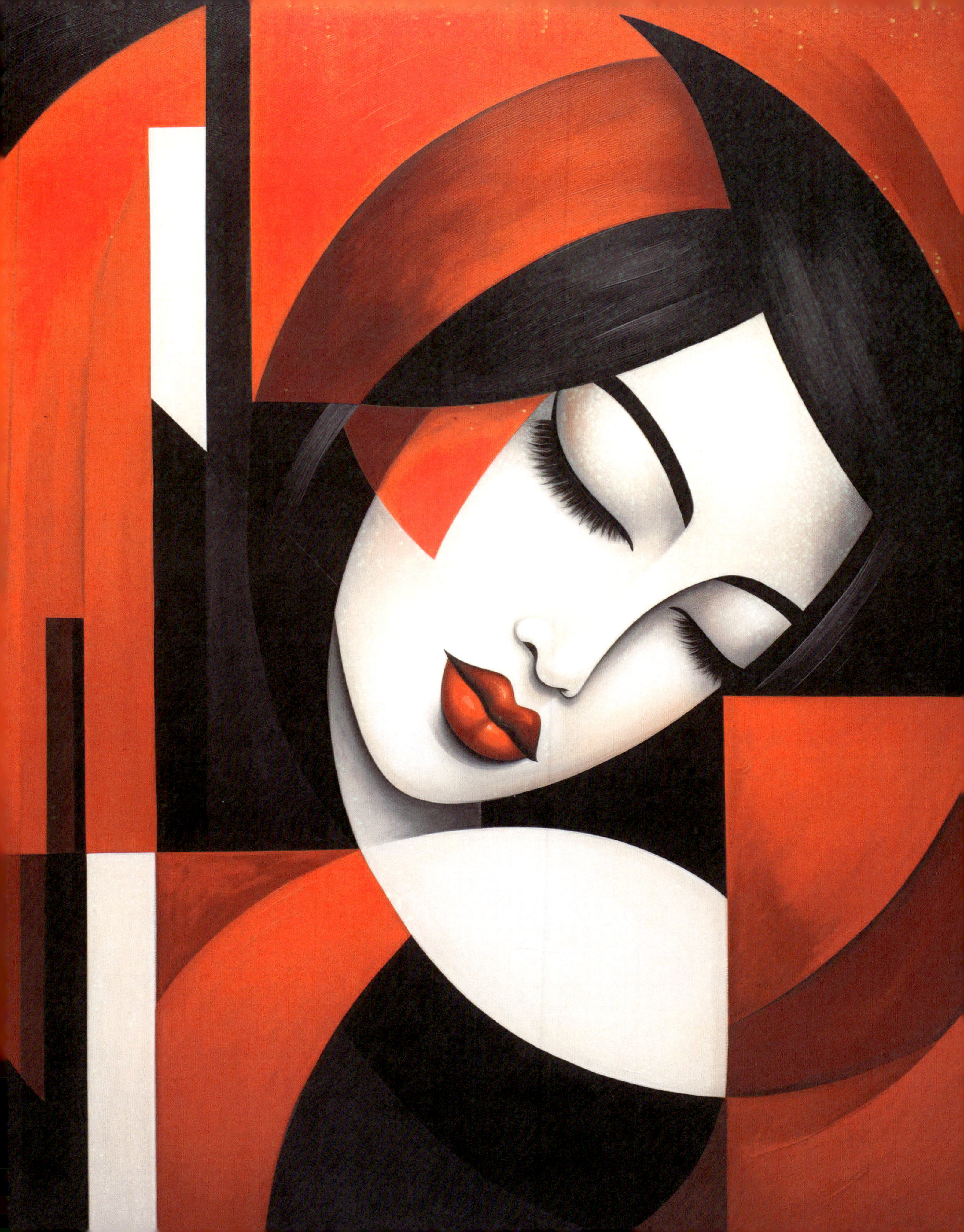

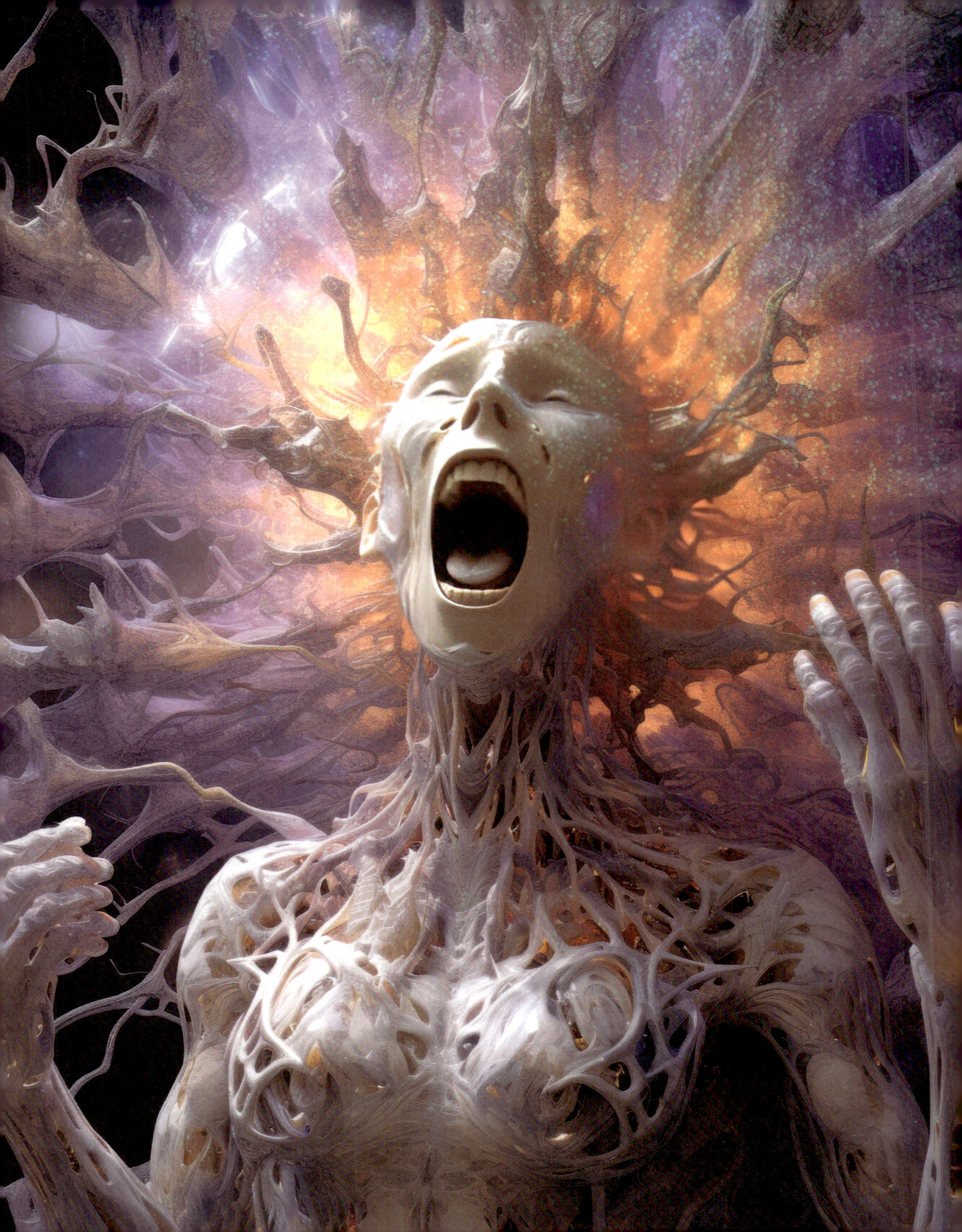

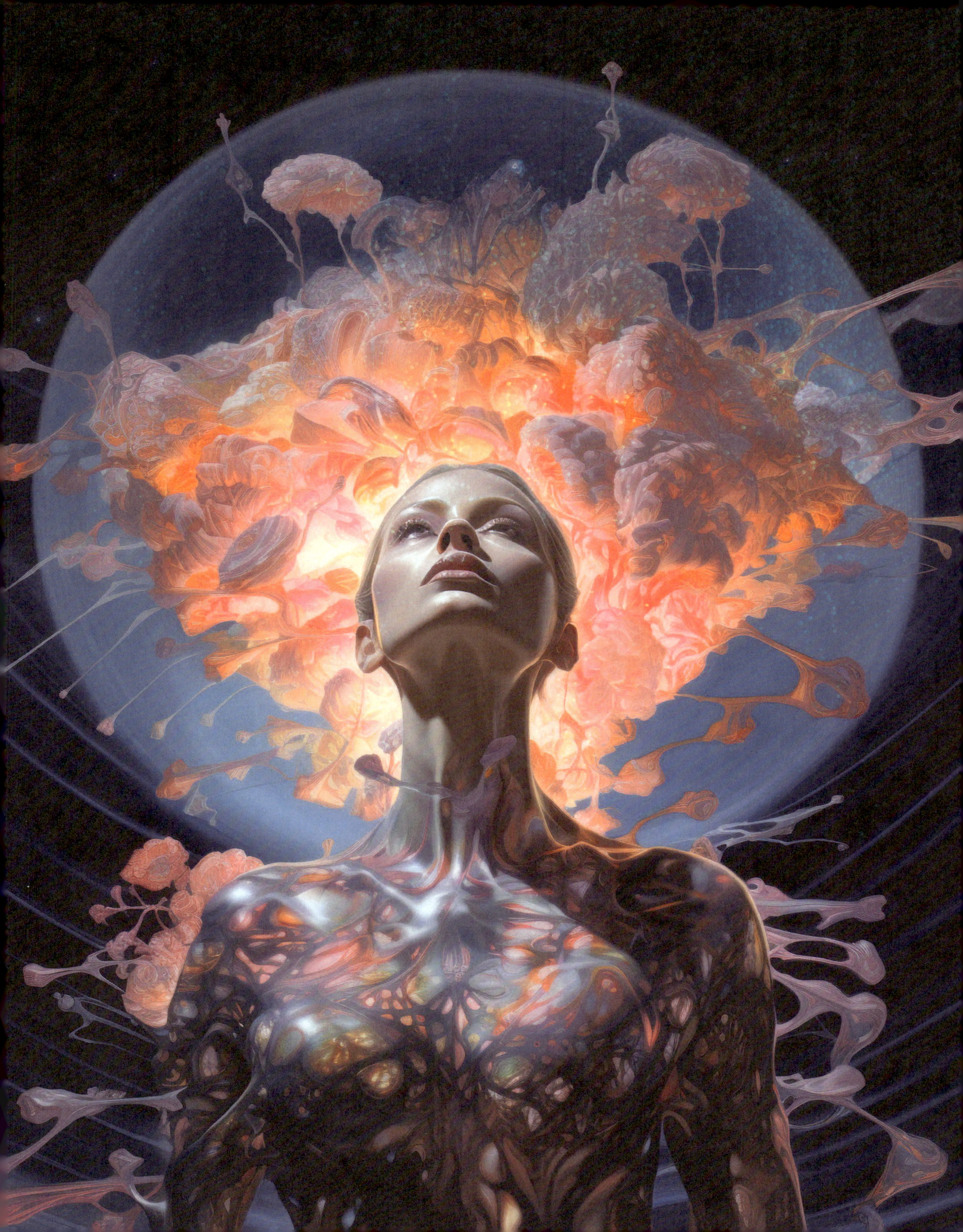

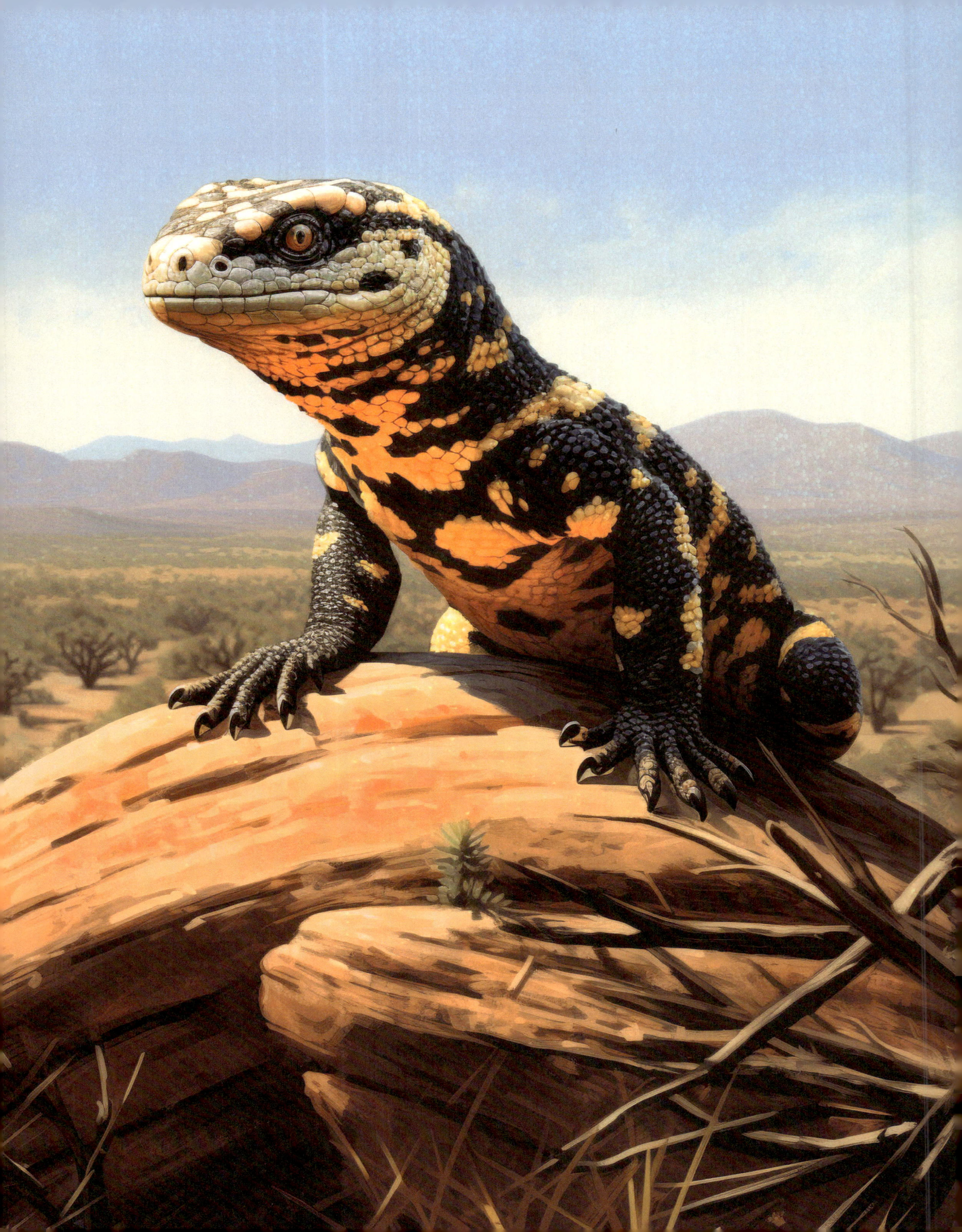

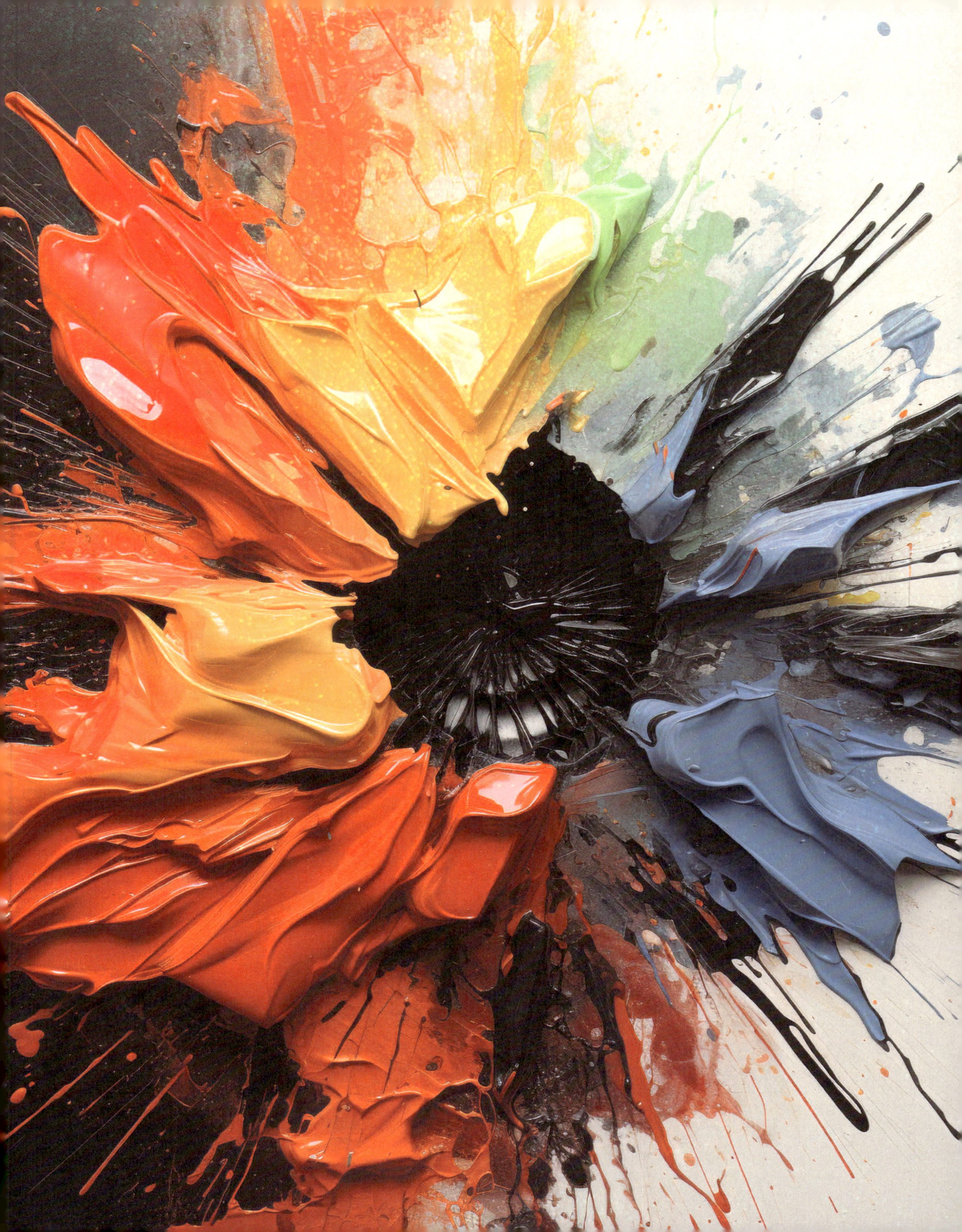

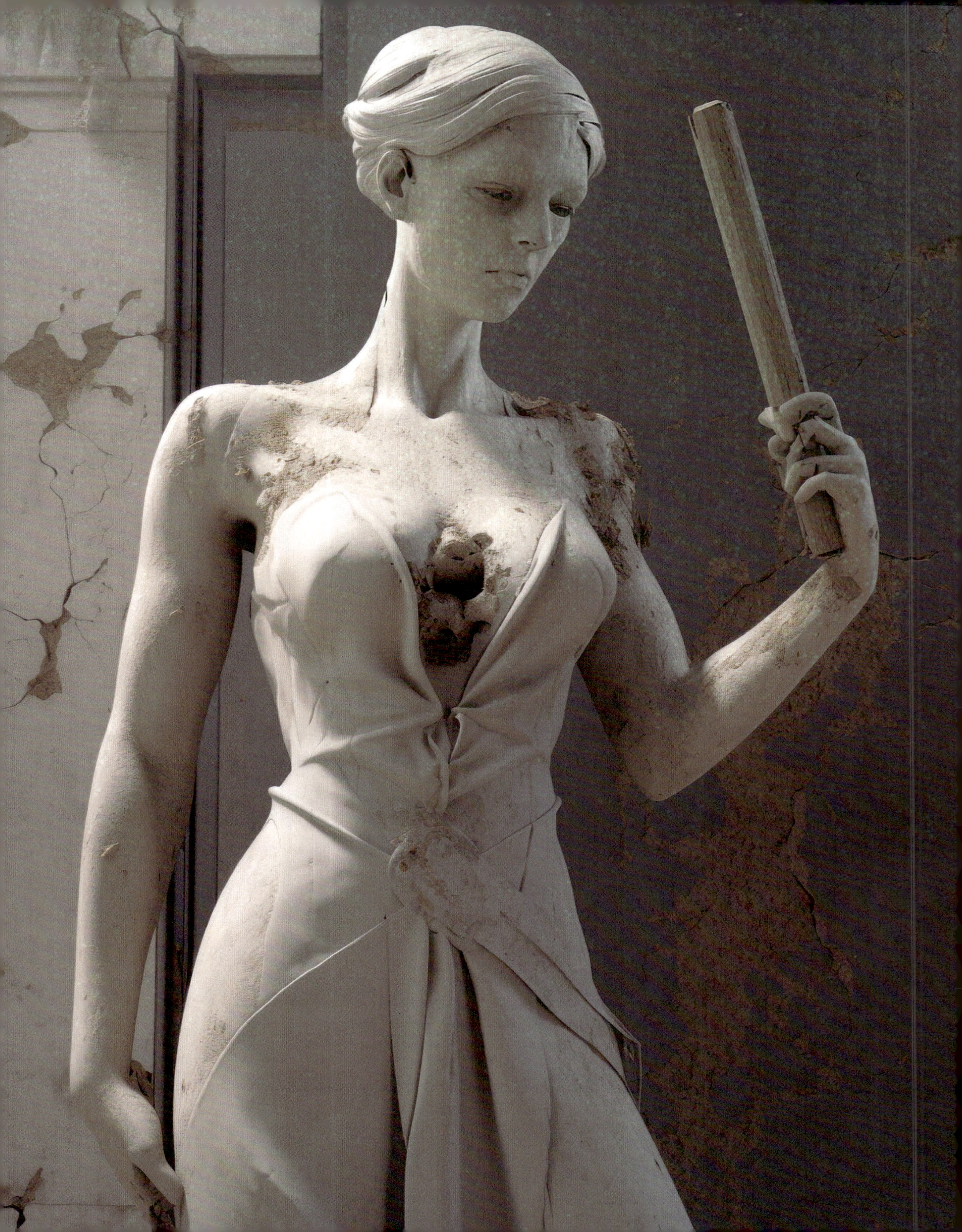

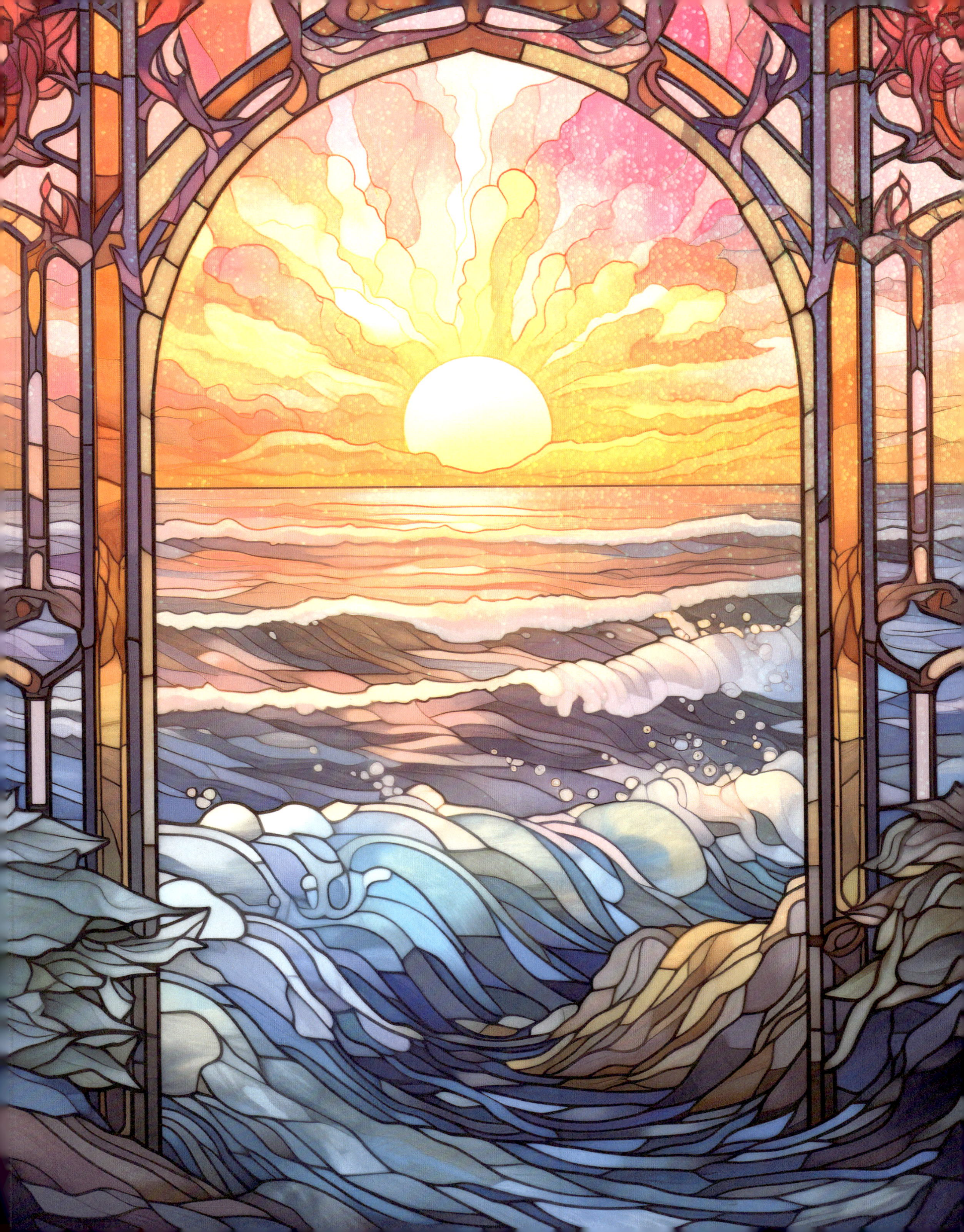

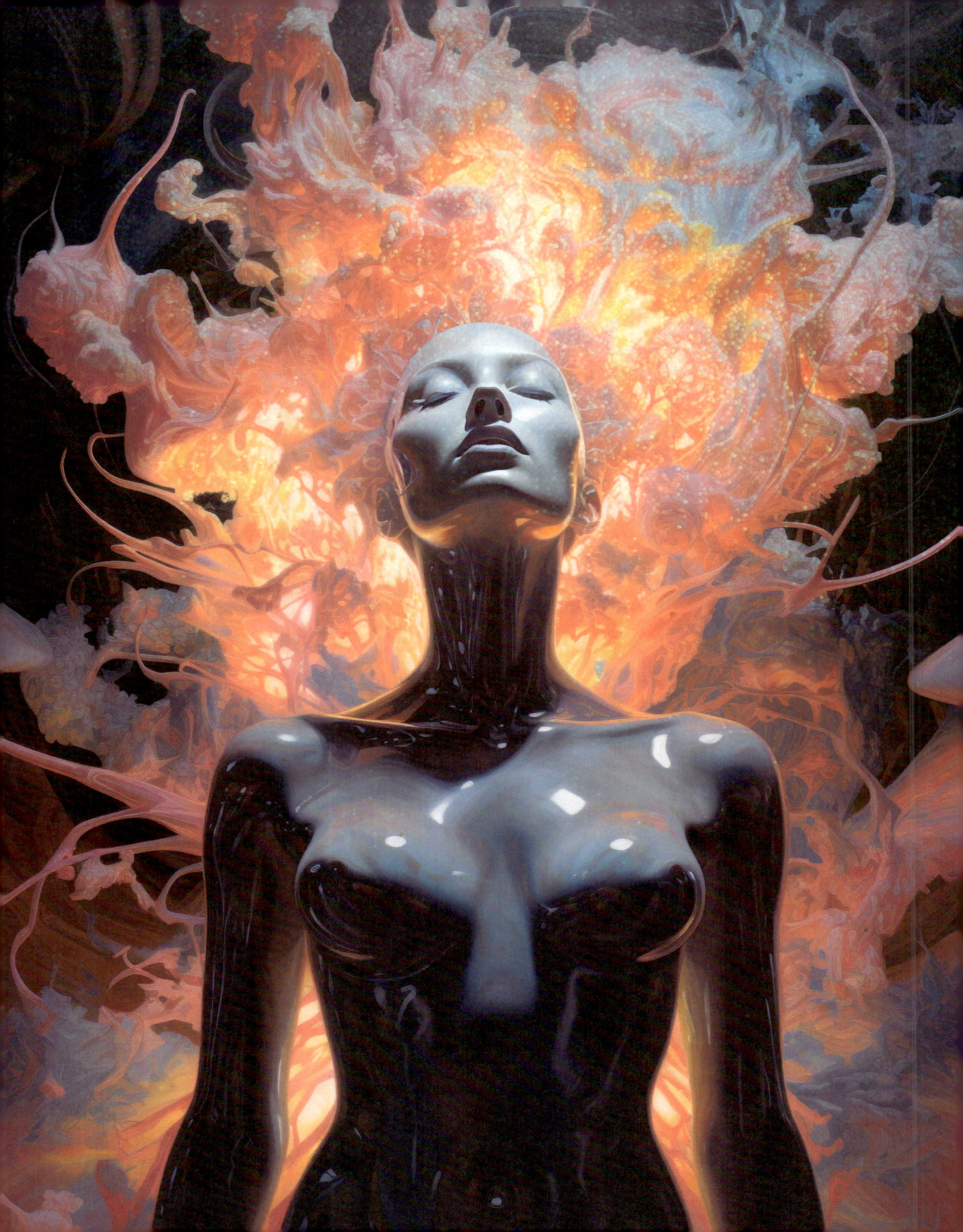

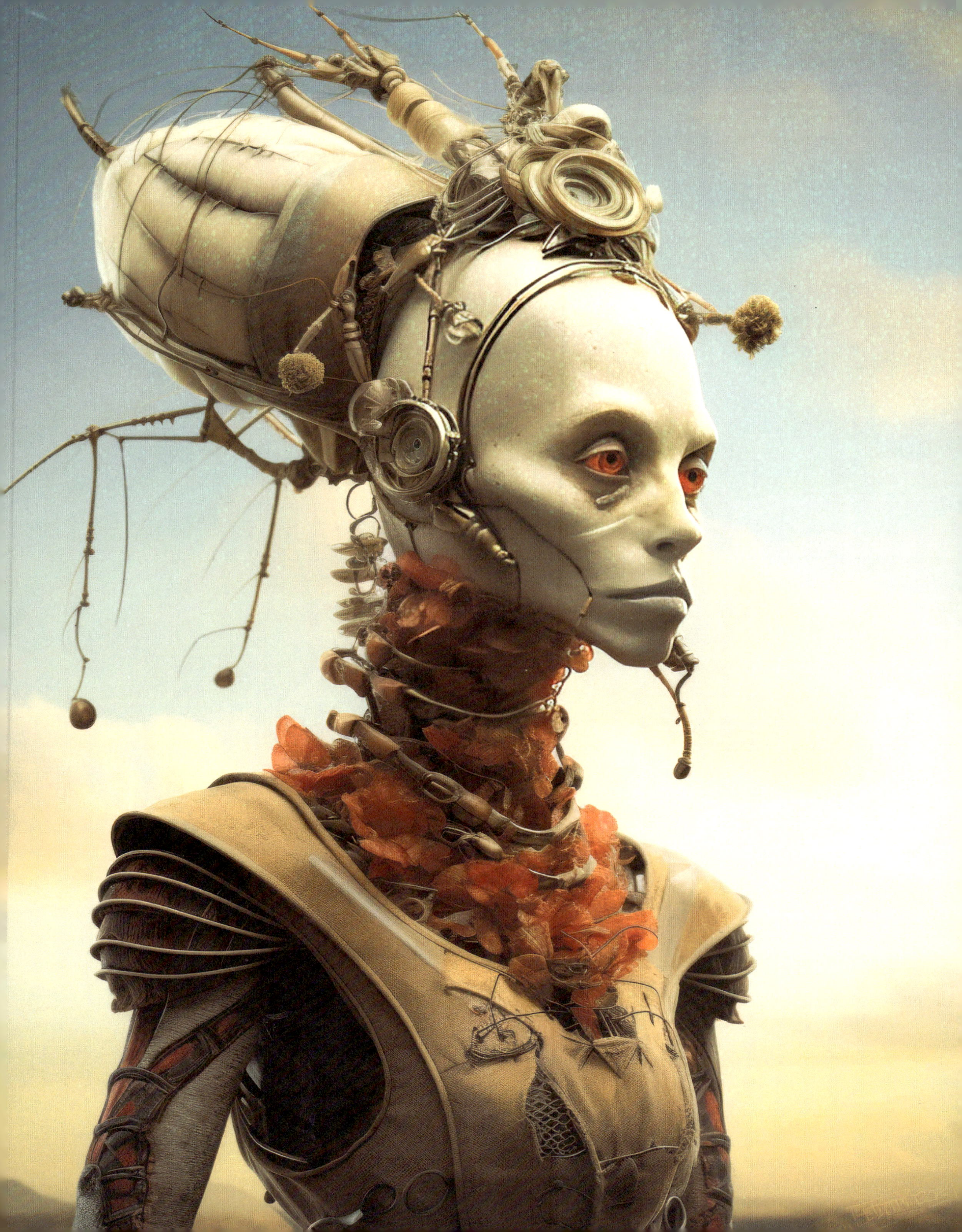

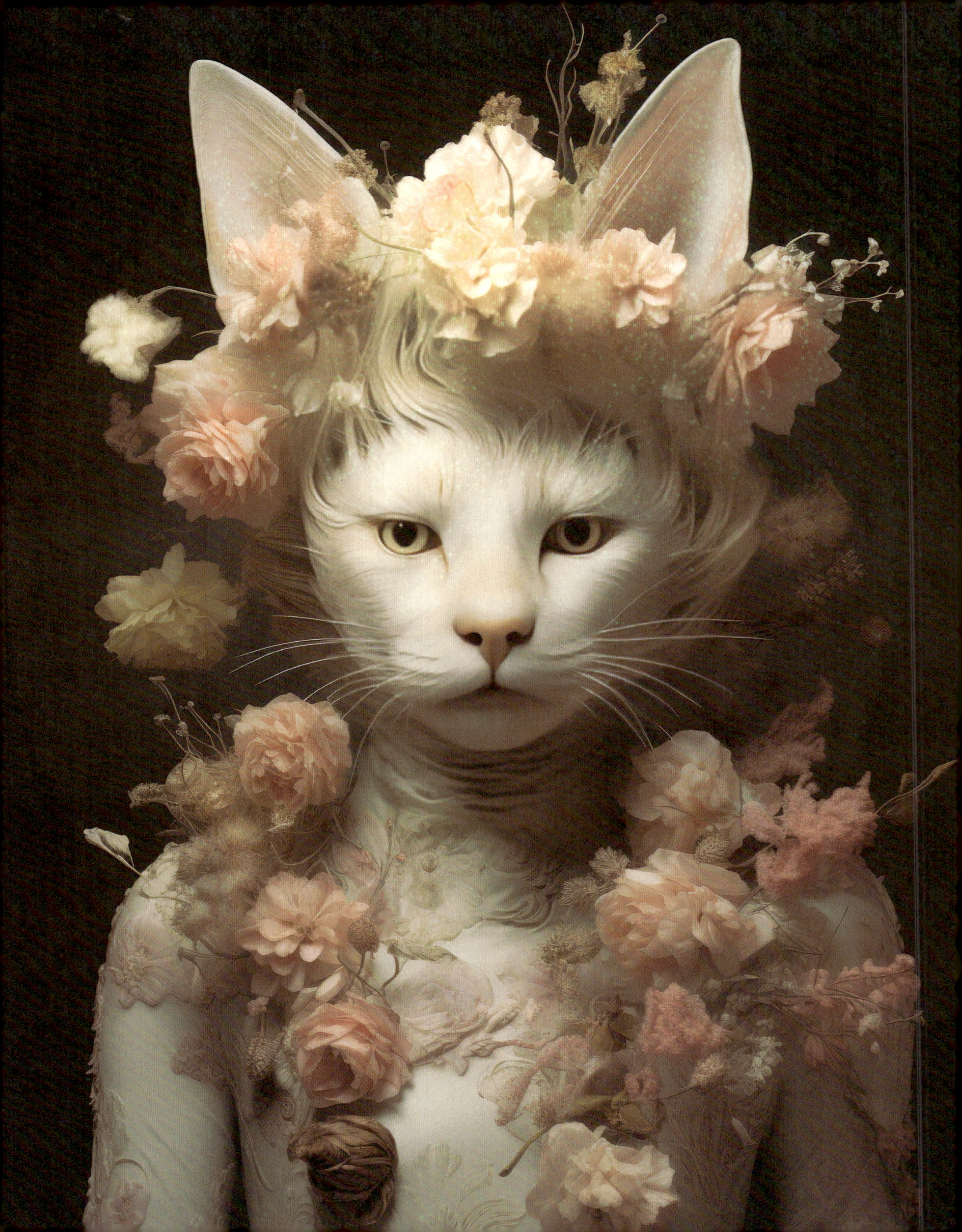

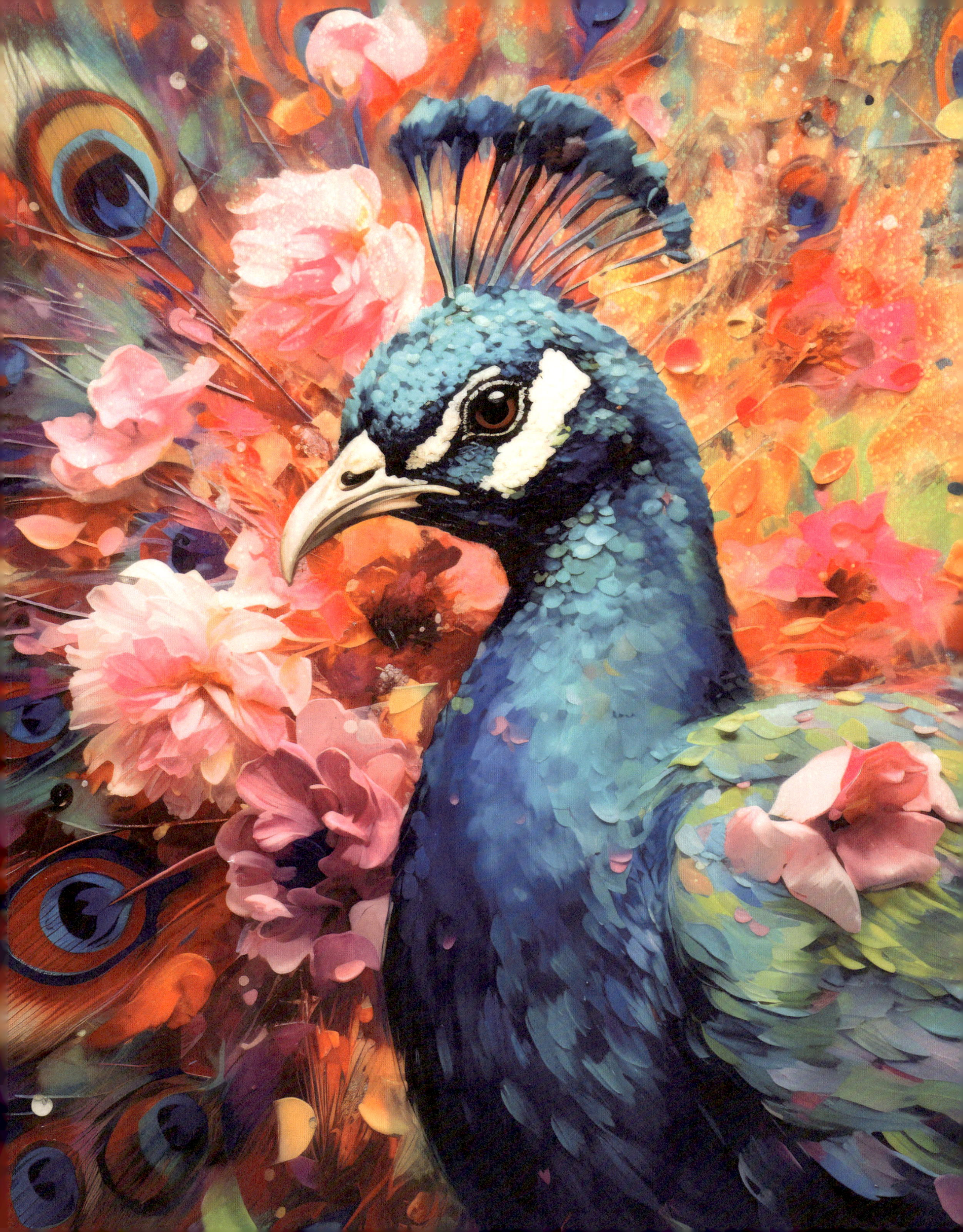

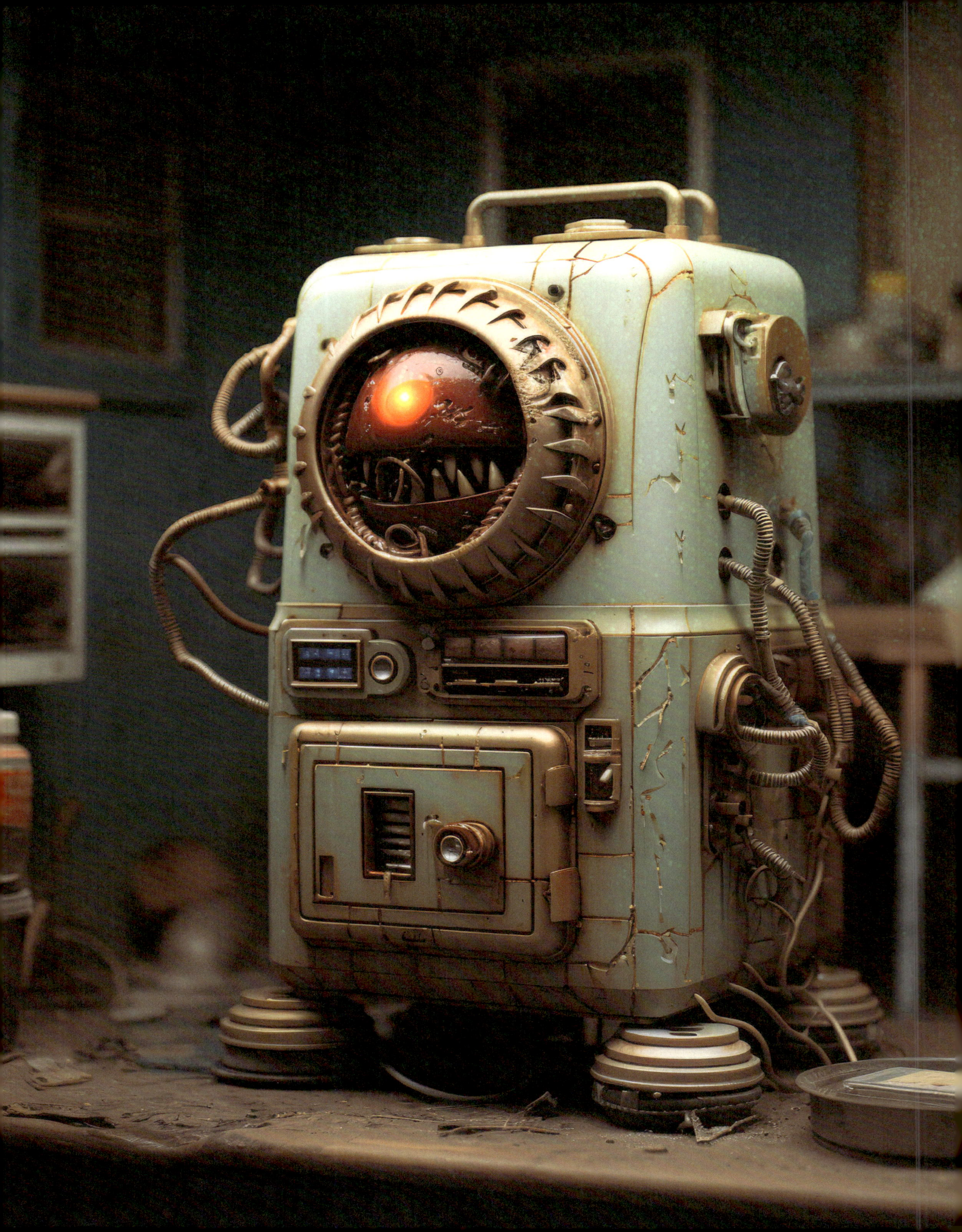

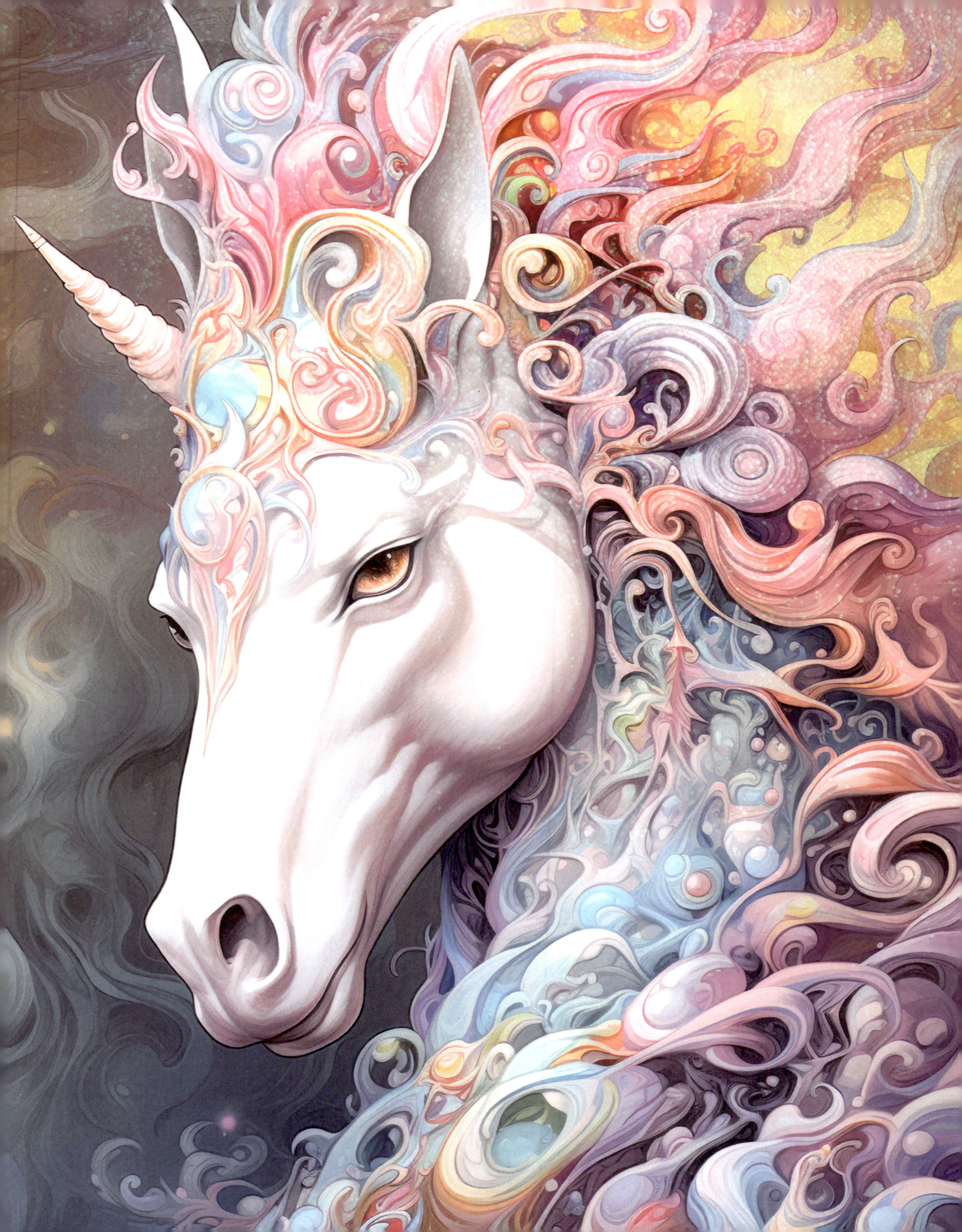

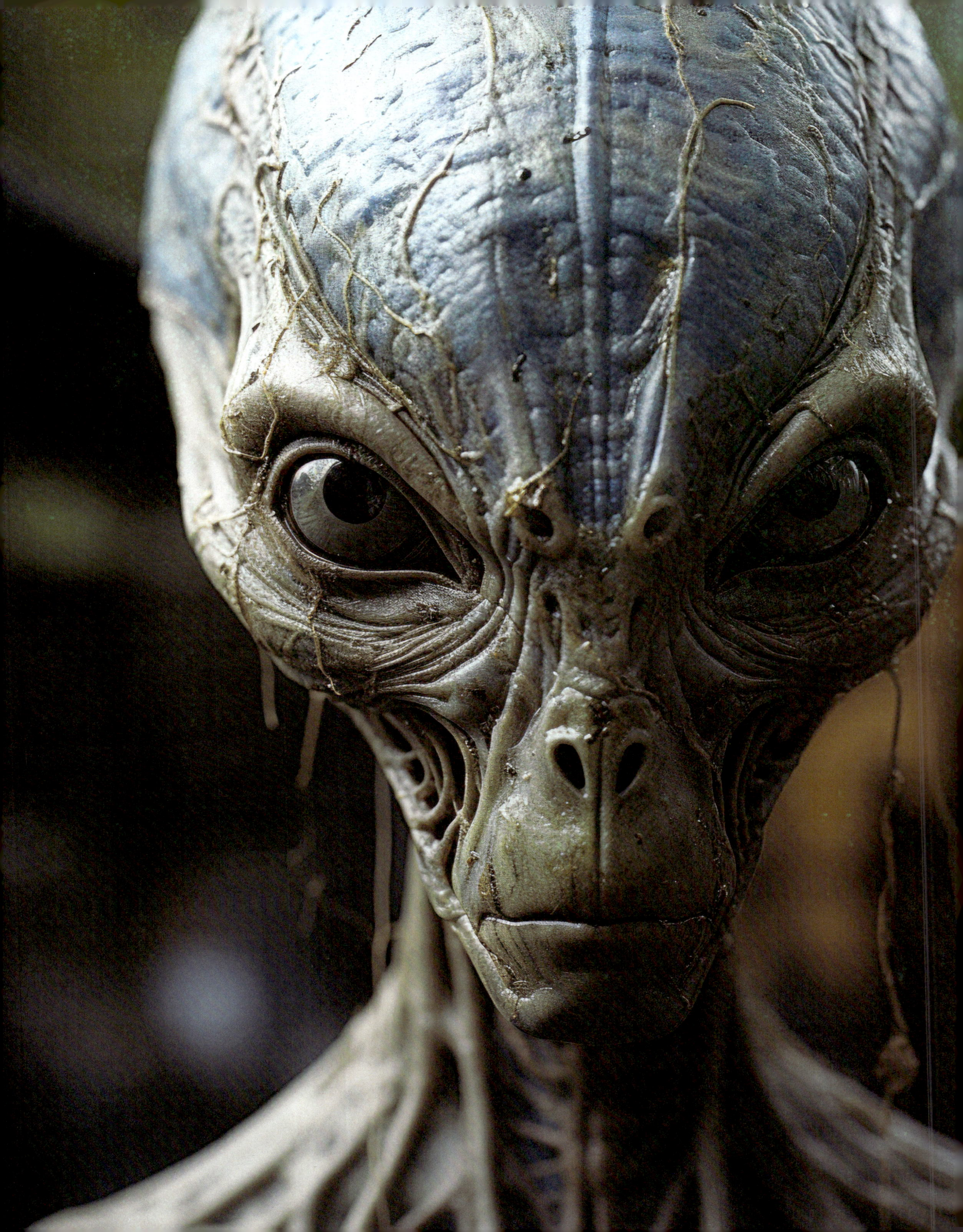

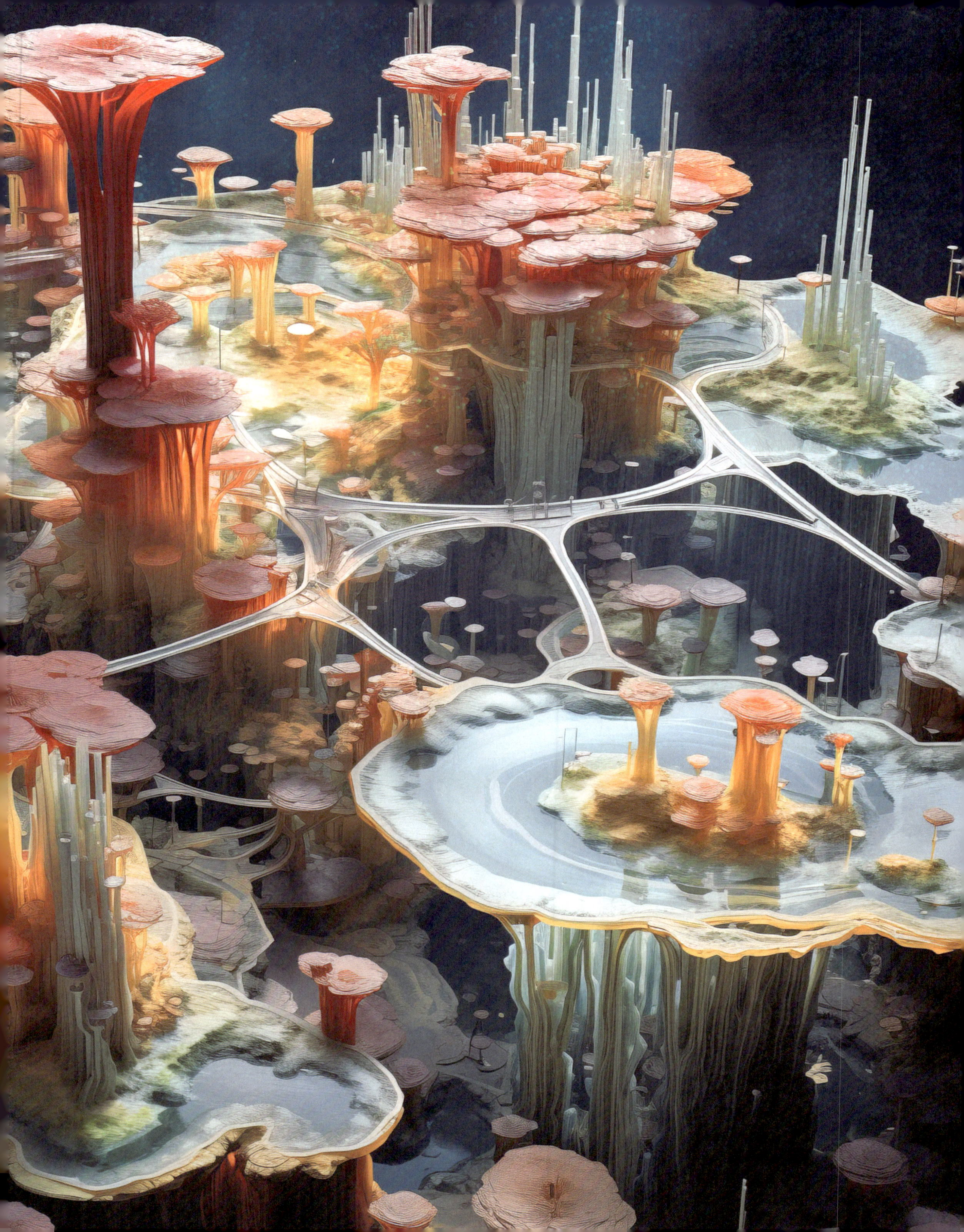

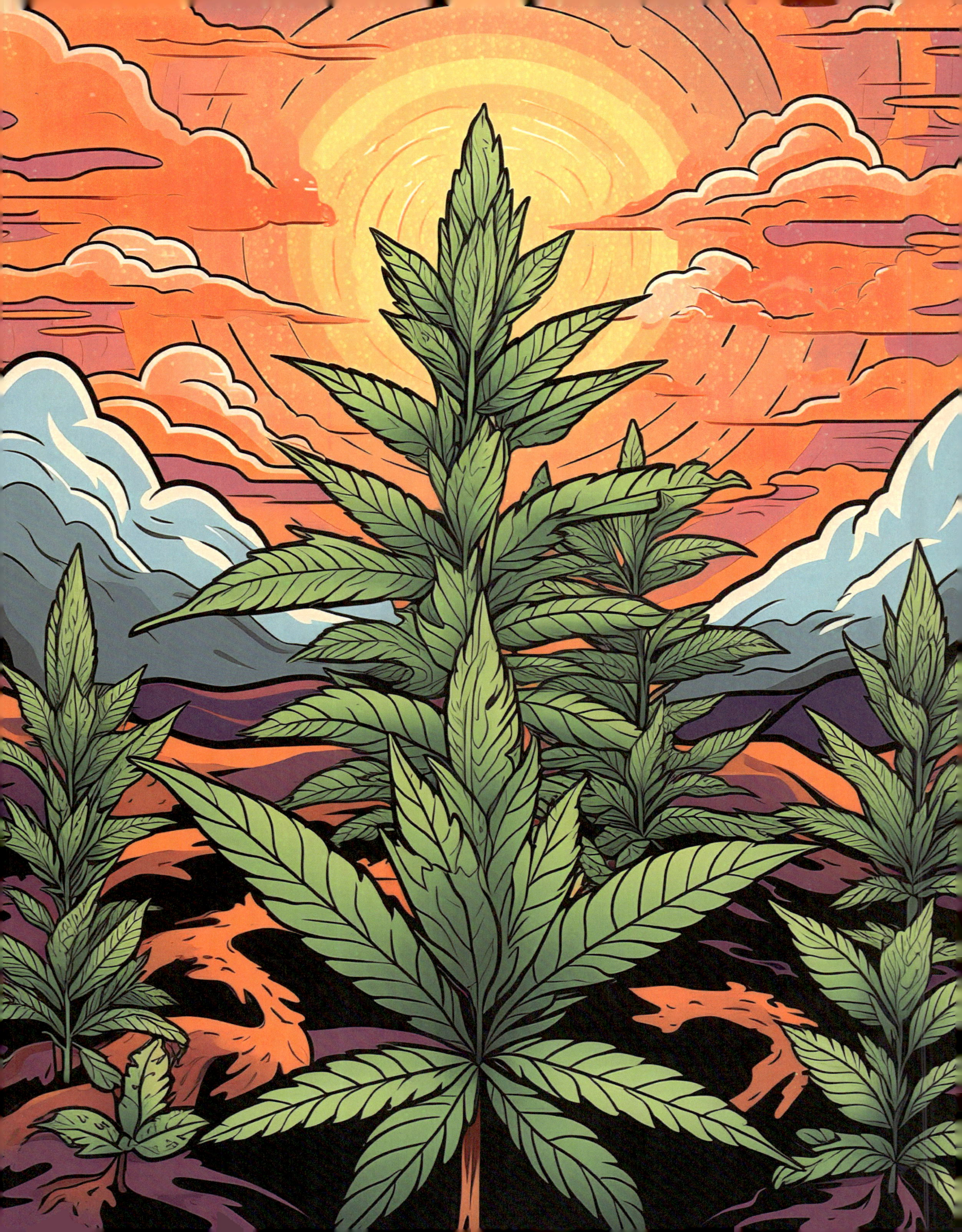

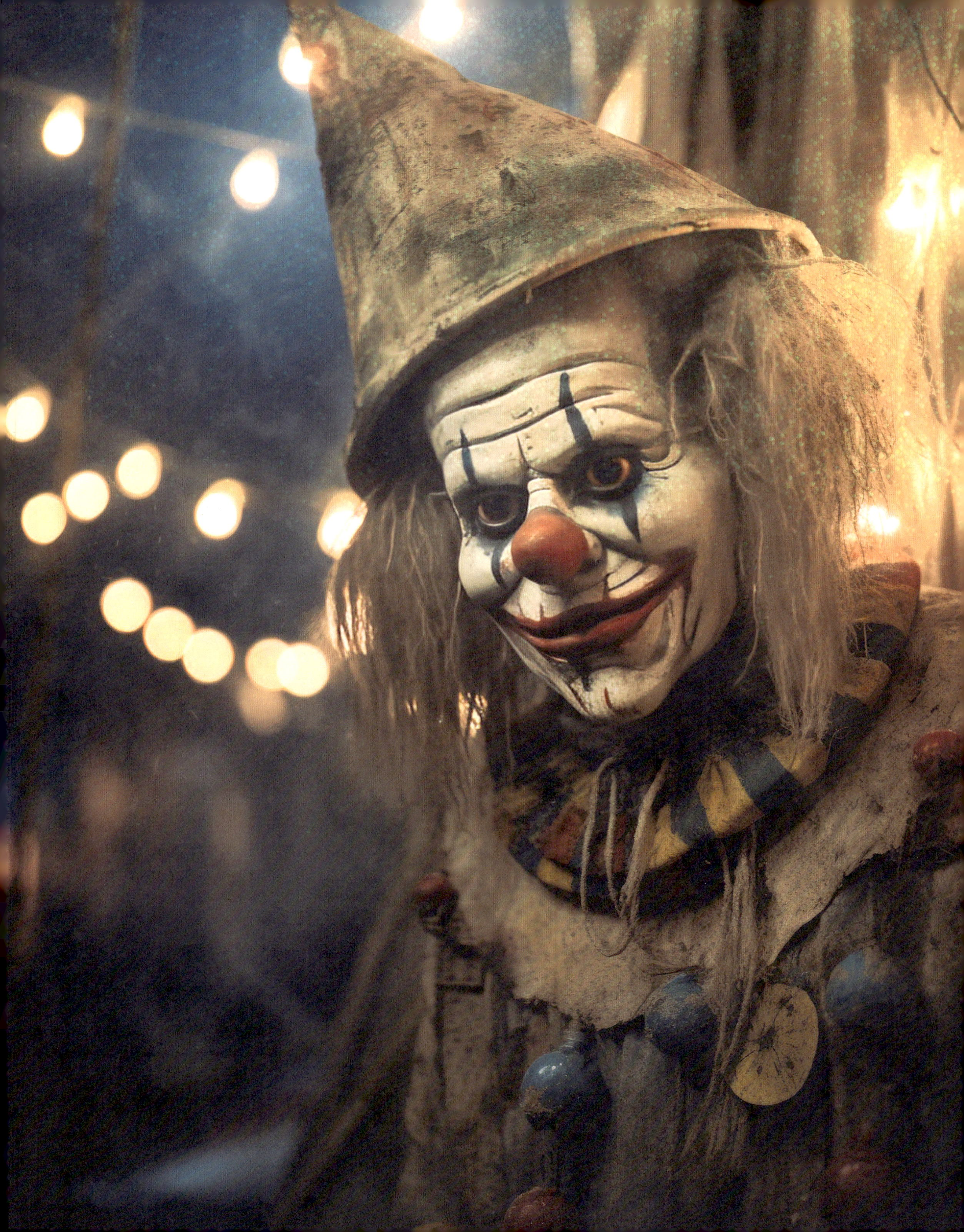

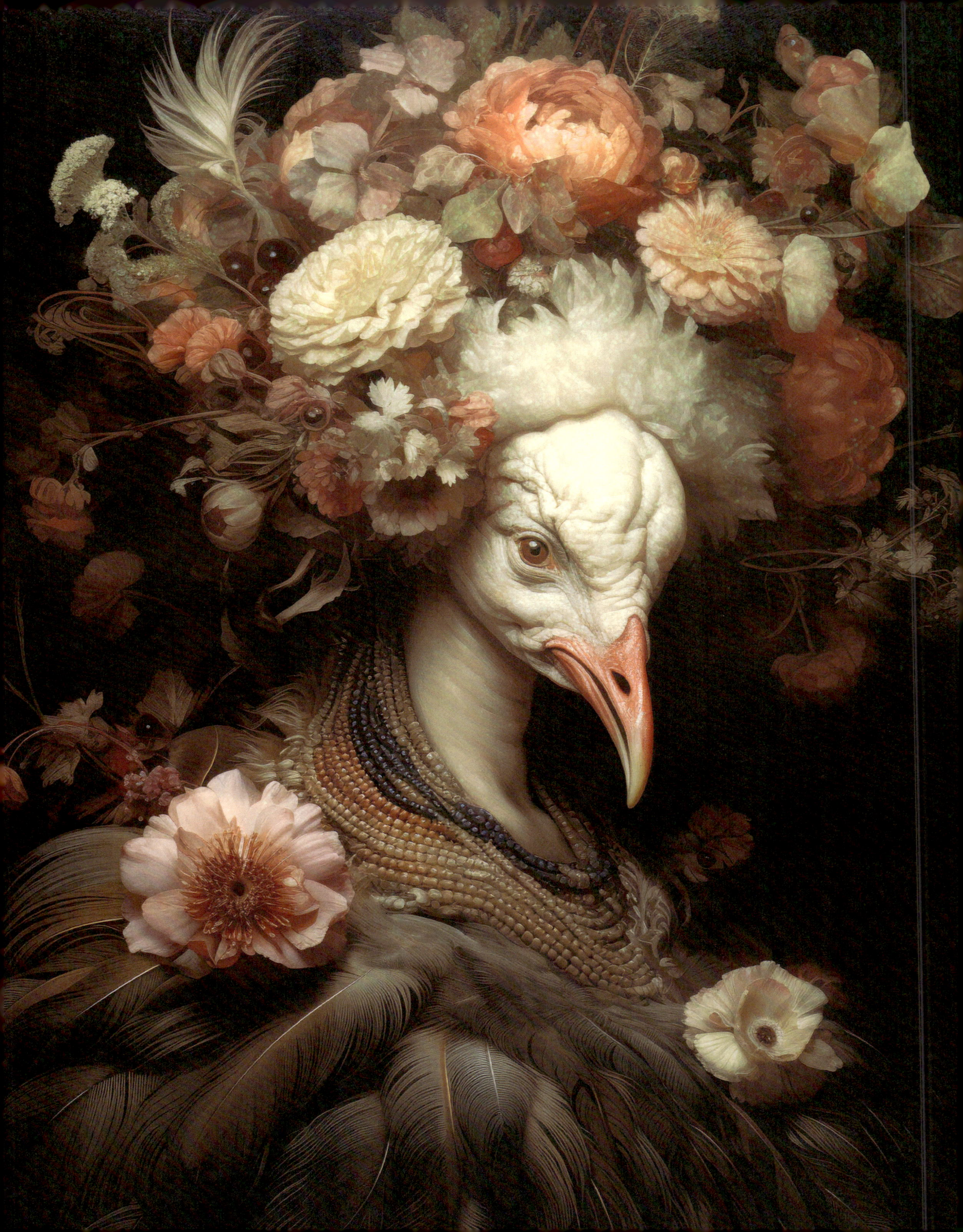

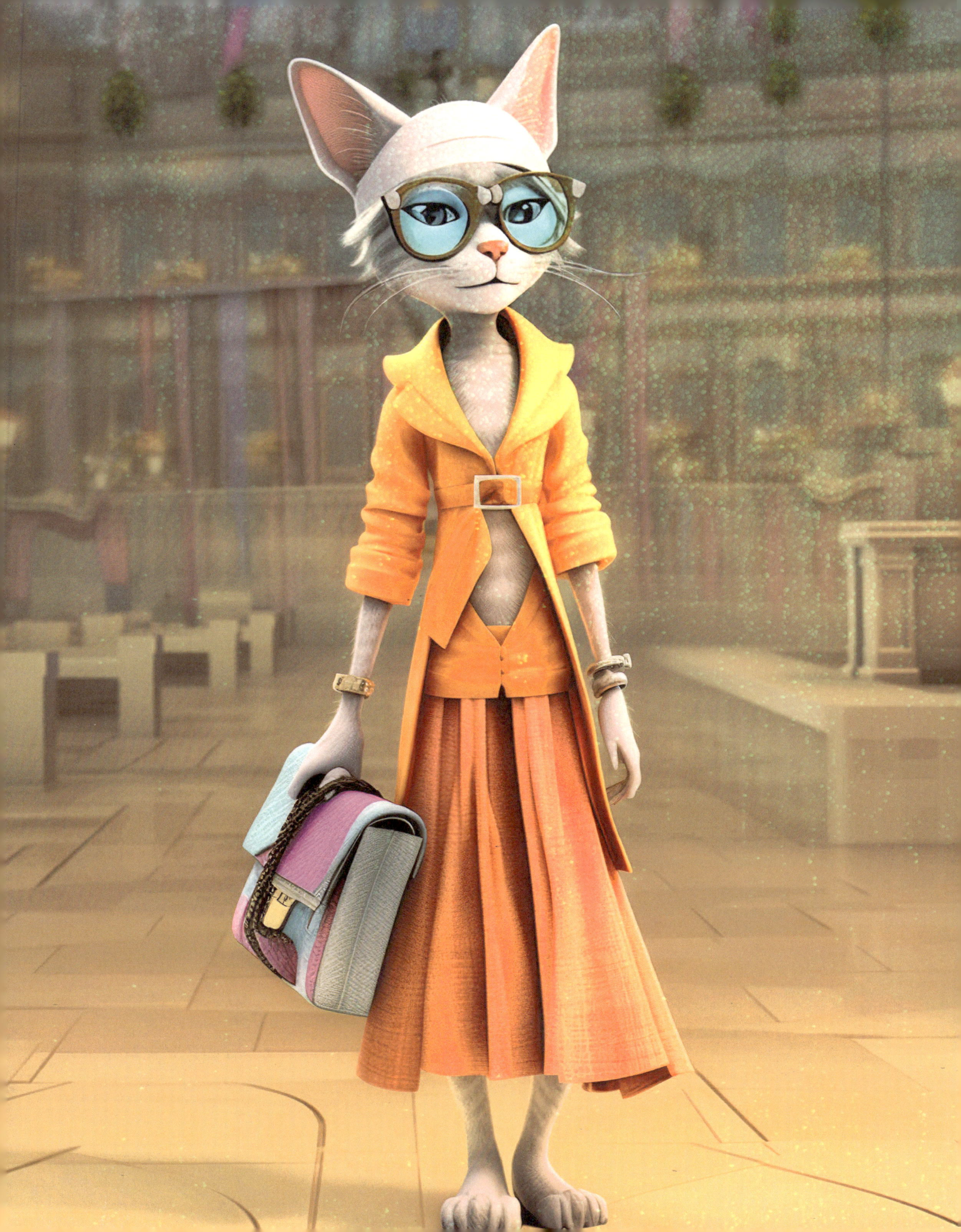

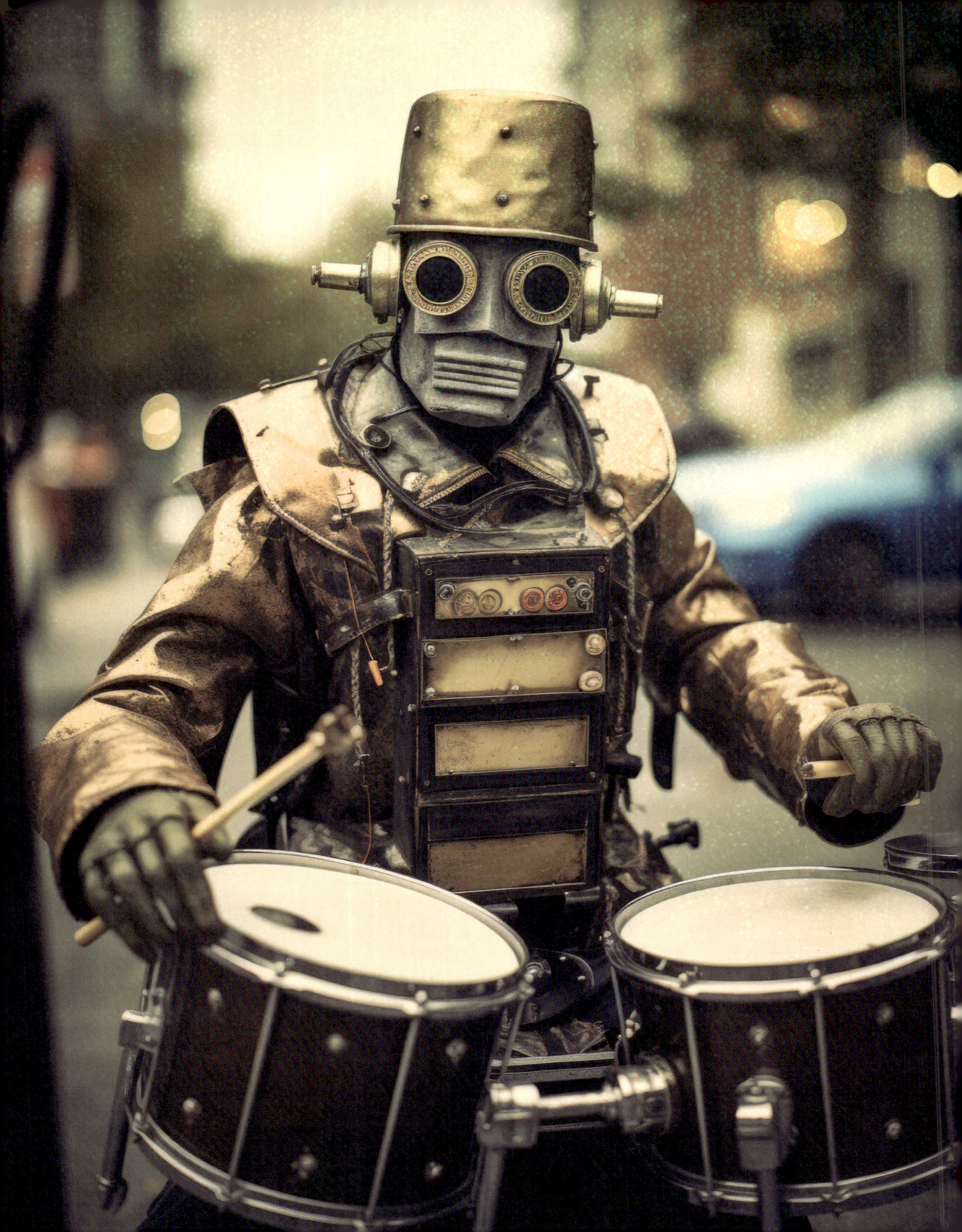

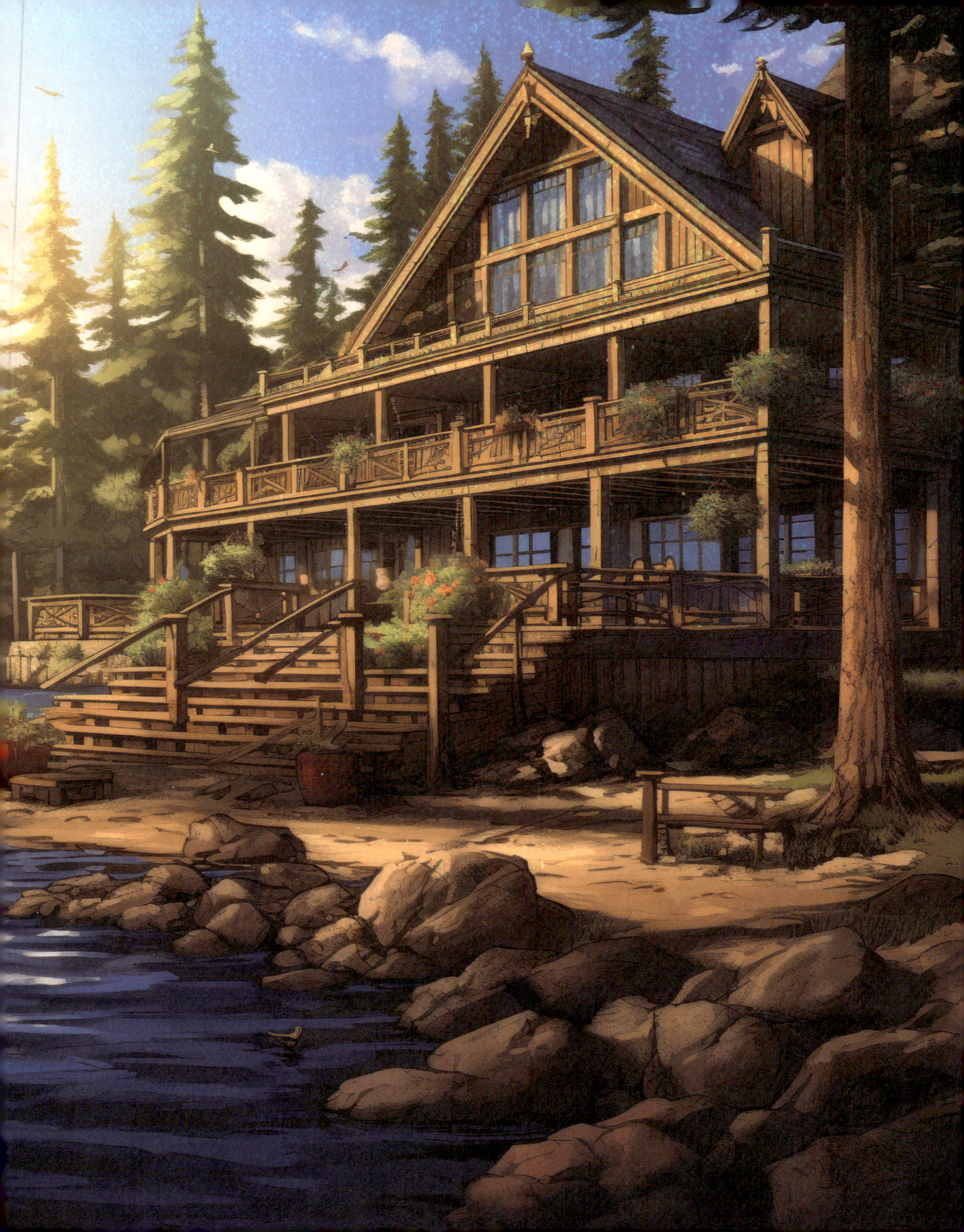

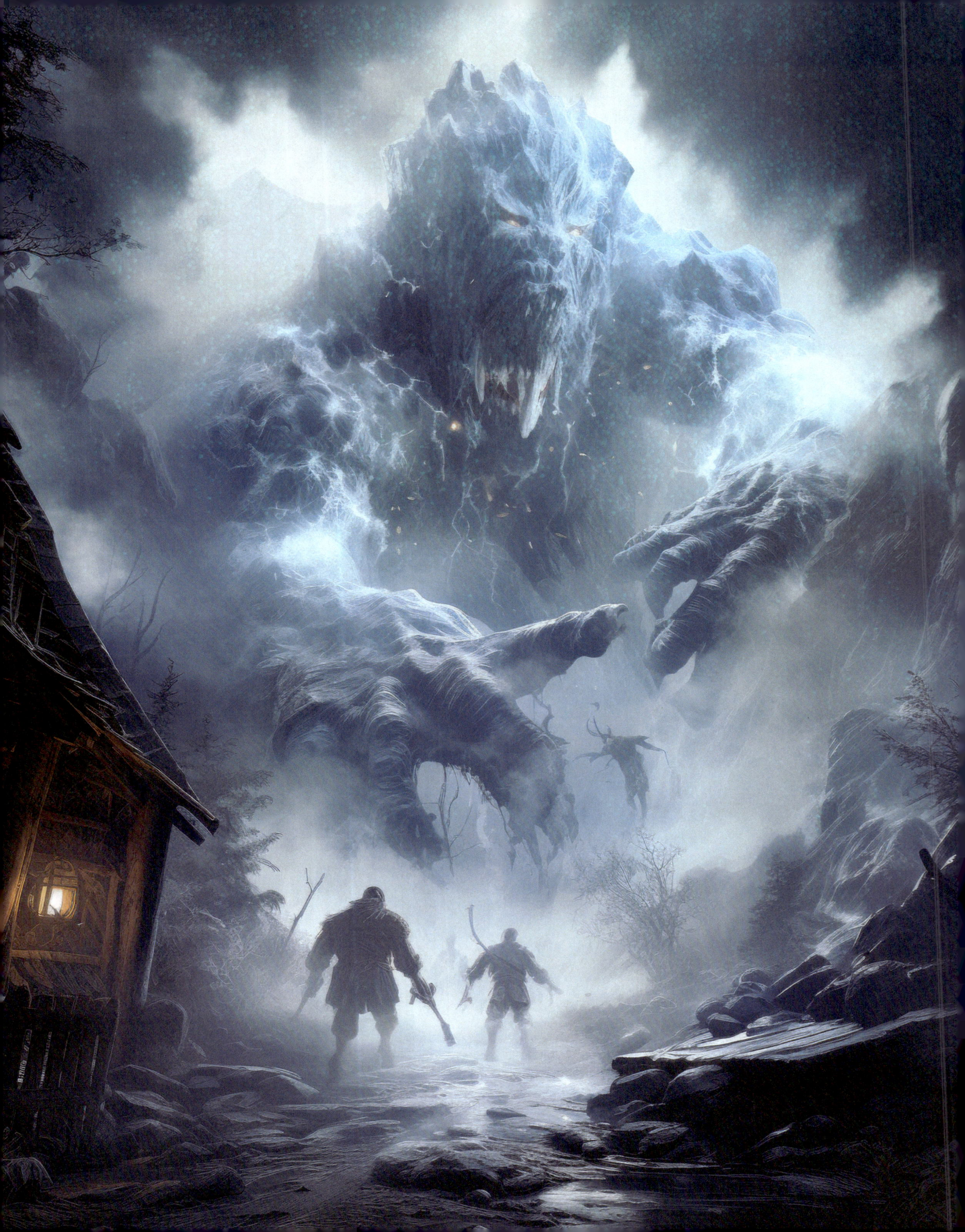

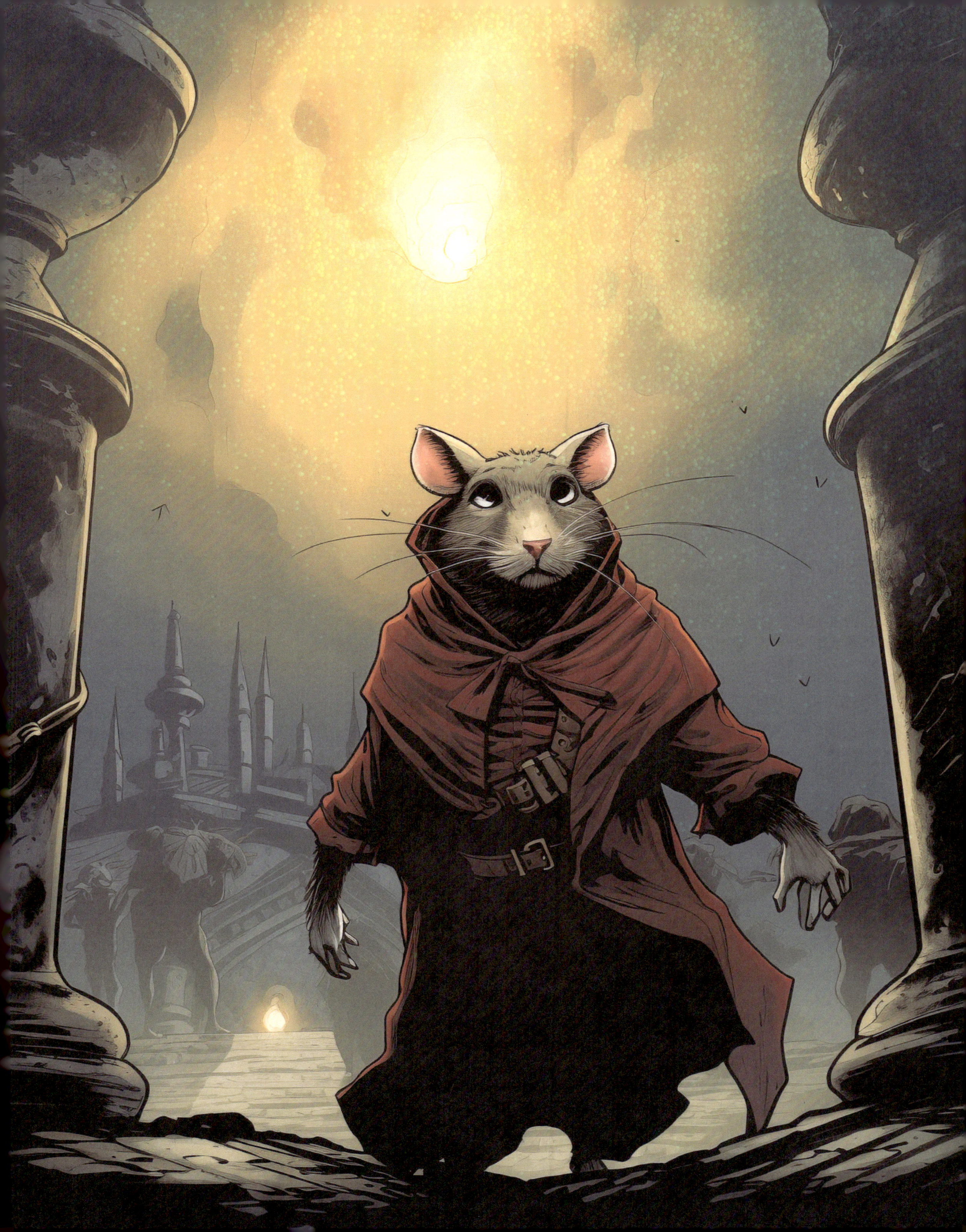

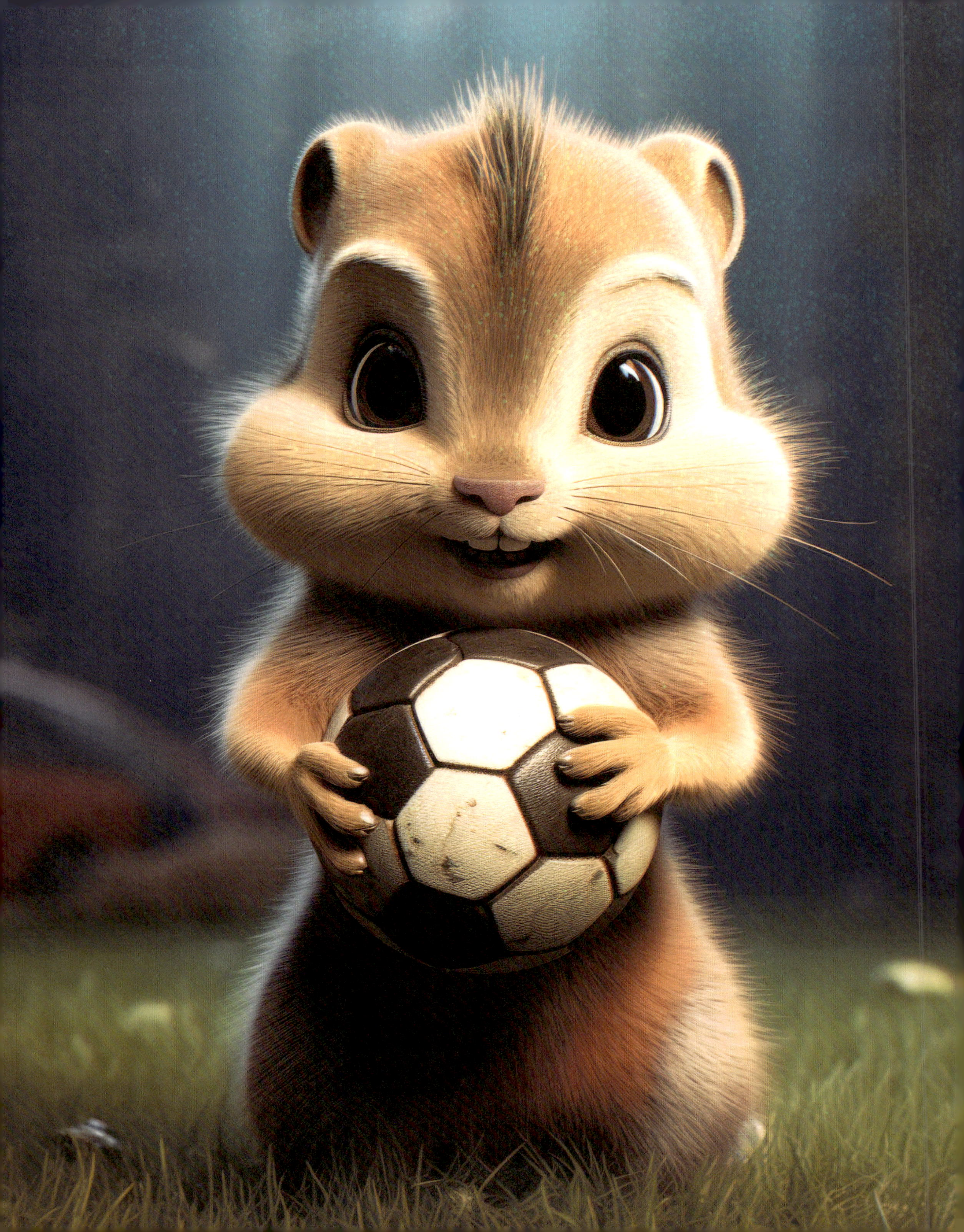

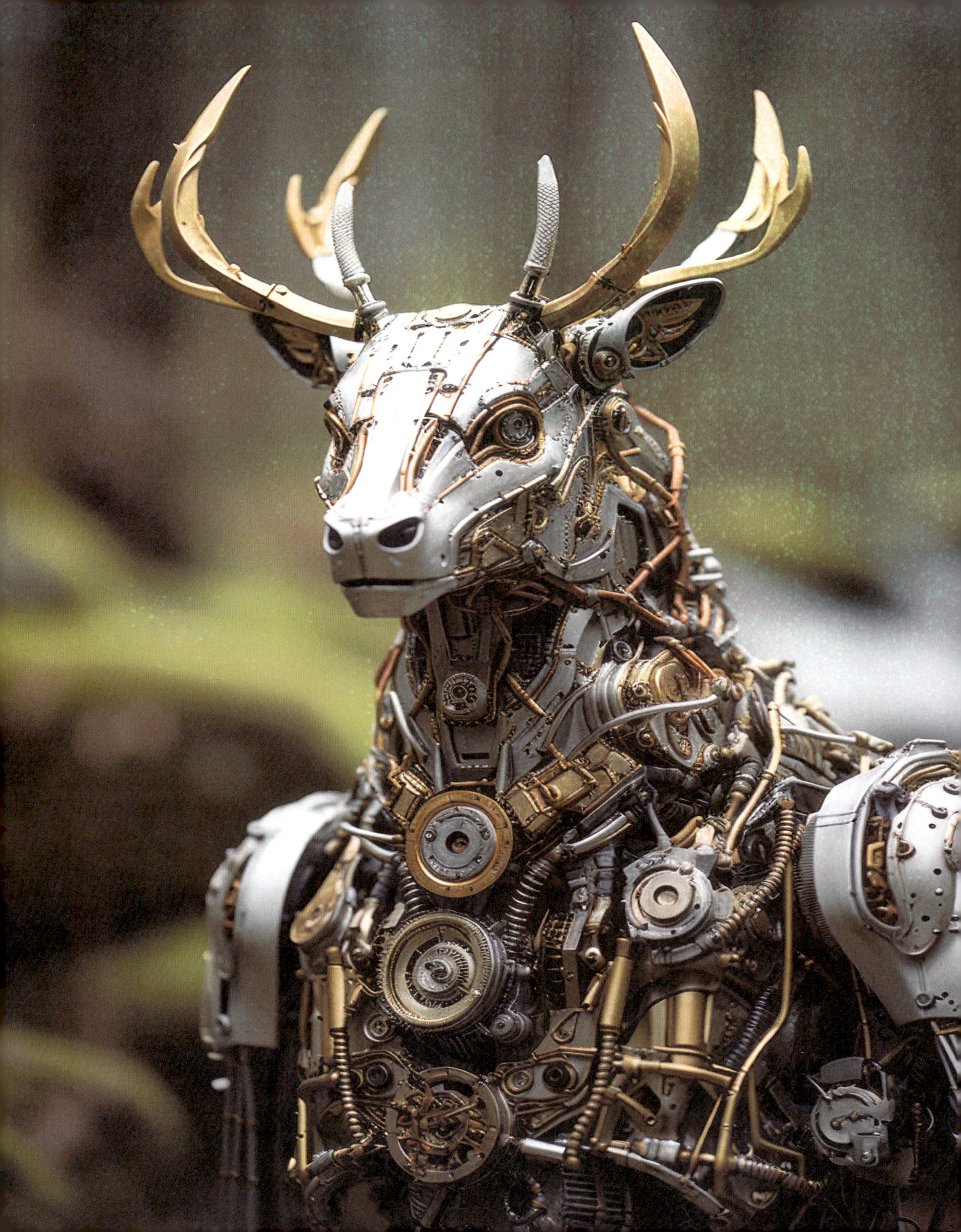

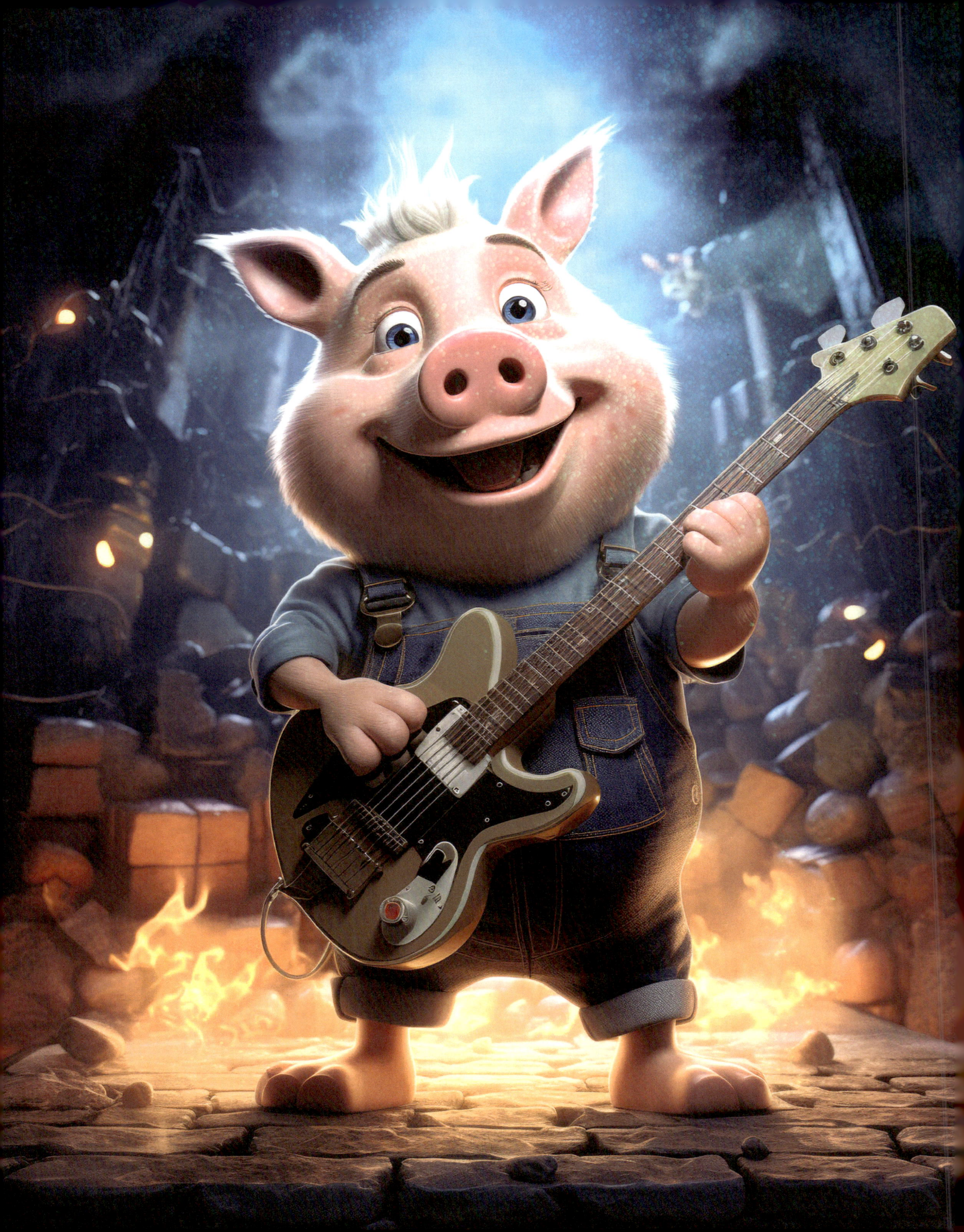

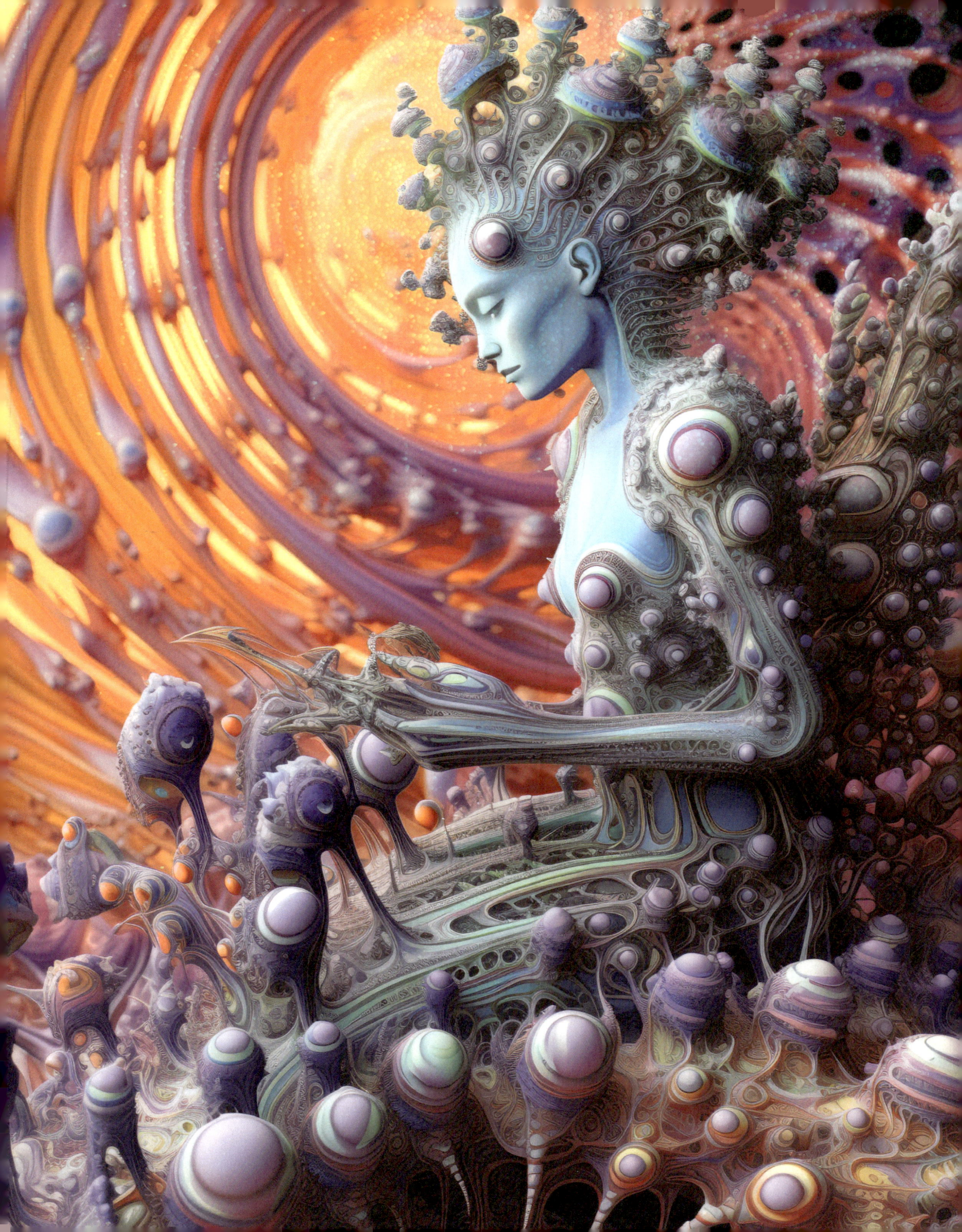

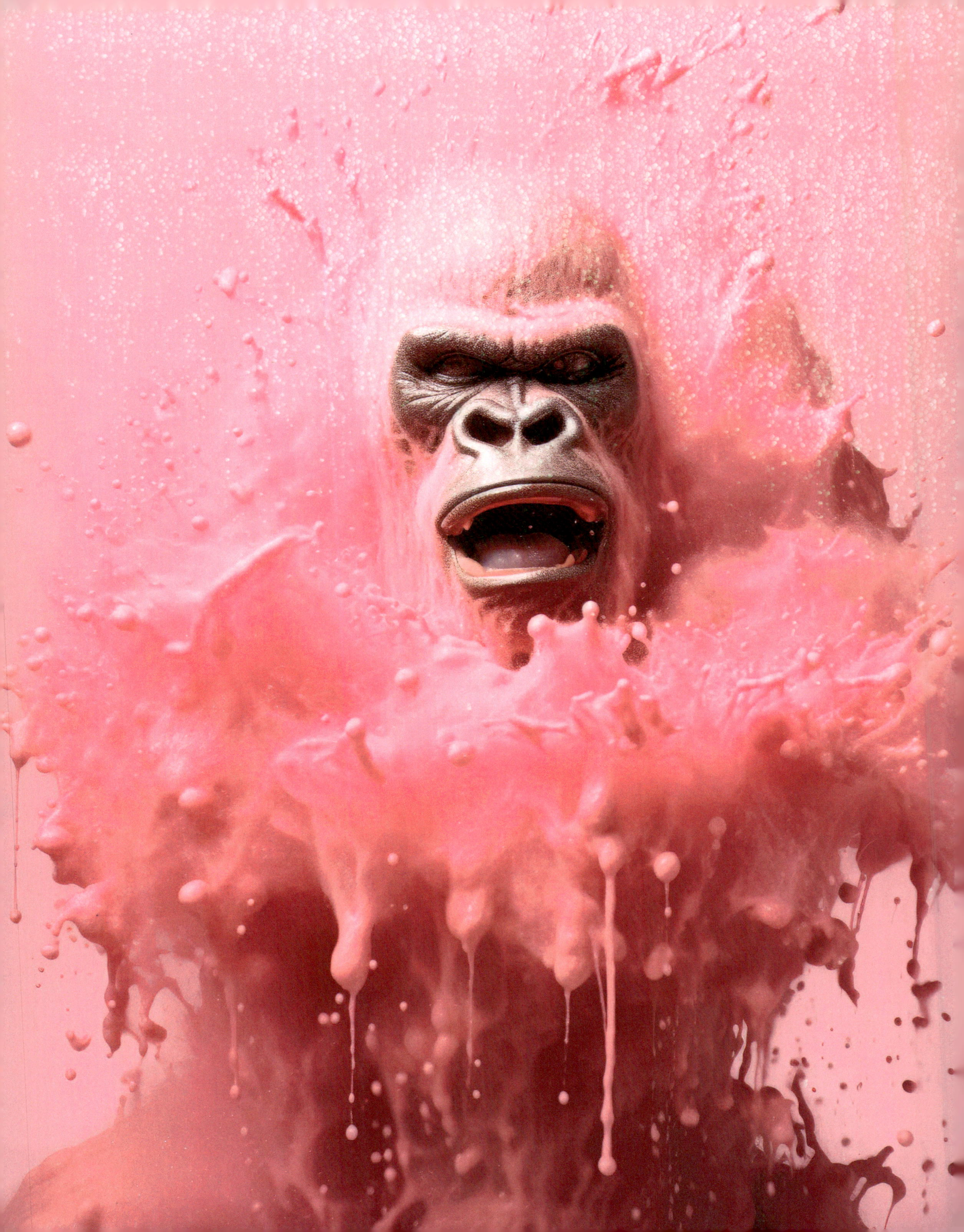

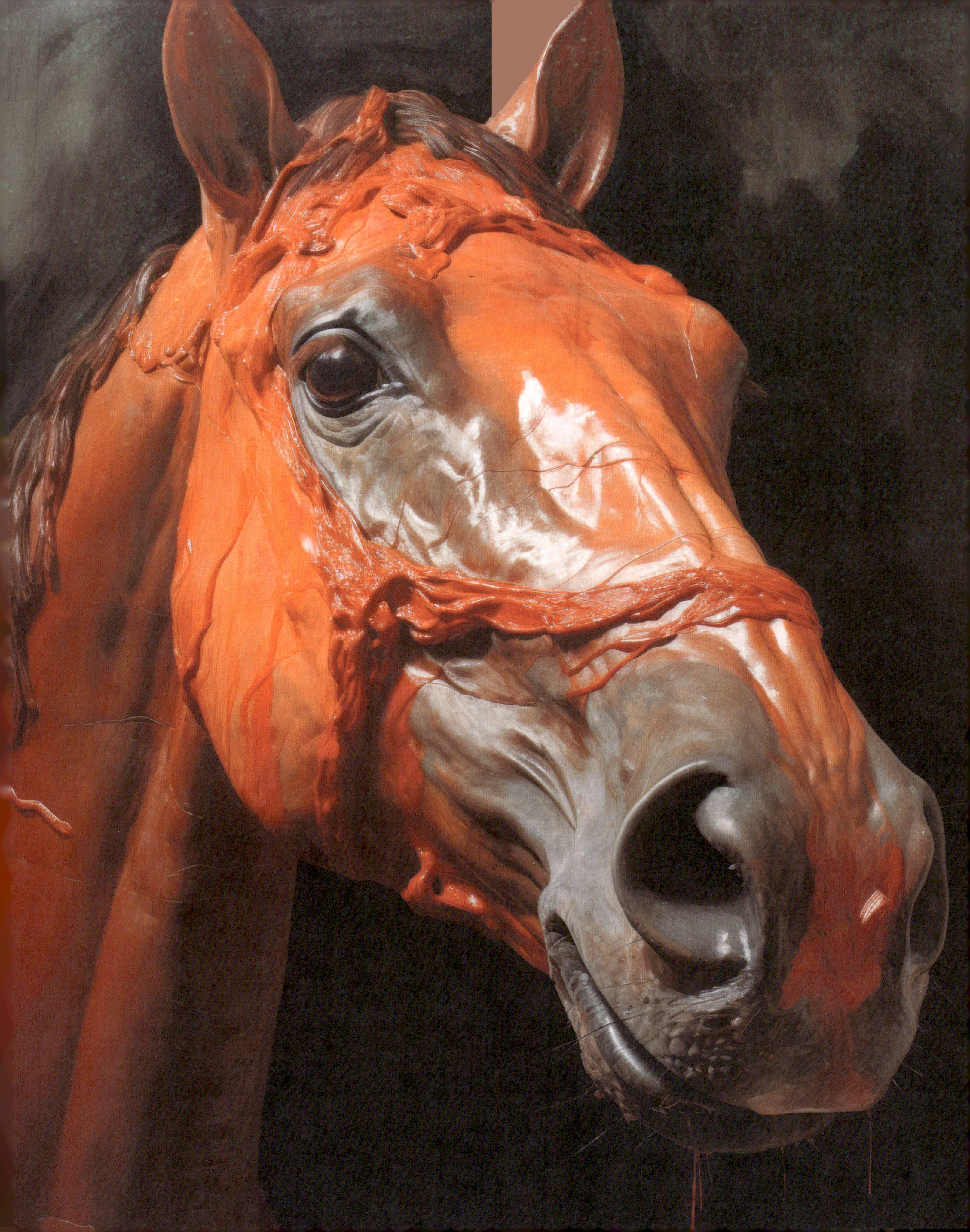

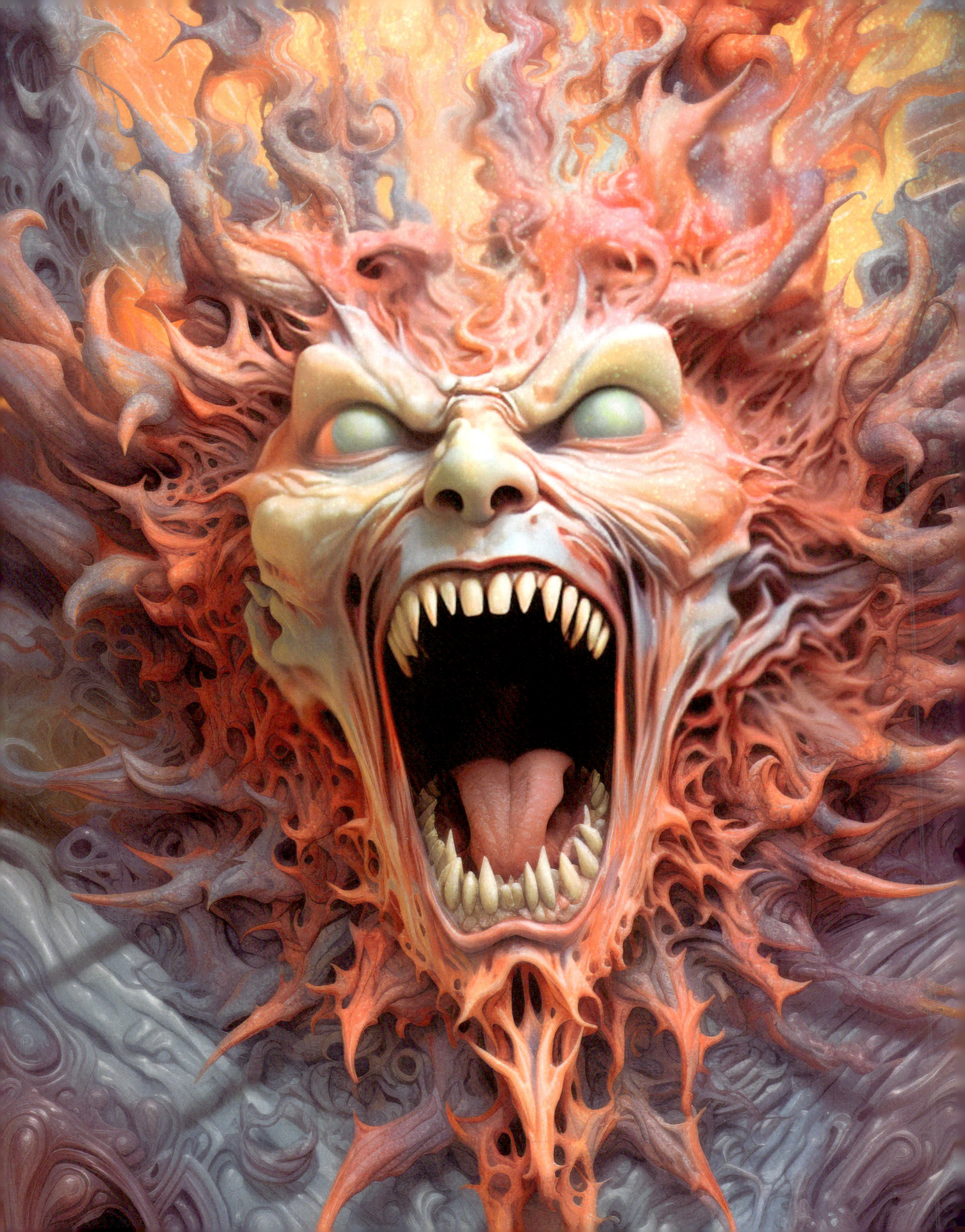

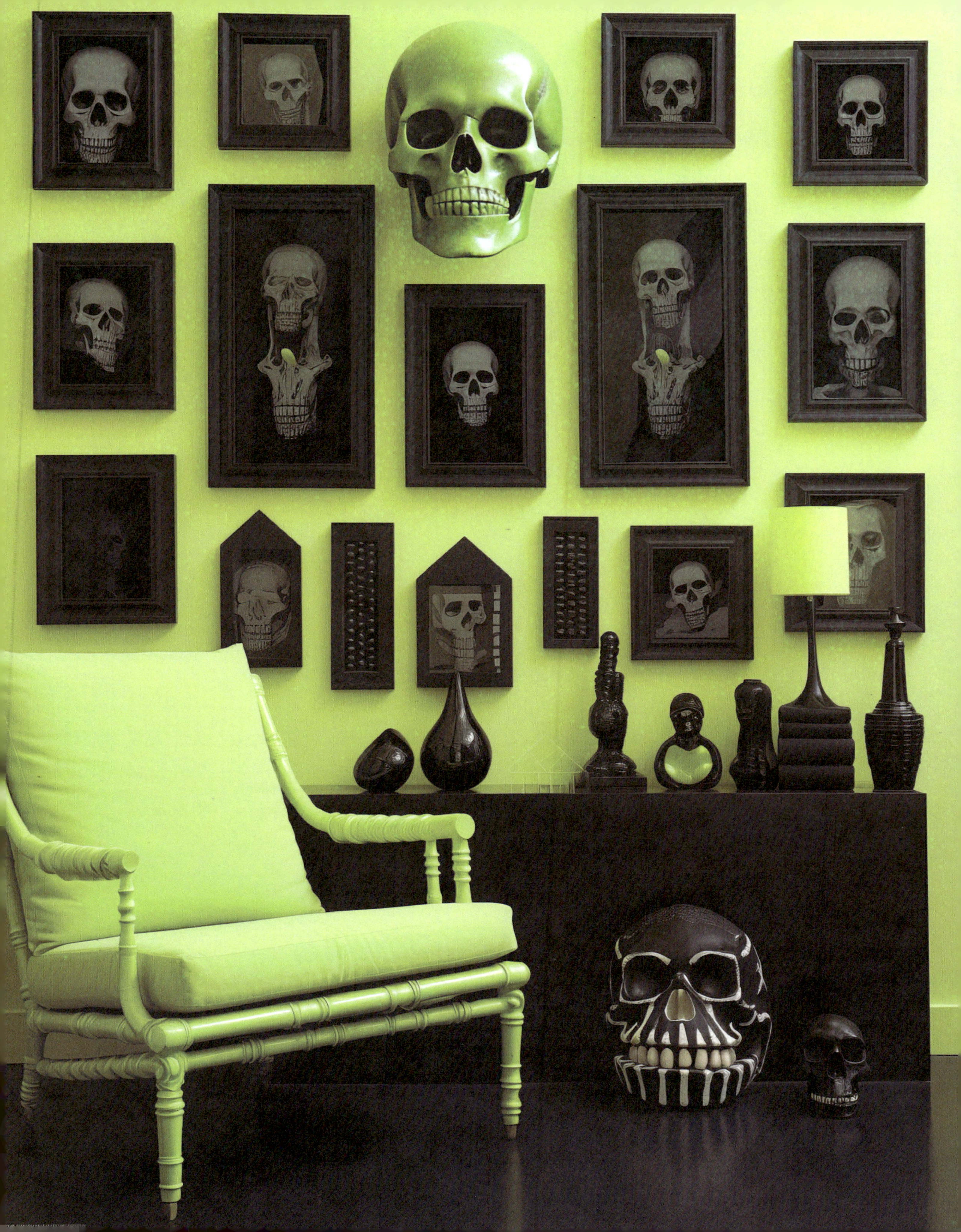

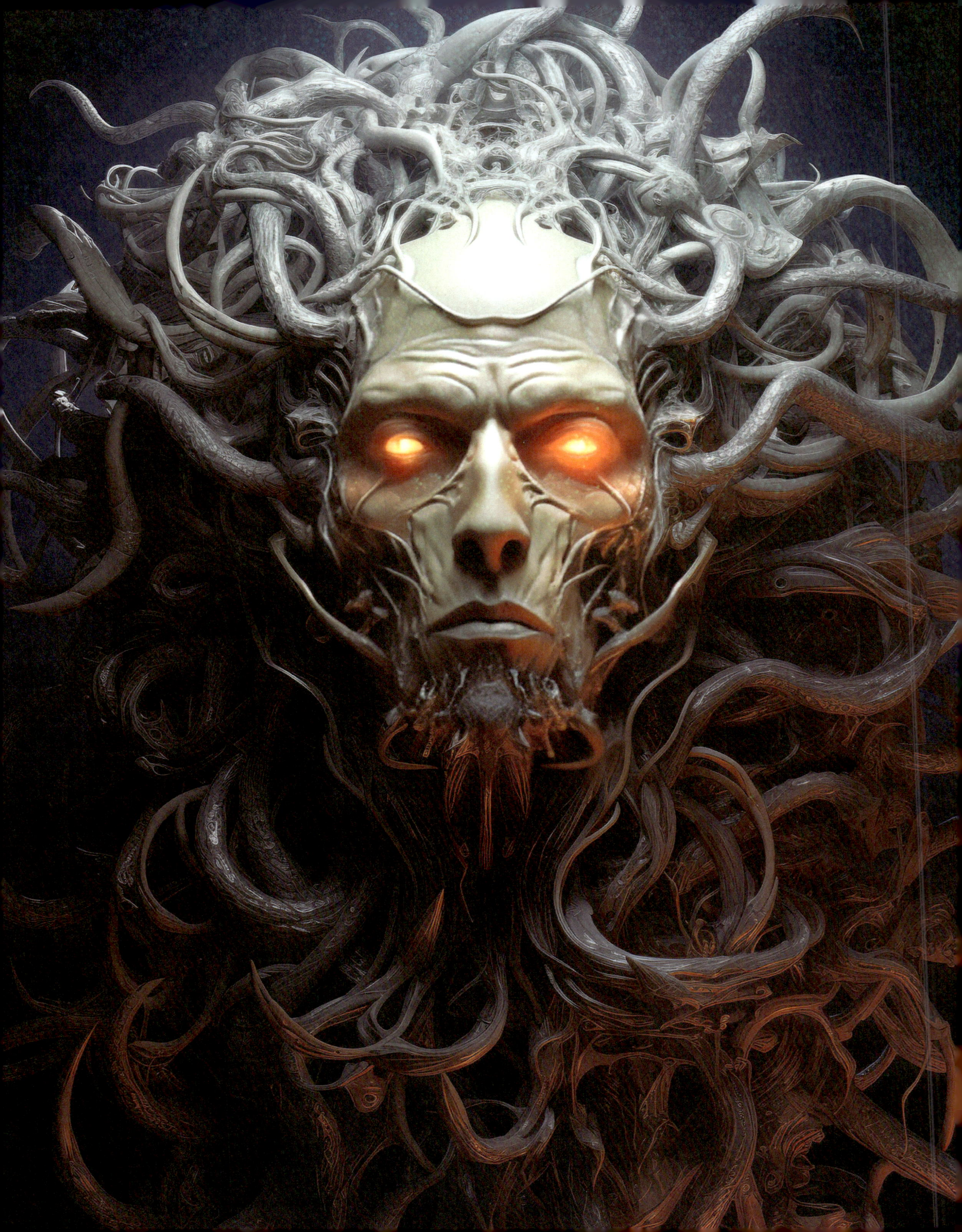

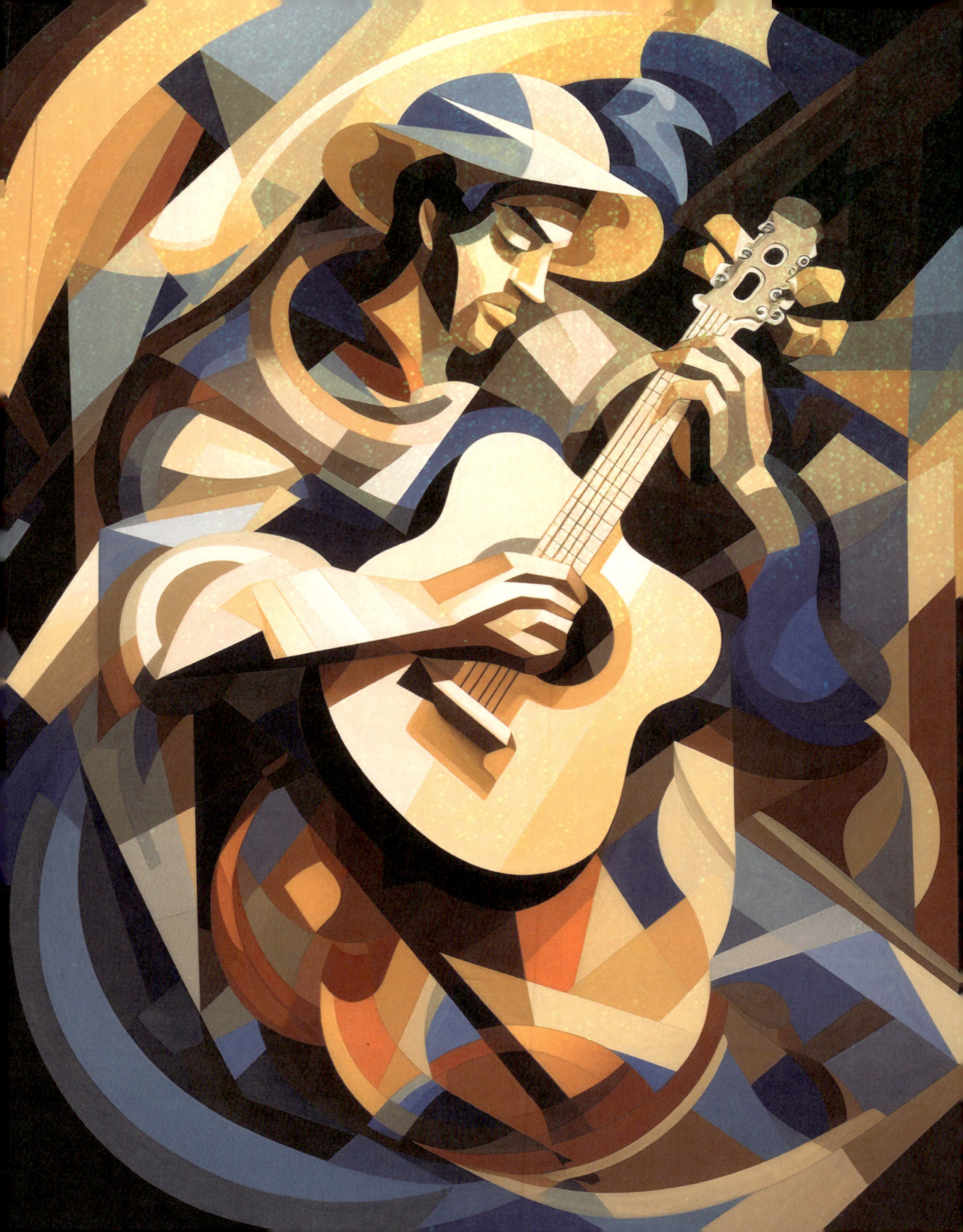

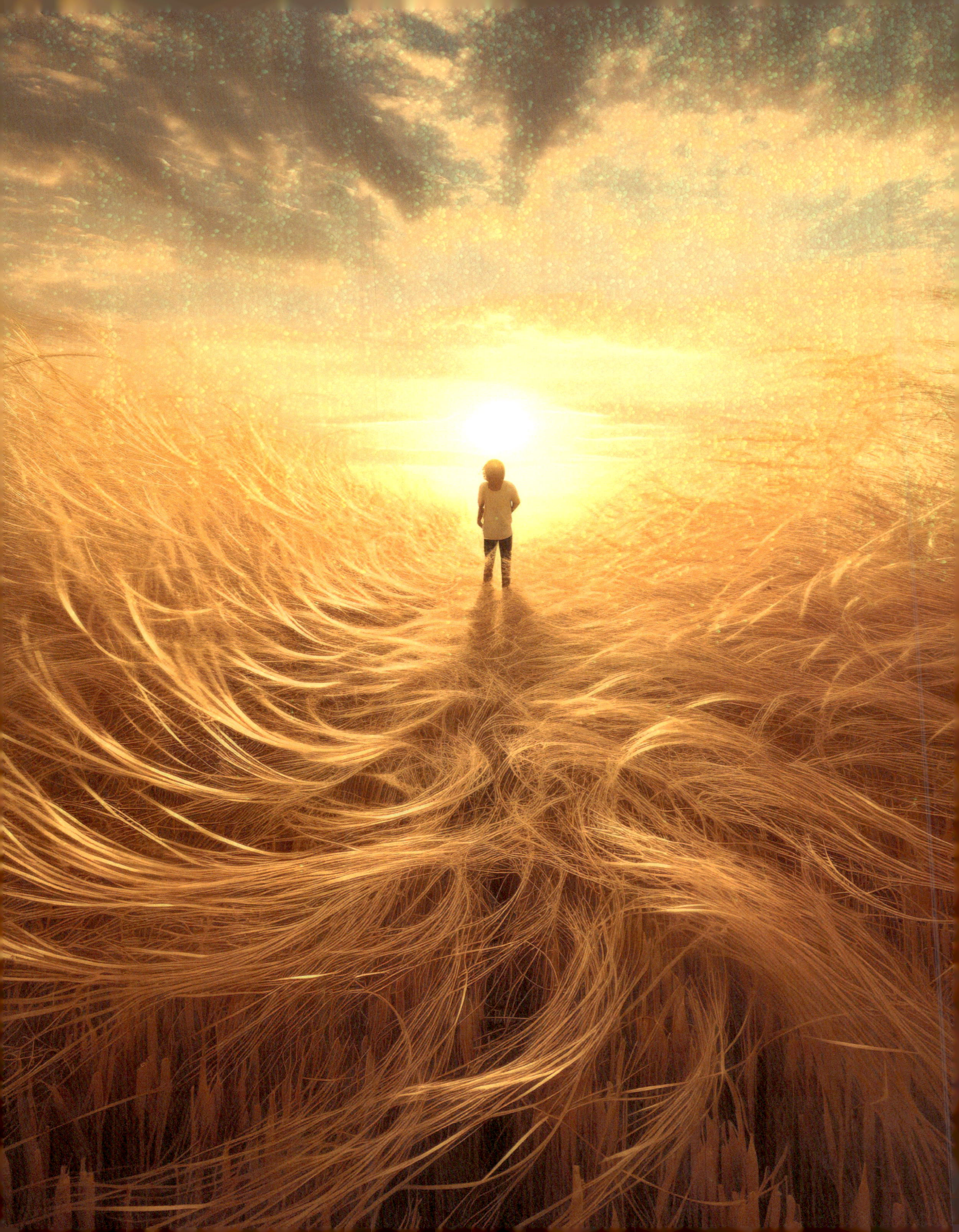

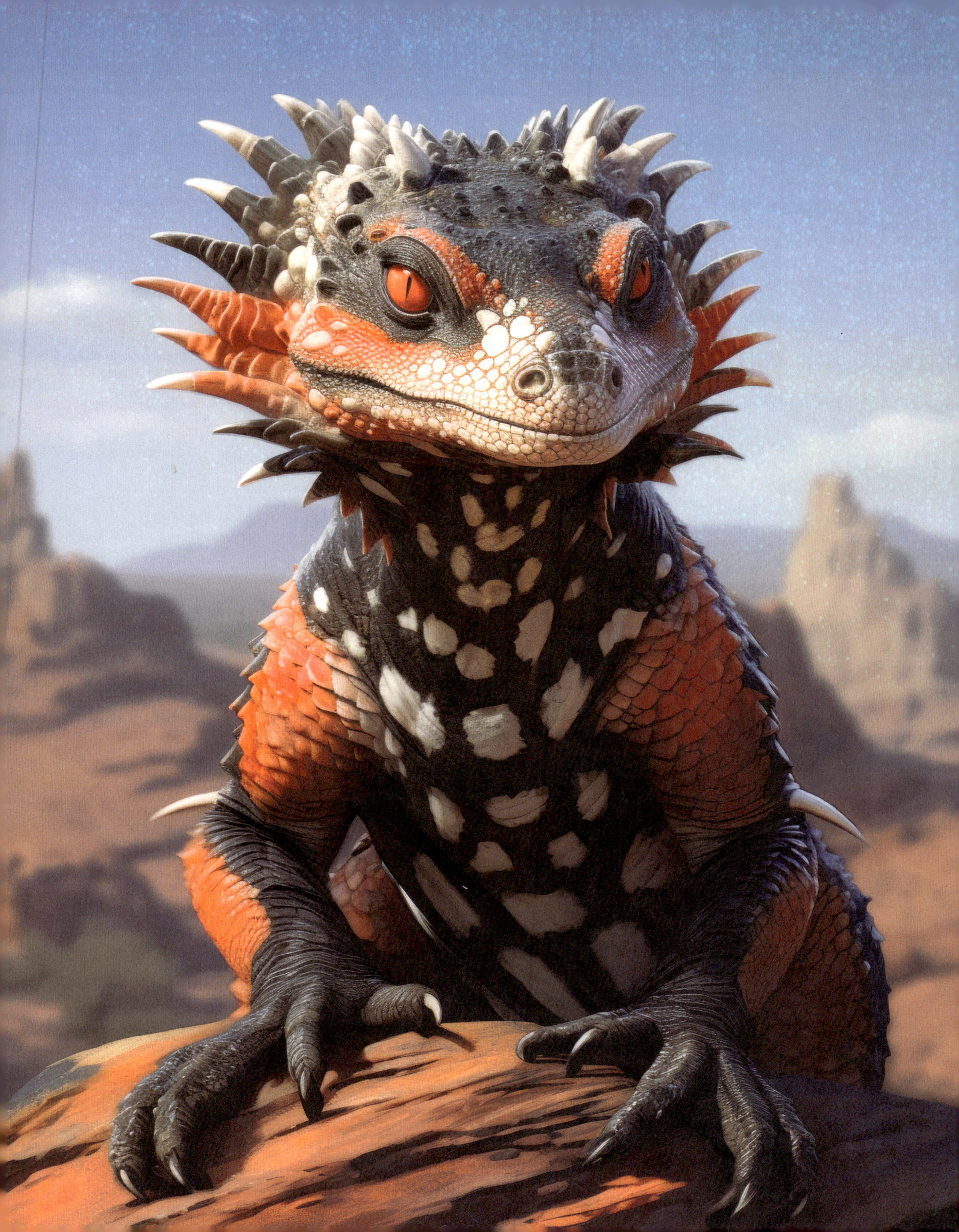

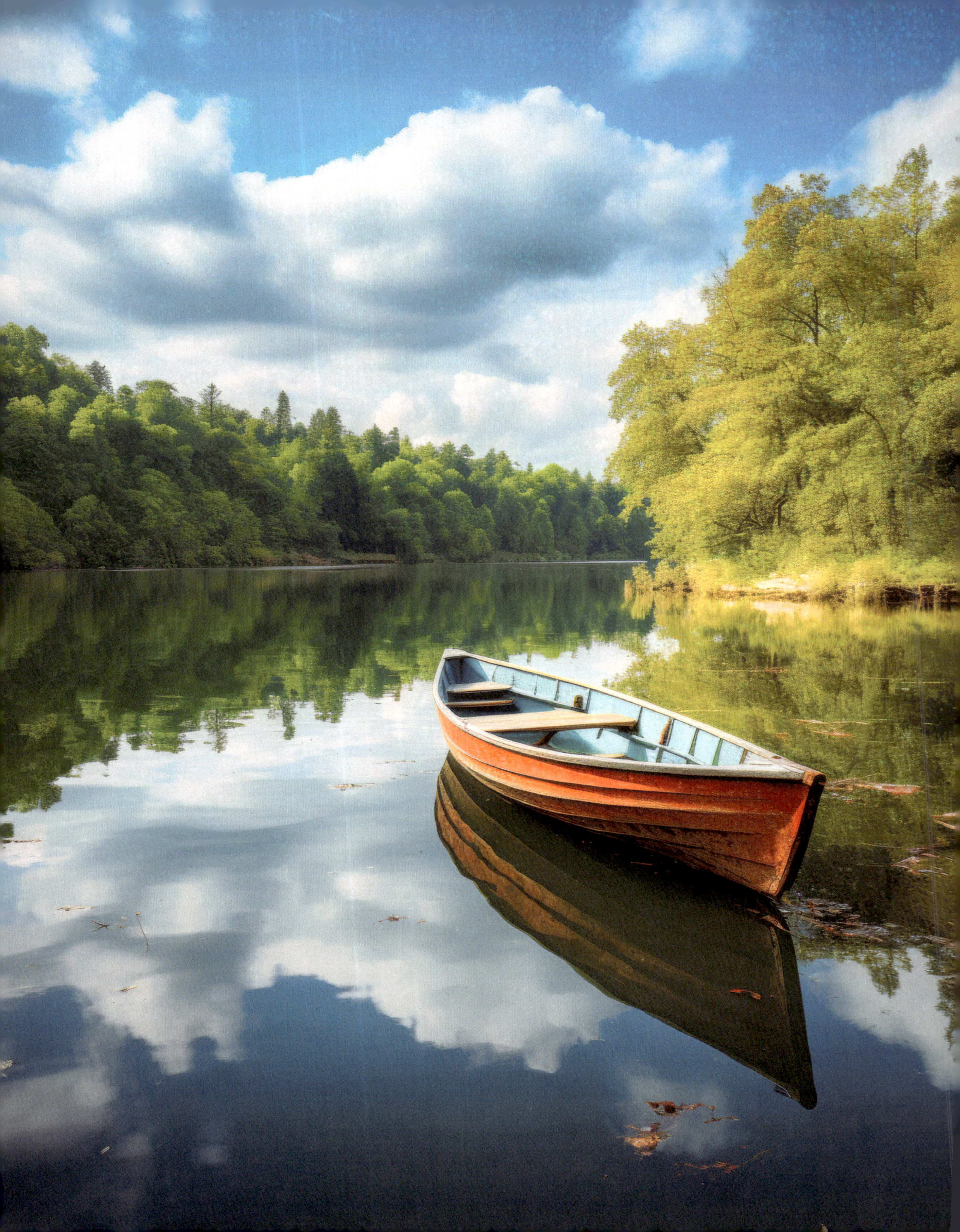

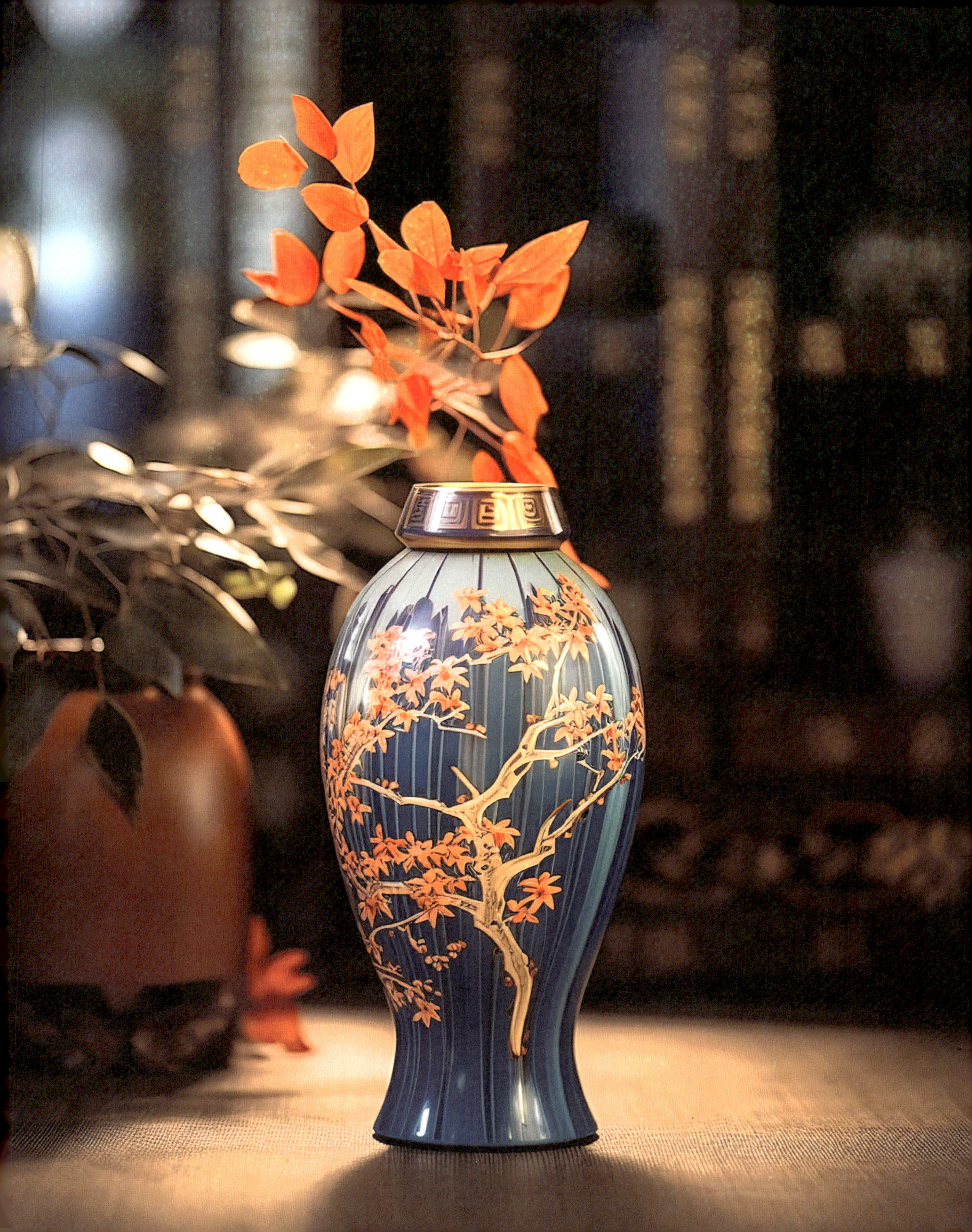

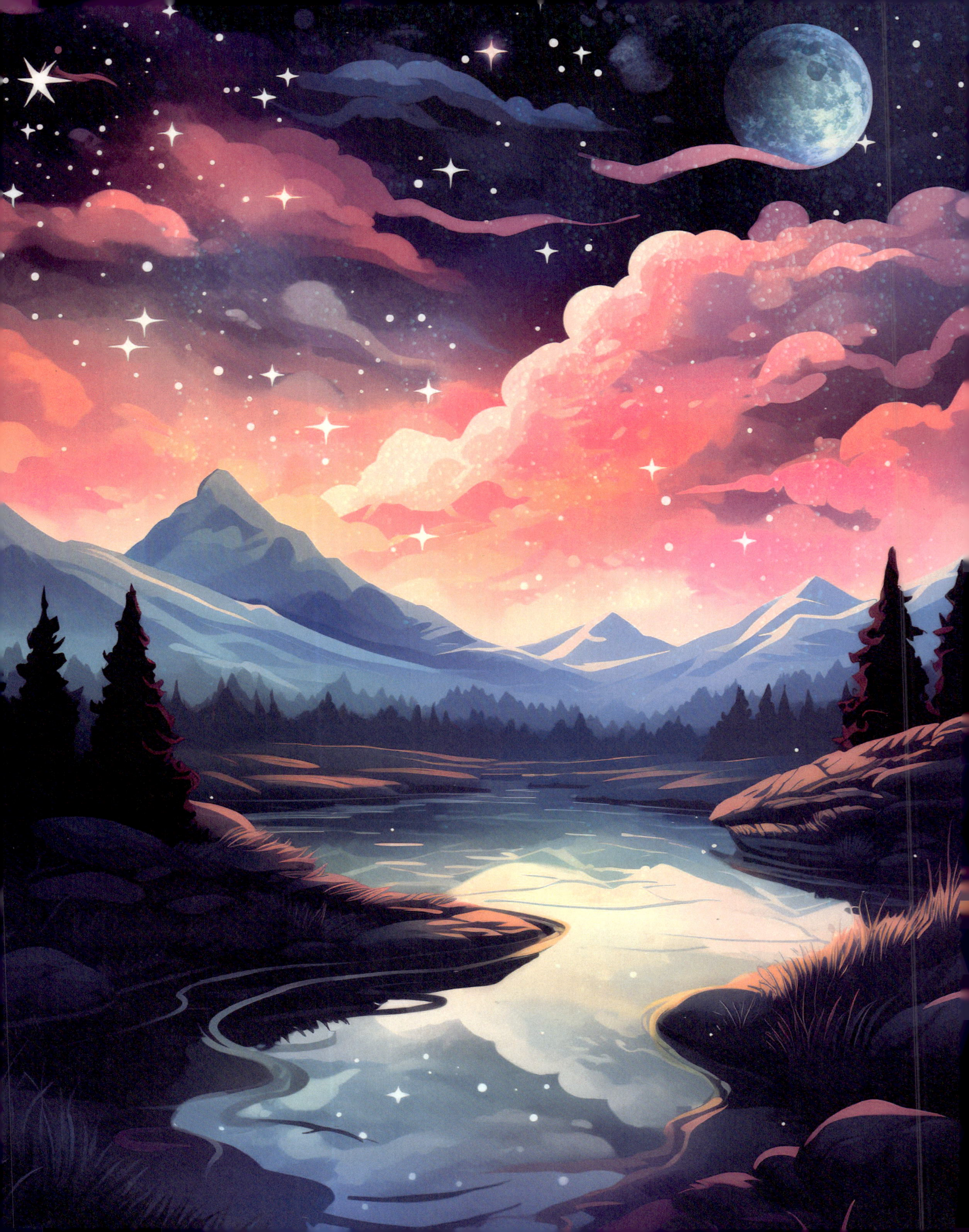

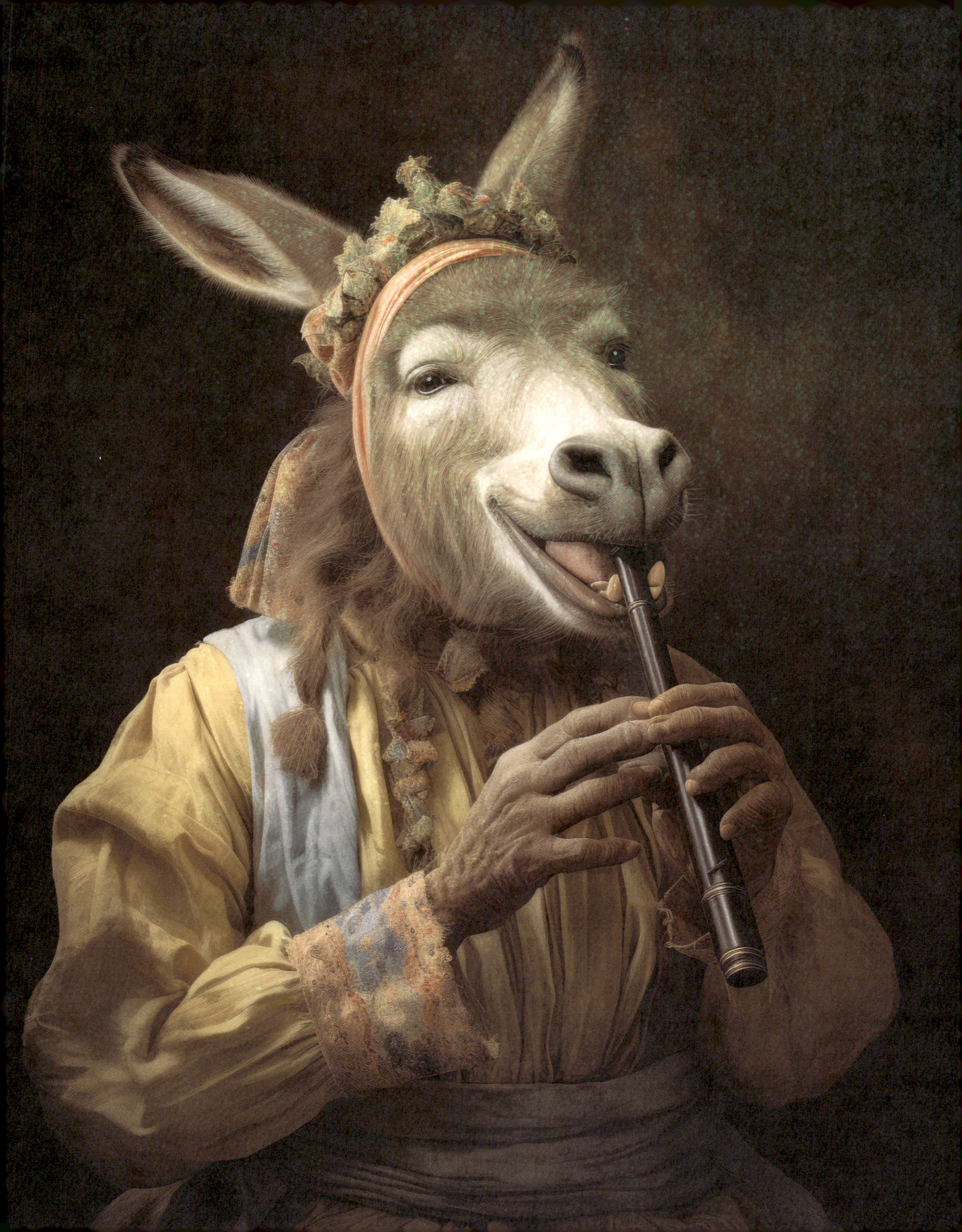

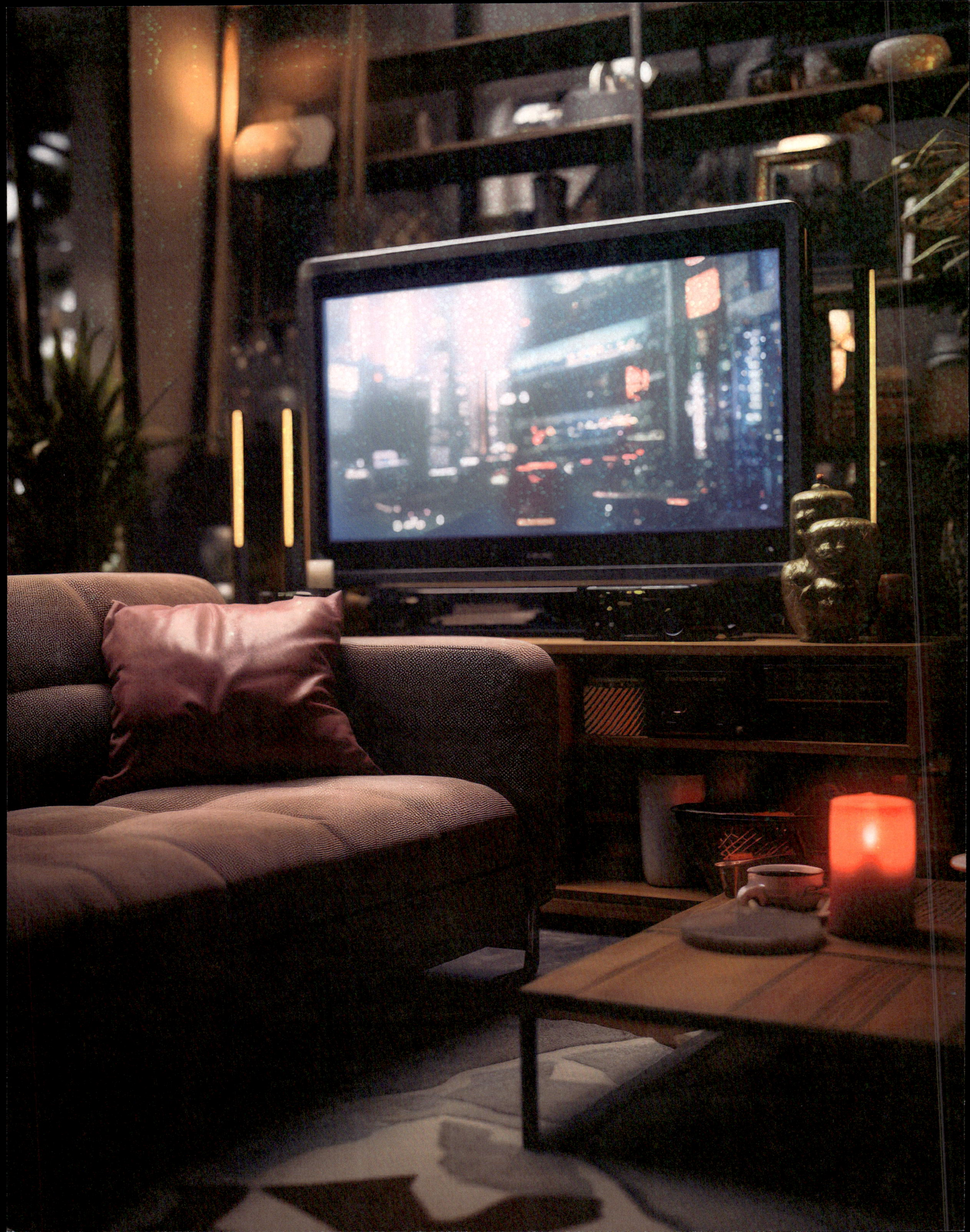

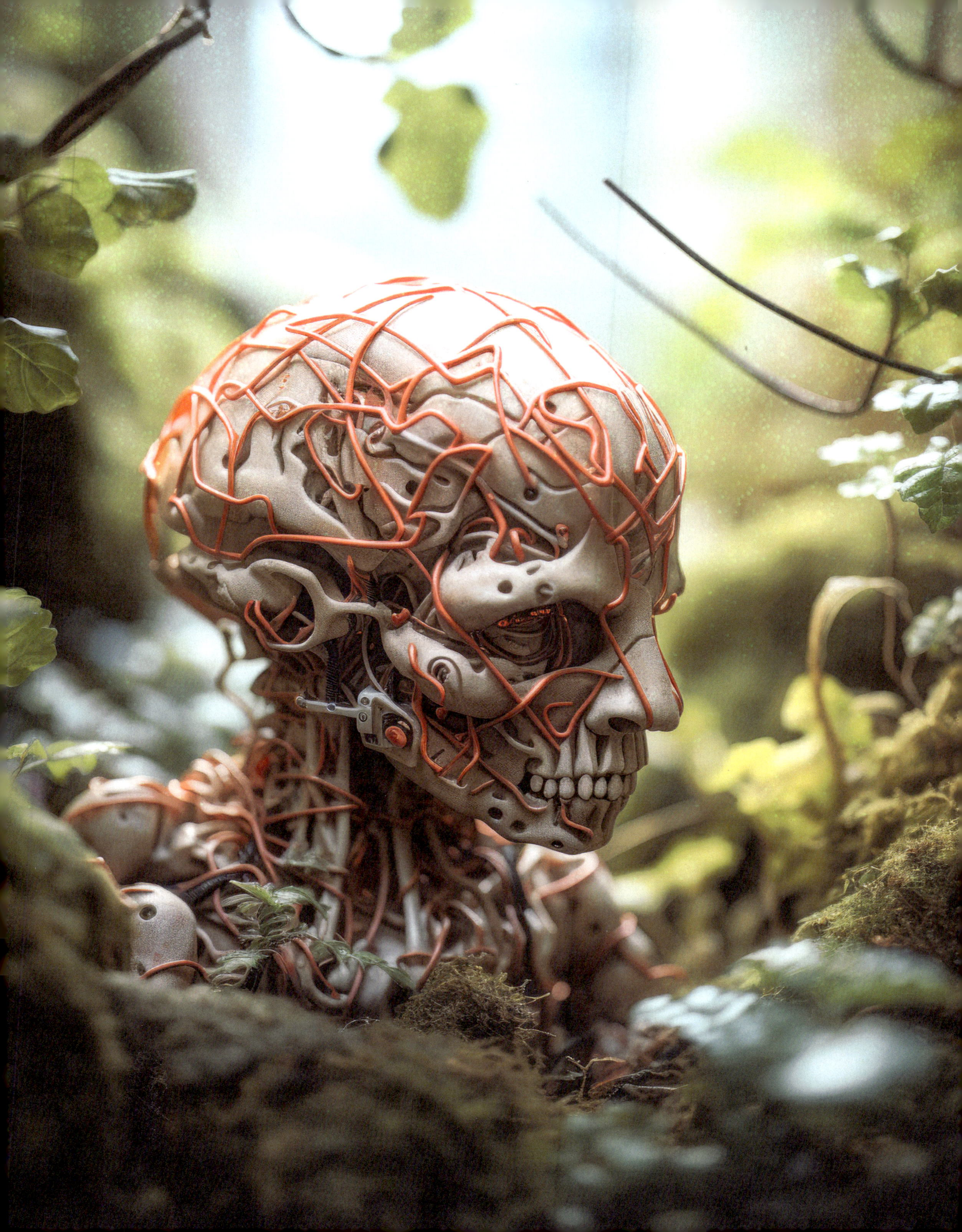

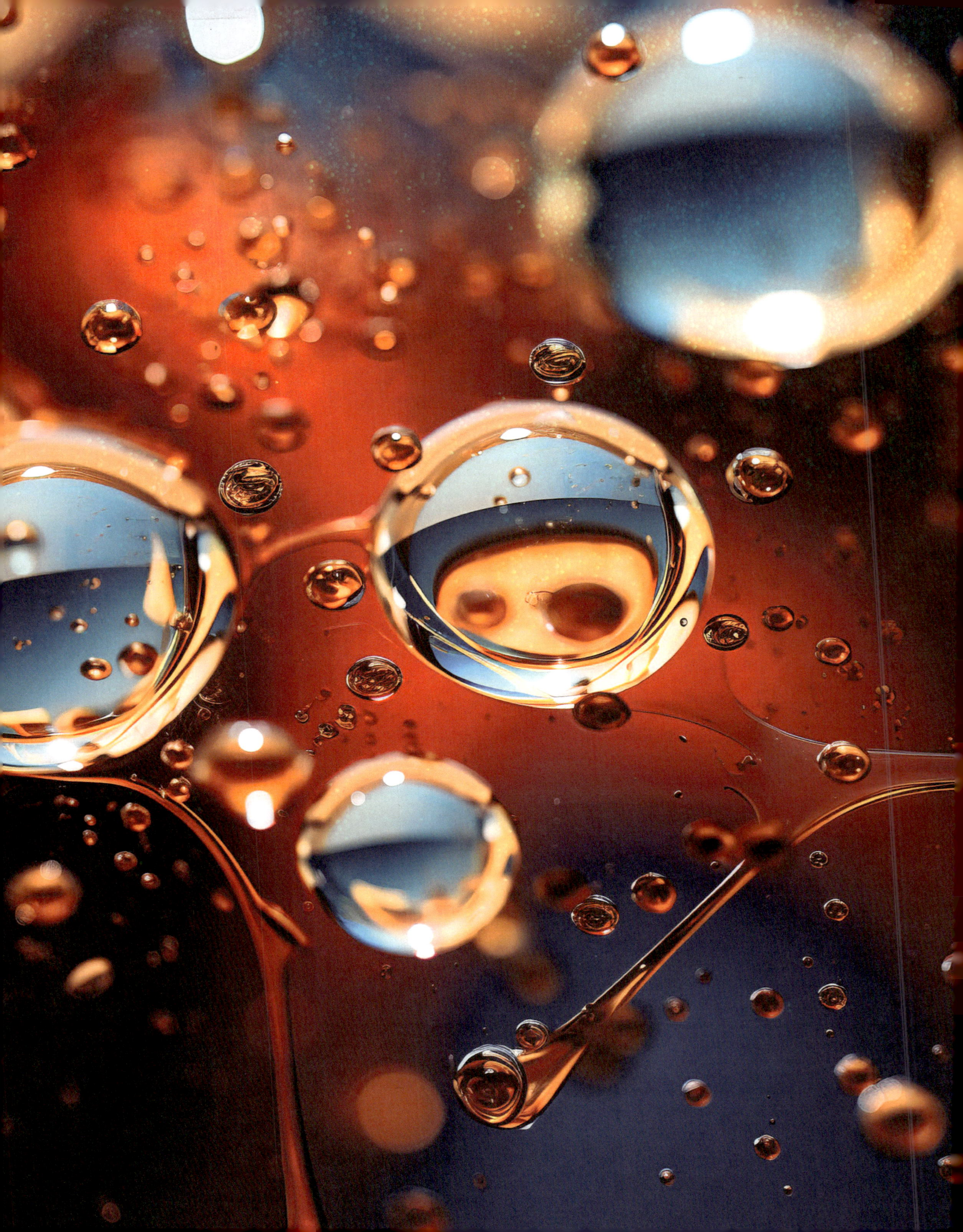

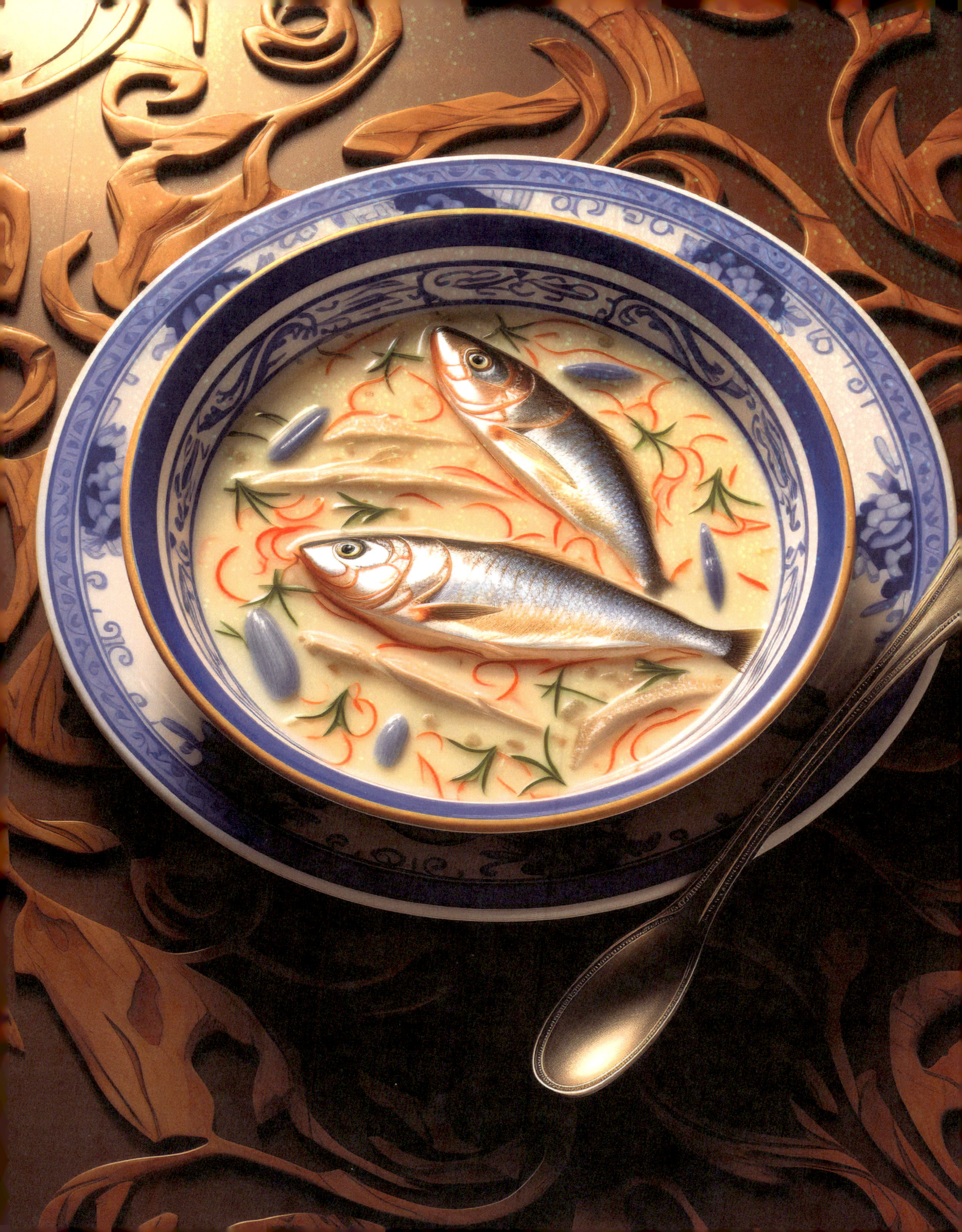

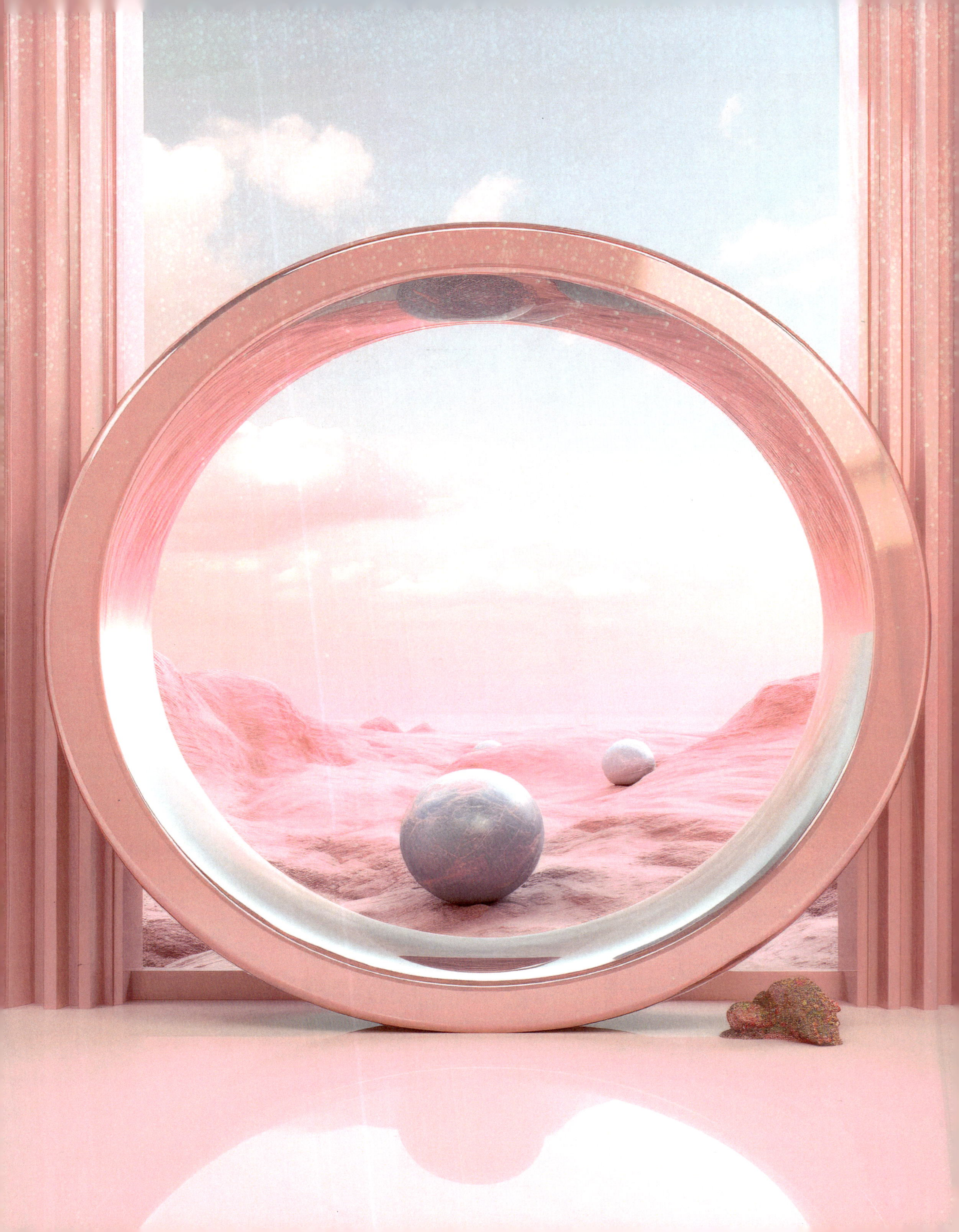

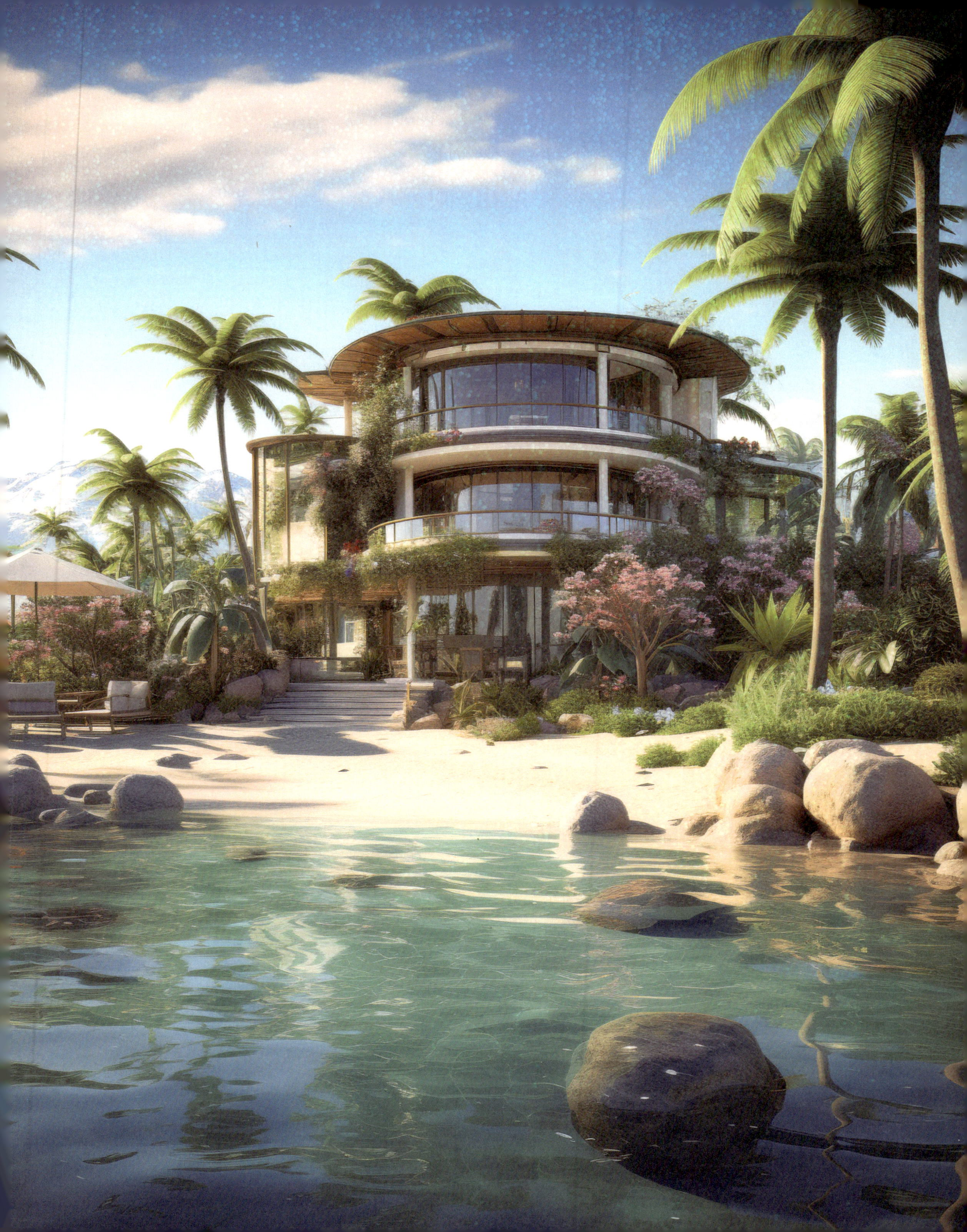

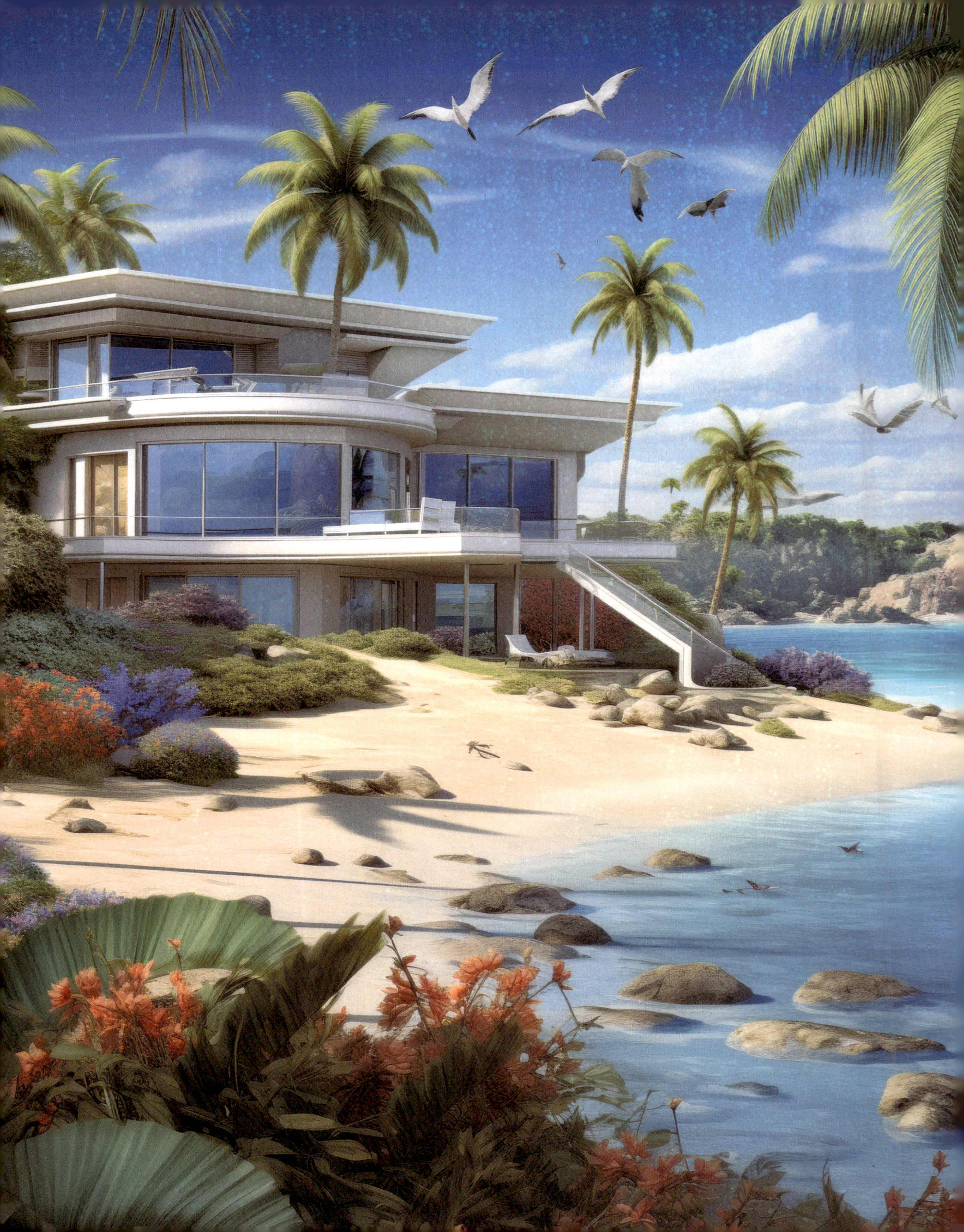

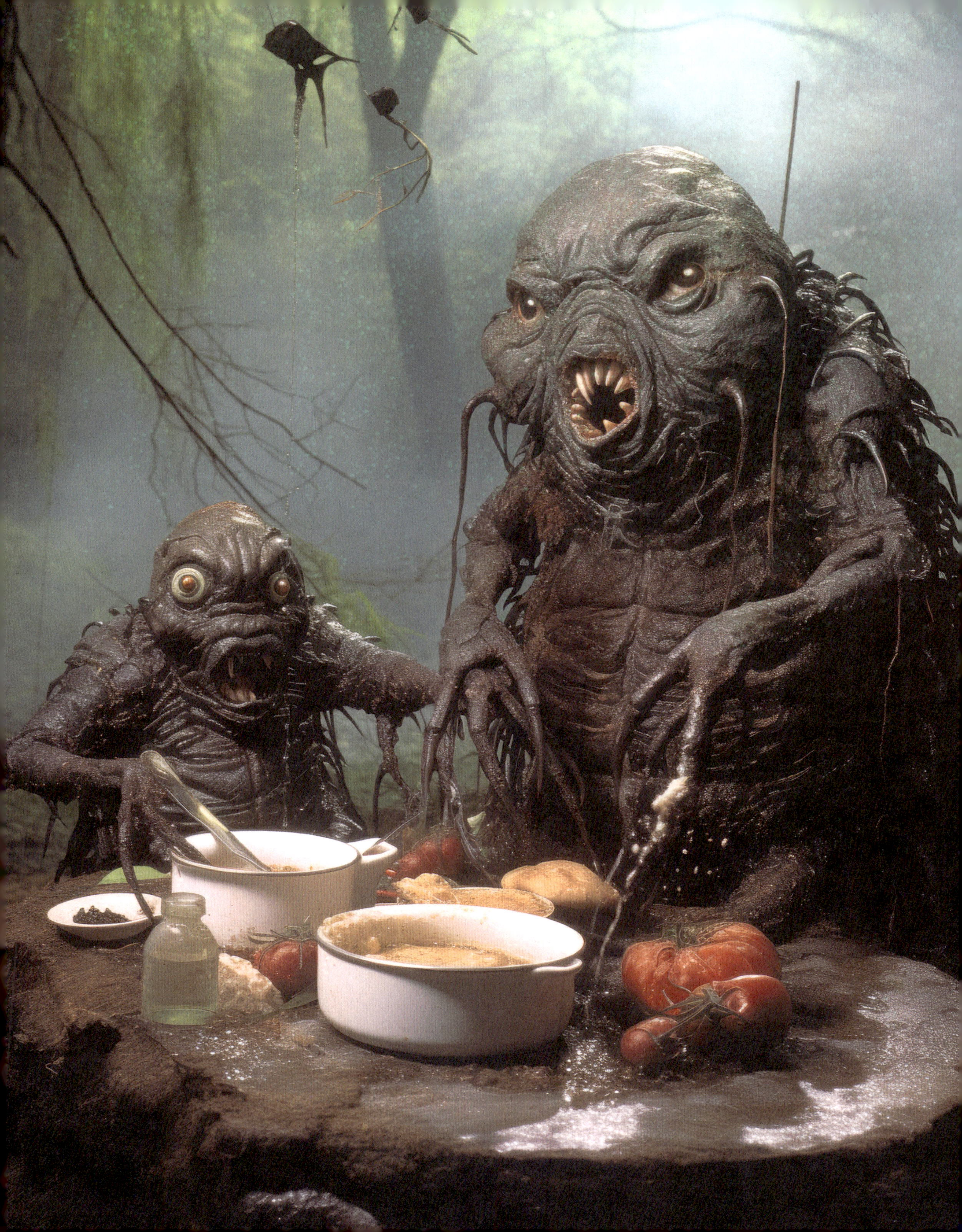

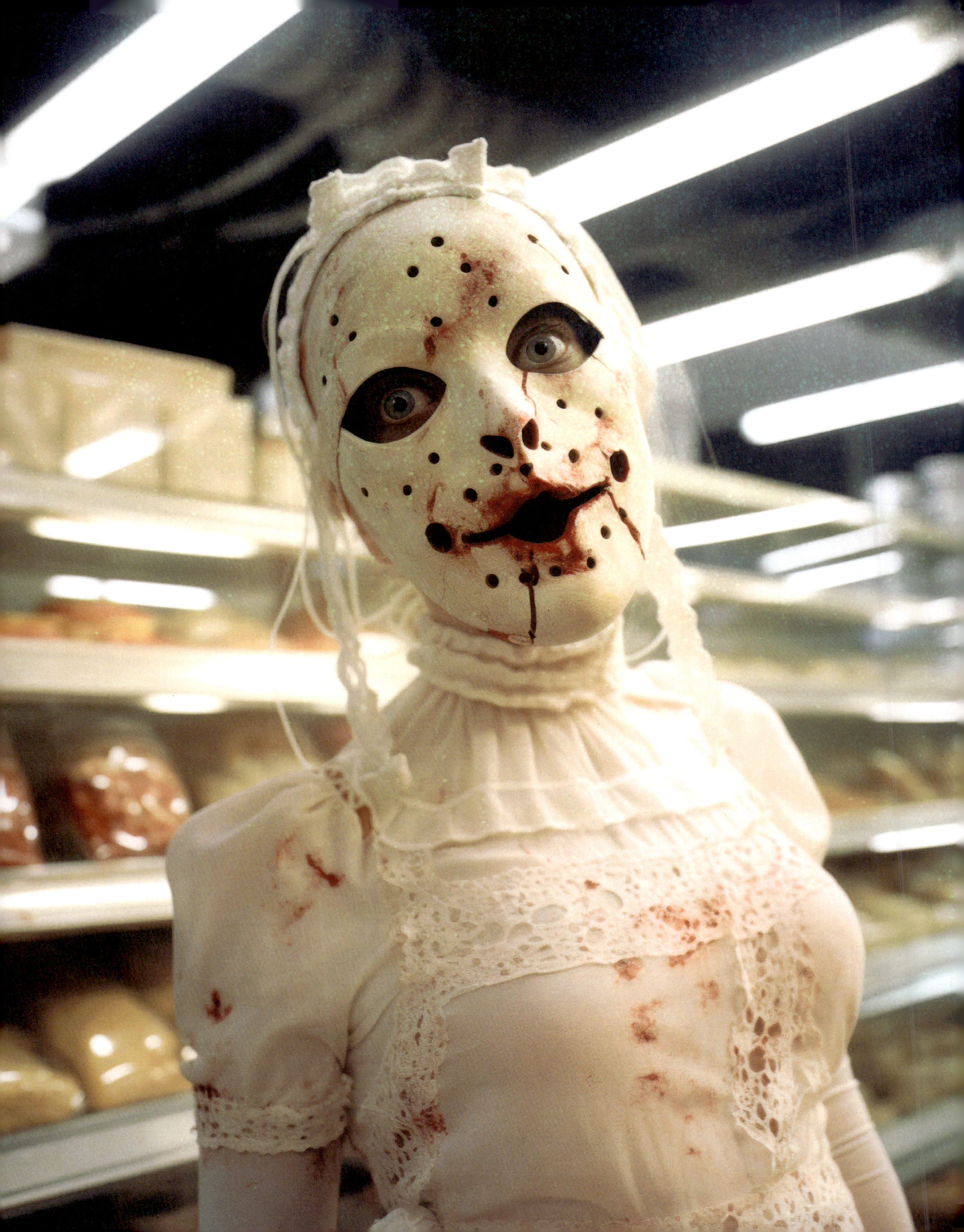

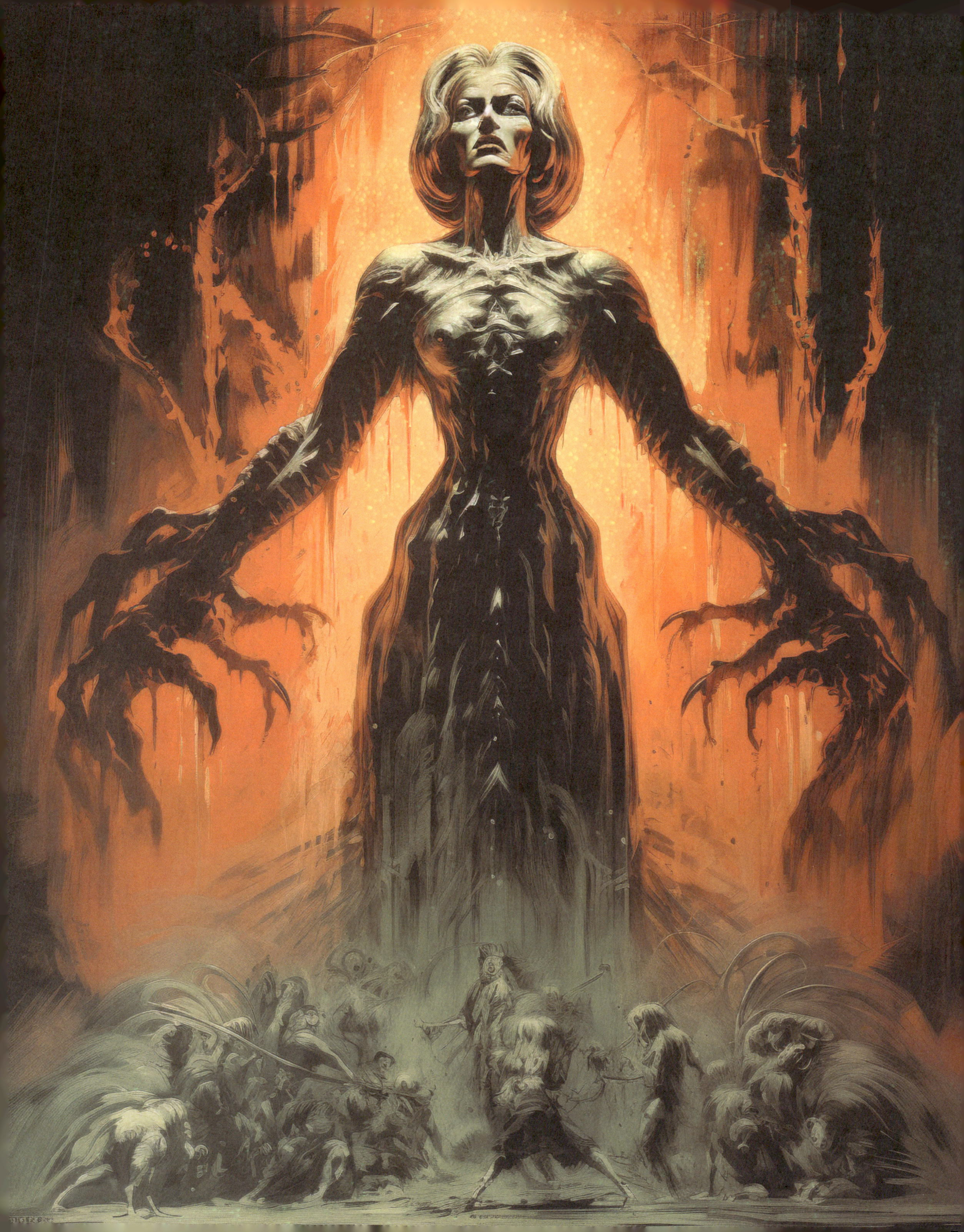

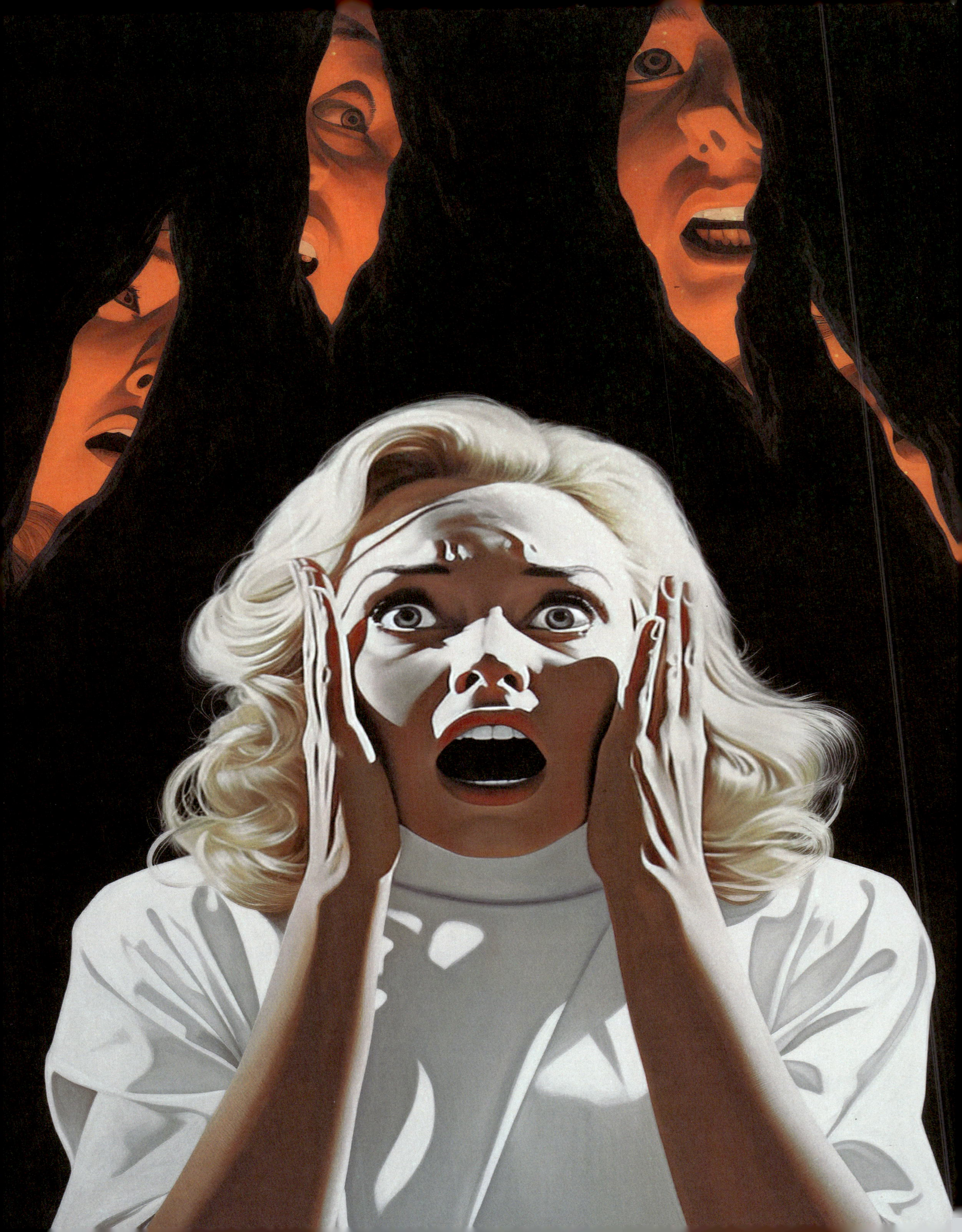

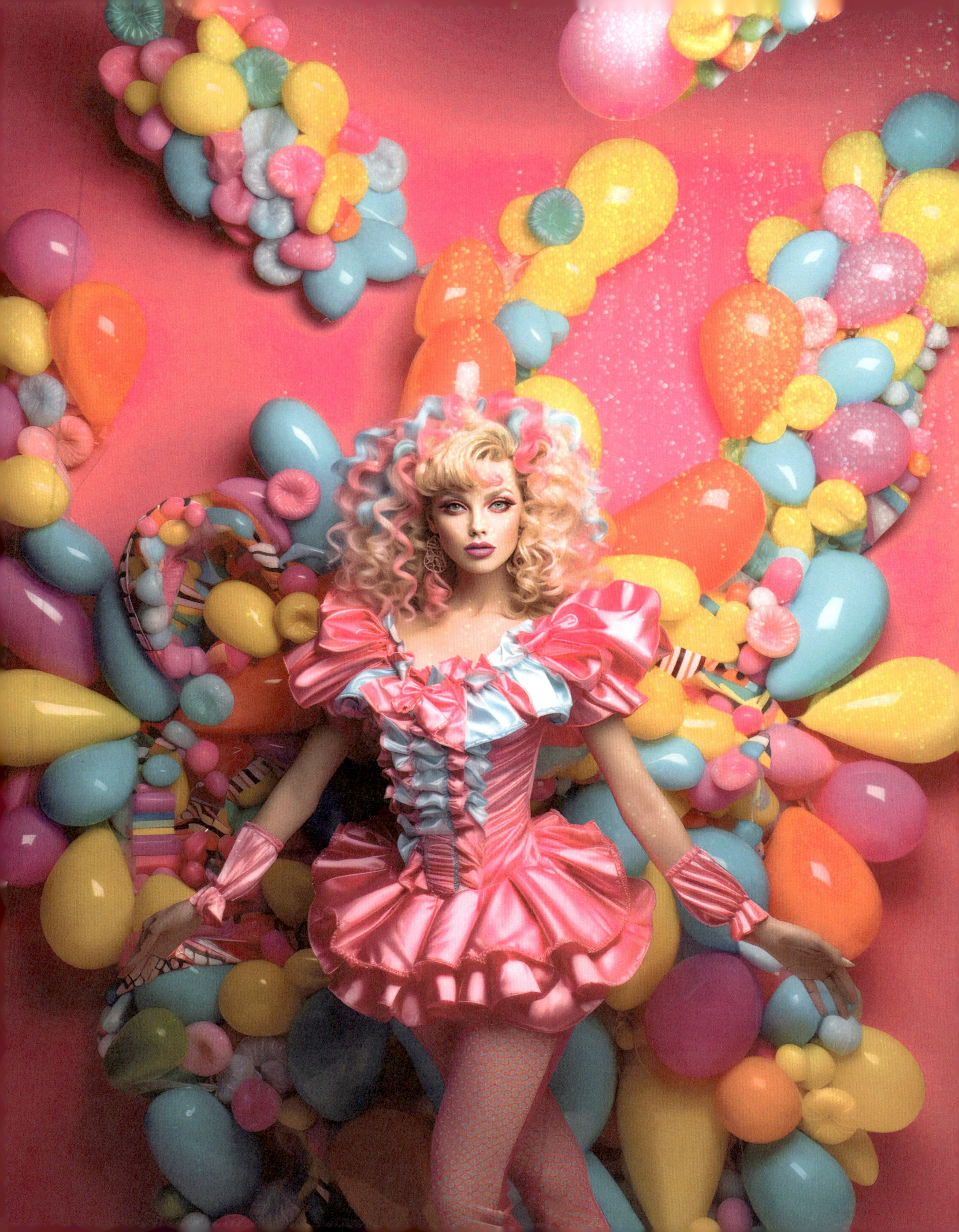

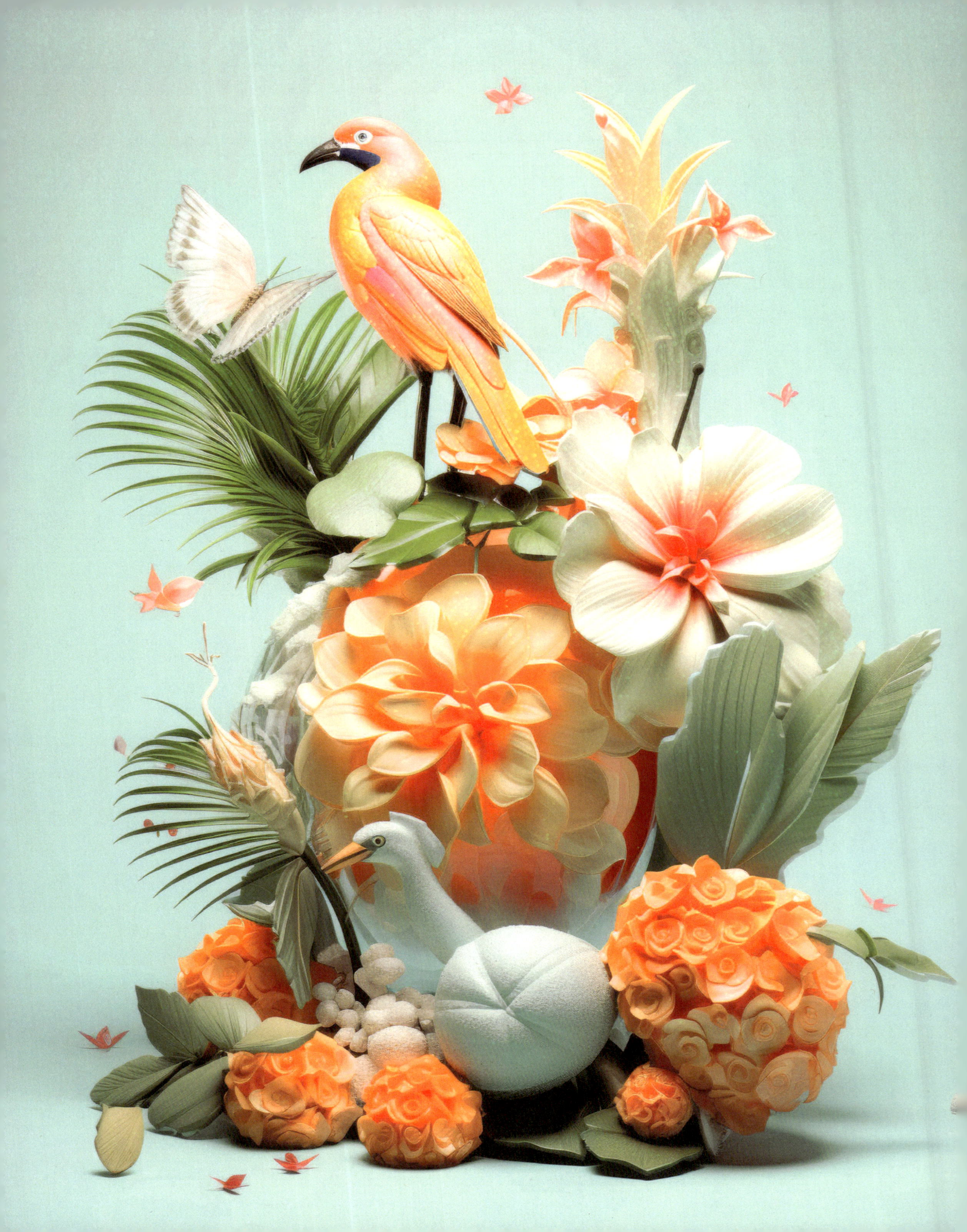

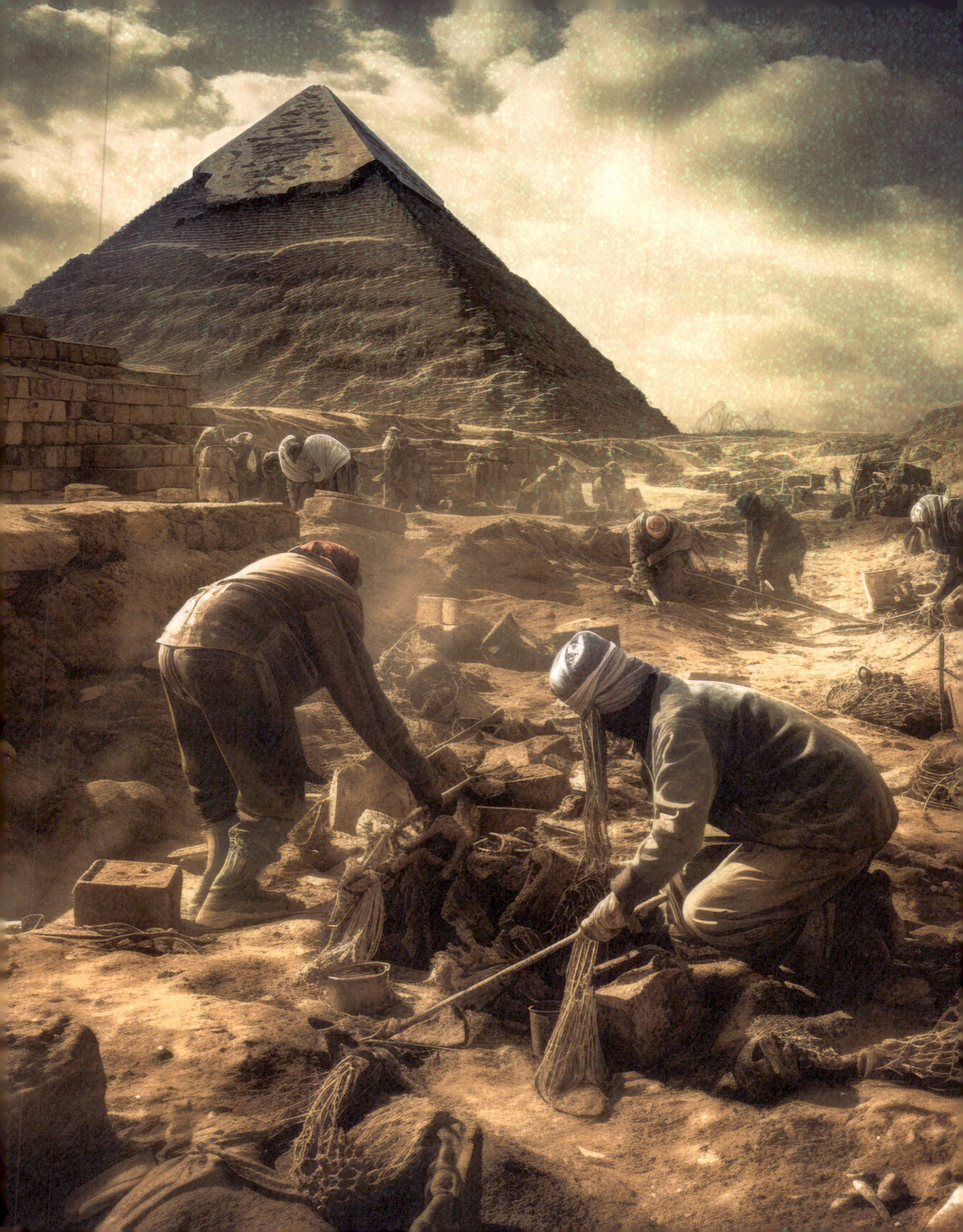

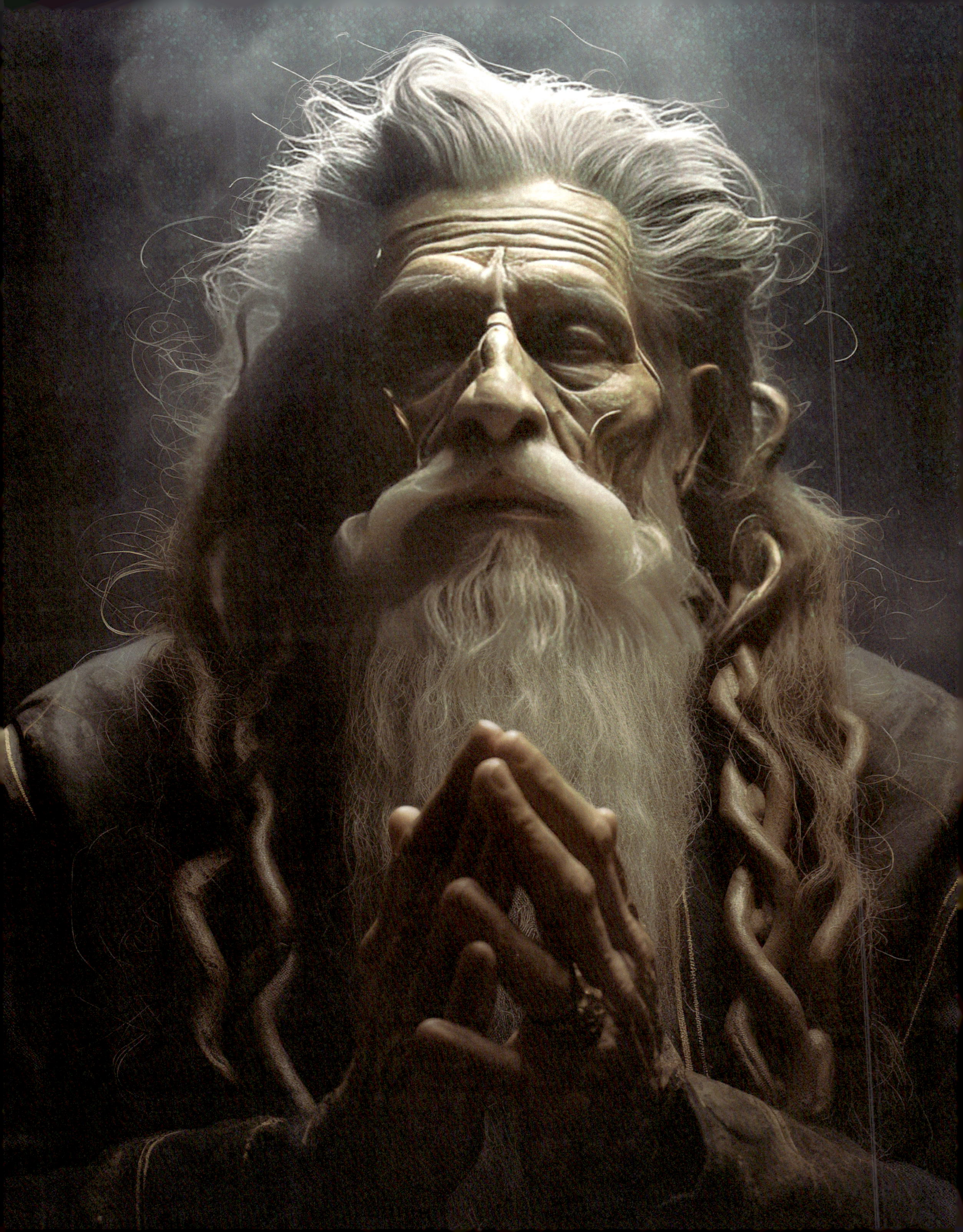

www.ingramcontent.com/pod-product-compliance
Lightning Source LLC
LaVergne TN
LVRC101547220926
848486LV00041B/393

* 9 7 8 1 7 3 8 1 3 5 5 0 9 *